Contents

Foreword		vii
Preface		xi
Acknowledgements		xv
1	Emergence of sustainable tourism	1
2	Issues in sustainable tourism	18
3	Alternative tourism	38
4	Conventional mass tourism	58
5	The facilitating sectors	73
6	Attractions	91
7	Quality control	110
8	Tourist destinations	132
9	Spatial strategies for destinations	153
10	Visitor management strategies for destinations	174
11	Ecotourism: the conscience of sustainable tourism	191
References		209
Appendix 1		227
Index		233

Sustainable Tourism:
Theory and Practice

Sustainable Tourism:
Theory and Practice

David Weaver

ELSEVIER
BUTTERWORTH
HEINEMANN

AMSTERDAM • BOSTON • HEIDELBERG • LONDON • NEW YORK • OXFORD
PARIS • SAN DIEGO • SAN FRANCISCO • SINGAPORE • SYDNEY • TOKYO

Butterworth-Heinemann is an imprint of Elsevier
The Boulevard, Langford Lane, Kidlington, Oxford, OX5 1GB
30 Corporate Drive, Suite 400, Burlington, MA 01803, USA

First edition 2006
Reprinted 2006, 2007, 2008 (twice)

Notice
No responsibility is assumed by the publisher for any injury and/or damage to persons
or property as a matter of products liability, negligence or otherwise, or from any use
or operation of any methods, products, instructions or ideas contained in the material
herein. Because of rapid advances in the medical sciences, in particular, independent
verification of diagnoses and drug dosages should be made

British Library Cataloguing in Publication Data
A catalogue record for this book is available from the British Library

Library of Congress Cataloging-in-Publication Data
A catalog record for this book is available from the Library of Congress

ISBN: 978-0-7506-6438-7

For information on all Butterworth-Heinemann publications
visit our website at www.elsevierdirect.com

Transferred to Digital Printing in 2010

Working together to grow
libraries in developing countries

www.elsevier.com | www.bookaid.org | www.sabre.org

ELSEVIER   BOOK AID International   Sabre Foundation

Foreword

This book has a rich, up-to-date and innovative didactical and pedagogical value, thus becoming an essential tool for tourism university students at the beginning of the century. It clearly responds to the unavoidable need to include the principles of sustainability in all study areas, but especially in tourism, which has become one of the main social and economic phenomena of our times.

If tourism is to continue growing and diversifying in the next decades according to the same patterns that were observed in the second half of the twentieth century, it is not conceivable to let it follow such an expansion without mastering its wide range of impacts, both positive and negative, upon the social, economic and environmental fabrics of societies. In this context, educating future tourism industry professionals is crucial, both for developing more awareness about sustainability issues, and for providing them with the necessary tools for addressing those issues in their concrete, day-to-day tourism operations and in the policy-making decisions in tourism.

This publication is also a practical handbook for current tourism destination, site or enterprise managers. It can help them in raising the level of sustainability in their activities. It allows them to learn about the different sustainability challenges facing the tourism industry today, how to redress current unsustainable operations, and how to take informed decisions regarding the expansion or refurbishment of existing facilities to make them more sustainable, or to plan and develop new tourism infrastructures that guarantee long term, sustainable operations.

For students and operators, the book clarifies the concept of sustainable tourism, which is not to be understood as a particular variety of tourism as it is sometimes wrongly thought, but rather as an overriding approach to tourism development and management applicable to all the segments of the tourism industry. In this respect, Chapter 4, dedicated to mass tourism, is an *a fortiori* example, showing that sustainable principles must be applied to all human activities, and tourism, in all its forms, must be included in the general sustainable development of territories and nations.

According to the Conceptual Definition established by the World Tourism Organization, sustainable tourism must:

- Make optimal use of environmental resources that constitute a key element in tourism development;
- Respect the socio-cultural authenticity of host communities, conserve their built and living cultural heritage and traditional values, and contribute to inter-cultural understanding and tolerance;
- Ensure viable, long-term economic operations, providing socio-economic benefits to all stakeholders that are fairly distributed, and contributing to poverty alleviation; and
- Maintain a high level of tourist satisfaction and ensure a meaningful experience to the tourists, raising their awareness about sustainability issues and promoting sustainable tourism practices.

In order to implement the equally important three dimensions of sustainability reflected in this definition (environmental, socio-cultural and economic), and to ensure the quality of the tourist experience, all stakeholders in the tourism sector are relevant and play complementary roles. Indeed, it is known that actors in the tourism industry are very numerous, and they all share a common responsibility towards sustainability. However, this responsibility is differentiated and each stakeholder should assume it and establish, whenever necessary, the appropriate partnership with other actors. The book reflects well this multi-stakeholder nature of tourism, as well as its trans-sectoral implications.

Quality, the notion of which is often linked to sustainability, is also dealt with in this book. Indeed, in today's world, no product or service can be considered of high quality if it does not comply with sustainability criteria. These criteria should be the basis on which tourism organizations, companies and destinations should establish quality labels, associating such labels with suitable indicators of sustainability. Indicators are crucial tools and help tourism managers at all stages, from planning decisions to monitoring process, but also in zoning and for determining carrying capacities. The book dedicates part of Chapter 3 to indicators, with corresponding references to the substantive work carried out in this field by the World Tourism Organization in recent years.

After explaining various managing tools and techniques, such as visitor management, and presenting some of the tourism destinations, like small islands or cities, this publication ends by dealing with one particular tourism segment: ecotourism. Ecotourism is no longer a vague, confusing concept or a marginal tourism segment. The International Year of Ecotourism in 2002 – which gave the opportunity to open a wide, participatory debate among all types of stakeholders that reached its peak at the World Ecotourism Summit in Québec (Canada) – recognized the leading role that ecotourism is playing in terms of the overall sustainability of tourism activities. The Québec Declaration on Ecotourism clearly defines the concept of ecotourism and has become a reference point in all ecotourism studies, publications and conferences. In many ways, ecotourism is a microcosm of all the issues of sustainable tourism, but focusing in a more concentrated way on specific ecosystems and traditional cultures. As a leading segment in sustainability issues, ecotourism should serve to open new windows in future research on tourism and its relation with major human challenges worldwide, contributing as far as possible to the UN Millennium Development Goals.

The book also deals with the main categories of infrastructure and services that make up a tourism product, avoiding a classical and somehow outdated description of each of these components, but rather grouping them into two major groups, irrespective of whether they are physical, infrastructural elements, or services. Yet, in both the so-called 'facilitating sectors' and in the 'attractions', the author stresses the need to adopt the sustainability approach, addressing first the ways in which each of these components affects the environment and generates impacts upon the social and cultural fabrics of societies. The facilitating sectors and the attractions come together in Chapter 8 of the book to constitute a 'destination', and it is here the role of the host community is examined, and especially the various ways in which communities can influence the level of sustainability of destinations.

In conclusion, there is an adequate and appropriate coverage in the book of the various denominations that are commonly, but not always rightly used by tourism professionals and academics, clarifying the concepts of :

- sustainable tourism – namely a condition that all types of tourism must fulfil;
- alternative tourism – referring to the variety of modern, special interest tourism niches that have appeared over the last couple of decades and that have tended

to remain outside the mass markets, although not necessarily being more
sustainable;

- conventional mass tourism – referring to the traditional forms of tourism, such as
  beach, city, congress and winter sports tourism, and the need for these forms of
  tourism to become more sustainable; and
- ecotourism, understood as the segment of the tourism industry operating in relatively wild natural areas.

Clarifying these concepts has become an unavoidable necessity, especially when
talking about sustainability in tourism, in order to erase, once and for all, the misunderstanding that it is only some segments of the industry that need to be more
sustainable. Perhaps the marketing and promotion of these segments need to be differentiated; perhaps also their operational management too, but the sustainability
conditions must apply to all of them.

Eugenio Yunis
Head, Sustainable Development of Tourism
World Tourism Organization

Preface

Introduction

The juggernaut of global tourism continues to roll inexorably in the early years of the new millennium, with major geopolitical events such as 9/11 and the Iraq war causing little more than minor and temporary interruptions in the pattern of increased tourist arrivals and revenues that has persisted since the end of World War II. Mass tourism destinations are now evolving into mega tourism destinations, ever more remote places are being incorporated into the global tourism system and the exploding domestic and outbound tourist markets of China and India are poised to propel global tourism into yet another period of accelerated expansion. Intensifying tourism activity is affecting more and more places – mostly on earth, but now also in outer space – and there can no longer be any doubt as to the potential of this sector to effect fundamental economic, environmental and sociocultural change on destination as well as origin and transit regions. This change, depending on how this sector is managed, can be either positive or negative and it is the understandable desire to maximize the former and minimize the latter that has given rise to the now ubiquitous engagement of stakeholders with the concept of sustainable tourism.

Premises

This book facilitates the engagement process by describing and critically analysing the extent to which sustainability-related considerations are being pursued within the global tourism sector. In effect, it engages the contemporary engagement with sustainable tourism. At least four basic premises inform the content, which is directed primarily toward senior university undergraduates taking a tourism management major or minor. First, all scales of tourism are inherently legitimate and it is a question of how appropriate alternative or mass tourism, or some combination of the two, is in any given place and time. Having said this, it makes sense to pay particular attention to the sustainability of 'mass tourism' since this accounts for most tourism activity and is the mode that has been implicated in most negative impacts. Second, both alternative and mass tourism always entail costs as well as benefits and neither is a panacea. It is for this reason that managers can only hope to minimize rather than eliminate the negative impacts. Third, any strategy aspiring to attain environmental, sociocultural and economic sustainability, to be viable, must additionally take into account the imperative of financial sustainability. The other dimensions of sustainability are moot if an operation goes out of business, while the ability to pursue those dimensions is enhanced if the operation is profitable. The ability of the public sector to pursue effective strategies is similarly dictated by the direct and indirect financial resources at hand. Sustainability deliberations are too often utopian, yielding superb paper plans for destinations that are unlikely to attract the necessary funding. Fourth and finally, comprehensive engagement with sustainability requires public/private partnerships based on mutual respect and cooperation, since neither sector can achieve sustainable tourism by itself.

Outline

The first two chapters are introductory, with Chapter 1 examining the historical origins of sustainable tourism and the extent to which the concept of sustainability has been adopted and institutionalized by organizations both internal and external to tourism. Chapter 2 discusses basic issues that complicate the practice of sustainability and introduces indicators as a critical component in sustainability-related strategies and management. Chapter 3 considers alternative tourism, which was conceived in the 1980s as a more appropriate or 'sustainable' form of tourism than mass tourism. But recognizing that alternative tourism is only a partial solution to the world's tourism-related problems, the next four chapters focus on the private sector mass tourism industry. Specifically, Chapter 4 examines the factors that have given rise to the industry's growing engagement with sustainability, including the emergence of the 'green' consumer and the advantages associated with size. Chapter 5 looks at the initiatives and issues of sustainability in facilitating sectors such as travel agencies, tour operators, transportation and accommodations, while Chapter 6 examines selected mass tourism attractions such as casinos, theme parks, ski resorts and golf courses. Chapter 7 addresses quality control mechanisms such as codes of conduct, ecolabels and awards that attempt to ensure adherence to the precepts of environmental and sociocultural sustainability. The next three chapters shift the focus to destinations (Chapter 8) and to the spatial strategies (Chapter 9) and visitor management strategies (Chapter 10) that can be employed by public sector managers to realize sustainable tourism outcomes. Finally, Chapter 11 illustrates and synthesizes issues raised in previous chapters to one particular sector, ecotourism, which is described here as the conscience of sustainable tourism because of its explicit focus on sustainability precepts.

Format

The 11-chapter format reflects the division of most senior university-level courses into a 12 to 14 week semester, so that allowing time for midterm exams as well as introductory and concluding housekeeping, one chapter can be covered each week. Each chapter begins with a list of expectations that the student should meet after reading and assimilating the text. The text that follows is organized into main sections (e.g. Section 1.0), primary subsections (e.g. Section 1.2.1) and secondary as well as tertiary subsections, neither of which are numbered. Important terms are italicized while asterisks identify organizations, initiatives, etc. for which a relevant web link is provided near the end of the chapter in the *On the net* feature. Other supportive features that follow the main text of each chapter include a Summary, a list of print resources, a *Beyond the Book* feature that provides relevant questions and exercises that go beyond mere reiteration of content and a case study that illustrates concepts and issues raised by the chapter.

Limitations

The topic of sustainable tourism encompasses an enormous body of information and knowledge that expands by the day. It is therefore inevitable that much important material will be excluded from this book. In some cases no coverage was available in English and in other instances my search for relevant information through personal contact, the web or other sources was unsuccessful. The author would appreciate being made aware of such material so that it can be considered for inclusion in the next edition. One result of this limited access to information is uneven geographic coverage. Most of the material pertains to developed regions such as North America and Western Europe where the involvement with sustainability is most pronounced, while regions such as Africa, the Middle East and Asia receive only sporadic attention. A major limitation beyond the author's control is the paucity of rigorous academic studies that assess the results of certification programmes, measure awareness of and support for such initiatives among consumers and operators and otherwise provide objective evidence by which progress in the realm of sustainable tourism can be assessed.

Acknowledgements

I am indebted to Eugenio Yunis, Head of the Sustainable Development of Tourism Department of the World Tourism Organization, for agreeing to write a foreword to this book, for providing critical WTO documents and for clarifying the administrative structure of WTO initiatives and bodies in this area. Thanks also to Dr Dirk Glaesser, Chief of the WTO Publications Section, for granting permission to reprint material from WTO publications. The following individuals also deserve to be recognized in respect to the provision of information and/or permission to reproduce information:

Jenny Dunhill, Editorial Assistant, CABI, for providing permission to reproduce Table 4.1 from Eagles and McCool (2002) *Tourism in National Parks and Protected Areas: Planning and Management*, Figure 1.1 from Font and Buckley (2001) *Tourism Ecolabelling: Certification and Promotion of Sustainable Management*, Table 1.4 from Weaver (1998) *Ecotourism in the Less Developed World* and Figure 18.3 from Lawton (2001b) 'Public Protected Areas'; Helen Gainford, Rights Manager, Elsevier, for permission to reproduce Figure 2 from Weaver (2000a) 'A broad context Model of Destination Development Scenarios' and Figure 2 from Weaver (in press) 'Comprehensive and Minimalist Dimensions of Ecotourism'; Annalisa Koeman, Customer Services Manager, Green Globe 21 for providing information about the organization's recent initiatives and the reasons for the current membership pattern by country; Fanny Langella, the Information Services Coordinator of the Global Reporting Initiative in the Netherlands, who gave permission to reproduce extracts of the Tour Operators Supplement for use in Figure 5.1; Francesca Leadlay, Administrator, Tourism Concern, for giving permission to reprint the Himalayan Tourist Code; Steve Noakes, Chair of the PATA Sustainable Tourism Committee, for providing information about the initiatives of PATA and Green Globe 21; Cathy Parsons, Global Manager of Green Globe 21 and Chief Executive Officer, Green Globe Asia Pacific, for permission to reproduce the three Green Globe 21 logos as well as the Company Standard Environmental Management System and Social Sustainability Policy; and Peter Semone, Vice President Development, PATA, who gave permission to reproduce the APEC/PATA Environmental Code for Sustainable Tourism. Thanks also to the Resort Municipality of Whistler for allowing the author to reproduce portions of their tourism zoning bylaw. Last but definitely not least, I want to thank Elsevier Butterworth-Heinemann team members Sally North, Senior Commissioning Editor – Hospitality, Tourism & Leisure, for her unflagging encouragement and support throughout the process of writing and producing this book and editorial assistant Fran Ford, who managed the production of the manuscript after it was submitted.

Chapter 1
Emergence of sustainable tourism

Chapter objectives

Upon completion of this chapter, the reader should be able to:

- **describe the growth and geographical diffusion of international tourism since World War II**
- **discuss how each of Jafari's four 'platforms' perceives tourism in terms of its potential impacts and sustainability**
- **explain why the destination life cycle model can be regarded as the culmination of the cautionary platform**
- **describe the relationship between sustainable development and sustainable tourism**
- **explain why sustainable tourism has become institutionalized and**
- **illustrate how sustainable tourism has been formally incorporated into the agendas of tourism and non-tourism organizations at the global, regional and national levels.**

1.1 Introduction

The paradigm of sustainable tourism emerged, and is still evolving, as a result of developments both internal and external to the tourism sector over the past half-century. The primary purpose of this introductory chapter is to trace the evolution of the now dominant sustainable tourism paradigm during this period, using the platform model of Jafari as a framework (Section 1.3). The extent to which the idea of sustainable tourism development has been formally recognized by international and regional organizations, both external and internal to the tourism sector, will also be considered (Section 1.4). As a prelude to this analysis, Section 1.2 briefly describes the status of the global tourism industry as of 2004 and broadly outlines its dramatic numeric growth and geographic expansion since World War II.

1.2 Status of global tourism in 2004

Among the most remarkable socioeconomic phenomena of the post-World War II era has been the expansion of the global tourism industry. International tourism statistics compiled by the World

Tourism Organization (WTO) are subject to periodic revision and should therefore not be regarded as absolute, but they nevertheless indicate a 30-fold increase in recorded international stayover tourists (i.e. those staying one or more nights in another country for reasons that qualify as 'tourism') between 1950 and 2004 (see Table 1.1). Concurrently, international tourism receipts are estimated to have increased by a factor of 235, from approximately US$2 billion to US$474 billion (WTO, 2003a). Allowing for inflation, this still represents a 'real' 23-fold increase. Conventional wisdom, moreover, maintains that a 10:1 ratio exists between domestic and international tourists (e.g. Goeldner and Ritchie, 2003), suggesting that the 750 million international tourist trips of 2004 were augmented by 7.5 billion instances of individuals travelling as tourists within their own country.

Having moved from relative obscurity in 1950 to one of the world's largest industries at the beginning of the twenty-first century, global tourism as of 2003 was attributed by the World Travel and Tourism Council (WTTC) with generating 67 million direct jobs and a direct US$1.28 trillion contribution (or 3.7 per cent) to global cumulative GDP (gross domestic product, or the value of all goods and services produced within a given country in a given year). If the indirect effects are factored in (e.g. the portion of the oil and automotive industries that are consumed by tourism), the respective statistics increase to 195 million jobs and a US$3.53 trillion contribution, or 10.2 per cent, to global GDP (WTTC, 2003a).

While individual destinations often experience dramatic fluctuations in the number of tourist visits from year to year and over the long term, the overall global pattern since 1950 has been one of almost uninterrupted growth. Stagnation in the early 1980s is associated with a severe global economic recession, while the Oil Crisis of 1973 and the Gulf War of 1991 succeeded only in slowing rather than reversing the rate of increase (see Table 1.1). One of only two actual declines occurred in 2001 as an aftershock of the September 11 terrorist attacks in the USA. But given the magnitude of those attacks and subsequent events such as the invasion of Iraq, the recovery in 2002 to a growth rate of 2.7 per cent is that much more notable and indicative

Table 1.1
Estimated international tourist (stayover) arrivals 1950–2004[1]

Year	Arrivals	Year	Arrivals	Year	Arrivals	Year	Arrivals
1950	25	1971	179	1983	293	1995	565
1960	69	1972	189	1984	320	1996	596
1961	75	1973	199	1985	330	1997	613
1962	81	1974	206	1986	341	1998	625
1963	90	1975	222	1987	367	1999	650
1964	105	1976	229	1988	394	2000	687
1965	113	1977	249	1989	425	2001	684
1966	120	1978	267	1990	457	2002	703
1967	130	1979	283	1991	463	2003	694
1968	131	1980	288	1992	503	2004	750
1969	144	1981	290	1993	520		
1970	166	1982	290	1994	551		

[1] in millions.
Source: WTO.

of tourism's resiliency. The subsequent 1 per cent decline in 2003 can also be considered an anomaly attributable in part to the US-led invasion of Iraq.

The environmental and sociocultural sustainability of the tourism industry may be highly contentious, as subsequent sections in this chapter will show. However, the sustainability of tourism *growth*, at least at the global level, seems quite clear. Accordingly, the WTO (2003a) retains confidence in its long-term forecast of one billion international stayover tourists by 2010 and 1.5 billion by 2020, despite persistent uncertainties such as those associated with the ongoing 'war on terrorism'.

1.2.1 Pattern of geographic expansion

The actual spatial expansion of global tourism since 1950 has occurred through three distinct stages (see Figure 1.1), as described below.

Stage 1: between and within the more developed countries

Initially, the rapid post-World War II increase in discretionary income and time within Europe, North America and Australia/New Zealand resulted in a surge of tourism activity both within and between these more developed countries (MDCs), which were later joined by Japan and the so-called Asian 'tigers' of South Korea, Taiwan, Singapore and Hong Kong. In 2003, travel among the MDCs accounted for more than 70 per cent of all international tourism traffic, or about 500 million tourist trips (WTO, 2003a). Moreover, eight of the top ten destination countries in terms of total stayover visitors in that year were MDCs (i.e. France, Spain, USA, Italy, UK, Austria, Germany and Canada), while just two (China and Mexico) were less developed countries (LDCs).

Stage 2: from more developed to less developed countries

In the second stage, which gained momentum during the 1960s, tourists from the MDCs, or 'North', travelled in significant numbers to LDC destinations, or 'South'.

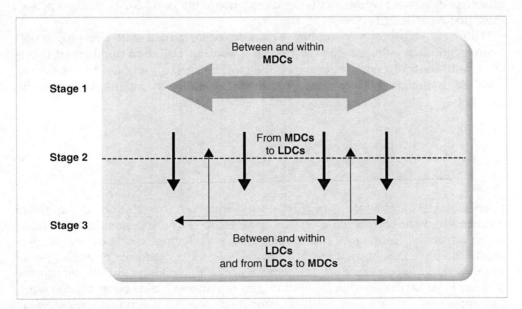

Figure 1.1
Three stages of global tourism diffusion.

Longitudinal demand/supply relationships evolved as North American tourists came to dominate Caribbean basin 'sunlust' destinations and Europeans accounted for most visitors to the emerging destinations of the Mediterranean and Indian Ocean basins. Developing countries such as Barbados, Bahamas (see case study at the end of this chapter), Antigua, Fiji, Cyprus, the Maldives and Seychelles, as a result, underwent a rapid transition toward a position of dependency on the tourism sector as part of their incorporation into what Turner and Ash (1975) termed the international *pleasure periphery*. By the early 2000s, approximately 25 per cent of international tourist traffic consisted of travellers from MDCs visiting LDCs, primarily within the pleasure periphery.

Stage 3: between and within the less developed countries

The third and most recent stage of global tourism diffusion results from the emergence of a significant middle class within the less developed world and involves its travel between and within the LDCs as well as to the more developed world. Examples of this phenomenon, which accounts for about 5 per cent of all international tourism, includes the movement of Indian tourists to Kenya, Brazilians to Uruguay, Malaysians to Thailand, Kuwaitis and other Arabs to Australia and Venezuelans to the USA.

China provides the most dramatic illustration of this latest stage, with the number of outbound Chinese tourists increasing from 620 000 in 1990 to 9.2 million in 1999 (Weaver and Lawton, 2002a). The WTO (2003b) projects 100 million Chinese outbound tourists by 2020. The number of domestic tourist trips within China, estimated at 694 million in 1998, was expected to exceed one billion in the early 2000s (Lew, 2001). Similar dynamics, while not as well articulated, are discernable in India, which had 3.5 million outbound and 131 million domestic tourists in 1997 (Singh, 2001). As population levels and travel proclivity reach a state of maturation within Europe and North America, it is the enormous potential of tourist markets in China and other less developed countries that lend credence to the WTO 2020 visitation projections that were described above.

With new stages of geographic expansion being added and previous stages being continually reinforced by additional growth in visitation numbers, it is reasonable to contend that *every* place on the world's surface can now be considered a tourist destination. The issue of tourism sustainability, as a result, is universally relevant.

1.3 Jafari's 'platform' model

Jafari (1989, 2001) contends that the post-World War II evolution of the global tourism sector has been both influenced and described by the sequential appearance of the 'advocacy', 'cautionary', 'adaptancy' and 'knowledge-based' platforms or perspectives. While they apply to tourism as a whole, these platforms provide a useful framework for understanding the emergence and development of sustainable tourism in particular, bearing in mind that each platform builds on its predecessors. The appearance of each new platform, moreover, does not mean that the preceding platforms disappeared or became less influential, with Jafari (2001) emphasizing that all four platforms coexist within the contemporary global tourism sector.

1.3.1 Advocacy platform

The first platform to appear in the post-war period is characterized by strong support for tourism. The appearance and dominance of this pro-tourism perspective in the 1950s and 1960s reflected the convergence of several facilitating factors during that era. These included the emergence of a strong middle class in the more developed world with a growing proclivity to travel for recreational purposes, the return of peace and stability to much of the world following World War II and the Korean War and the introduction of technological innovations that reduced the real cost of travel, making more destinations accessible to a larger market. Tourism, especially for the newly independent but impoverished countries of the South, was touted as a benign avenue to economic development that would be sustained by an inexhaustible supply of tourism resources such as beaches, local culture and scenery.

Economic benefits

The broad economic arguments for tourism that dominate the advocacy platform literature are summarized in Table 1.2. These include the generation of direct revenues, but also substantial indirect revenues realized through the subsequent dynamic of the multiplier effect as other local economic sectors, such as agriculture, respond to tourism's demand for an extensive array of affiliated products and services. A parallel effect is argued with respect to employment, wherein the labour-intensive tourism industry would provide a large number of direct and indirect jobs suitable in particular for largely unskilled labour forces bedevilled by high unemployment and underemployment. Tourism is additionally regarded as a stimulus of

Table 1.2
Contrasting tourism contentions of the advocacy and cautionary platform

Advocacy platform	Cautionary platform
• Generates direct revenues	• Direct revenues eroded by seasonality and costs (marketing, administration, public infrastructure, incentives)
• Generates indirect revenues (multiplier effect, linkages to other sectors)	• Leakages created by importation of goods and services and profit repatriation
• Creates employment (labour intensive, unskilled)	• Employment is low-paying, seasonal, part-time, low benefit
• Stimulates regional development	• Not necessarily best alternative (see problems)
• Strong global performance	• Performance fluctuates at national and local level (global curve cannot be extrapolated to local level)
• Promotes cross-cultural understanding	• Promotes cross-cultural conflict due to disparities, congestion
• Provides incentive to preserve culture, natural environment	• Culture is commodified, crime is stimulated and environment is degraded by development and tourist activities, as well as induced effects

economic development in peripheral regions experiencing stagnation or decline in the primary sector but lacking the potential to accommodate large-scale industrialization or other alternatives. Conversely, tourism is thought to provide a way of revitalizing declining industrial cities such as Lowell, Massachusetts (USA) through the presentation of its industrial heritage as tourist attractions (McNulty, 1985). In the context of modernization theory (Rostow, 1960), tourism serves as a propulsive activity within select growth poles to stimulate economic growth and consequent 'trickle-down' effects. This stimulus, moreover, would be sustained by tourism's record of robust growth, as evidenced in the visitation statistics of Table 1.1.

Sociocultural and environmental benefits

Purported social and cultural benefits augment the economic arguments that dominate the advocacy platform. One of these is the idea that tourism promotes cross-cultural understanding and, ultimately, world peace, through direct contact between host and guest (D'Amore, 1988). Moreover, tourism provides an incentive to preserve a destination's unique environmental, cultural and historical assets, from which a portion of the revenue can be allocated for ongoing restoration and maintenance purposes. By this logic, iconic heritage sites such as the Great Wall of China, the Egyptian pyramids and the Civil War battlefields of the UK and USA would be seriously compromised in the absence of tourist-related interest and revenue.

Mings (1969), in supporting tourism as an ideal economic sector for the Caribbean region, offers a good illustration of the advocacy perspective as it was presented earlier in the post-war period. His argument is essentially that the small islands of the Caribbean lack the resources and scale to base their economic development on a policy of industrialization, but are ideally suited because of their resources and large cheap labour forces to offer resort-based tourism opportunities to proximate markets such as the USA. Characteristic of this and much of the other advocacy literature is an uncritical approach that views tourism as a panacea. Accordingly, representatives of this platform usually implicitly or explicitly endorse a 'continual growth' approach to tourism development which holds that if a little tourism is a good thing, then more tourism must be even better. This pro-growth sentiment is consistent with the widespread support within this platform for free market capitalism as a vehicle that best facilitates this growth and yields significant economic benefits.

Representatives of the advocacy platform, however, as with all the other perspectives, are not homogeneous in their beliefs. An interventionist element, for example, is evident among supporters of the above-mentioned growth pole theory, who hold that government should take the lead role in establishing conditions conducive to market-sustained economic development and spatial diffusion through tourism. Cancún and the other tourism-based growth poles of Mexico are a good example of this approach (Truett and Truett, 1982).

1.3.2 Cautionary platform

Several factors contributed in the late 1960s and early 1970s to the emergence of the cautionary platform, which basically argues that unregulated tourism development eventually culminates in unacceptably high environmental, economic and sociocultural costs for the residents of destinations, who have the most to lose as a result of these costs. A major factor was the intensification of tourism development in many places (assisted by planners and officials supportive of the advocacy approach) and within less developed regions in particular, to a level where the negative impacts became increasingly evident. Concurrently, 'dependency theory' and other neo-Marxist commentaries provided a convenient framework within which these impacts, and the international tourism system in general, could be contextualized. Focusing especially on the pleasure periphery, the dependency theorists contended that tourism, like plantation agriculture in a previous era, was a means through which the developed core regions continued their exploitation and domination of the 'underdeveloped' periphery (Hills and Lundgren, 1977; Britton, 1982). It is through this logic that Finney and Watson (1975) consider tourism as 'a new kind of sugar', while Harrigan (1974) accuses tourism of perpetuating the master–slave relationships of slavery.

An additional factor was the emergence of the environmental movement and its popularization through such breakthrough works as *Silent Spring* (Carson, 1962), *Small is Beautiful* (Schumacher, 1973) and *Gaia: A New Look at Life on Earth* (Lovelock, 1979). Knill (1991) associates this movement more broadly with the appearance of a green paradigm that has challenged the alleged exploitative and anthropocentric premises of the 'dominant western environmental paradigm' (see Chapter 4). Representatives of this environmental strand of the cautionary platform include Crittendon (1975), who emphasized the negative impacts of tourism on wildlife, and Budowski (1976), who maintained that the relationship between tourism and the natural environment was mostly one of neutral 'coexistence' that was, however, moving toward 'conflict' as tourism continued to expand haphazardly into relatively unspoiled areas. The ideal scenario of 'symbiosis', according to Budowski, is rarely encountered.

Economic costs

As outlined in Table 1.2, supporters of this platform, many of who are not strict dependency theorists or environmentalists (e.g. English, 1986; Lea, 1988), typically cite a counter-argument to every supposed benefit put forward by tourism advocates. Where the advocacy platform extols the generation of substantial direct revenues, supporters of the cautionary platform cite accelerating marketing, incentive and administrative costs that significantly erode these revenues as destinations become more competitive and bureaucracies more bloated. Where the former note the auxiliary benefits of the multiplier effect, the latter contend that this is minimal or non-existent due to revenue leakages associated with local economies too weak to generate meaningful linkages with tourism. Tourism employment, moreover, is decried as chronically low-wage, part-time and seasonal, as well as bereft of employee benefits or opportunities for upward mobility. And while a long-term pattern of sustained growth exists at the global scale, individual destinations are subject to unpredictable and potentially devastating fluctuations due to competition from other tourism destinations and products as well as the sensitivity of tourist markets to political and environmental instability. The seasonal nature of tourist demand, moreover, tends to create a regular 'drought–deluge' cycle that respectively induces periods of under-capacity and over-capacity. These factors combine, ultimately, to reduce the effectiveness of tourism as an agent of economic development in peripheral or depressed regions.

Sociocultural and environmental costs

In the sociocultural arena, supporters of the cautionary platform contend that tourism is just as likely to foster misunderstanding and conflict, rather than harmony and world peace, due to the cultural divide and disparities in wealth that often occur between host and guest and to the *in situ* nature of tourism consumption (i.e. tourism products are 'produced' and 'consumed' at the same location). Frustration over congestion and the diversion of services and resources to tourists may also increase the likelihood of conflict. The incentive effect may be offset by the *commodification* effect as residents adapt products and services to the demands of the tourist market rather than the needs of their own community (Cohen, 1988). Increased tourism activity is also associated with increased crime in destinations such as the Gold Coast of Australia (Prideaux and Dunn, 1995), in part because the tourist is an attractive target and in part because some tourists (e.g. paedophiles visiting Cambodia, or football hooligans from the UK travelling to France) intend to engage in illegal or criminal activity.

With regard to the natural environment, foundation assets such as beaches, forests and lakes, as per Budowski (1976) and Crittendon (1975) (see above), become congested and polluted due to pressures arising from tourism-related construction, waste generation and visitor activity, thereby neutralizing the incentive effect. Indirect construction and waste, often on a much greater scale, is also associated with the need to provide housing and services for workers in the tourism industry and their dependents (Weaver and Lawton, 2002a). It is argued that these cultural and environmental modifications ultimately give rise to a homogeneous 'international' tourism landscape that destroys the destination's unique 'sense of place'.

Destination life cycle model

The well-known destination life cycle model of Butler (1980) may be regarded as the culmination of the cautionary platform given its contention that unregulated tourism development eventually undermines the very foundation assets that support the growth of a tourist destination in the first instance. The S-curved model begins with a low-level equilibrium 'exploration' stage during which the impacts of the embryonic tourist flow, either positive or negative, are negligible. Local responses to the incipient tourist traffic eventually give rise to a transitional 'involvement' stage, which is soon in turn superseded by a period of rapid tourism 'development' as the destination experiences and responds to accelerated demand. It is during this stage of mass tourism onset that the problems cited above become significant and eventually cause the critical environmental, sociocultural and economic carrying capacities of the destination to be breeched. 'Consolidation' and 'stagnation' and then 'decline' successively occur if industry or government undertakes no remedial intervention. Alternatively, 'rejuvenation' is possible if such measures are implemented. The assumptions of the destination life cycle model, like the cautionary platform in general, are not inherently hostile to tourism, but contend that unregulated tourism contains within itself the seeds of its own destruction. Hence, it is assumed that a high level of public sector intervention is necessary to ensure that deterioration does not occur.

1.3.3 Adaptancy platform

The cautionary platform identified the potential negative *impacts* of tourism, but did not articulate models of tourism that would avoid these effects and actually realize the array of benefits described by the supporters of the advocacy platform. The appearance in the late 1970s and early 1980s of discussion on perceived *solutions* marks the beginning of the adaptancy platform, a perspective aligned ideologically with the cautionary platform that is so called because it espouses tourism that is adapted to the unique sociocultural and environmental circumstances of any given community.

Many umbrella terms were used to describe these adaptations, but the one to gain the widest recognition was 'alternative tourism', meaning specifically that these options were alternatives to mass tourism, which was regarded as the antithesis of the adaptive tourism cited above (Dernoi, 1981; Holden, 1984; Gonsalves, 1987; Cazes, 1989). Alternative tourism characteristics, accordingly, are distinguished by the degree to which they contrast with mass tourism, as for example in supporting locally owned small-scale enterprises rather than those that are externally owned and large-scale (see Section 3.4). Ecotourism, notably, first appeared in the mid-1980s as a manifestation of alternative tourism that emphasizes attractions based on the natural environment (see Chapter 10).

1.3.4 Knowledge-based platform

According to Jafari (2001), several factors gave rise in the late 1980s and 1990s to what he terms the 'knowledge-based' platform. One of these was the growing realization among tourism stakeholders that the sector had evolved into an enormous global industry and that the alternative tourism espoused by the adaptancy platform is not a practical or even appropriate option for the many destinations already dominated by mass tourism, which 'is here to stay'. Alternative tourism, accordingly, is at best only a partial solution to broader problems of global tourism. Secondly, it became increasingly apparent that *any* mode of tourism in any destination gives rise to both positive and negative impacts, suggesting that the ideologically polarized advocacy, cautionary and adaptancy platforms offer a limited and biased world view of an increasingly complex global tourism sector that defies such simplistic analysis.

What is required, according to Jafari, is a holistic, systematic approach that utilizes rigorous scientific methods to compile the knowledge needed to properly assess and manage the tourism sector. He argues that tourism stakeholders, and academics in particular, have started to pursue the 'scientification' of the field and that this is increasingly manifest in the introduction of tourism into university curricula, increased funding of tourism-related research and the proliferation of peer-reviewed tourism and hospitality journals (see Weaver and Lawton, 2002a). In this context, it is untenable to contend (as with the adaptancy platform) that small-scale tourism is inherently superior to large-scale tourism or vice versa (as with the advocacy platform). Rather, the decision as to what mode(s) of tourism is best for a particular destination should be based on a sound scientific analysis of its characteristics and the subsequent implementation of appropriate planning and management strategies.

Sustainable development

By the early 1990s, the term *sustainable tourism* was gaining currency among academics and practitioners to describe desired and (in theory) scientifically informed outcomes that, depending on circumstances, could potentially range from the most rudimentary forms of alternative tourism to the most intensive manifestations of urban and resort tourism. The term itself emerged from a broader discourse on the idea of 'sustainable development', which according to Bramwell and Lane (1993) was first articulated in 1973 and gained momentum through the 1980 World Conservation Strategy (IUCN, UNEP and WWF, 1980). However, it was the report of the World Commission on Environment and Development (popularly known as the Brundtland Report, after the name of the Commission's Chair) which popularized the concept in the late 1980s, defining sustainable development as 'development that meets the needs of the present without compromising the ability of future generations to meet their own needs' (WCED, 1987, p. 43). Essentially, sustainable development 'advocates the wise use and conservation of resources in order to maintain their long-term viability' (Eber, 1992, p. 1).

The subsequent extent to which the concept of sustainable development has become almost universally endorsed as a desired process is truly remarkable. Aside from the credentials of the Commission and the high level endorsement by the United Nations that followed (in evidence for example at the 1992 Rio Earth Summit), this support can be explained in part by the appealing semantics of the term, which offers the prospect of *development* for the supporters of continued growth, but the prospect of *sustainability* for environmentalists and other advocates of a slow growth or steady state approach. Synthesizing these two contradictory strands, sustainable development represents the attractive possibility of continuing economic development that does not unduly strain the earth's environmental, socio-cultural or economic carrying capacities.

Sustainable tourism

Sustainable tourism may be regarded most basically as the application of the sustainable development idea to the tourism sector – that is, *tourism* development that meets the needs of the present without compromising the ability of future generations to meet their own needs or, in concert with Budowski's (1976) 'symbiosis' scenario (see Section 1.3.2), *tourism* that wisely uses and conserves resources in order to maintain their long-term viability. Essentially, sustainable tourism involves the minimization of negative impacts and the maximization of positive impacts. Yet, while sustainable tourism may therefore be regarded as a form of sustainable development (i.e. development as a process) as well as a vehicle for achieving the latter (i.e. development as a goal), there is not as direct a relationship between the two terms as might be expected. The Brundtland Report, curiously, makes no mention of tourism even though the latter had already attained 'megasector' status by the mid-1980s. This neglect was evident several years later in the *Agenda 21* strategy document that emerged from the seminal Rio Earth Summit in 1992, which made only a few incidental references to tourism as both a cause and potential ameliorator of environmental and social problems (UNCED, 1992).

It was, rather, among tourism academics and organizations, or those especially aware of the sector's great potential to generate both costs and benefits, that discussions explicitly using the term sustainable tourism first emerged in the early 1990s (see for example Pigram, 1990; Dearden, 1991; Inskeep, 1991; Lane, 1991; Manning, 1991; Bull, 1992; D'Amore, 1992; Eber, 1992; Zurick, 1992). A notable development was the inauguration of the peer reviewed *Journal of Sustainable Tourism* in 1993. Preceding this literature is earlier material, notably by Murphy (1985) and Krippendorf (1987), that does not use the term 'sustainable tourism' explicitly (they respectively refer to 'community-based tourism' and 'soft tourism'), but espouse similar principles in reference to mass tourism, which they regard as legitimate. Similar sentiments are evident in contemporary deliberations involving the World Tourism Organization and the United Nations (WTO, 1985, 1989; WTO and UNEP, 1982, 1983). Distinguishing the work of the 1990s, however, was reference to the broader discourse on sustainable development as a basis for proposing strategies that would achieve a more sustainable tourism sector.

1.4 Institutionalization of sustainable tourism

Since the pioneering work of the 1980s and early 1990s, the amount of research and literature related to sustainable tourism has increased exponentially in volume and sophistication as the idea has moved rapidly from a position of peripherality to centrality within the knowledge-based platform. This centrality is evident in the extent to which the concepts of sustainable development and sustainable tourism (or sustainable tourism development) have been officially recognized or 'institutionalized' (Frazier, 1997) in organizations both internal and external to the tourism sector. The array of organizations described below is not inclusive, given the large number of institutions engaged with sustainable tourism and the frequency with which new organizations are becoming involved. Other more specialized sustainable tourism-related organizations are described in chapters where they are more relevant to the topic areas (e.g. the IHEI in Chapter 5 and Green Globe 21 in Chapter 7).

1.4.1 External (non-tourism) institutions

Global organizations

The primary example of the formal recognition of sustainable tourism within global multilateral organizations is the United Nations, which has increasingly if belatedly attended to tourism-related issues since the 1992 Rio Earth Summit. Matters pertaining to sustainable tourism are officially addressed through the Production and Consumption Unit of the United Nations Environment Programme (UNEP), whose Tourism Programme* is mandated by the UN Commission on Sustainable Development to facilitate the implementation of *Agenda 21* within the tourism sector, primarily through local governments (UNEP, 2002, 2003a). The Seventh Session of the UN Commission on Sustainable Development in 1999 was largely focused on the issue of sustainable tourism.

The Organization for Economic Cooperation and Development (OECD) is a major international organization focused on fostering free markets and democratic governance. Through its Tourism Committee*, the OECD, among other objectives, 'aims to enhance the capacity of OECD governments (which include most MDCs and some LDCs) to adjust their policies and actions to support sustainable growth in tourism' (OECD, 2003).

Regional organizations

At a regional level, European multilateral institutions have been especially proactive in formally promoting sustainable tourism since the Rio Earth Summit. The European Commission* (the executive body of the European Union), for example, has identified sustainable tourism as one of five priority areas in the *Fifth Community Programme for Environment and Sustainable Development*, while its environmental policy wing has developed a European Charter for sustainable tourism in protected areas. Deliberations took place through the Commission during 2003 toward the articulation of a formal sustainable tourism policy for the European Union (EC, 2003). The Council of Europe* (a 45-member group encompassing most European states and concerned with regional human rights, standardization of social and legal practices, etc.) has established a programme to support the dissemination of sustainable tourism in Eastern Europe (Blangy and Vautier, 2001).

Elsewhere, the Organization of American States (OAS) is increasingly involved with sustainable tourism through its Inter-Sectoral Unit for Tourism*, which sponsored the Seventeenth Inter-Sectoral Travel Congress in 1997 with the theme of 'Partnership for the Sustainable Development of Tourism'. In 2000, the Asia-Pacific Economic Cooperation (APEC) region's Tourism Working Group* passed the Seoul Declaration on an APEC Tourism Charter*, which presented as one of four goals its intent to 'sustainably manage tourism outcomes and impacts' (APEC, 2000). In addition, APEC cooperated with a major regional promotional body to produce a sustainable tourism code for member states and organizations (see below).

The sustainable tourism initiatives of the Association of Caribbean States (ACS) are notable because of the extent to which the Caribbean has become regionally dependent upon large-scale tourism (Weaver, 2001a). Through its Special Committee on Sustainable Tourism, the ACS in 2001 formulated a Convention Establishing the Sustainable Tourism Zone of the Caribbean.

Engagement with this topic, however, is not universal among regional multilateral organizations. The tourism arm of the Association of South-East Asian Nations (ASEAN), for example, was focused at the time of publication on promoting the region as a tourist destination, liberalizing international travel regulations and ensuring the safety of tourists from terrorism. Concurrently, the recently formed African Union (AU, which supersedes the Organization of African Unity or OAU), is concentrating on addressing basic issues of security, good governance and economic development and thus is not yet positioned to regard tourism, including sustainable tourism, as a priority.

Environmental organizations

Sustainable tourism is also being formally advocated within prominent worldwide environmental organizations such as Conservation International (CI) and The Nature Conservancy (TNC), each of which has established an Ecotourism Programme* to promote nature-based sustainable tourism as one strategy for protecting global biodiversity. The World Wide Fund for Nature (WWF) is collaborating with partner organizations to support sustainable tourism through regional initiatives such as the International Arctic Programme and the Mediterranean Programme*.

1.4.2 Tourism-related institutions

World Tourism Organization (WTO)

The World Tourism Organization* (WTO) has played a lead role in the formulation and diffusion of sustainable tourism policies and practices since the early 1980s. Early milestones include the 1980 Manila Declaration, which claimed that tourism resources 'cannot be left uncontrolled without running the risk of their deterioration, or even destruction' (WTO, 1980, p. 4) and subsequently called for the 'orderly growth' of the sector. In 1985, the Joint Declaration of the WTO and UNEP advocated the 'rational management' of tourism (Inskeep, 1991). The 1989 Hague Declaration on tourism proclaimed similar sentiments, but for the first time used the terminology of sustainable development and sustainable tourism, while supporting integrated planning as the vehicle for attaining these objectives.

Following through on the Rio Earth Summit's call for all sectors to embrace the principles and practices of sustainable development, the WTO, in partnership with the WTTC and the Earth Council, released *Agenda 21 for the Travel and Tourism Industry* in 1996. This document offers practical suggestions to businesses and governments for implementing sustainable tourism. It was the WTO that 3 years later brought the issue of sustainable tourism to the Seventh Session of the UN Commission on Sustainable Development (see above) and which was then called upon by the Commission to take the lead global role in this area. The Sustainable Development of Tourism Department, whose head reports directly to the WTO Secretary-General, is the WTO unit through which this role is primarily exercised. In this operational capacity, it is advised and supervised in matters of policy and priority action by a Sustainable Development of Tourism Committee consisting of representatives from eight rotating member states who serve a 4-year term.

The year 2002 was particularly significant for sustainable tourism in the global arena as the International Year of Ecotourism, which was organized by the WTO, and also because of the plenary address given by the Secretary-General of the WTO to the World Summit on Sustainable Development in Johannesburg (the largest global environmental forum since the Rio Earth Summit in 1992), which called for the creation of a formal plan of implementation. Indicating the extent to which the idea of sustainable tourism has become recognized and formalized at the highest levels of international discourse, the WTO subsequently launched its ST–EP* (Sustainable Tourism – Elimination of Poverty) initiative which under the rubric 'Liberalization with a Human Face' called for the establishment of an international Foundation, a systematic research base, an operating framework to provide incentives and disseminate information, and an annual forum. The Foundation, based in Seoul (Republic of Korea), seeks $100 million of funding by 2015 primarily for the purposes of supporting 5000 community-based projects.

World Travel and Trade Council (WTTC)
The WTTC is the main international forum and interest body for the private sector tourism industry, comprising most of the world's largest tourism-related corporations. Beyond its collaboration with the WTO in the *Agenda 21* report, the WTTC has embraced sustainable tourism through its Blueprint for New Tourism*, launched in 2003 (WTTC, 2003b). The involvement of the WTTC is notable given this organization's longstanding adherence to an advocacy platform approach to tourism development.

PATA
Like the WTTC, the Pacific Asia Travel Association (PATA), as the lead promotional organization for tourism in the Pacific Asia region, actively promotes the cause of sustainable tourism. This is done through its Office of Environment and Culture and through the Sustainable Tourism Committee in particular. Relevant initiatives include the 2001 APEC/PATA Code for Sustainable Tourism*, a code of ethics for travellers (approved in 2002), the hosting of conferences and environmental awards (see Chapter 7) and the commissioning of expert Task Forces to investigate options for sustainable tourism in member destinations.

National and subnational recognition
A growing number of countries, at least on paper, are engaging in the effort to foster sustainable tourism development, usually under the auspices of their national

tourism organizations and often in cooperation with relevant international organizations. One example of the latter is a group of APEC members (Australia, Brunei, Chile, Hong Kong, Indonesia, Japan, Korea (Republic), Malaysia, Mexico, New Zealand, Peru, Philippines, Singapore, Taiwan and Thailand) that have agreed to develop Individual Action Plans* for implementing the APEC Tourism Charter (see above), with 2005, 2010 and 2020 designated as key delivery dates.

Other regional state-level initiatives are being coordinated through the Association of Caribbean States and the Council of Europe (see above), while the WTO has assisted countries such as Pakistan, Rwanda, the Palestinian Territory and Moldova to develop sustainable tourism master plans. Such organizations, especially in regard to the less developed regions, are important as stimulators of sustainable tourism to the degree that they (a) obligate member states to make commitments and also to move from a position of rhetoric to implementation and (b) provide tangible assistance for attaining designated objectives.

Substate units (e.g. provinces) in some of the larger and/or federally constituted countries are also actively involved with sustainable tourism. Examples include the states of Australia (e.g. Queensland), the regions of Spain (e.g. Cataluña), the internal Russian republics (e.g. Tatarstan) and the Canadian provinces (e.g. Newfoundland and Labrador).

1.5 Summary

Since World War II, tourism has evolved from a relatively minor activity to arguably the world's largest industry, entailing travel mainly within and among the MDCs as well as from the MDCs to the LDCs, but increasingly also travel by the burgeoning middle classes of the LDCs within the less developed world but also to the MDCs. Accordingly, the WTO is confident that international stayover arrivals will effectively double between 2000 and 2020 despite uncertainties such as the ongoing 'war on terrorism'. Already, it can be argued that *every* place in the world is now a tourist destination for which the issue of sustainability is relevant.

Four distinct perspectives have successively appeared during this era of global tourism expansion. The first of these is the advocacy platform, which touts the positive economic impacts of tourism as well as its auxiliary sociocultural and environmental benefits. Free market forces are the mechanism through which these benefits are realized. The cautionary platform, in contrast, emphasizes the costs of unregulated mass tourism and stresses the need for public intervention. Butler's destination life cycle model, which holds that a destination's carrying capacities are eventually breeched by unconstrained tourism development and that this mode of tourism therefore carries within itself the seeds of its own destruction, best summarizes this platform. The adaptancy platform maintains the same ideological premises as the cautionary platform, but differs in promoting 'alternative' or small-scale, locally controlled tourism as a vehicle for achieving positive impacts.

The knowledge-based platform emerged in the early 1990s from the realization that *any* tourism results in both costs and benefits and that alternative tourism is only a partial solution to the problems of the global tourism industry given the entrenchment of mass tourism in many destinations. In contrast to the polarized biases of earlier platforms, this perspective advocates the use of science to provide the knowledge that will determine the mode of tourism that is most appropriate under given circumstances.

Large-scale and small-scale tourism are both regarded as inherently legitimate. 'Sustainable tourism', derived from the broader concept of sustainable development, emerged in the early 1990s as a central principle of this platform, largely on the strength of its broadly appealing and seemingly neutral semantics.

Early deliberations on sustainable tourism were undertaken mainly by academics and it was only after the release of the catalytic *Agenda 21* during the 1992 Earth Summit that the concept became more broadly engaged and institutionalized by organizations such as the United Nations, the APEC region, Conservation International, the World Tourism Organization, the WTTC and PATA. The ST–EP initiative of the WTO, in particular, provides an ambitious global framework for coordinating international action. In association with the above organizations, numerous countries are also engaging with sustainable tourism through their national and subnational tourism organizations. Indeed, destination tourism bodies that do *not* espouse such policies are now the exception rather than the rule.

On the net

APEC Tourism Charter: Individual Action Plan for Australia
http://www.dfat.gov.au/apec/meetings/apec1997/action_plan.pdf

APEC Tourism Working Group
http://apecsun.apecsec.org.sg/loadall.htm?http://apecsun.apecsec.org.sg/workgroup/tourism.html

Conservation International Ecotourism Program
http://www.conservation.org/xp/CIWEB/programs/ecotourism/ecotourism.xml

Council of Europe: deliberations on the pursuit of sustainable tourism
http://assembly.coe.int/Documents/AdoptedText/TA02/ERES1285.htm

European Commission: deliberations on the pursuit of sustainable tourism
http://europa.eu.int/comm/enterprise/services/tourism/consultation/cons_en.pdf

OAS Inter-Sectoral Unit for Tourism
http://www.oas.org/main/main.asp?sLang=E&sLink=http://www.oas.org/TOURISM/home.htm

OECD Tourism Committee
http://www.oecd.org/about/0,2337,en_2649_34389_1_1_1_1_1,00.html

PATA Code for Sustainable Tourism
http://www.pata.org/frame3.cfm?pageid=55

ST–EP (Sustainable Tourism – Elimination of Poverty) WTO initiative
http://www.world-tourism.org/step/step.htm

The Nature Conservancy Ecotourism Programme
http://nature.org/aboutus/travel/ecotourism/

UNEP Tourism Programme
http://www.uneptie.org/pc/tourism/home.htm

WTO and sustainable tourism
http://www.world-tourism.org/frameset/frame_sustainable.html

WTTC Blueprint for New Tourism
http://www.wttc.org/frameset1.htm

WWF Mediterranean Programme sustainable tourism initiatives
http://www.panda.org/about_wwf/where_we_work/europe/where/mediterranean/tourism_initiatives.cfm

For further reading

Finney, B. and Watson, K. (eds) (1975). *A New Kind of Sugar: Tourism in the Pacific*. East–West Centre.
This collection of papers effectively reflects the cautionary platform and its interpretation by dependency theorists in particular. The case studies are obtained from the small island states and dependencies of the South Pacific.

Jafari, J. (2001). The scientification of tourism. In *Hosts and Guests Revisited: Tourism Issues of the 21st Century* (V.L. Smith and M. Brent, eds) pp. 28–41, Cognizant.
This is Jafari's updated discussion of his four platforms, with the emphasis on the recent 'scientification' that is occurring within the field of tourism studies.

Weaver, D.B. and Lawton, L.J. (2002). *Tourism Management*, 2nd edn. John Wiley & Sons, Australia.
Chapters 1 and 2 provide a general introduction to tourism, while Chapters 3 and 4, respectively, examine the demand and supply factors that have stimulated tourism growth since 1950. Economic, sociocultural and environmental impacts are described in Chapters 8, 9 and 10.

Beyond the book

1. Obtain a copy of the article on Caribbean tourism by Mings (1969). (a) Describe his main arguments for advocating expanded tourism development in the Caribbean and (b) outline the counter-arguments that would be put forward by supporters of the cautionary platform.
2. As depicted in Table 1.1, international stayover numbers increased steadily throughout the 1970s and 1980s despite the presence of the cautionary and adaptancy platforms during that period. Provide three reasons that help to explain the apparent lack of influence of these platforms.
3. Select any organization from among those included in Section 1.4. (a) Find out when it first became involved with sustainable tourism and describe how this involvement evolved formally (e.g. through the creation of units using the term 'sustainable tourism'). (b) Outline the sustainable tourism initiatives that have been undertaken by this organization and indicate the extent to which other organizations have collaborated in these initiatives.

On the ground: the development of tourism in the Bahamas

The Bahamas emerged after 1950 as a major pleasure periphery destination because of its proximity to the USA, ample 'sunlust' resources, political stability and the diversion of tourism activity from Cuba after 1960 following that country's revolution. From a level of 39 000 in 1937, international stayover arrivals increased to 100 000 in 1953 and 1.1 million by 1969, which represented about six arrivals for each permanent resident. A facilitating factor was successive Bahamian governments that actively supported tourism development and which were, according to Wilkinson (1997), 'fascinated by [its] short-term benefits' and closely tied to local business elites that stood to profit from the sector's expansion. Government enthusiasm also stemmed from an appreciation of tourism's viability in a country where agriculture, fishing, mining or manufacturing lacked the capacity to support economic development.

By the early 1970s, tourism accounted for about 70 per cent of GDP and receipts that exceeded $470 million in 1978 helped to position the Bahamas as one of the wealthiest Caribbean countries. Serious vulnerabilities, however, were also exposed in the early 1970s as a result of the 'oil crisis', the attainment of independence and increased competition from other regional destinations. Stayover arrivals subsequently declined to 900 000 by 1975, leading to high losses and a restive labour force. Other problems included a 90 per cent leakage rate (i.e. the loss of direct revenues to imported goods and services), a growing sex trade, foreign dominance of the hotel sector, an eroding Caribbean identity, rising incentive costs, high inflation and reliance on the short-stay US market, which accounted for four-fifths of all visitors.

Additional problems, associated with the concentration of tourism on just three of the archipelago's 700 islands (New Providence, adjacent Paradise Island and Grand Bahama) and the virtual lack of public sector tourism planning, included congestion, pollution and severe stresses on services (Wilkinson, 1997). Moreover, the rapidly growing cruise ship sector resulted in hyper-concentrations of activity and damage to the marine environment during ship visits, while generating only modest economic benefits in return (see Section 5.5.2). Archer (1981) estimated that one job was created for every 350 low-spending excursionists, compared with one for every 30 stayovers.

Master planning for Bahamian tourism commenced in 1981 in response to these problems (Wilkinson, 1997), though the proffered solutions ironically included further tourism expansion, increased incentives and the diffusion of tourism to other islands. Subsequent master plans emphasized product diversification, authenticity and 'up-scale' tourism products focused on the relatively undeveloped 'Out Islands'. The transition in the 1990s to an approach centred on sustainable development resulted in part from government's participation in the Earth Summit. Another influence was continuing product deterioration and market stagnation, with stayover arrivals hovering around 1.5 million through most of the 1980s and early 1990s. A third factor was the influence of Poon (1993), a consultant who contrasted the 'old' tourism of New Providence and Grand Bahama with the 'new' tourism potential of the Out Islands.

Sustainable tourism was first explicitly recognized in a 1995 OAS-funded consultant's report outlining development options for the Out Islands (MacGregor, 1995). The report also led to the 1996 establishment of a Sustainable Tourism Unit within the Ministry of Tourism as the driving force for implementing a national sustainable tourism strategy. In 2001, the government signed the ACS Convention Establishing the Sustainable Tourism Zone of the Caribbean. This obligates signatories to protect and promote Caribbean culture, foster community participation, protect natural resources, promote sustainable technology, provide incentives for sustainable tourism enterprises, educate tourists, develop sustainable tourism indicators and create an Information Centre on Sustainable Tourism Development accessible to all ACS members. Concurrently, a document, National Policies for Sustainable Development of Tourism in the Bahamas Islands, has been prepared under the auspices of the OAS Plurinational Tourism Project.

It remains to be seen whether this new-found focus on sustainability will revitalize the Bahamian tourism sector, which as of the mid-1990s was described by Wilkinson (1997) as a 'house of cards'. Clearly, there are fundamental differences between the 'mature' mass tourism destinations of New Providence and Grand Bahama, where strategies must take into account the reality of casinos, golf and duty-free shopping and the Out (or Family) Islands, where the relative lack of tourism activity creates opportunities for alternative tourism products such as ecotourism and locally owned guest houses.

Exercises

1. How are Jafari's four platforms evident in the development of the Bahamian tourism sector since the 1950s?
2. (a) Using the Internet and other sources, find evidence of the advocacy, cautionary and adaptancy platforms in current Bahamian tourism. (b) How would you convince these individuals or organizations to support the concept of sustainable tourism?
3. (a) What opportunities and threats to the Out Islands derive from the proximity of mass tourism in New Providence, Paradise Island and Grand Bahama? (b) What could be done to take advantages of the opportunities associated with this proximity while minimizing its threats?

Chapter 2
Issues in sustainable tourism

Chapter objectives

Upon completion of this chapter, the reader should be able to:

- discuss the problems associated with flexibility and complexity that arise when managers and planners attempt to implement strategies of sustainable tourism
- differentiate between a comprehensive and minimalist model of sustainability and explain the circumstances under which each is warranted
- rationalize the importance of financial viability in any model of sustainable tourism
- describe the crucial role played by indicators
- discuss the problems associated with selecting, measuring, monitoring and evaluating sustainable tourism indicators
- understand the work undertaken by the World Tourism Organization to assist destinations with the process of indicator selection and use
- employ the Bellagio Principles as a basis for selecting relevant sustainable tourism indicators and
- rationalize the pursuit of sustainable tourism strategies despite the many challenges that these entail.

2.1 Introduction

With its alluring premise of continued development that does not unduly harm a destination's natural and sociocultural environment, the idea of sustainable tourism has emerged as a priority objective of the global tourism sector since the mid-1990s. This is indicated in part by the extent to which it has been officially recognized and internalized by a broad array of international, regional and national organizations both internal and external to tourism. Yet, as attempts have subsequently been made to operationalize the concept in the actual planning and management of tourism businesses and destinations, various attendant issues and challenges have become increasingly apparent. This chapter introduces these interrelated challenges and in so doing provides a framework to better inform the discussion of actual tourism products, businesses and destinations in the chapters that follow.

The first issue to be discussed below (Section 2.2) is the inherent flexibility of sustainable tourism and the resulting possibility of weak and strong interpretations. A second issue (Section 2.3) is the degree to which the semantics of sustainable tourism encourage the perpetuation of a possibly unsustainable status quo. Third, the complexity of tourism systems, including their fuzzy boundaries, indirect and induced impacts, the influence of external (non-tourism) systems and the often unpredictable nature of relationships between cause and effect, are discussed (Section 2.4). Comprehensive and minimalist composite models of sustainable tourism that emerge from this discussion are presented in Section 2.5. The fourth and final issue involves sustainable tourism indicators (Section 2.6). The chapter concludes with a presentation of the Bellagio Principles for implementing sustainable development (Section 2.7) and a synoptic set of arguments for pursuing a sustainable tourism agenda (Section 2.8).

2.2 Flexibility

Hall (1998, p. 13) notes that sustainable development, like earlier terms such as 'conservation', seemingly 'emerged in an attempt to reconcile conflicting value positions with regard to the environment'. Yet, Hall (1998, p. 13) also describes sustainable development as an 'essentially contested concept', the 'application of which is inherently a matter of dispute', depending on the 'values and ideologies of various stakeholders'. This suggests that the consensus of support that has developed around the concept might simply disguise continued and largely opportunistic support for the more ideologically polarized platforms of the past. As discussed in Chapter 1, the semantics are appealing to both the pro-growth and slow or anti-growth supporters, with 'development' having particular resonance with the former and 'sustainable' being attractive to the latter.

Sustainable development (and, by extension, sustainable tourism), as a result, can mean just about anything to anyone, rendering it vulnerable to appropriation by either group (Romeril, 1994). For supporters of the advocacy platform, it represents continued tourism growth and intensification, while for supporters of the cautionary and adaptancy platforms, it often represents alternative tourism and a halt to mass tourism development. Accordingly, the consensus surrounding the principle is liable to dissolve once a diverse group of stakeholders begins the process of implementation and the different strategies and outcomes associated with the attainment of the principle become apparent. For Wheeller (1993, p. 122), sustainable tourism is therefore 'an intellectually appealing concept with little practical application'.

Wheeller (1993), MacLellan (1997) and Mowforth and Munt (1998), among others, raise a more sinister implication of this excessive flexibility, alleging that some businesses and governments deliberately use 'sustainable' and allied terms such as 'ecotourism' in their marketing as a form of *greenwashing* to give a false impression of environmental and social responsibility to the public. In combination with a failure to address the broader problems of appropriation and implementation, the exposure of such practices could cause sustainable tourism to be perceived by the public as nothing more than a discredited, cynical and empty cliché (MacLellan, 1997).

2.2.1 Weak and strong interpretations

Not everyone regards the malleable semantics of sustainable development and sustainable tourism as a liability. If one accepts the premise of the knowledge-based platform that both small-scale and large-scale tourism development are legitimate and sustainable under appropriate circumstances, it follows that the issue of sustainable tourism will need to be engaged in environments ranging from wilderness to intensely developed urban cores. To allow for these dramatically diverse baseline settings, Hunter (1997) suggests that sustainable tourism must be regarded as an 'adaptive paradigm' that accommodates both weak and strong interpretations of the sustainable development idea.

Weak sustainable tourism strategies, on one side of the planning/management spectrum, apply to extensively modified environments such as the inner city where the absence of undisturbed natural habitat makes the protection of the latter irrelevant and extremely high densities of tourism activity are not necessarily associated with environmental or social stress. The same applies to massively degraded or modified rural settings such as an abandoned strip mine, where large-scale tourism development may represent a significant improvement over the environmental status quo. Large resort hotels and theme parks are modes of tourism that could be appropriate in weak sustainable tourism strategies, which emphasize the 'development' component of sustainable development and are influenced by the advocacy platform.

This highly anthropocentric approach contrasts on the other side of the spectrum with *strong sustainable tourism* strategies, which are regarded by Hunter (1997) as relevant in relatively undisturbed natural or cultural settings where even a small increase in tourism-related activity could result in unacceptable environmental or sociocultural costs. Accordingly, the *precautionary principle*, or idea that a course of action should be avoided if its consequences are unknown, is a premise of this approach, which stresses the 'sustainable' component of sustainable development and is basically compatible with the cautionary and adaptancy platforms. In extreme cases, this may entail the prohibition of all tourism activity from certain areas. Where tourism is allowed, alternative options such as small-scale ecotourism are usually preferred.

2.3 Status quo or enhancement?

Another issue germane to sustainable tourism is whether the term actually encourages the perpetuation of an unsustainable status quo. The term 'sustainability' itself has steady state connotations that suggest the maintenance of the existing situation. If the natural and sociocultural environment of a destination is not unduly stressed, as might be the case with a wilderness area or bucolic rural setting, then this is not problematic and a *status quo sustainability* approach is warranted. However, if those environments are degraded, as in the case of blighted inner cities, polluted beaches or grasslands infested with exotic plants, then an *enhancement sustainable tourism* approach is necessary to redress an unsustainable status quo.

2.3.1 Intergenerational and intragenerational equity

This distinction between status quo and enhancement dynamics is implicit in the Brundtland Report's definition of sustainable development, which espouses *intergenerational equity* in suggesting that the actions of the present generation should not unduly inhibit the options of future generations (see Section 1.3.4). According to

Frazier (1997) and MacLellan (1997), this dangerously focuses attention away from the need to address the inequitable status quo that exists within the world today and thereby to attain *intragenerational equity*. At worst, intergenerational sustainability can be seen as an elitist principle that deliberately perpetuates societal and regional inequities in the distribution of power and wealth.

2.4 Complexity of tourism systems

The complexity of tourism and the subsequent preference for a holistic approach to sustainable tourism are major premises of the knowledge-based platform, yet actually taking these into account greatly complicates the planning and management of tourism destinations and businesses and requires the application of new approaches and strategies (Faulkner and Russell, 1997; McKercher, 1999). Related issues include the fuzzy boundaries of tourism systems, tourism's indirect and induced effects on other systems, the impacts of those external systems on tourism and the unpredictable relationships between cause and effect.

2.4.1 Fuzzy boundaries

An aspect of complexity is the absence of clear boundaries around tourism systems. This is especially true in the food services sector as well as transportation and shopping, where tourism accounts for a substantial but by no means overwhelming share of all activity. In the USA, the National Restaurant Association estimates that tourists account for one-half of all sales at table service restaurants (TIA, 2003). However, the actual portion within a given array of individual establishments will range from almost all tourists to almost all local residents, with further variability occurring on a seasonal and monthly basis. Tourism is much more clearly dominant among travel agencies, accommodations and tour operators, while attractions in general occupy an intermediate position. In all cases, however, it is extremely difficult to isolate the component for which the tourism industry is responsible.

2.4.2 Indirect and induced impacts of tourism

Complexity is further evident in tourism's indirect and induced impacts on other sectors and environments. In the multiplier effect, indirect impacts involve the ongoing expenditure of direct revenues on goods and services within the destination. For example, a hotel allocates a portion of tourist receipts to purchase local food, while the farm supplying the food uses some of the receipts from the hotel to purchase fertilizer and extra labour from local sources. At each round of indirect impact, induced impacts are created when the wages paid out by the hotel and farm are in turn used to purchase other goods and services (Weaver and Lawton, 2002a). The implication is that a certain amount of food and fertilizer production, with its attendant effects on the natural and cultural environment, would not otherwise occur except for the demand created by tourism, both inside and outside the destination. The same applies to housing and related induced construction that occurs in a destination when a new hotel adds 500 jobs to the community, as well as the concomitant extraction of natural resources.

The magnitude of these indirect and induced impacts is indicated by the fact that the global tourism *economy*, which takes into account direct as well as indirect impacts, is approximately three times larger than the global tourism *industry*, which quantifies only the direct impacts (see Section 1.2). Hence, a hotel that appears to operate in a sustainable manner may actually be generating substantial negative impacts within the sectors and land uses that link with that hotel – impacts and links, moreover, which may be extremely difficult to isolate beyond the first round of indirect and induced effects. Whether the tourism industry, in its quest for sustainability, should assume at least some culpability for its impacts in agriculture, mining, construction and other external sectors is a contentious ethical question (see Section 2.4.5). More fundamentally, to what extent should the assessment of tourism as a sustainable or unsustainable industry take into account these indirect and induced impacts?

Equally contentious is the culpability of tourism in bringing about social and cultural change through the demonstration effect and commodification. While direct social and commercial contacts between hosts and guests clearly do have some impact, it is also likely that changes are inordinately attributed to tourism that are more likely associated with a society's exposure to mass media.

2.4.3 Influence of external systems

Although it is not reflected adequately in the frequently myopic tourism literature, complexity is also evident in the pervasive extent to which external sectors and systems profoundly influence tourism. For example, some ecolodges in the rainforests of southern Peru have been threatened by the deforestation of adjacent properties settled by farmers from other parts of the country (Yu et al., 1997). Similarly, attempts to foster sustainable tourism in parts of coastal Indonesia are impeded by the continued use of dynamite and poison to capture fish in coral reefs (Elliott et al., 2001). Political and social unrest can severely disrupt tourism, whether the latter is a target or an incidental casualty (Beirman, 2003). The latter scenario is illustrated at a national level by the Fiji coup of 1987 (Lea, 1988), prolonged unrest in Indonesia in the late 1990s (Soemodinoto et al., 2001) the suicide bombings in Israel in the early 2000s (Fleischer and Buccola, 2003) and the 9/11 experience of the USA in 2001 (Blake and Sinclair, 2003). In contrast, Egypt provides one of the best examples of a country where tourism has been deliberately targeted for disruption by dissident groups (Aziz, 1995).

The Caribbean island of Montserrat, where a promising small-scale tourism sector was devastated in 1994 by the eruption of a dormant volcano that rendered most of the island uninhabitable, illustrates the negative impacts of natural systems. The effects of cataclysmic flooding on the Northern Australia town of Katherine were examined by Faulkner and Vikulov (2001, p. 331), who states that 'one of the certainties in the evolution of a tourist destination is that, at some point of its history, one of its visitors will be a disaster of one kind or another'. This statement is especially relevant given the unprecedented post-World War II diffusion of tourism into disaster-susceptible settings such as coastlines and mountains. More broadly, all these examples demonstrate that sustainable tourism is an essentially meaningless construct if the external context, and its effects on sustainability, are not taken into account in the planning and management of destinations and businesses.

2.4.4 Unpredictable cause and effect relationships

Complex systems such as tourism are associated with non-linear and unpredictable cause and effect relationships, so that it is extremely difficult, if not impossible, to anticipate the location and timing of all significant consequences associated with an action such as the construction of a new hotel or the opening of a rainforest to tour groups. When stresses reach a critical level, long periods of calm (indicating apparently sustainable levels of activity) may suddenly give way to an *avalanche effect* after seemingly minor catalysts. This is illustrated by the sudden appearance in coastal areas of 'red tide', or the explosive multiplication of toxic single-cell algae that can be caused in part by the indiscriminant discharge of fertilizer and human waste. A sociocultural equivalent occurs when ostensibly content local residents suddenly engage in hostile actions against tourists following a relatively minor incident. The opposite scenario is revealed in research showing that most campsite vegetation damage and soil compaction occurs during the first few visits, with subsequent visits resulting in relatively small increments of additional damage (Marion and Farrell, 1998).

Spatial and temporal discontinuities between cause and effect are an aspect of complexity that further complicates the implementation of sustainable tourism strategies. The former scenario is illustrated by the ski resort of Aspen, Colorado, where strict internal controls on development in the early 1990s exacerbated the problem of tourism-related sprawl in nearby communities inadequately positioned to accommodate this extra pressure (Gill and Williams, 1994). Problems may therefore be deliberately or inadvertently diverted from one location to another when a narrow view of planning is taken. At a larger scale and within the external arena, terrorist actions and other forms of instability often reverberate throughout an entire region, as when the civil war in Sri Lanka destabilized the tourism industries of nearby India and the Maldives in the mid-1980s (Richter and Waugh, 1986).

2.4.5 Confined and holistic sustainability

The above complexity warrants a holistic approach toward sustainability that entails indirect, 'macro', intersectoral and pan-realm assumptions about the scope of engagement with sustainable tourism, as described below. This contrasts with a confined approach that considers only the destination or business itself, considers direct impacts only, does not go beyond the tourism sector and emphasizes only environmental *or* sociocultural impacts.

Direct and indirect impacts

The confined approach considers only the direct impacts, or those that emerge directly from the actual tourism sector. The holistic approach goes beyond these to incorporate tourism's indirect and induced effects, insofar as these can be identified and quantified.

Micro and macro spatial context

A macro approach accommodates the indirect and induced impacts by extending the spatial and temporal context of sustainability beyond the 'micro' perspective of the immediate destination or business. In the case of Aspen (see above), the inclusion of the surrounding area or functional region in planning considerations may have prevented the displacement of tourism-related congestion to adjacent communities in subsequent months. In extreme form, a macro approach considers the long-term global implications of such actions, as when a hotel manager takes measures to compensate for the hydrocarbon emissions produced by the travel of occupants to that facility.

Intrasectoral and intersectoral foci

Intersectoral sustainability is similar to the macro approach in that it looks beyond tourism to incorporate interrelationships with relevant external sectors and systems. The intrasectoral approach, which complements the micro perspective, focuses only on tourism and is far more prevalent because of its relative simplicity.

Environmental, economic and sociocultural realms

It was a common practice prior to the emergence of the knowledge-based platform to limit discussions of tourism effects to a limited impact 'realm'. The dependency theory manifestation of the cautionary platform, for example, emphasized economic and sociocultural impacts, as did the earliest proponents of alternative tourism (see Chapter 3). In contrast, early discussions of ecotourism were focused on the effects of tourism on the natural environment. While these limitations can still be discerned in some quarters, they have largely been superseded by a 'pan-realm' approach that assumes the need to address environmental, economic and sociocultural (sometimes separated into social and cultural) objectives simultaneously. As with the macro and intersectoral approaches, this is consistent with the scientific and systematic premises of the knowledge-based platform, which stress the interrelationships between these realms.

While laudable in principle, the 'pan-realm' approach is hindered in practice by the possibility of incompatible outcomes and undesired trade-offs, at least in the short term. For example, the preservation of wildlife and natural habitat in the African savannah and elsewhere has often been pursued at the expense of indigenous inhabitants who have been expelled from National Parks in the interests of fulfilling a Eurocentric perception of conservation (Akama, 1996; Butler and Boyd, 2000). Similarly, the closure of a hotel that consistently violates pollution laws results in the loss of jobs and income for local residents. Positive environmental effects in both cases are offset by negative sociocultural and economic repercussions, which in complex systems can lead to further unanticipated and undesirable consequences, both internal and external to the destination or the tourism sector. These could include disaffected local residents who in the first example deliberately kill off wildlife to drive ecotourists away and, in the second example, become employed in industries that result in even greater environmental costs.

2.5 Minimalist and comprehensive composite models

The above discussion of selected sustainable tourism issues suggests the possibility of two composite *ideal types* (i.e. polarized models against which real life situations

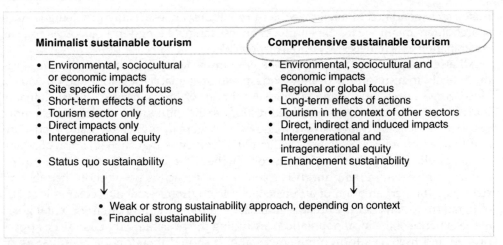

Minimalist sustainable tourism	Comprehensive sustainable tourism
• Environmental, sociocultural or economic impacts • Site specific or local focus • Short-term effects of actions • Tourism sector only • Direct impacts only • Intergenerational equity • Status quo sustainability	• Environmental, sociocultural and economic impacts • Regional or global focus • Long-term effects of actions • Tourism in the context of other sectors • Direct, indirect and induced impacts • Intergenerational and intragenerational equity • Enhancement sustainability

• Weak or strong sustainability approach, depending on context
• Financial sustainability

Figure 2.1
Minimalist and comprehensive sustainable tourism ideal types.

can be assessed and compared). Since ideal types are rarely encountered in the real world, it is generally useful to describe a destination or business as 'tending towards' rather than adhering to one model or the other.

In *minimalist sustainable tourism* (see Figure 2.1), which broadly aligns with the confined approach described above, priority is given to either the biocentric (environmental) or anthropocentric (sociocultural and economic) impacts within a particular site or product, without considering sectors other than tourism or intragenerational equity. Attention is also focused on sustaining the status quo and addressing short-term direct impacts only. Whether a weak or strong approach is adopted depends on the nature of the product or destination, though a combination may be warranted if the latter incorporates diverse settings or elements.

At the other end of the spectrum, *comprehensive sustainable tourism* is holistic in approach, simultaneously taking into account environmental, sociocultural and economic impacts within a global and intersectoral context that includes considerations of intragenerational equity as well as indirect and induced impacts over the long term. It is enhancement-based, since much of the world is environmentally degraded as well as economically impoverished and thus requires rehabilitation as well as wealth redistribution. This context encompasses the entire array of destination settings and therefore weak and strong approaches will both be incorporated into strategic planning and management, as warranted by the characteristics of any given context.

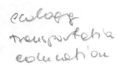

2.5.1 Financial sustainability

Both composite ideal types assume that the destination or business must maintain its financial viability. Discussions of sustainable tourism generally ignore or downplay the issue of financial sustainability (as opposed to economic sustainability), even though a tourism product that is not financially viable will not survive, no matter how sustainable it is from an environmental or sociocultural standpoint. All sustainable tourism strategies therefore must be formulated within the financial capabilities of the managing body, which can substantially constrain the scope of these strategies.

Businesses mandated to maximize their profitability are especially problematic since shareholders might regard expenditures on less tangible long-term outcomes such as 'sustainability' as unnecessary and irresponsible.

All else being equal, the comprehensive composite model is preferable since it is more likely to result in the desired widespread sustainable development outcomes. However, for destinations and businesses without prior experience with sustainable tourism, or with seriously constrained resources, the minimalist model offers a more realistic and feasible framework that allows managers to engage the issue of sustainability in a non-intimidating way. Miller (2001) contends that such an approach may attract public interest, paving the way for a higher level of engagement in the future. But as pointed out in the prior discussion, this approach is not without its inherent risks (e.g. the perpetuation of an unsustainable environmental and economic status quo, failure to consider the broader impacts, and the pursuit of environmental goals at the expense of the local population), including the possibility that it may be appropriated and used as a form of greenwashing. It should therefore be regarded as an entry point rather than a long-term strategic imperative. As the destination or business becomes more experienced and public support increases, a more comprehensive model should gradually supersede the minimalist framework.

2.6 Sustainable tourism indicators

Whichever approach is adopted, effective planning and management decisions require knowledge that is both relevant and adequate to the complexity of the situation at hand. Tourism-related information has proliferated dramatically during the past decade, but much of it is useless or misleading. Moreover, while giving the impression that an adequate and relevant database is available, this plethora of 'knowledge' masks the fact that strategic information on key aspects of sustainability is still seriously lacking. There is, according to T. Manning (1999), both too much information and not enough.

Indicators, or variables that can be measured and monitored to reveal the changing condition of a particular phenomenon, are a means through which existing information can be filtered and new information collected. This new body of essential condensed information makes it easier to recognize trends as well as more immediate threats and to take appropriate actions. According to the WTO (1996, p. 9), 'indicators measure information with which decision-makers may reduce the chances of unknowingly taking poor decisions'. While elegant in theory, however, an indicators-based sustainable tourism strategy is complicated by the actual process of selecting, measuring, monitoring and evaluating a viable set of relevant variables.

2.6.1 Selection

Given the complex nature of tourism systems, there are in theory an infinite number of tourism-related indicators to choose from. Factors that influence the actual selection of working indicators in a particular destination or business include policy relevance, the type of approach to sustainability that is adopted (i.e. weak or strong,

minimalist or comprehensive), measurability, financial and other resource constraints, stakeholder interests, level of public support and politics. Thus, a wealthy
beach resort utilizing a comprehensive approach toward sustainability requires an
indicator set that overlaps but is generally distinct from the set required by a large,
financially constrained inland urban centre where more of a minimalist model is followed. An interesting consideration is that while the selection process should follow
from the definition of sustainability that is adopted, the creation of the indicator set
may actually serve in turn to fine-tune this definition (Miller, 2001).

Referring to sustainable development more generally, Bossel (1999) argues that
the indicator set should be compact yet comprehensive, so that it is not too time-
consuming and expensive to operate but still captures critical information. In addition, individual indicators should be understandable, practical, clearly defined and
reproducible. A useful analogy can be made with statistical sampling, wherein the
characteristics of a few hundred carefully selected and surveyed respondents can
be considered an accurate representation of a much larger overall population.
Similarly, a handful of carefully selected and monitored indicators can accurately
depict the condition of an entire tourism system.

Internal and external indicators

An indicator set should incorporate variables that describe the condition, viability
and potential influence of the system itself (e.g. number of tourists, annual growth,
units of accommodation, percentage of labour force employed in tourism) as well as
those that show the effects of the target system on the viability of other systems (e.g.
levels of water pollution and greenhouse gas emissions produced by tourism activities, amount of domestic and imported food consumed by the tourism industry)
(Bossel, 1999). Especially where a comprehensive sustainability approach is taken, it
is additionally important to include indicators that measure the overall condition
of external systems (e.g. infant mortality rate, percentage of overall labour force
unemployed, per capita GDP), since problems in these areas could have direct and
dire consequences for tourism whether or not the latter significantly contributes to
those values. In essence, these three types of indicator combine to capture the internal
and external dimensions of a tourism system.

Aggregate indicators

One method for simplifying indicator sets is to construct *aggregate* or *composite*
indicators. A well-known example is the Human Development Index (HDI) of the
United Nations Development Programme, which combines economic variables
such as GDP per capita with social indicators such as life expectancy and literacy to
obtain a score that profiles a country's overall level of development (UNDP, 2003).
Such scores, however, may be misleading if inappropriately high or low weightings
are given to the constituent variables, or if they are all simply given equal weight.
Accordingly, Dahl (1997) argues that any such approach should be regarded as
suspect and especially subjective.

2.6.2 Measurement and monitoring

Data measurement and collection procedures must be rigorous in order to increase the
likelihood of obtaining valid and reliable information. Indicators such as the change in
the number of hotel rooms or employees directly employed in tourism are relatively

easy to collect, although the difficulty in compiling an accurate and comprehensive database increases as the destination becomes larger. Other indicators, like water quality, spatial distribution of tourists and the psychological well-being of residents, tend to vary substantially through space and time even within a small area, so that the compilation of a robust database requires a long-term commitment to sampling rigour and concomitant financial support. In the case of psychological well-being, an added complication is the subjectivity of this type of critical information, which requires careful attention to measurement techniques and to the maintenance of consistency in the latter over many years. The problems posed by such variables may, in practice, bias the selection process toward indicators that are readily quantifiable (Miller, 2001).

2.6.3 Evaluation

Timing is a fundamental issue in indicator evaluation. Minimally, the results of an indicator set should be assessed once a year against the outcomes of prior annual assessments, as is the practice of British Airways (see Section 5.5.1) and other companies that monitor long-term sustainability performance. Measures such as the seasonality of visitation and tourism employment should be included in these annual indicator sets to ensure that important shorter-term variations are not neglected. In between these annual assessments, critical indicators should be identified for more frequent evaluation, since sudden deteriorations in bellwether variables such as tourist satisfaction, tourist receipts, resident attitudes toward tourism, tourism-related crime rates and tourism-induced water pollution could indicate an imminent crisis in the tourism system, as per the avalanche effect.

Benchmarks and critical thresholds

The identification of benchmarks and critical thresholds is another important aspect of evaluation. *Benchmarks* are values against which the relative performance of an indicator is assessed, often in terms of what is desired. These may be based on a prior state (e.g. the level of tourist arrivals in the destination 10 years ago) or a desired future state (e.g. a target reduction of 50 per cent in tourism-related air borne particles). The frame of reference of the benchmark may be the destination or business itself (as in the first example) or it may derive from a similar external destination or business and sometimes one that is perceived to demonstrate sector *best practice*. This value depends in large part on whether a strong or weak model of sustainability is adopted (see Section 2.2.1), so that the benchmark number of accommodation units and visitors in a large urban centre is likely to be much higher than in a wilderness area.

A *threshold* is a value or value range (i.e. threshold range) indicating critical change in a variable, usually demarcating in tourism the perceived transition between sustainable and unsustainable outcomes. Benchmarks in some cases may also be thresholds. When a threshold has been breeched or a threshold range entered, managers must respond with appropriate and timely remedial actions in order to restore the indicator (and by extension the tourism system) to a sustainable level. As with benchmarks, thresholds vary depending on the type of destination and sustainability model. For example, the critical threshold number for tourists in any given overnight period may be logically set at 50 000 in the site-hardened commercial core of a large urban centre, but only 25 in a traditional indigenous community in the Amazon basin.

In addition to this relativity, there is still much that is confounding and controversial about tourism indicator thresholds. This is in part because of the complexity factor (e.g. the unpredictable nature of cause and effect relationships) as well as the fact that tourism in many types of settings has not been established long enough to reveal stress levels that would allow thresholds to be identified. The political and ideological nature of the evaluation process is another factor, wherein a managing authority or government may deliberately set a higher than warranted threshold so that it does not appear responsible for unsustainable outcomes and/or is not obligated to allocate scarce resources for remediation when those thresholds have been crossed.

Indicator prioritization

While the selection of an indicator set implies that priority has rightly or wrongly been given to certain variables over those that are excluded, it cannot be assumed that all indicators within that set are equally important as barometers of sustainability. During the evaluation process, it is likely that managers will need to weigh or prioritize the available indicators, especially if contradictory trends are evident, or if the apparent breeching of critical thresholds in several variables requires decisions to be made about prioritizing the disbursement of remedial resources. One basis for making such decisions is to identify cause-and-effect relationships among indicators. If for example the alleviation of tour bus congestion is known to create more positive community attitudes toward tourism as well as reduce tourism-related air pollution and road accidents, then the former indicator (i.e. tour bus-related congestion) would be a logical choice for priority ranking and action.

Even where thresholds or benchmarks are not arbitrarily manipulated for political or ideological purposes, there is a possibility that such ends can be achieved through the manipulation of the prioritization process. For example, a manager might give priority to the indicators that show less stress in the system, or are less expensive to redress.

2.6.4 Sustainable tourism indicators and the WTO

In keeping with its leadership role in the sustainable tourism field, the WTO has been involved with indicators since the early 1990s. In 1993, a Task Force was established to identify a set of relevant sustainable tourism indicators that were subsequently tested through local pilot projects in Canada, The Netherlands, Mexico, Argentina and the USA. These projects culminated in the publication of a guide suitable for destination managers (WTO, 1996). More recent regional application workshops were held in Hungary and Mexico (1999), Sri Lanka and Argentina (2000), Croatia (2001) and Cyprus (2003). A new study of sustainable tourism indicators in 20 countries was begun in 2003.

Reconciling demands for both a large and a minimal number of indicators, the WTO process identified 11 core indicators that would provide a basic framework for sustainable tourism management in any destination (see Table 2.1). Supplementing these are indicators particularly relevant to specific environments and sites, such as coastal zones, mountains, urban areas and small islands (see Table 2.2). Three additional aggregate indicators, quantifying 'carrying capacity', 'site stress' and 'attractiveness', were conceived that combine core and environment-specific variables. The 'site stress' index, for example, measures intensity of use at selected 'hot spots' and incorporates visitor numbers, type and frequency of tourist activity and spatial/temporal

Table 2.1
WTO core indicators of sustainable tourism

Indicator	Specific measures
1. Site protection	Category of site protection according to IUCN index
2. Stress	Tourist numbers visiting site (per annum/peak month)
3. Use intensity	Intensity of use in peak period (persons per hectare)
4. Social impact	Ratio of tourists to locals (peak period and over time)
5. Development control	Existence of environmental review procedure or formal controls over development of site and use densities
6. Waste management	Percentage of sewage from site receiving treatment (also structural limits of other infrastructural capacity on site, such as water supply)
7. Planning process	Existence of organized regional plan for tourist destination region
8. Critical ecosystems	Number of rare/endangered species
9. Consumer satisfaction	Level of satisfaction by visitors (questionnaire-based)
10. Local satisfaction	Level of satisfaction by locals (questionnaire-based)
11. Tourism contribution to local economy	Proportion of total economic activity generated by tourism only

Source: WTO (1996).

Table 2.2
Sample WTO supplementary indicators of sustainable tourism for selected environments

Environment	Indicator	Suggested measures
Coastal zones	Levels of beach erosion	% of beach eroded
	Beach use intensity	Persons per metre of accessible beach
Mountains	Extent of erosion caused by tourists	% of surface in eroded state
Managed wildlife parks	Human population in park and surrounding area	Number of people within 10 km of boundary
	Level of poaching in park	Number of poaching incidents reported
Urban environments	Air pollution measurements	Number of days exceeding specified pollutant standards
	Use intensity	Traffic congestion
Cultural sites	Restoration costs	Estimated costs to maintain/restore site per annum
	Measures of disruptive behaviour	Traffic vibration, number of vandalism incidents per year
Unique ecological sites	Changes in flora mix and concentration	Primary flora species as a % of total plant cover
Traditional communities	Social impacts	Average net income of tourists/average net income of local population
Small islands	Measures of capital flight	% of exchange leakage from total tourism revenues
	Fresh water availability	Volume of water used by tourists/ volume used by local population on a per capita basis

Source: WTO (1996).

patterns of concentration, as well as appropriate idiosyncratic variables. However constituted, all of the WTO indicators are regarded as being 'demand driven' in that they are specifically intended to be useful to managers for making practical decisions (WTO, 1996).

Model for selecting site-specific indicators

The WTO has produced a simple schema that assists local managers to select an appropriate set of site-specific indicators to augment the core set discussed above. This consists of five criteria against which candidate indicators can be ranked as 'high', 'medium' or 'low' in terms of their fulfilment of those criteria. 'Obtainability' describes whether data are available, while 'understandability and credibility' describe whether the indicator is easy to understand and is supported by reliable information. 'Temporality and comparability' considers whether the indicator allows for the identification of trends both internal and external to the study area and over time. The 'predictive of sustainability' criterion assesses the early warning capacity of the indicator, while 'threshold value' describes whether the latter is available for that variable. An indicator that achieves a 'high' ranking on all or most of the criteria is a strong candidate for selection (WTO, 1996).

2.7 Bellagio Principles

In 1996, a group of experts met in the Italian town of Bellagio to establish a set of general guidelines that would inform the implementation of sustainable development strategies, including those associated specifically with tourism (see Figure 2.2). The first of these Bellagio Principles* stresses the need for any organization to have a clear vision and practical definition of what they mean by sustainable development. This is the point, for example, where either a comprehensive or minimalist model of sustainable tourism and a weak or strong approach to sustainability, would be adopted. The next three principles, however, indicate a clear preference for the comprehensive model in advocating a holistic, systems-based approach that takes an adequate spatial and temporal scope into account. Subsequent principles stress the need for practicality (including a small, workable set of indicators), openness and accountability to avoid political problems such as those cited above, broad-based participation by stakeholders and appropriate ongoing monitoring procedures. The final principle also alludes to sufficient capacity for evaluation in citing the need for organizations to properly fund sustainable development strategies so that they do not fall short in their objectives.

2.8 Pursuing sustainable tourism

The numerous challenges associated with the implementation of sustainable development and sustainable tourism make it impossible to say whether a given destination or product is ever definitively 'sustainable'. Tourism managers may therefore

1. Guiding vision and goals
Assessment of progress toward sustainable development should be guided by a clear vision of sustainable development and goals that define that vision.

2. Holistic perspective
Assessment of progress toward sustainable development should:

- include review of the whole system as well as its parts
- consider the well-being of social, ecological and economic sub-systems, their state as well as the direction and rate of change of that state, of their component parts and the interaction between parts
- consider both positive and negative consequences of human activity, in a way that reflects the costs and benefits for human and ecological systems, in monetary and non-monetary terms

3. Essential elements
Assessment of progress toward sustainable development should:

- consider equity and disparity within the current population and between present and future generations, dealing with such concerns as resource use, over-consumption and poverty, human rights and access to services
- as appropriate consider the ecological conditions on which life depends
- consider economic development and other, non-market activities that contribute to human/social well-being

4. Adequate scope
Assessment of progress toward sustainability should:

- adopt a time horizon long enough to capture both human and ecosystem time scales thus responding to current short-term decision-making needs as well as those of future generations
- define the space of study large enough to include not only local but also long distance impacts on people and ecosystems
- build on historic and current conditions to anticipate future conditions: where do we want to go, where could we go

5. Practical focus
Assessment of progress toward sustainable development should be based on:

- an explicit set of categories or an organizing framework that links vision and goals to indicators and assessment criteria
- a limited number of key issues for analysis
- a limited number of indicators or indicator combinations to provide a clearer signal of progress, standardizing measurement wherever possible to permit comparison of indicator values to targets, reference values, ranges, thresholds, or direction of trends, as appropriate

6. Openness
Assessment of progress toward sustainable development should:

- make the methods and data that are used accessible to all
- make explicit all judgments, assumptions and uncertainties in data and interpretations

7. Effective communication
Assessment of progress toward sustainable development should:

- be designed to address the needs of the audience and set of users
- draw from indicators and other tools that are stimulating and serve to engage decision-makers
- aim, from the outset, for simplicity in structure and use of clear and plain language

8. Broad participation
Assessment of progress toward sustainable development should:

- obtain broad representation of key grass-roots, professional, technical and social groups, including youth, women and indigenous people to ensure recognition of diverse and changing values
- ensure the participation of decision-makers to secure a firm link to adopted policies and resulting action

9. Ongoing assessment
Assessment of progress toward sustainable development should:

- develop a capacity for repeated measurement to determine trends
- be iterative, adaptive and responsive to change and uncertainty because systems are complex and change frequently

Figure 2.2
The Bellagio Principles.

- adjust goals, frameworks and indicators as new insights are gained
- promote development of collective learning and feedback to decision-making

10. Institutional capacity
Continuity of assessing progress toward sustainable development should be assured by:

- clearly assigning responsibility and providing ongoing support in the decision-making process
- providing institutional capacity for data collection, maintenance and documentation
- supporting development of local assessment capacity

Figure 2.2
(*continued*).

well ask why scarce resources should be committed to a sustainability-based strategy. Bramwell and Lane (1993) provide one rationale in emphasizing that the active pursuit of sustainability is preferable to the alternative of inaction, which greatly increases the likelihood of unsustainable outcomes as per the destination life cycle model. Empirical evidence from destinations that have experienced decline, such as the US beach resort of Atlantic City (Stansfield, 1978), indicates that rejuvenation is possible despite such circumstances, but only after painful and costly adjustments have been made. As with human illness, it is better to emphasize prevention rather than remediation.

A second consideration is historical perspective. The formal pursuit of sustainable tourism commenced as recently as the early 1990s and, with all the issues and complications that have emerged, it is easy to underestimate the actual amount of relevant knowledge that has accumulated and momentum that has been gained during this brief period of time. Indeed, the revelation of problems and issues should be regarded as a necessary and desirable step in the identification of appropriate solutions and strategies rather than an excuse for disengagement. This leads to a third rationale, which is that sustainable tourism, according to MacLellan (1997), provides at the very least a focal point for continued debate and one moreover that has attracted a high level of support at the conceptual level at least. The growth in interest, which constitutes a fourth rationale, is discussed in subsequent chapters that examine the increasing demand for alternative and conventional tourism products that adhere to principles of sustainability.

Fifth, the fact that an indicator is an *indication* of a condition and not necessarily a definitive assessment, needs to be more fully appreciated. As long as a trend towards an unsustainable state has been identified (e.g. density of tourists on the beach is increasing and resident attitudes are becoming less positive toward tourism), appropriate managerial decisions can be made even though the critical threshold values of specific indicators are still speculative. A sixth and final rationale is the availability of a minimalist model of sustainable tourism that simplifies the parameters of engagement and makes it attractive for destinations and businesses who are otherwise daunted by the comprehensive approach to become involved with its implementation.

2.9 Summary

The ongoing engagement with tourism sustainability has revealed a number of issues that complicate the pursuit of strategies based on this principle. One of these involves the semantic flexibility of terms such as sustainable development and sustainable tourism, which makes the terms vulnerable to appropriation but also facilitates the construction of weak and strong approaches to sustainability that together address the full range of tourism settings and products. A second issue is whether sustainability should encourage maintenance or enhancement of the status quo and intragenerational as well as intergenerational equity. The complexity of tourism is a third major issue, entailing the fuzzy boundaries of tourism systems, the role of indirect and induced impacts and the crucial influence played by external human and natural systems. Unpredictable cause and effect relationships are another element of system complexity that complicate the engagement with sustainable tourism.

Two sustainable tourism ideal types arise from this analysis. The more desirable comprehensive model is predicated on holistic, pan-realm assumptions that focus on enhancement sustainability, intragenerational as well as intergenerational equity and indirect and induced impacts that occur within an expanded space/time continuum. Minimalist sustainability, in contrast, is characterized by more restricted parameters of engagement. It is appropriate primarily as a temporary framework that expedites entry into the sustainability arena. Both models can adopt a weak and/or strong approach to sustainability depending on the nature of the destination or product and both include the premise of financial sustainability, without which the pursuit of environmental and sociocultural sustainability is effectively irrelevant.

Indicator implementation is another major issue in sustainable tourism. Problems arise initially in the selection of appropriate indicators and then in their measurement and monitoring. Evaluation issues include timing, the identification of benchmarks and thresholds and indicator prioritization. Within the tourism arena, the WTO has played a lead role in developing core and site-specific indicators through a series of local pilot projects. Such efforts to identify appropriate indicators and to implement sustainable tourism strategies more broadly, are enhanced by the application of the Bellagio Principles. In general, the pursuit of such strategies is rationalized by the non-viability of the 'do nothing' alternative, the progress that has been made in a short period, the concept's role as a focus for debate, growth in support, the imprecise nature of indicators and the availability of the minimalist entry point.

On the net

Bellagio Principles
http://www.iisd.org/measure/principles/1.htm

Network Evolution for Sustainable Tourism (NEST) project
http://destinet.ewindows.eu.org/nest

For further reading

Beirman, D. (2003). *Restoring Tourism Destinations in Crisis: a Strategic Marketing Approach.* CABI Publishing.
Beirman discusses an array of tourism crisis possibilities associated with external sectors and systems, such as war, international terrorism, coups, earthquakes, foot-and-mouth disease and crime. He describes the Philippines as an example of 'combination crises' and considers how such situations can be strategically managed.

Bossel, H. (1999). *Indicators for Sustainable Development: Theory, Method, Applications.* International Institute for Sustainable Development.

Although the focus of this publication is on sustainable development indicators in general, its implica-tions are applicable to tourism systems. Issues of selection and implementation follow an overview of sustainable development and systems theory.

Faulkner, B. and Russell, R. (1997). Chaos and complexity in tourism: in search of a new para-digm. *Pacific Tourism Review*, 1, 93–102.
The authors argue for the need to take chaos theory into account as part of a new paradigm in planning and management that recognizes the complexity of tourism systems. Butterfly and lock-in effects, as well as bottom up synthesis, are among the concepts discussed.

Frazier, J. (1997). Sustainable development: modern elixir or sack dress? *Environmental Conservation*, 24, 182–93.
This article provides a comprehensive critical analysis of the concept of sustainable development (or 'susdev') and, by extension, sustainable tourism. Issues of intergenerational and intragenerational equity are discussed.

Hunter, C. (1997). Sustainable tourism as an adaptive paradigm. *Annals of Tourism Research*, 24, 850–67.
Hunter provides a very useful discussion of the concepts of weak and strong sustainability, situating this within a tourism context.

WTO (1996). *What Tourism Managers Need to Know: a Practical Guide to the Development and Use of Indicators of Sustainable Tourism*. Madrid.
This important publication considers the practical management of sustainable tourism indicators, including the identification of site attributes and issues, indicator selection, data collection and analy-sis and evaluation.

Beyond the book

1. (a) Using either Haiti, Bosnia Herzegovina, Indonesia, Solomon Islands or Zimbabwe as a case study, describe the natural and cultural factors external to the tourism system that impede the implementation of national sustainable tourism strategies. (b) Indicate how the tourism sector in your case study can best respond, proactively and/or reactively, to each of these factors.
2. For each of the core WTO indicators included in Table 2.1, design a strategy for measure-ment, monitoring, evaluation and costing that is relevant to a case study destination of your choice.
3. (a) For the destination selected in question no. 2, use the Bellagio Principles (Figure 2.2) to help identify a set of five additional case study-specific indicators to augment the core WTO indicator set. (b) Design a strategy for measurement, monitoring, evaluation and costing each of these supplementary indicators.

On the ground: employing sustainable tourism indicators in Scandinavia

Among the sustainable tourism initiatives being undertaken by organizations other than the WTO is the Network Evolution for Sustainable Tourism (NEST) project*, which was co-financed by the Nordic Industrial Fund and the Nordic tourism industry and undertaken between 2001 and 2003. Designed to assess the role of stakeholder networks in implementing sustainable tourism at the local destination level and to create a management tool to expedite this, the project included the selection and implementation of sustainable tourism indicators in four communities. Lillehammer (Norway), the site of the 17th Winter Olympic Games in 1994, is a city of 36 000 residents that received 760 000 overnight visitors in 2002 along with an unknown number of day-only visitors. Præstø Fjord (Denmark) is a rural coastal community

Table 2.3
NEST core sustainable tourism indicators

Indicator	Measurement criteria
1. Area of destination	km^2
2. Resident population	Number of residents
3. Tourists	Number of tourists
4. Room occupancy rate	Room occupancy rate in %
5. Tourism's economic contribution to local economy	Tourism revenues as a % of local economy
6. Employment in tourism industry	Total number of person-years
7. Range of labelled tourism products[1]	Number of products labelled
8. Attractions	Number of tourist attractions
9. Ecolabelled ecotourism or other tourist package activities[1]	Number of products
10. Natural/cultural/historical guided tours	Number of tours carried out
11. Ecolabelled restaurants[1]	Number of restaurants
12. Accommodation businesses with ecolabel or certified environmental management system[1]	Number of businesses
13. Blue Flag beaches and marinas[2]	Number of beaches and harbours
14. Protected nature conservation areas	% of destination's total area
15. Red listed animal species[3]	Number of species
16. Signage translated to different languages	% of signage in destination with translation to different languages
17. Bike paths and footpaths	km
18. Bicycle hire	Total number of bikes for hire
19. Eco-friendly product marketing information	% of the total number of publications that is produced in an eco-friendly manner
20. Action plan approved for sustainable tourism	Yes or no
21. Security	Total number of thefts (house, car and shop) and violence against persons reported to the police in destination

[1] see Section 7.4.
[2] see Section 7.4.5.
[3] Red-listed species are those deemed by the IUCN (World Conservation Union) to be most in need of conservation actions.
The NEST project was financed by the Nordic Innovation Centre and undertaken by Ramboll DK.

of 34 000 that hosted 528 000 overnight visitors in 2002, while Suomenlinna (Finland) is a district of Helsinki with 860 residents that hosted 3000 overnight visitors and 700 000 day-only visitors in that year. Finally, Söderslätt (Sweden) is a rural coastal community of 120 000 that in 2002 accommodated 455 000 overnight visitors and 400 000 day-only visitors.

The implementation of indicators in each case is preceded by the need to define clearly the boundaries of the destination, to establish a 'destination network' to implement the strategy and to complete a visitor survey that identifies tourism-related issues requiring priority attention. Through regular meetings, the Network should complete a Tourism Potential Analysis, which profiles the destination's tourism sector and sets the foundation for the development of a Vision for tourism, which outlines the type and volume of tourism that the destination wishes to attract. This vision subsequently informs the destination's Baseline Analysis, which measures the performance and impacts of tourism in the destination and gives rise to the Action Plan, which details the actions and strategies necessary to achieve the vision.

The Tourism Potential Analysis, Baseline Analysis and the Action Plan all require the collection of relevant tourism-related data. Twenty-one core sustainable tourism indicators, suitable for any type of destination, were selected by the NEST coordinators for these purposes (see Table 2.3). Ten of the indicators, including the presence of bicycle rentals and ecolabelled tourism products, emphasize environmental concerns, while others (e.g. number of tourists, tourism-related employment) provide fundamental baseline information about the sector. It is estimated by the project managers that one person-month of work is required to collect this information. As part of the Action Plan, short-term and long-term targets for tourism in the destination should be identified, which could involve the identification of benchmarks and thresholds for each of the 21 criteria. As part of the Baseline Analysis and Action Plan, it is also suggested if feasible that more detailed information be collected for some of the indicators, including the number of overnight and day-only visitors, its distribution by month and country of origin, information about the consumption of water, heat and electricity by tourists and wastes produced by tourism accommodations.

Exercise

1. As appropriate, identify more detailed indicators that should be collected under each of the 21 more general indicators presented in Table 2.3. In each case, explain why this 'sub-indicator' is important and what difficulties are likely to be encountered, if any, in obtaining this information.

Chapter 3
Alternative tourism

Chapter Objectives

Upon completion of this chapter, the reader should be able to:

- describe the major differences between alternative tourism and conventional mass tourism ideal types
- list and describe relevant subsectors
- differentiate between circumstantial and deliberate alternative tourism and explain why the distinction is important
- evaluate the differences and similarities in major alternative tourism subsectors, including farm-based tourism, volunteer tourism, guesthouses, backpacking, urban alternative tourism and education tourism and
- discuss the potential problems and weaknesses associated with alternative tourism.

3.1 Introduction

As discussed in Chapter 1, alternative tourism emerged in the early 1980s as part of the adaptancy platform. The term was conceived to encompass products and activities that were thought to be more appropriate than conventional mass tourism. Alternative tourism may therefore be regarded as an early form of engagement with the idea of sustainability. The first part of this chapter (Section 3.2) traces the early development of alternative tourism and this is followed in Section 3.3 by a typology of alternative tourism products. Section 3.4 examines the contrasts between alternative tourism and conventional mass tourism ideal types, while Section 3.5 considers the crucial distinction between circumstantial and deliberate alternative tourism. Subsequent sections profile selected subtypes with the intent of depicting the diversity and commonalities within alternative tourism. The target subtypes are farm-based tourism (Section 3.6), volunteer tourism (Section 3.7), guesthouses (Section 3.8), backpacking (Section 3.9), urban alternative tourism (Section 3.10) and education tourism (Section 3.11). Ecotourism is another major form of alternative tourism, but is addressed separately in Chapter 11 because of its concurrent existence as a form of mass tourism. Section 3.12 concludes the chapter by examining the potential shortcomings of alternative tourism.

3.2 History of alternative tourism

Alternative tourism existed long before the term itself was coined (Jones, 1992). Medieval pilgrimage travel and the Grand Tour, for example, are antecedents that both resonate in the modern day pursuit of religious tourism, education tourism and backpacking. Farm-based tourism, moreover, has been established in Europe for more than 100 years (see Section 3.6). More broadly, it can be argued that most if not all tourism prior to Thomas Cook and the era of 'industrial' tourism was alternative tourism by default, since it did *not* resemble what we now call 'mass tourism' in any substantive way.

Early discussions of alternative tourism as a formal concept tended to adopt a restricted perspective. Dernoi (1981), for example, defined it as a form of tourism in which visitors are accommodated in the houses of local residents. This mode of alternative tourism, commonly referred to as *homestay* tourism, was in fact well articulated by the late 1970s, with formal programmes in Denmark ('Meet the Danes'), Jamaica ('Meet-the-People'*) and the US state of Connecticut ('Friendship Force'), among other destinations. Dernoi (1981) estimates that home-based alternative tourism at that time accounted for about 15 per cent of all foreign stayover nights in Bulgaria, 9 per cent in Slovenia, 1 per cent in Mauritius and 0.1 per cent in India. Wall (1997a) describes the homestay sector as a significant indigenous initiative that included over 1600 available rooms in the early 1990s. One of the most widely cited examples of pioneering alternative tourism, though not strictly home-based, is the cultural villages of the Casamance region in southern Senegal, which were established beginning in the mid-1970s and accommodated 20 000 visitors in 1990 (Echtner, 1999).

3.2.1 Role of ecumenical church groups

The early emphasis on sociocultural attractions and Third World venues arose partly in response to the cautionary platform's focus on the social, cultural and economic costs of mass tourism in pleasure periphery destinations, where the need for more appropriate forms of tourism was deemed to be most urgent (see Section 1.3.2). Ecumenical church groups in both the developing and developed regions played a lead role not only in pointing out the problems with Third World tourism, but also in working toward 'pro-poor' solutions, as during the 1980 International Workshop on Tourism in Manila, Philippines (Roekaerts and Savat, 1989). This conference led to the establishment of the Ecumenical Coalition on Third World Tourism* (ECTWT) which forged stakeholder networks and initiated grassroots projects and the Third World Tourism Ecumenical European Network* (TEN), a loose coalition of alternative tourism organizations which was involved in efforts to effect change in the origin regions (Gonsalves, 1987). Other significant milestones included the 1984 Chiangmai Workshop on Alternative Tourism, where the latter was defined in terms of mutual understanding, equality and solidarity among all participants (Holden, 1984).

3.3 Typology of alternative tourism products

The contours of alternative tourism are still being defined as new forms of activity emerge for scrutiny. Figure 3.1, which depicts a typology of candidate subtypes based on the extent to which they are defined by their relative orientation toward attractions, accommodations or motivations, is therefore tentative. Nevertheless, it appears that many alternative tourism subtypes gravitate toward one of the three

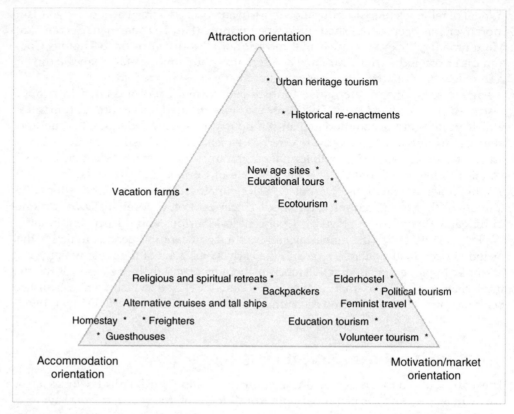

Figure 3.1
Types of alternative tourism.

criteria, while several combine attraction and motivation. These subtypes vary in the extent to which relevant organizations explicitly market their products as 'alternative tourism', in part because some of them occur both as alternative tourism and mass tourism (e.g. ecotourism and historical re-enactments). In addition, each subtype has internal variations that may fall in different positions within the triangle. For example, alternative cruise expeditions specializing in Antarctic science would be located in the centre of the diagram, since the specialization reflects a specific attraction (Antarctica) and motivation (interest in science). Figure 3.1 does not take into account the possibility of alternative tourism hybrids, such as backpackers seeking accommodation in guesthouses, or visits to New Age sites by female followers of the Earth Goddess.

3.4 Mass conventional tourism and alternative tourism ideal types

Table 3.1 profiles unsustainable mass tourism and alternative tourism as ideal types. As with the conventional and minimalist models of sustainable tourism described

Table 3.1

Unsustainable mass tourism and deliberate alternative tourism ideal types

Characteristics	Unsustainable mass tourism	Deliberate alternative tourism
Markets		
Segment	Psychocentric to midcentric	Allocentric to midcentric
Volume and mode	High; package tours	Low; FIT arrangements
Length of stay	Brief	Extended
Seasonality	Distinct high and low season	No distinct seasonality
Origins	One or two dominant markets	No dominant markets
Attractions		
Character	Generic, purpose built, 'contrived'	Idiosyncratic, pre-existing, 'authentic'
Emphasis	Highly commercialized	Moderately commercialized
Orientation	Tourists only or primarily	Tourists and locals
Accommodation		
Size	Large scale	Small scale
Spatial pattern	Concentrated; obvious tourism districts	Dispersed; no obvious tourism districts
Density	High	Low
Architecture	Obtrusive international style	Unobtrusive vernacular style
Ownership	Non-local; corporate	Local; community or small business
Economic status		
Tourist receipts	High	Low
Linkages	With non-local sectors	With local sectors
Leakages	High	Low
Multiplier effect	Low	High
Role of tourism	Dominant	Supplementary
Regulation		
Control	Non-local corporate	Local community
Amount	Low	High
Ideology	Free markets	Public intervention
Emphasis	Economic growth; profits	Community well-being
Timeframe	Short-term	Long-term

Source: adapted from Weaver, 1998, Ecotourism in the Less Developed World, CAB International, with permission.

in Section 2.5, it is prudent to assess particular tourism destinations, business or products as leaning towards rather than conforming exactly to one ideal type or the other. Cazes (1989), for example, stresses that it is difficult to identify any products that completely fulfil the criteria associated with the alternative tourism ideal type. For discussion purposes, characteristics can be grouped into the five categories of markets, attractions, accommodation, economic status and regulation.

3.4.1 Markets

Alternative tourists lean towards the allocentric pole of the psychographic continuum, which is characterized by intellectual curiosity, self-confidence, openness to new experiences and respect for other cultures. Also described as 'venturers' (Plog, 1998), *allocentric tourists* are risk takers who prefer to explore offbeat places perceived to be more authentic than 'tourist destinations'. In contrast, *psychocentric tourists* (or 'dependables'), who prefer to avoid risk and are comfortable with established destinations and brands, dominate unsustainable mass tourism. Alternative tourists, in contrast, are *FITs* (free and independent travellers) who avoid high volume package tour arrangements and instead travel as individuals or in small groups, often remaining in a destination for an extended period. They often prefer to travel in the off season knowing that there will be fewer tourists and hence alternative tourism tends to be less susceptible to the pronounced seasonality that often characterizes unsustainable mass tourism. In addition, visitors typically originate from a diverse array of countries, since the mass marketing systems that skew markets to one or two dominant sources are not in place.

Alternative tourism guidebooks

The growth of the alternative tourism market has spawned a specialized guidebook industry characterized by obscure publishers, low print runs and an emphasis on offbeat destinations as well as budget services and attractions. Examples include Ocko (1990), Holing (1991), Wood and House (1991), Daniel (1993), LaPlanche (1995), Elander and Widstrand (1998), Mann (2002) and McMillan et al. (2003).

3.4.2 Attractions

The allocentric proclivities of the alternative tourist engender a preference for 'authentic' cultural, historical and natural attractions that are perceived to capture a destination's unique sense of place and allow for interactions between visitors and local residents. This contrasts with the generic and purpose built theme parks, casinos and other 'contrived' attractions favoured by mass tourists. Alternative tourism attractions may in some instances be non-commercial, but it is more likely that there is a degree of commercialization because of the need for the product to be financially viable.

3.4.3 Accommodation

Alternative tourism accommodations tend to be small-scale facilities that adhere to unobtrusive vernacular standards and are dispersed at a low density throughout the destination. Options include the homes of residents (i.e. homestay), small guesthouses, scientific research stations, monasteries and retreats, tents, yurts (Mongolian-style tents), bed and breakfasts, youth hostels, dormitories, kibbutzim, ecolodges and freighters. In contrast to the non-local corporate ownership of large hotels and resorts, alternative tourism accommodations are controlled by local small businesses or residents, or by the local community more generally.

3.4.4 Economic status

Small visitor numbers result in low overall tourist receipts in alternative tourism destinations, but allegedly most of this revenue is retained and leakages minimized due to the high level of local control and the preference of alternative tourists for 'authentic' goods and services. These factors indicate strong intersectoral linkages within the destination economy and thus a high multiplier effect, as local farmers, fishers and artisans fill the demand for these products and services. Whereas tourism in mass tourism destinations gradually displaces other sectors and becomes dominant, alternative tourism supposedly functions as a supplementary sector within a diversified and interlinked local economy.

3.4.5 Regulation

Mass tourism is associated with support for free markets and only enough regulation to ensure stability and facilitate short-term profitability for shareholders. External corporate interests overtly or covertly play a dominant role in establishing these regulations. Ideally, alternative tourism regulations, in contrast, are established and monitored by the local community and are intended to maintain the above constellation of structural characteristics in the long-term interests of community well-being. They may therefore involve 'anti-market' measures such as restricting visitor numbers and infrastructural capacity, requiring accommodations to have majority local ownership, designating architectural standards and height limits and requiring that most goods and services be obtained from local sources.

3.5 Deliberate and circumstantial alternative tourism

Table 3.1 uses the heading *deliberate alternative tourism*. What makes this ideal type 'deliberate' is the existence of the regulatory framework that deliberately keeps it alternative. Without these regulations, the ideal type can be more appropriately described as *circumstantial alternative tourism* (Weaver, 1991), meaning that the apparent adherence to alternative tourism simply reflects the fact that the destination is experiencing 'exploration' or 'involvement'-type circumstances within the destination life cycle model (see Section 1.3.2). It is, in essence, alternative tourism by default rather than intent. It is crucial to determine whether a destination adheres to deliberate or circumstantial alternative tourism, since in the absence of such a regulatory framework there is no insurance against the possibility that tourism will evolve into something more intensive and/or less benign. The existence of regulations, however, does not in itself provide this insurance; rather, it must be determined whether the regulations are effective in maintaining a sustainable alternative tourism status quo.

3.6 Farm-based tourism

Farm-based tourism, under a variety of guises (e.g. *vacation farms* and *Gîtes ruraux*), is one of the longest established forms of organized (and hence deliberate) alternative tourism, having been in existence in Europe as a formal industry since the late 1800s (Frater, 1983; Roberts, 2002). To qualify as a form of alternative tourism, farm-based tourism should involve operations that are locally owned and derive most of their income from agriculture (i.e. they are 'working' farms). Individual operations should also be small, with maximum thresholds of five or ten units of overnight accommodation usually stipulated. As an industry, farm-based tourism is a relatively small sector in the USA, Canada, New Zealand and Australia, where the number of such farms varies from 700 to 2000. In contrast, the UK, France, Germany and Austria each host 20–30 000 vacation farms (Weaver and Fennell, 1997). With the exception of Namibia (Shackley, 1993), there is scant evidence of a formal farm-based tourism industry in the less developed world, although its potential in such areas appears high.

Farm-based tourism is attractive from an economic perspective because of its potential to supplement and diversify rural economies in peripheral areas such as the North American Great Plains or the far north of England that have long suffered from declining agricultural economies (Weaver and Fennell, 1997; Ilbery et al., 1998; Roberts, 2002). Critically, tourism typically accounts for only a small portion of a vacation farm's total income, but this revenue is perceived by many operators in Austria, Saskatchewan, northern England and elsewhere to constitute the difference between survival and failure (Frater, 1983; Weaver and Fennell, 1997; Ilbery et al., 1998; Nickerson et al., 2001). Inskeep (1991) describes farm-based tourism as a symbiotic opportunity for areas where neither agriculture nor tourism is independently viable. Investment costs, moreover, can be minimal for farmers who have rooms available in their homes when children leave the household and there is evidence that the tourism component provides income and power for female adult household members who provide most of the relevant labour (Dernoi, 1991; Ilbery et al., 1998; Busby and Rendle, 2000; Nilsson, 2002). Many female participants cite contact with guests as an outlet for relieving stresses caused by social isolation (Oppermann, 1997; Nickerson et al., 2001).

3.6.1 Issues of regulation and scale

While urban tourists seeking contrast with their usual environment may regard spatial peripherality and underdevelopment as assets, these can hinder the marketing and accessibility of vacation farms. Another barrier consistently cited in the literature is a government regulatory environment perceived to be time-consuming, expensive, restrictive, irrational and intrusive with regard to taxation, health and safety regulations, licences, liability and access to government loans and other forms of assistance (e.g. Weaver and Fennell, 1997, Ilbery et al., 1998). The small size of individual operations and the marginal revenues obtained from tourism are major complications that make these restrictions and costs even less bearable and also reduce the likelihood that an operator will possess the range of skills and knowledge necessary to undertake efficiently all aspects of the operation (Nilsson, 2002). With less available resources and due to the fact that peak farm work often coincides with peak visitation periods, the requirements of tourism may distract from essential farm work, while the latter may in turn distract from tourism-related responsibilities necessary to ensure high levels of customer satisfaction. Dernoi (1991) suggests that Canadian vacation farms often do not meet basic standards of service for these reasons and hence are less likely to survive as long-term propositions.

Consortia

The vacation farm sector in several European countries employs the concept of *consortia* to compensate for the disadvantages associated with small size. A consortium is a group of farms (often between 10 and 20) that pools member resources to pursue integrated marketing and product development strategies, more effectively represents the interests of the members and provides access to relevant information and financing. Ideally, a consortium creates efficient economies of scale without compromising the autonomy and character of the individual units. The Cartwheel cooperative* in southwestern England, with 200 member vacation farms in 2000 (or about 5 per cent of all farms in the region), is an interesting example of a large consortium that engages in innovative practices such as the provision of local food supplies to visitors and the utilization of rural development grants from the European Union (Roberts, 2002).

3.7 Volunteer tourism

Volunteer tourism encompasses a diverse array of experiences and settings that involve tourists who receive no financial compensation while undertaking various forms of, usually, organized social and/or environmental work in the destination (Wearing, 2001). It is explicitly associated with enhancement sustainability, notably not just from the destination perspective, but also in terms of the personal development of the participating tourist. Another distinctive characteristic is the extent to which volunteer tourism is associated with environmental, religious and social non-profit NGOs (non-governmental organizations) based in major origin regions. Prominent NGOs that have been featured in the tourism literature include the US-based Earthwatch Institute* (McGehee, 2002) and Habitat for Humanity* (Gaillard, 1996), the Gibbon Rehabilitation Project in Thailand (Broad, 2003), Conservation Volunteers Australia* (Townsend, 1999; Davies, 2002), the UK-based British Trust for Conservation Volunteers* and Canadian-based Youth Challenge International* (Wearing, 2001) and Volunteer for Nature* programmes (Halpenny and Caissie, 2003).

3.7.1 Sample accomplishments

Conventional tourism benefits are usually quantified in terms of direct tourist revenues that eventuate in economic growth and lifestyle enhancement of residents within the destination. Volunteer tourism, in contrast, entails a more immediate connection between tourist activity (i.e. the volunteer work) and tangible benefits for residents (e.g. improved housing, education and medical care) or the natural environment. Habitat for Humanity, for example, has constructed more than 100000 houses for low-income residents around the world. The Earthwatch Institute claims the participation of more than 65000 volunteers and the establishment of at least five high order protected areas as a result of their sponsorship of more than ten million hours of research. In 2001, volunteers for Conservation Volunteers Australia logged 45000 days of work, valued at AUS$5 million, on conservation projects within Australia (Davies, 2002). The British Trust for Conservation Volunteers claims 330000 conservation workdays undertaken each year in the UK and abroad by 130000 volunteers. McGehee (2002), moreover, cites evidence from a sample of Earthwatch volunteers to suggest that participation in such activities stimulated further social and environmental movement involvement by its volunteers, reinforcing the organization's claims that it fosters a sense of global citizenship among participants.

3.7.2 Potential negative impacts

There is as of yet no overt criticism of volunteer tourism in the literature, in part because little research has been undertaken on this topic, but also because its laudable character and outcomes may render it more resistant to critical scrutiny. It may be speculated, however, that problems can arise from a motivation mix that is concurrently altruistic and egotistical, that is, focused on destination enhancement but also personal development. Added to Wearing's (2001) observation that the opportunity to travel is a fundamental influence in the decision to become a volunteer, it may be that the egotistical aspect often outweighs other considerations, producing participants who are more interested in adventure and résumé enhancement (i.e. ego satisfaction) than the long-term betterment of disadvantaged communities or degraded natural environments. In such cases, the righteous veneer of volunteer tourism masks an activity that is not essentially different from less regarded forms of tourism. Problems can also emerge if volunteers are insufficiently trained to perform adequately their assigned tasks, or if rapid turnover of participants reduces accountability and hinders continuity.

Corporatization, vested interests and preserving the status quo

Organizations that sponsor volunteer tourism projects, while ostensibly non-profit oriented, often become more like large corporations in their marketing and management sophistication as they expand. Hence, they may lose site of the grassroots issues that prompted their establishment and spend more time on improving their public image, lobbying, establishing complex and expensive bureaucracies and enhancing revenue flows. Concurrently, the volunteer component might be seen as a form of exploitation if it becomes used as a way of offloading or minimizing costs.

As with all organizations, volunteer tourism organizations are also fundamentally ideological in nature and it is likely that their agendas will be consciously or subconsciously projected on destinations even if ulterior motives are adamantly denied. Habitat for Humanity, for example, is an ecumenical Christian organization that is motivated by biblical injunctions. Hence, it cannot be discounted that the priority objective of some volunteers working in non-Christian locales is covert or even overt proselytization. It has also been suggested, at least in the case of Seattle (Washington state, USA) that the organization is neglecting homeless single males, the group most in need of housing, because of its bias for 'family values'. Finally, some leftist academics contend that the activities of volunteer organizations such as Habitat for Humanity are counterproductive in that they fail to address the systemic forces that give rise to poverty and may actually reduce the pressure for change.

3.8 Guesthouse tourism

Whereas volunteer tourism is defined in terms of tourist motivation, *guesthouse tourism* is defined, like homestay and farm-based tourism, primarily by accommodation type. There is no standard definition of a 'guesthouse', though the latter is usually perceived as a specialized tourist facility that has a small number of accommodation units and is usually locally owned. To the extent that owners often reside on-site, the guesthouse sector overlaps with homestay tourism.

3.8.1 Guesthouses in the Caribbean

The guesthouse sector of the Caribbean, because it coexists with conventional mass tourism in the heart of the pleasure periphery, may offer valuable insights as to how alternative tourism can persist in areas otherwise dominated by more intensive forms of tourism. Most Caribbean islands have a concentration of guesthouses in the central business districts of major port cities, in peripheral residential neighbourhoods and in local villages near beach resorts (Weaver, 1993). Cumulatively, they account for only a very small portion of all accommodation units, but a disproportionate share in the dominant urban centres. Although guesthouse owners have their own specialized organizations in most destinations, much of the industry is situated within the unregulated informal sector and relies on word of mouth marketing and happenstance to attract customers, a high proportion of whom originate in other parts of the Caribbean or consist of backpackers from the more developed regions (see Section 3.9). This informal component is indicative of a circumstantial alternative tourism sector that could be undermined or subsumed by conventional mass tourism.

It is interesting, especially from a gender perspective, that African Caribbean females account for a large share of guesthouse owners and operators in the region. More remarkable is the historical continuity of this pattern, with Weaver (2005c) noting the extent to which such individuals apparently dominated the guesthouse sector in cities such as Bridgetown (Barbados), Kingston (Jamaica) and Port-of-Spain (Trinidad) in the nineteenth and early twentieth centuries. Ironically, this survival occurred even as the tourism involvement of the dominant white elite shifted dramatically from providing accommodation in plantation homes to establishing resort hotels. Further research on this little known topic is warranted.

3.9 Backpacking

Relative to the guesthouse sector with which it overlaps, the *backpacking tourism* sector has been extensively studied in recent years. It is defined mainly in participant terms as involving usually young and budget-minded tourists (i.e. the 'backpacker') travelling for extended periods of time. Research indicates that backpackers adhere to many core tenets of alternative tourism, such as the preference for small-scale, locally owned accommodations and independent travel arrangements, as well as a desire to interact with local residents (Loker-Murphy and Pearce, 1995; Murphy, 2001; Richards and Wilson, 2004). Backpackers can be regarded as a distinctive subculture in particular because of their tendency to travel and socialize with other backpackers while avoiding other types of tourist, constructing and demonstrating in the process an overt 'anti-tourism' identity (Welk, 2004).

An interesting pattern of behaviour that results from this tendency is exceptionally flexible itineraries and travel parties that change impulsively in response to encounters with other backpackers and exposure to the backpacker 'grapevine' (Murphy, 2001; Sorensen, 2003). It is ironic, however, that while backpackers identify themselves in strongly individualistic terms, they can often be readily distinguished by their appearance (and by their backpacks in particular) and they are predictable in terms of what they eat and where they congregate. The 'backpacker hostel' is a specialized type of accommodation that encourages these cliquish and predictable yet unpredictable tendencies by serving as a 'gathering place' for the subculture (Westerhausen and Macbeth, 2003).

A contentious form of tourism

Backpacking, more than other forms of alternative tourism, is controversial as to whether it constitutes a desirable type of tourist activity or even qualifies as alternative tourism. Some destinations, and notably Australia through its National Backpacker Tourism Strategy (CDOT, 1995), have deliberately cultivated this market in recognition of its substantial economic impact. At the beginning of the twenty-first century, backpackers comprised about 10 per cent of all international tourists in Australia after growing by a rate of 9 per cent per year in the 1990s. With long average lengths of stay compensating for low daily per capita expenditures, international backpackers in Australia spent an estimated AUS$1.5 billion in 1999, much of it accruing to peripheral destinations such as the Northern Territory that otherwise do not benefit proportionately from international tourism receipts (Buchanan and Rossetto, 1997; Mohsin and Ryan, 2003).

In other destinations, and Third World ones in particular (e.g. Bhutan, Maldives and the Indian state of Goa), some residents and decision-makers continue to decry backpackers as 'hippies' who produce few economic benefits to compensate for behaviour that is perceived as antisocial and harmful to local communities (Scheyvens, 2002). Hence, their tendency has been to discourage or 'demarket' this segment (see Section 10.5.1) (Ateljevic and Doorne, 2004). Mohsin and Ryan (2003) suggest that this stereotype had some validity in the 1970s when international backpacking was dominated by members of the ultraliberal counter-culture, but now persists despite the sanitized and overwhelmingly middle class nature of the phenomenon, which Spreitzhofer (1998) refers to as 'post hippie' backpacking.

Yet, promiscuity and drug taking are still undoubtedly common within the subculture and serve to perpetuate and amplify the negative stereotype. Unfavourable reactions also result from the perceived frugality of backpackers, which may be exacerbated by the status gained within the subculture by individuals who are able to keep trip expenditures to an absolute minimum (Scheyvens, 2002; Sorensen, 2003). Spreitzhofer (1998) maintains that the overall character of backpacking tourism in much of Southeast Asia and elsewhere positions this sector closer to mass tourism at a low budget level than to alternative tourism, especially given the relative lack of specialized backpacking tourism organizations that would help to maintain the alternative character of this sector.

Yet, Hampton (1998) and Scheyvens (2002), among others, argue that backpacking can be highly beneficial to developing countries. One positive effect for local residents is the willingness of backpackers to purchase non-luxury goods and services from informal sector businesses whose access to conventional tourists is often deliberately curtailed by government and/or the formal tourism industry (Timothy and Wall, 1997). New informal sector businesses, in addition, might be created as a result of the backpacker clientele, since capital and skill requirements are much less restrictive than those required by conventional businesses within the formal sector.

Once established, their continuing response to the alternative needs of backpackers may help to arrest the transition of certain locations into more intensive phases of the resort cycle (Hampton, 1998).

3.10 Urban alternative tourism

With the exception of urban guesthouses and volunteer social activities focused on poor inner city neighbourhoods, alternative tourism is not typically associated with urban settings. Yet, large resident numbers, the need for economic revitalization and diversification, concentrations of cultural and heritage attractions and proximity to services and amenities all combine to suggest an alternative tourism subtype with great potential to reach the large tourist markets that visit urban areas.

3.10.1 Urban cultural heritage tours

The phenomenon of *urban cultural heritage tourism* is one area where this potential is being realized. As opposed to the mass tourism that has developed in the 'Chinatowns' and 'Little Italys' of large American cities, this refers mainly to nascent tourism opportunities such as those undertaken in the African American neighbourhoods of Harlem (New York), Watts (Los Angeles) and Shaw (Washington, DC – see case study at the end of this chapter) that are peripheral to the mass tourism circuits of the central business district. One example is Boston's MYTOWN, which offers summer tours of the South End neighbourhood conducted by local high school students who acquire relevant skills and gain pride in their own community. In 2003, such tours involved 43 local residents and 1500 visitors, not all of who were necessarily tourists (Lund, 2004). The emphasis on civil rights-related attractions in the MYTOWN tour suggests an overtly political dimension that is also apparent in tours of Soweto, the South African township adjacent to Johannesburg.

Boyd's (2000) study of Chicago's Bronzeville community provides one of the few analyses of heritage tourism in an African American urban context. The essential argument in this study is that the commodification of race and the emphasis on racial identity through heritage tourism makes it difficult to justify the displacement of the local working class African American population in the face of gentrification and other pressures. However, ironically, it also *encourages* gentrification by making the neighbourhood more attractive, which benefits middle class more than low-income African American residents. Issues of particular importance to the latter group, such as exclusion from unions, segregation, overcrowding and crime, are omitted from or at least not emphasized in heritage interpretation and the establishment of place meaning. Rather, the latter according to Boyd (2000) focus on what the neighbourhood could and should be from the perspective of the often newly-arrived middle class (e.g. a creative hotbed of jazz), rather than what it presently is.

3.10.2 Other urban activities

Urban alternative tourism initiatives that do not adhere to the cultural or racial heritage model include Hong Kong's Family Insight Tour, which allows tourist groups of no more than 12 individuals to visit ordinary residents in public housing estates.

In the early 1990s, approximately 1000 visitors per year went on the tour. Reported problems include disruptions to the schedule of estate managers, residents not home at scheduled visit times, limited space in homes for tourists to sit or stand and language barriers (Hobson and Mak, 1995). In Canada, the Green Tourism Association promotes a broader 'green' tourism product for Toronto that offers visitors interesting alternatives to iconic attractions such as the CN Tower. The Association has produced alternative guides and maps that employ assumptions of environmental responsibility, local economic vitality, cultural diversity and experiential richness (Dodds and Joppe, 2001).

3.11 Education tourism

Education tourism overlaps with urban alternative tourism to the extent that most of the post-secondary institutions that host international and domestic student tourists are located in urban centres. However, it is distinct from other forms of alternative tourism in that few students who meet the WTO definition of an 'educational tourist' intuitively identify themselves as tourists. Similarly, the businesses and organizations that have been spawned by international education are only tangentially associated with the larger tourism industry. Patterns of motivation (education, learning), travel arrangements (FIT), interactions with local residents, spatial distribution (widely dispersed, usually away from conventional tourism spaces) and consumption of locally produced goods and services, nevertheless, all serve to situate education tourism within alternative tourism.

3.11.1 A growth sector

The relatively small numbers and low daily per capita expenditures of education students, as with backpackers, are offset by the length of time they spend in the host destination. International students in Australia, for example, account for just 3 per cent of all stayover arrivals but about 20 per cent of all stayover expenditures (Leiper and Hunt, 1998). This has also been a growth market, with Australian visas issued to international students (post-secondary and other) increasing from 1900 in 1960 to 100 000 in 1994 and 167 000 in 2000 (Weaver, 2004). The stability of the international student market is demonstrated by the fact that international student numbers in the USA did not decline following the terrorist attacks of September 11, 2001 (Marklein, 2002).

Education students as tourism magnets

In a study of 139 international students who had graduated from a major university in southeastern Queensland, Australia, Weaver (2004) found that all had visited tourist attractions in the city where they had studied, while 83 per cent had travelled in Australia as leisure or social tourists while completing their degree. Seventy-eight per cent reported at least one visit from an overseas relative or friend during this time and 53 per cent had returned to Australia as a visitor since their graduation. Two-thirds claimed that they had influenced one or more individuals from their home country to study in Australia. These data indicate that international students function as efficient long-term 'tourism magnets' for Australia even though they themselves are not associated with the tourism sector. These findings amplify their disproportionate economic impacts and support the argument of Leiper and Hunt (1998) that national tourism marketing bodies should become more proactive in attracting and satisfying international student tourists.

3.12 Potential problems

Supporters of the knowledge-based platform discourage value judgments based on the scale of tourism alone and therefore are willing to expose the potential problems of alternative tourism and challenge its claims to the moral high ground (see for example Butler, 1990; Pearce, 1992; Griffin and Boele, 1997; Weaver, 1998). Ideally, such a critique positively influences alternative tourism by forcing managers to challenge long-held assumptions about its appropriateness and to reflect on the actual impacts of their products. Associated issues that are discussed below include the sector's links with mass tourism, the disadvantages of small-scale operations, Eurocentrism and community disruption.

3.12.1 Links to mass tourism

Attempts by the adaptancy platform to disassociate alternative tourism from mass tourism (see Table 3.1) are disingenuous to the extent that almost all alternative tourism activity involves some interaction with the conventional tourism industry. Indeed, it is arguable that alternative tourism could not exist but for its utilization of mass tourism infrastructure and services at various stages in the tourism system (Pearce, 1992). The large international airlines illustrate this association most clearly, since the vast majority of alternative tourists travelling from the more developed to the less developed regions travel by air. Alternative tourists also commonly use credit cards, travellers' cheques and other devices of the corporate world that support mass tourism.

Alternative tourism is therefore at least partly implicated in global economic systems and structures that are alleged to perpetuate intragenerational and inter-regional inequities. These linkages may be unavoidable, but alternative tourists could respond by selecting smaller alternative providers wherever possible. Where it is not feasible, they may at least voice their concerns to public relations departments of these conventional corporations and select providers with stronger 'green' credentials (see Chapter 5).

Transformation to mass tourism

As discussed in Section 3.5, the idea of deliberate alternative tourism is important because it entails regulations that attempt to maintain the integrity and identity of the sector. Yet, even with these regulations, there is a possibility that alternative tourism can be transformed into more intensive and potentially less benign forms of tourism. Such a transformation may be the ironic outcome of a product's popularity, wherein increased visitation to an 'outstanding alternative tourism' destination or product prompts restructuring or expansion that causes it eventually to resemble a conventional tourism product. This is evident in the establishment of backpacker hostel chains and in increasingly corporatized backpacker guidebook products such as *Lonely Planet* and *Rough Guide*. It is also the basis for the claim of Busby and Rendle (2000) that the vacation farm sector is moving from a 'tourism on farms' to a 'farm tourism' modality, implying its emergence as a large industry. As noted in Section 3.7, many of the organizations involved with volunteer tourism already bear some resemblance to large corporations. In this regard, it should be borne in mind that most of today's large-scale conventional tourism products started out as alternative tourism.

Such 'up-sizing' is not necessarily problematic if sustainability is maintained, but there remains the risk that this new and possibly oxymoronic 'corporate alternative tourism' will absorb or otherwise outcompete smaller alternative tourism products and/or eventually become indistinguishable from other mass tourism operations. They will be more likely to use their growing leverage to seek better rates from airlines and other mass tourism facilitators, thereby increasing their integration into the conventional tourism system.

Precursor to mass tourism

Alternative tourism, however deliberate, can also facilitate the introduction of more intensive and potentially less benign forms of tourism from outside. It can do this by functioning as a spearhead that initiates tourism-friendly services and draws publicity, subsequently attracting more conventional tourism operators and tourists. In this sense, alternative tourists may act as 'explorers' who inadvertently open the destination to more invasive stages of the destination life cycle. Butler (1990) captures this precursor effect in alluding to alternative tourism as a Trojan horse, although such outcomes are as or more likely to result from inadvertent actions than from malicious intent. Northern Thailand, which was opened to mass tourism through trekking, appears to illustrate both the precursor and transformation effects (Cohen, 1989; Dearden, 1991; Silver, 1992; Petry, 1996).

3.12.2 Limitations of scale

In their celebration of the 'small is beautiful' approach, proponents of alternative tourism often ignore or downplay the disadvantages inherent to small-scale dynamics. These may be counteracted to some extent by the formation of organizations and strategic alliances such as consortia, but the individual unit is still hindered by restricted economies of scale that, among other impacts, limit the skills and access to capital available to the entrepreneur (Buhalis and Cooper, 1998). Ironically, small local businesses are thus often ill suited to implement technologies that are more environmentally sustainable (Ioannides and Petersen, 2003). As with the guesthouses of the trekking regions in Nepal (Gurung and De Coursey, 1994; Shackley, 1996), growth in visitation is therefore not necessarily accompanied by the implementation of measures to cope sustainably with resulting pressures on the environment and local community. The level of service (e.g. cleanliness, quality of food) may also be such that even the allocentric alternative tourist is dissatisfied. Small tourism businesses such as those found in alternative tourism ultimately experience a high rate of failure (McKercher, 1998, 2001) and this creates economic and social instability within local communities, especially as the loss of even a few visitors may make the difference between survival and collapse, as evidenced by the responses of vacation farm operators (see above).

At a broader scale, it can be argued that alternative tourism lacks sufficient scale to serve as a meaningful vehicle of economic development for a peripheral region.

According to Oppermann (1997), this is especially so for farm-based and other tourism organizations that impose artificial ceilings on the number of units that member farms can offer for accommodation, which nicely adheres to the ideal of deliberate alternative tourism, but essentially constrains the capacity of the sector to support struggling rural economies.

3.12.3 Elitism and ecoimperialism

Alternative tourism, while it emphasizes local control and presentation of the locality's unique sense of place, may ultimately be regarded as an elitist Eurocentric or 'Western' creation that in many cases is imposed on residents in peripheral and Third World destinations (Butler, 1990). As such, it can represent an image of what the tourists and aid agencies believe the community *should* be rather than what it really is or wants to be. According to Carter (1998) guidebooks written for backpackers often adopt a stereotypical and patronizing approach to featured LDC destinations. The reality, if it includes gender inequities and activities such as hunting or slash and burn agriculture, may be unpalatable to the alternative tourists, who may boycott the product or confront local residents engaged in practices deemed to be unacceptable. Alternative tourism at worst may be interpreted as a form of 'ecoimperialism' in which the economic and sociocultural development and modernization of a peripheral destination is curtailed by organizations, tour operators and alternative tourists who wish to maintain the destination in an 'authentic' traditional small-scale condition to satisfy the demands of the alternative tourist market. Local residents, encouraged to uphold the principles of deliberate alternative tourism, may actually prefer to pursue a mass tourism trajectory.

3.12.4 Community disruption

Resources and power are not equally distributed within any given community and the benefits from new activities such as alternative tourism will therefore not usually be equally distributed. Alternative tourism can actually exacerbate existing inequalities by increasing the power of the local elites who are most likely to control such projects. Yet, those assessing its impacts from the outside may be satisfied that control and benefits are invested within the local community. For example, the non-European females historically dominating the Caribbean guesthouse sector have belonged mainly to the mixed race urban middle class, while working class women of unmixed African descent have been conspicuous by their low level of representation within this group of entrepreneurs (Weaver, 2005c).

Internal conflict

Alternative tourism may also serve to upset delicate balances of power within local communities. A case study of this effect is provided by Ranck (1987), who examined the impacts of alternative tourism on a traditional community in Papua New Guinea. Aside from chronicling the myriad challenges faced by small alternative tourism business owners, this research reveals the relationship between the growth of tourism activity and increased clan rivalry. One guesthouse's acquisition of two outboard motors as a gift from the New Zealand High Commission, for example, positioned the owners' clan well above its neighbours and provided it with a competitive advantage over other guesthouses, thereby inviting resentment and retaliation from other clans.

Intrusiveness

Alternative tourists often seek a high level of personal interaction with local residents, but in doing so, they may disrupt the community by invading for extended periods the personal spaces where the community is normally sheltered from exposure to tourists (Butler, 1990) (see Chapter 9). Casual liaisons and relationships between tourists and local residents may cause or exacerbate conflicts and change within the community that persist long after the tourist has departed, especially if these involve sexual activity or the use of drugs. Macleod (1998), for example, describes how contact with alternative tourists substantially altered social relationships and norms within the traditional society of La Gomera in the Canary Islands.

3.13 Summary

Early deliberations in alternative tourism were closely associated with ecumenical church groups, third world destinations and homestay-style accommodations. Subsequently, the sector has expanded and diversified to the point where a tentative typology of subtypes as well as an alternative tourism ideal type can be presented. The latter offers a distinct contrast to the unsustainable mass tourism ideal type in terms of markets, attractions, accommodation, economic status and regulation, with local control and small-scale dynamics being core principles. Without the regulation component, alternative tourism is 'circumstantial' rather than 'deliberate', meaning that it is essentially an 'involvement'-stage situation within the destination life cycle that could move toward a less sustainable position.

Profiles of selected alternative tourism subtypes reveal commonalities as well as distinct characteristics. The vacation farm sector, for example, is long established, well organized, found mainly in the more developed countries and fundamentally coexistent with another sector (i.e. agriculture). Volunteer tourism, in contrast, is closely defined by tourist motivation, is controlled mainly by social and environmental non-governmental organizations and is associated with tangible enhancement-based accomplishments within local communities. In regions such as the Caribbean, the guesthouse sector is distinguished by its spatial concentration and high level of local female participation. Much of it is informal and thus indicative of circumstantial alternative tourism. Backpacking is defined largely through the characteristics of 'backpackers', who constitute a tourist subculture. The behaviour of this subculture combines with the increased corporatization of this sector to make backpacking a particularly controversial form of alternative tourism and one that also has circumstantial characteristics. Urban alternative tourism is demarcated by locales and attractions, which often entails the presentation of racial or ethnic heritage, while education tourism has perhaps the weakest intuitive association with tourism or tourism organizations despite its significant role in generating tourism income and ongoing activity.

It cannot be assumed that alternative tourism is always sustainable, given its association with potential problems such as its links with mass tourism and the possibility that it can be transformed into or function as a precursor to the latter.

Limitations of scale also hinder its effectiveness as a business and exemplar of environmental sustainability, while its Eurocentric origins and premises raise questions of elitism and the imposition of alien value systems and preferences. Finally, communities are at risk of disruption if alternative tourism exacerbates or creates power inequities, or if contact between local residents and alternative tourists is overly intrusive.

On the net

British Trust for Conservation Volunteers
http://www.btcv.org/

Cartwheel cooperative (southwest UK)
http://www.cartwheelholidays.co.uk/cartwheel-about.asp

Conservation Volunteers Australia
http://www.conservationvolunteers.com.au/

Earthwatch Institute
http://www.earthwatch.org/

Ecumenical Coalition on Third World Tourism (ECTWT)
http://is6.pacific.net.hk/~contours/

Green Tourism Association
http://www.greentourism.on.ca/indexflash.html

Habitat for Humanity
http://www.habitat.org/

Meet-the-People program (Jamaica Tourist Board)
http://meetthepeople.visitjamaica.com/home/default.aspx

Third World Tourism Ecumenical European Network (TEN)
http://www.eed.de/fix/ten-tourism/

U Street/Shaw Heritage Tours
http://www.sustainabletravel.org/docs/communityProfile_shaw.pdf

Volunteer for Nature
http://www.ontarionature.org/action/

Youth Challenge International
http://www.yci.org/

For further reading

Buchanan, I. and Rossetto, A. (1997). *With my Swag upon my Shoulder: a Comprehensive Study of International Backpackers to Australia*. Bureau of Tourism Research. Occasional Paper No. 24.
A highly detailed study of backpackers in Australia is provided in this report, which is based on data collected through a special survey of 1100 individuals. Variables include reasons for visiting Australia, spatial patterns of travel, activities, satisfaction levels and market profiles.

Butler, R. (1990). Alternative tourism: pious hope or Trojan horse? *Journal of Travel Research* 28 (3), 40–5.
Butler's classic article offers one of the earliest and best articulated critiques of alternative tourism.

Green Tourism Association (2000). *The Other Guide to Toronto: Opening the Door to Green Tourism.*

The Guide is one of the first examples of an urban tourist guidebook that takes an alternative tourism approach, the promotion of which is the goal of Toronto's Green Tourism Association.

Holden, P. (ed.) (1984). *Alternative Tourism: Report of the Workshop on Alternative Tourism with a Focus on Asia.* Ecumenical Coalition on Third World Tourism.
The Report is a remarkable collation of pioneering alternative tourism perspectives and case studies presented at a 1984 conference in Chiang Mai, Thailand, in response to the negative effects of mass tourism in Asia and other Third World regions.

Richards, G. and Wilson, J. (eds) (2004). *The Global Nomad: Backpacker Travel in Theory and Practice.* Channel View.
The academics contributing to this edited volume explore the behaviour, attitudes and motivations of backpackers and examine from an interdisciplinary perspective the development of backpacking as a global social phenomenon.

Wearing, S. (2001). *Volunteer Tourism: Experiences that Make a Difference.* CABI Publishing.
This analysis of volunteer tourism, which focuses on the author's experience in the Santa Elena Rainforest Reserve of Costa Rica, is one of the few books written on this form of alternative tourism. A strongly sociological perspective is employed.

Beyond the book

1. (a) Write a 500-word promotional piece that would attract an allocentric tourist to a proposed alternative tourism product of your choice. (b) Design a marketing strategy that will expose the piece to as many allocentric tourists as possible. (c) Prepare a 500-word document that explains to the local community why they should support your promotional efforts.
2. Formulate a set of ten regulations, half from the local government and half from the industry association, that would maintain the alternative tourism character of a growing farm-based tourism sector in your country, while maximizing its economic and sociocultural contributions.
3. The government of Bhutan opposes the presence of backpacker tourism, which it regards as unsustainable. Write a 1000-word consultant's report proposing a backpackers strategy for Bhutan that would be acceptable to the Bhutanese government on grounds of environmental, economic, sociocultural and financial sustainability.
4. (a) Design a combined bus and walking heritage tour that features an interesting urban neighbourhood or rural district of your choice. (b) Explain how this tour will satisfy the participants while stimulating local economic and sociocultural development.
5. Obtain a copy of Butler's 1990 article critiquing alternative tourism. (a) Explain what he means by referring to alternative tourism as a 'pious hope' and a 'Trojan horse'. (b) How can this critique be used to ensure that alternative tourism has minimal negative impacts?

On the ground: sharing African American heritage in Washington, DC

The Shaw district of Washington, DC is an inner city neighbourhood that was once a leading centre of African American urban culture and business. It fell into disrepair following the race riots of the late 1960s, but has been experiencing renewal and gentrification since the mid-1990s. One consequence of this revitalization has been the establishment of U Street/Shaw Heritage Tours*, a grassroots urban alternative tourism initiative of the DC Heritage Tourism Coalition, which includes most of the city's museums and cultural organizations as well as neighbourhood associations, churches, community development organizations, professional tour guides, the Metropolitan Transit Authority, the official DC marketing agencies and the National Park Service.

In partnership with the Manna Community Development Corporation (one of its members) and the DC Chamber of Commerce, the Coalition operates a guided bus tour ('Duke Ellington's DC') and a walking tour ('Before Harlem, There Was U Street'). The goal of these tours is to (a) utilize heritage tourism as a mechanism for stimulating economic development in the neighbourhood, (b) generate employment for Shaw residents, especially as tour guides, (c) attract some of the estimated 20 million tourists who visit DC each year but congregate in the Mall area just one mile to the south and (d) celebrate and enhance the district's rich African American heritage (Peckham, 2003).

The first bus and walking tours were given in 1999 and 2000, respectively, and 20 bus tours were booked for 2001. The bus tour is a 4-hour experience that includes stops at the Lincoln Theater, the Thurgood Marshall Center, the African American Civil War Memorial and the Whitelaw Hotel, which was once the only inner city hotel to accept African American travellers. Neighbourhood restaurants cater lunches and the tour ends with a performance focused on local oral history. A local scholar wrote the scripts for both tours based on research, focal groups and interviews with present and former residents.

The diversity of the Coalition and its partners allows for extensive marketing through conventional mechanisms such as websites, trade shows, media advertisements and free publicity brochures distributed in tourist areas and unconventional mechanisms such as churches, universities and their alumni associations and local hotels and youth hostels. Familiarization tours are also provided for tour operators, meeting planners and others who might in turn provide additional bookings and publicity. The marketing effort includes an exit survey that identifies strengths and weaknesses and compiles visitor addresses to which ongoing information about the tours is sent. These visitors, about one-third of whom are DC residents, are invited to the annual DC Open House, in which Coalition members offer free walking tours and museum admission in Shaw and other DC neighbourhoods.

According to Peckham (2003), problems encountered in the first few years of operation include resident complaints about buses idling in the streets as well as scheduling and cost issues associated with the renting of the tour buses. Catered lunches have proven problematic because of the diverse requirements and preferences of participants and many interested residents have failed to pass Washington's restrictive tour guide licensing requirements. Many local residents are participating informally in the tours by talking with the tourists. This adds authenticity and richness to the tours, but there is also a danger that panhandlers, drug dealers, swindlers and other questionable individuals who frequent the DC inner city could exploit such opportunities for contact.

Exercises

1. With regard to marketing and managing the Tours, what are the advantages and disadvantages of having an operating partnership that is as diverse as the one described above?
2. What are the relative strengths and weaknesses of the bus and walking tour options, in terms of their environmental and sociocultural impacts, as well as their effects on visitor satisfaction?
3. How can the operators of the Tours protect participants from interactions with questionable individuals without alienating opportunities for legitimate contacts with local residents?

Chapter 4
Conventional mass tourism

Chapter objectives

Upon completion of this chapter, the reader should be able to:

- describe the structure and major components of the formal tourism industry
- assess the role of ethics in accounting for the involvement of the tourism industry in sustainability
- explain why the *in situ* nature of consumption in tourism supports the case for greater sustainability within the industry
- provide and critically assess evidence for the emergence of the 'green consumer' and 'green tourist'
- differentiate between committed and veneer environmentalism among tourists as well as consumers more generally
- explain the concept of a paradigm shift and discuss the possibility that the green consumer and tourist are evidence that such a shift is currently underway and
- assess the conventional mass tourism industry with respect to the advantages it has over small businesses in implementing sustainable tourism measures.

4.1 Introduction

As discussed in Chapter 1, alternative tourism constitutes at best only a partial solution to the problems of a global tourism sector that is overwhelmingly dominated by conventional mass tourism products and activities. Mass tourism, moreover, not only resists conversion into alternative tourism, but also is often the model that government and communities prefer to pursue because of the perceived economic benefits that are conferred by size. Efforts to make global tourism more sustainable must therefore focus primarily on conventional mass tourism. Fortunately, there are compelling reasons for the latter to pursue strategies of sustainability, in addition to the factors described in Section 2.8 and in conformance with the 'stamp of authority' given to sustainable tourism policies by numerous organizations as outlined in Chapter 1. Chapter 4 begins by outlining the structure and components of the formal tourism industry (Section 4.2) and this is followed in Section 4.3 by a consideration of the role played by ethics in influencing the

tourism industry to pursue sustainability. Section 4.4 considers the incentives arising from the *in situ* nature of tourism consumption, while Section 4.5 discusses the
emergence of the 'green consumer' and 'green tourist'. The possibility that these
emerging market segments provide evidence for a societal paradigm shift is considered. Section 4.6 concludes by examining the advantages associated with larger
economies of scale in achieving sustainable tourism outcomes.

4.2 Structure of the formal tourism industry

The formal tourism industry that forms the core of conventional mass tourism may
be defined as 'the sum of the industrial and commercial activities that produce
goods and services wholly or mainly for tourist consumption' (Weaver and Lawton,
2002a, p. 471). As depicted in Figure 4.1, eight main sectors constitute the tourism
industry, three of which (travel agencies, specialized merchandise and tour operations (wholesale component only)) have a major presence in the origin regions of
the tourism system. Transportation is the only sector that is located mainly within
transit regions, while all sectors except travel agencies have a substantial direct
presence in the destination region, which accommodates most of the industry's

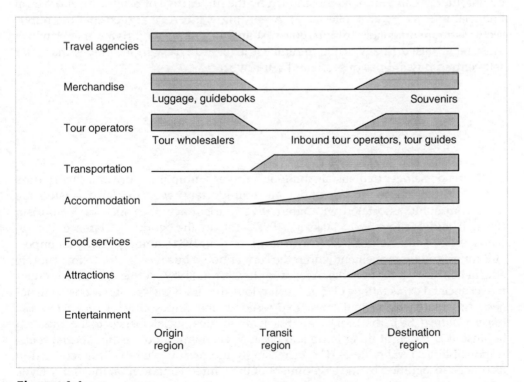

Figure 4.1
Distribution of tourism industry segments in origin, transit and destination
regions.

activity. This concentration helps to explain why the impact and sustainability literature focuses overwhelmingly on the destination region (see Section 1.3).

Figure 4.1 also depicts tangential linkages, including the presence of accommodation and attraction interests in the origin region through marketing and administrative activities and the presence of travel agencies in destinations through the provision of consultative and intervention services to their clients while they are in the destination. These linkages are important because they reveal the role sectors can play in fostering sustainability throughout the tourism system. Managers of attractions, for example, can disseminate information about appropriate behaviour to potential clients in origin regions, while travel agents can provide feedback to influence the behaviour of tourists while they are travelling (see Chapter 10).

4.2.1 Dominance of the private sector

Most of the tourism industry in MDCs is controlled by the private sector, with public sector ownership in major tourist origin countries being limited to certain types of attraction (e.g. National Parks and major historical sites in the USA) and some transportation providers (e.g. government-owned Singapore Airlines). Public involvement, by contrast, is more extensive in major planned economies such as China, although government participation in tourism within that country has diminished recently as a result of globalization and economic reform (Zhang et al., 2000). Such patterns are relevant from a sustainability perspective since the public sector is normally mandated to represent the population as a whole rather than particular interests and is not as constrained by the imperative of producing short-term financial returns (Swarbrooke, 1999). Accordingly, it can be argued that the public sector is more amenable to pursuing sustainability than the private sector, which must be attracted (likely at the minimalist level at first) with incentives that offer self-centred possibilities of profit and self-advocacy.

4.3 Ethics

The focus on self-centred sustainability incentives within the tourism industry does not mean that ethical considerations are unimportant, even though the latter are more commonly associated with alternative tourism activities such as ecotourism (Fennell and Malloy, 1995; Jaakson, 1997). Yet, in the work of Clarence Walton (Duska, 1998) and Keith Davis (Davis and Fredrick, 1984), among others, an important longstanding movement within the conventional business sector to incorporate ethical concerns is discernable. According to Carroll (1989), 'ethical responsibilities' reflect societal expectations of 'right' behaviour that for a variety of reasons have not been articulated by formal laws. Expressed in the philosophy of *corporate social responsibility* (CSR), the ethical approach advocates social justice to be pursued because it is the right thing to do and because economic clout creates special social responsibilities (Walle, 1995). The increasingly important role of CSR is reflected in its official recognition by the government of the United Kingdom* at the policy level.

In marketing, this is reflected in Kotler's 'societal marketing concept', which advocates 'long-run consumer welfare' as a core principle that needs to be taken into consideration in addition to the more traditional goals of customer satisfaction and profitability (Crane, 2000). An ethical foundation for business decisions may derive from religious fiat ('Do unto others . . .') and/or from a realization that the failure to behave ethically will eventuate in disastrous consequences, in which case the foundation is an expression of the principle of enlightened self-interest.

4.3.1 Empirical evidence of an ethical focus

In the world of business, there is evidence of ethical decision-making in which the shorter-term profitability considerations are transcended by longer-term social and environmental considerations. The prevalence of such behaviour, however, is debatable (Walton, 1998). It is safe to assume that the tourism industry is similarly conflicted by a mixed pattern of adherence to ethical imperatives. One difficulty in determining the extent to which ethical precepts are incorporated into tourism decision-making is that notions of 'right' and 'wrong', however semantically absolute, are still open to interpretation. A transnational entity, for example, may find that societal perceptions of proper behaviour vary from one country to another. The financial state of the business at any given time, in addition, may dictate the priority given to ethics.

Codes of ethics have become a common feature of tourism-related organizations since the early 1990s as part of the institutionalization of sustainable development principles. However, they remain contentious for a variety of reasons and the possession of such a code therefore does not necessarily indicate adherence to the ethical tenets they contain (see Chapter 7). The Blueprint for New Tourism put forward by the WTTC (see Section 1.4.2) might be viewed sceptically for similar reasons.

A 1991 study by Schmidgall (as cited in Wheeler, 1994), which solicited the reactions of American hotel managers to various ethical scenarios, provides empirical evidence of this conflicted arena. Fifty-five per cent of respondents in this research regarded it as appropriate to hire their own employees to do yard work at the homes of their bosses, while 40 per cent disagreed due to the undue pressure and conflict of interest it places on these employees. Twenty-five per cent believed that there was no ethical problem in accepting a free case of wine from a business supplier, while 65 per cent thought that this is unacceptable.

4.4 *In situ* nature of tourism consumption

A strong argument for ethical behaviour in tourism arises from the *in situ* nature of consumption in the sector, which means that the tourism product is 'produced' and 'consumed' simultaneously in place and time within the destination. This renders tourism especially vulnerable to disruption as a result of social or environmental upheaval, while making it at the same time an especially formidable agent of social and environmental changes that can induce such upheaval (Walle, 1995). Even without dramatic upheavals, tourists are less likely to consume a tourism product as the surrounding environment becomes crowded and polluted, as per the destination life cycle. Hence, the components of the conventional tourism industry with large capital investments in a destination have a particularly strong vested interest in maintaining the environmental integrity of their surrounds. This contrasts with non-*in situ* industries such as the production of textiles for export, where the consumer is not directly affected by the environmental conditions at the point of production and is likely to express such concerns only as a matter of personal ethics.

4.5 Emergence of the 'green consumer'

Elements of the conventional mass tourism industry may also decide to pursue an agenda of sustainability because of the alleged growth in the so-called 'green consumer' market, which encompasses individuals whose purchasing decisions are substantively influenced by ethical motives and not just by egotistical considerations of a satisfying holiday in pleasant surroundings, or cost considerations. Crucial factors that influence the response of the industry to this phenomenon are the size of the green market, internal variations, demographic profile, rate of growth and what green consumption actually means in the marketplace.

4.5.1 Magnitude and growth of green consumption

Green consumers appear to constitute a large and growing portion of society in the more developed countries. This is illustrated by the increase in the 'green products' share of all new US product introductions from 2.8 per cent in 1988 to 9.5 per cent in 1997 (Fuller, 1999). A similar trajectory characterizes the growth of organizations such as the Organic Consumers Association* as well as the revenue growth of US organic products, which increased from $178 million in 1985 to over $3 billion in 1996 (Ottman, 1998). Such products have been relocated from peripheral to central locations in many supermarkets and large transnational corporations have been enticed to become involved in their production (Roberts, 1996; Ottman, 1998). In the UK, it was expected that organic products would account for 10 per cent of all food purchases by 2005 (Miller, 2003). Concurrent elevations in concern over genetically engineered (GE) foods have stimulated this trend, especially in Europe, as has the fact that Socially Responsible Investment (SRI) portfolios accounted for about 12 per cent of all professionally managed funds in 2003, or more than $2.16 trillion in assets, compared with just $40 billion in 1984 (Social Investment Forum*, 2003).

The seriousness with which such trends are viewed by the corporate world is evidenced by the branding transformation of the oil company BP*, which once stood for British Petroleum but is currently being marketed as Beyond Petroleum. The participation of BP and many other large corporations in emissions trading is further indication of the corporate greening that has occurred in response to the increased consumer demand for green products.

Consumer segments

Various studies have attempted to quantify and position the green market within the larger consumer population, since it is clear that green consumer tendencies are not equally shared within the population. A well-known example is the Roper Survey, which in 1996 used clustering techniques to identify five relatively homogeneous groups of American adult consumers (Ottman, 1998). Two of these groups ('true-blue greens' and 'greenback greens') consist of active environmentalists who together account for about 15 per cent of the population, down from about 22 per cent in 1990. These individuals are most likely to fulfil the litmus test of active environmentalism by purchasing more expensive 'environmentally friendly' products and by otherwise taking environmental and social considerations into account in their everyday lives. Two other groups ('grousers' and 'basic browns') account for over one-half of the population and are characterized by indifference and/or unwillingness to take environmental considerations into account in their behaviour unless they are required to. Making up the remaining one-third of the population are 'sprouts' or conditional environmentalists whose environmental engagement vacillates in accordance with convenience and other factors.

A study by Ray and Anderson (2000) in the late 1990s identified 26 per cent of American adults as 'cultural creatives' whose activist and holistic world view includes strong environmentalist tendencies and core 'green' values. At the other end of the spectrum, 25 per cent are socially and culturally conservative 'traditionals' who are less likely to ascribe to strong environmentalist views, although many do hold strong desires to restore the environment to 'the way it used to be'. The remaining one-half of the population consists of mainstream 'moderns' who are comfortable with the commercialized urban-industrial world and notions of growth and 'progress', which they regard as normative and desirable. Career advancement and material well-being are priorities, but most cultural creatives also claim pro-environment credentials. Important from the perspective of market trends is that this cohort accounted for only about 5 per cent of the adult American population in the 1960s while traditionals at that time accounted for over one-half.

Similar consumer surveys have been undertaken in other major tourist-generating regions. Two UK studies, for example, have found that environmental 'activists' respectively account for about 14 and 16 per cent of the British population. A third study by the private firm Marketing Diagnostics provided a range of 5–15 per cent, but contextualized this group within a broader segment of 'green thinkers' (30 per cent) who are not activists but do make an effort to purchase green products and services. They in turn are part of a 'green consumer base' (45–60 per cent) that has changed its habits at least partially in response to perceived environmental problems. Finally, the green consumer base is a segment of the 90 per cent of the British population that claims to be 'generally concerned' about the natural environment (as cited in Webster, 2000).

Veneer and other environmentalists

According to Roper Starch Worldwide, a US-based consultancy, major social issues such as environmentalism pass through three stages of societal reaction: (a) high anxiety but low response; (b) greater activity as people become more informed and less anxious; and (c) integration of the new ethos into peoples' everyday lives (as cited in Ottman, 1998). Ottman (1998) argues that environmentalism is now in the second stage overall in the USA, but it is more meaningful to stress the high level of internal variation. That is, somewhere between 10 and 25 per cent of the population has already reached the third stage, while approximately one-half (i.e. the 'sprouts' and 'moderns') are in stages one and two. Large portions of overlapping groups such as the 'traditionals' and 'basic browns', which account for about one-quarter of the population, have not yet entered the first stage.

In broad terms, about one-quarter of the American population can be considered *non-environmentalists* in that they do not make any particular concessions to environmental concerns in their everyday lives or voting patterns and do not identify themselves as environmentalists. Another quarter consists of *true environmentalists* who place a priority on 'green' issues and actualize this on a daily basis through their consumer behaviour and overall lifestyle. Significantly, this appears to be the most rapidly growing consumer segment.

The remaining one-half of the population, as with UK consumers, appears to consist of *veneer environmentalists* who claim to be environmentalists, but engage only in green behaviour that is convenient and does not threaten their standard of living or consumer lifestyle. These superficial environmentalists, for example, are enthusiastic proponents of 'soft' green activities such as recycling, but would be reluctant to support an environmental tax on gasoline that would significantly increase their transportation costs. Similarly, they usually avoid green products that are 'too expensive' or 'less effective' even though they indicate an intention and preference for consuming such products (Roberts, 1996). Factors that may induce these fickle consumers to purchase green products include their personal household financial situation, their perception of the national economic situation as a whole and their changing feelings about the seriousness of environmental issues such as global warming and ozone depletion (Ackerstein and Lemon, 1999). Significantly, it is from this group that many new recruits to the cultural creative group are obtained as they become more aware of environmental and social issues.

Overall, it may be concluded that 'green consumers', loosely defined as those who express concern about environmental issues and consciously engage in green consumer behaviour at least some of the time, account for about three-quarters of the American population and a similar proportion in the UK. This is consistent with the high proportion of respondents in various surveys that claims to be 'environmentalists' (Roberts, 1996; Ottman, 1998; Ackerstein and Lemon, 1999).

Demographics

Research conducted on green consumers between the late 1960s and mid-1990s have generally yielded an 'upscale' profile of higher income professional females with strong post-secondary education credentials (Roberts, 1996; Ottman, 1998). Ray and Anderson (2000) similarly found that cultural creatives are disproportionately female (about 60 per cent). They also have higher than average income and education, although the actual spread around these means is considerable. The apparently greater female proclivity for green behaviour is associated with various factors, including the contention that gender role expectations make it more likely for females to take into account the consequences of their actions (Roberts, 1996). Roberts (1996) also found green consumers to be significantly older than other consumers. Ottman (1998) goes further in contending that green consumption is being led by a baby boomer generation whose formative years included exposure to high profile environmental disasters such as the Three Mile Island nuclear incident in 1979, the Bhopal chemical leak of 1984 and the Chernobyl nuclear disaster of 1986 and to popular classics of environmentalism such as Rachel Carson's *Silent Spring*, Ernst Schumacher's *Small is Beautiful* and James Lovelock's *Gaia*.

Incipient green markets

High levels of green consumerism are characteristic of the USA and UK, as well as similarly developed Canada, Australia and Western Europe. In contrast, environmental and green sentiments in less developed countries such as China and India are more incipient. Chan (2001) provides insight on the situation in China by finding that consumers in two large cities (Beijing and Guangzhou) tend to hold strong views about the environment, largely as an outcome of Taoist and collectivist tendencies in the culture. However, these sentiments did not translate into a strong pattern of green purchasing, although an earlier survey by Chan (as cited in Chan, 2001) found that one-third of the respondents had purchased an eco-friendly product in the previous 6 months. This behaviour appears to fall into the first stage of 'high anxiety but low response' as cited above, though it is notable that the results apply only to a more educated urbanized sample that is probably not representative of average Chinese consumption patterns.

4.5.2 The 'green tourist'

The growth of alternative tourism (see Chapter 3) attests to the robustness of green and socially responsible consumption within at least one facet of the tourism sector. However, the conventional tourism industry is more likely to meaningfully pursue sustainability-based strategies if there is compelling evidence of green proclivities and behaviour within the much larger conventional mass tourist market. As with green consumption in general, the patterns within conventional tourism are variable but generally indicative of a significant green component.

Perhaps the most widespread evidence of green sentiment among conventional tourists, as discussed in Section 4.4, is the almost ubiquitous desire to experience one's holidays in a scenic, unpolluted environment. A 1996 study by Horner and Swarbrooke (as cited in Swarbrooke and Horner, 1999), for example, found that seven of ten criteria cited by British consumers for a 'quality holiday' were environment-related. Miller (2003) found in a survey of travel show participants that 78 per cent 'always' (34 per cent) or 'sometimes' (44 per cent) sought information about the environmental conditions of intended destinations and that 84 per cent were influenced in their destination selection by environmental information. Survey work by the Danish Tourist Board in the late 1990s found that high environmental standards were an 'important' or 'very important' destination selection criterion for 74 per cent of Germans (20 and 54 per cent respectively), but only 47 per cent of Danes (20 and 27 per cent respectively), who probably already assume these standards to be high in their home country (Hjalager, 1999).

Green proclivities and altruism

Green proclivities arising from more altruistic motivations are evident in several recent empirical studies, although all of these must be qualified by the likely discontinuities between stated intentions and actual behaviour. One example is a 1997 survey of UK consumers (as cited in Miller, 2003) in which 61 per cent of respondents felt that it was 'very' or 'fairly' important that travel companies take into account environmental issues in their operations. On average, the respondents indicated a willingness to pay £7–8 more for a tour operator or accommodation provider that is committed to environmental protection. Another survey conducted around the same time (as cited in Miller, 2003) found that 73 per cent of Co-op Travel customers in the UK want information about the environmental and social effects of tourism in destinations, while 67 per cent want to know about the human rights record of destination countries. In the USA, a survey of 489 air travellers revealed that 70 per cent were more likely to select a hotel with strong environmental credentials, while 91 per cent stated that hotels should use energy efficient lights (as cited in Webster, 2000).

Horneman et al. (1997) revealed in a survey of Australian consumers that 62 per cent were willing to pay a 10 per cent premium for environmentally quality assured tourism products. This alleged willingness was especially high among females, younger respondents, urban residents and higher income earners. Determining willingness to pay was also the aim of research by Hudson and Ritchie (2001), who found that skiers visiting the Banff/Lake Louise area of Canada were willing to pay an additional CAN$16 per day to patronize a 'green' ski resort. However, Americans (CAN$20.20) and British (CAN$18.60) were willing to pay more than Canadians (CAN$10.40). Three-quarters of the total sample said that they would be more likely to visit a ski resort that paid attention to its impacts on wildlife and habitat and about two-thirds said the same about resorts that monitored visitor numbers, offered environmental education programmes and used sustainability principles in water management.

Shades of green

Green sentiments among conventional tourists, in general, appear to be stronger in countries such as Sweden, Germany, Austria and The Netherlands than in the UK or USA, reflecting a longer tradition of green consumerism in northern Europe (Swarbrooke and Horner, 1999). Variations, however, are also discernable within individual markets, with veneer environmentalism evident in the high proportion of 'light green' tourists (Swarbrooke and Horner, 1999) who say that they are 'somewhat more likely' to purchase a green product, who 'sometimes' seek out environmental information or who regard environmental issues as 'fairly important'. As with green consumerism more generally, females and those with higher levels of education and income are more likely to display green tourist proclivities, though the number of studies seeking this information is limited.

Factors underlying the relative obscurity of the green tourist

While the green tourist and green consumer profiles are similar, it has been argued that the former has not attained the same level of recognition as the latter (Swarbrooke and Horner, 1999). One plausible explanation for this is that much of the 'green' attention in tourism has been monopolized by the alternative tourist, who is something of a surrogate green tourist and for which green consumerism in general has no obvious equivalent. A second factor is that green conventional tourism products tend not to be as conspicuous to the conscientious traveller as conspicuously packaged and aggressively marketed organic products are to the conscientious grocery shopper. Hence, informed choice is limited by a lack of visual clues and knowledge from the actual product and also, thirdly, by the scarcity of sources that provide sustainable tourism product information to the consumer. Among the few exceptions is the Travel Planner* section on the website of Green Globe 21 (GG21), an international tourism certification organization that is profiled in Section 7.4.5. This website allows viewers to identify easily GG21 certified conventional tourism products (e.g. hotels, attractions, tour guides, etc.) in any selected country and also provides sustainable travel suggestions. Another nascent example from the USA is the GreenBiz Leaders* website, which allows for the reader to select from several tourism/hospitality categories to receive a list of businesses whose environmental credentials and leadership have been acknowledged by government agencies or a 'credible third-party organization'. Along with a growing array of tourist-oriented codes of conduct and 'green guides', these websites represent incipient attempts to educate tourists into behaving more sustainably (see Section 10.4.1).

Fourthly, travel-related purchase decisions are far less frequent than food purchase decisions, thus hindering the development of environmental purchasing habits (Hjalager, 1999). Infrequent purchasing, combined with the spatial and temporal disconnect between the individual and their experience as a tourist, could in addition mean that the environmental and social concerns of tourism destinations are not a matter of daily concern to most consumers.

A fifth factor is that the literature and theories of the cautionary and adaptancy platform, while well known among tourism academics, are virtually unknown even among the more aware elements of the general public. There is no equivalent of a Rachel Carson or David Suzuki to advocate for responsible tourism and there is also no powerful global tourist consumer interest group equivalent to a Sierra Club or Greenpeace to lobby aggressively for change in the industry. Those that do exist are not yet well known (such as the church-based organizations outlined in Chapter 3) or are not yet operating at a level of critical mass (see case study at the end of this chapter) (Turner et al., 2001). It may therefore be that the adoption of sustainable tourism principles and practices among tourism businesses (see Chapters 5 to 7) is at present primarily an industry-led phenomenon motivated partly by the other factors discussed in this chapter and partly by industry's assessment that the green tourist market is a small but growing presence that may become a much stronger force in the future as green consumerism continues to permeate into the conventional tourism realm.

4.5.3 Paradigm shift

Whether the infiltration of green proclivities into conventional tourism is a significant trend or not depends in part on whether this can be situated as part of a broader paradigm shift in society. A paradigm is a collective world view more or less accepted as normative within a particular culture and a paradigm shift begins when the currently dominant paradigm can no longer adequately explain or internalize evidence that contradicts its core assumptions. Gradually, one or more competing paradigms emerge that more convincingly explain these contradictions and eventually one of these new paradigms becomes dominant (Kuhn, 1970). The superseding of the theological paradigm by the scientific paradigm during the sixteenth and seventeenth centuries in Europe is an example of a societal paradigm shift. Notably, the transition can take centuries and the new paradigm usually is itself a synthesis that incorporates non-contradictory aspects of the old paradigm.

Dominant western environmental paradigm and green paradigm

It is widely contended that a paradigm shift is again underway in reaction to the perceived contradictions of the scientific paradigm insofar as it relates to environmental and social issues. This *dominant western environmental paradigm* is associated with environmentally destructive technologies, 'rational' economic theories that value GDP growth and material acquisition above all else and a social Darwinian approach to human relationships (Knill, 1991). As the consequences of environmental degradation (e.g. global warming, deforestation, desertification) and social inequity have become more apparent, a *green paradigm* (Knill, 1991) or *new environmental paradigm* (Dunlap and Van Liere, 1978) has allegedly emerged to challenge the dominant western environmental paradigm. The popular environmental movement, as cited in Section 1.3.2, is a manifestation of this new paradigm, as is presumably the subsequent emergence of green consumerism and alternative tourism.

If these new developments do indicate an actual paradigm shift, then there are several implications for the conventional tourism industry, whose actions and impacts in the latter half of the twentieth century manifest the dominant western environmental paradigm. First, the process of transition will last well into the twenty-first century and periods of rapid change (as with the great increase in public environmental awareness in the 1970s and 1980s) will be interrupted by possibly longer periods of consolidation and quiet or surreptitious change, similar to the stages identified by the Roper Starch Worldwide survey (Section 4.5.1). Second, the polarized ideal types that typically emerge in the initial stages of paradigm confrontation (e.g. as represented by the cautionary and adaptancy platform) are eventually replaced by a synthesis of characteristics from both paradigms (as has occurred as part of the knowledge-based platform). Thus, while alternative tourism can be regarded as a more or less 'pure' expression of the green paradigm ideal type, efforts to make conventional tourism sustainable are more representative of the synthesis that occurs as a part of a paradigm shift. That is, notions of scale, commercialism, etc. are maintained, but restructured within an environmentally and socioculturally responsible framework. The popularity of 'sustainable development', as discussed in Chapter 1, may in this light be explained by the term's implication of synthesis. The dominance of veneer environmentalism may also provide evidence for synthesis, since such conflicted individuals essentially want to retain the best elements of both paradigms – high tech creature comforts and conveniences, but also a just world and a healthy natural environment to enjoy them within.

4.6 Advantages of large economies of scale

In addition to ethical considerations and the growth of green consumerism, conventional businesses may be encouraged to pursue sustainability by the interrelated advantages that are conferred by size and by participation in the formal tourism system, unlike the situation faced by small alternative tourism businesses (see Section 3.12.2). These include the availability of diverse skills and competencies, an enhanced capacity to innovate, the higher probability of profiting from some sustainability practice and the ability to influence distribution systems and consumers.

4.6.1 Diverse skills and competencies

The larger a business or corporation, the more likely it is to possess or otherwise be able to access the diverse skills and competencies that are required to operate efficiently. From a sustainability perspective, this means that a larger business is more likely to allocate resources to establish departments where specialists can focus on the pursuit of more sustainable environmental and social practices, including market and community research as well as indicator monitoring and environmental auditing. British Airways, for example, has two departments, Environmental Affairs and Community Relations, vested specifically with sustainability-related responsibilities.

4.6.2 Enhanced capacity to innovate

Scale of operation and the ability to access the necessary capital both facilitate innovation in a larger business. For example, the fact that a large hotel has 500 units of accommodation as well as a 50-metre swimming pool justifies the implementation of co-generation technology in which the waste heat from the air conditioning system is used to heat the water in the swimming pool. Moreover, the corporation would have little difficulty in funding, or securing funds at favourable rates, to implement this technology.

4.6.3 Profiting from sustainability

Economies of scale also mean that practices such as recycling and product re-use and reduction can be highly profitable or at least cost effective. Webster (2000) cites the experience of the UK hotel corporation Trusthouse Forte, which by negotiating the reduction of packaging in deliveries of sugar sachets saved £30 000 in a one-year period. A recycling programme by Sheraton Hotels reduced waste tonnage by 13 per cent and saved $7000 per month through revenue from the sale of the plastic as well as the reduction in dumping fees (Webster, 2000).

4.6.4 Influencing distribution systems

The Trusthouse Forte case study demonstrates how a large business can influence its suppliers to 'go green', if it so chooses, through its power to negotiate customized bulk purchases. More proactively, large chains can pressure suppliers by giving bidding preference to green companies. Similarly, corporations that are integrated both horizontally (e.g. a hotel chain that controls bargain and luxury chains) and vertically (e.g. they own backward suppliers such as tour operations and travel agencies) can impose sustainability policies extensively within the tourism industry because of their breadth of coverage.

4.7 Summary

There are several compelling reasons why the eight main sectors of the conventional tourism industry should vigorously pursue policies of environmental and sociocultural sustainability. The most altruistic of these is the argument that it is the right thing to do, although awareness of the negative consequences of not doing so suggests that the adoption of an ethical approach, as with the other reasons, is ultimately a matter of enlightened self-interest for many or most companies. A second reason involves the *in situ* nature of tourism consumption, which means that industry must be especially sensitive to environmental and social problems in their surroundings that could result in the loss of tourist arrivals as the destination becomes more risky and less attractive.

The emergence of green consumerism and the green tourism consumer in particular is a third factor. Evidence from major tourist origin countries such as the USA and UK suggests that consumers who consciously seek and purchase environmentally and socially friendly travel products and experiences beyond alternative tourism are still a minority of about 25 per cent, though a rapidly growing one that barely existed prior to the 1970s. Females, professionals and those with higher levels of income and education appear to be over-represented in this group. Veneer environmentalists, who express environmental and social concern but purchase compatible products sporadically and selectively as a matter of convenience, still constitute the normative majority. If, however, the emergence of green consumerism is indicative of a broader paradigm shift, then it is likely that the active environmentalist segment will become the normative majority group in coming decades in the major tourist-generating regions, though probably with some incorporation of materialist and other traits from the current dominant paradigm. Concurrently, veneer environmentalism will become increasingly normative in emerging tourist markets such as China and India. This shift towards the green tourist, however, does not appear to be occurring as rapidly as the shift to green consumerism more generally, due to the relative obscurity of green tourism products and advocates and the infrequency with which consumers make such purchases.

Finally, the conventional tourism industry may be compelled to become more sustainable by the advantages that are associated with its larger economies of scale. These include the ability to allocate resources to create specialized departments focusing on sustainability-related practices and an enhanced capacity to innovate by capitalizing on high volume flows of energy and preferred access to investment funds. Additional advantages include the ability to generate substantial profit and reduce costs through bulk recycling and use reduction and the potential for influencing distribution systems such as product suppliers and subsidiaries to engage in green practices.

On the net

BP (British Petroleum/Beyond Petroleum)
http://www.bp.com/home.do

GreenBiz Leaders.com
http://www.greenbizleaders.com/about.cfm

Green Globe 21 Travel Planner
http://www.greenglobe21.com/TravelPlanner.aspx

Organic Consumers Association (USA)
http://www.organicconsumers.org/

Social Investment Forum (USA)
http://www.socialinvest.org/

Tourism Concern (UK)
http://www.tourismconcern.org.uk/

United Kingdom (corporate social responsibility)
http://www.societyandbusiness.gov.uk/

For further reading

Ottman, J. (1998). *Green Marketing: Opportunity for Innovation*. 2nd edn. NTC Business Books.
The author provides a thorough discussion of green consumer trends and describes how various companies are responding to these trends through the introduction of green products and marketing strategies.

Ray, P. and Anderson, S. (2000). *The Cultural Creatives: How 50 Million People are Changing the World*. Three Rivers Press.
Ray and Anderson identified the 'cultural creatives' through their consultancy research and this book gives a detailed analysis of this rapidly growing consumer market. Indications of relevant travel and leisure behaviour are provided.

Walle, A. (1995). Business ethics and tourism: from micro to macro perspectives. *Tourism Management*, 16, 263–8.
This article considers the role of generic business ethics in the tourism industry, but also considers how this role is limited by the unique structure of tourism, which requires its own ethical precepts.

Beyond the book

1. (a) Among conventional tourism businesses and destinations, is the inclusion of an ethical imperative compatible with financial sustainability? (b) If so, how can they both be accommodated at the same time?
2. (a) Design a survey of ten statements that measures green travel intentions and behaviour. (b) Administer this survey to a random or convenience sample of 100 students. (c) What do the results indicate about the status of 'green tourists' relative to the tourist market in general? (d) What are the weaknesses in this survey-based research project?
3. What could businesses, government and advocacy groups do to encourage the conversion of tourist veneer environmentalists into activists?

On the ground: advocating for sustainable travel at Tourism Concern

Among the few relatively high profile specialized organizations that campaign for greater sustainability in the conventional tourism industry is UK-based Tourism Concern*. It was founded in 1989 to raise awareness of the environmental, sociocultural and economic costs of tourism within less developed regions in particular and 'to effect change in the tourism industry by campaigning for fair and ethically traded tourism' (Swarbrooke, 1999; Tourism Concern, 2004). A central tenet of Tourism Concern is to work cooperatively rather than confrontationally with the tourism industry and with government. This is being pursued in part through publications such as the industry-focused *Corporate Futures: Corporate Social Responsibility in the Tourism Industry, A Consultation on Good Practice*, which is used to educate and train businesses to pursue more responsible courses of action. Tourism Concern has also facilitated the development of a sustainable tourism policy for a major UK-based travel agency and has established training modules for one of the largest UK-based tour operators, with funding provided by the Foreign and Commonwealth Office (Tourism Concern, 2003). With regard to government, Tourism Concern is working for sustainable outbound tourism by lobbying government to create specific ministerial responsibilities for outbound UK tourists.

A major aspect of campaigning involves an outreach programme that raises public awareness at talks and exhibitions (e.g. the Destinations 2004 travel show in London) and provides educational videos (such as *Looking Beyond the Brochure*) and other material to schools and universities. The organization's views are also frequently publicized in the media and through lectures featuring tourism fair trade advocates from various destination countries. To focus public and industry attention, Tourism Concern concentrates on specific campaigns, including a boycott of tourism in Burma, a focus on the displacement of Maasai people from their land in Eastern Africa and, during 2002 and 2003, awareness of working conditions among those employed in the trekking industry. The intent of this campaign was to induce trekkers to demand decent conditions for porters and to patronize only those tour operators who insisted on such conditions, as well as to work with tour operators so that this issue influences the contractual arrangements that are made between the tour operators and the destination-based agents who hire the porters.

A larger campaign running from 1999 to 2002 involved the creation of the International Fair Trade in Tourism Network (FriT), with funding from the European Commission and the UK Department for International Development. Involving more than 150 members from industry, non-governmental organizations and universities, the Network facilitates the exchange of 'best practice' experience and monitors progress in the implementation of sustainable practices.

The impact of Tourism Concern's advocacy is not easy to quantify, in part because limited funds restrict the amount of follow-up research that can be undertaken and also because education and awareness raising tend to be long-term propositions whose effects are not immediately or directly discernable. Moreover, the membership appears to have remained steady at just 1000, a level that does not yet indicate a broad base of public support or a critical mass sufficient to induce widespread change within the industry or among the travelling public. An analysis of income and expenditures raises further concern, since Tourism Concern received 55 per cent of its revenue in 2002 from bilateral government grants and only 14 per cent from membership subscriptions (9 per cent) and publications and other resources (5 per cent). Conversely, 43 per cent of expenditures were administrative, even though volunteers account for much of the work performed by the organization (Tourism Concern, 2003).

Exercises

1. (a) Identify three additional international tourism-related issues that would be appropriate for Tourism Concern to pursue in one of their campaigns and indicate why the campaign is necessary. (b) How could Tourism Concern publicize each of these issues? (c) What actions should they recommend in each case?
2. Design a 500-word strategy that would increase the membership of Tourism Concern to 10 000 members within 2 years of implementation.

Chapter 5
The facilitating sectors

Chapter objectives

Upon completion of this chapter, the reader should be able to:

■ describe the strategic role and significance of travel agencies, guidebooks, outbound tour operators, air carriers, cruise ships and the hospitality sector within the broader tourism system
■ provide examples and identify patterns of sustainability-related practices within the featured sectors of the tourism industry
■ assess the extent to which each of these sectors, as a whole, has become more environmentally and socioculturally sustainable
■ discuss the opportunities and obstacles faced by each sector in its pursuit of sustainability and
■ indicate how each of these sectors influences the sustainability of other industry sectors, as well as the tourism industry as a whole.

5.1 Introduction

Sustainable tourism is now formally recognized as an important objective by many international organizations as well as governments and there are several compelling reasons for the conventional tourism industry to imitate the alternative tourism sector by seriously pursuing a sustainability-focused agenda. Not the least of these reasons is the possibility that the emerging green consumer, and the green tourist market in particular, indicates a societal paradigm shift that businesses ignore at their peril. The purpose of this and the two subsequent chapters is to investigate the extent to which the conventional tourism industry has actually pursued the objective of environmentally and socioculturally sustainable tourism. Under the assumption that the 'tourism industry' is no monolithic entity, this chapter focuses on the constituent travel agencies (Section 5.2), specialized guidebook merchandisers (Section 5.3), outbound tour operators (Section 5.4), transportation providers (Section 5.5) and hospitality providers (Section 5.6) that facilitate the tourism experience. (Attractions are featured in Chapter 6 and local tour guides are discussed in Chapters 10 and 11 in the context of visitor education.) The strategic function and influence of each sector within the broader tourism system is outlined and examples of sustainability-related practices are provided as part of a broader effort to assess how each has collectively engaged the issue of sustainability. The opportunities and obstacles encountered in this process are also examined, as is the influence of each sector in reinforcing or hindering the attempts of other sectors and the tourism industry in general, to become more sustainable.

5.2 Travel agencies

Travel agencies operate primarily in origin regions and provide a combination of retail services to travellers on behalf of other facilitators such as carriers, car rentals, tour operators and accommodations on a commission basis. They can therefore be characterized as brokers who also provide ancillary services such as travel insurance and travellers' cheques (Medlik, 2003). Because they are often the first point of contact within the formal tourism system for a potential traveller, travel agencies are 'gateway' facilitators or intermediaries that play a critical but usually understated role in shaping which destinations are visited and which businesses throughout the system are patronized (Oppermann, 1998). Potentially, travel agencies can also play a crucial role in fostering sustainability throughout the tourism system by providing travellers with information about appropriate behaviour as well as 'green' tourism businesses and products and by giving preferential exposure to the latter (Hjalager, 1999).

5.2.1 Sustainability initiatives

Unfortunately, within the tourism literature there is very little information about or commentary on the sustainability practices of travel agencies. Swarbrooke (1999), for example, omits this sector from his otherwise comprehensive coverage of sustainable practices within the conventional tourism industry. There is minimal evidence of engagement with sustainability on the website of ASTA* (American Society of Travel Agents), which is the world's largest travel agency organization with more than 20000 members in 170 countries (Goeldner and Ritchie, 2003). The 'For Travelers' section of this site makes no mention of tourist responsibilities in destinations, focusing instead on travellers' rights, avoidance of risk and 'hot destinations'. ASTA does have an annual Environmental Award (see Section 7.5) and espouses 'Ten Commandments on Responsible Tourism', but these are buried under the 'Awards' section of the 'About Us' feature and are not linked to the 'For Travelers' section.

One US-based travel agency that stands out by its exceptional attention to sustainability is the Better World Travelers Club*, which aggressively markets its alleged environmental credentials. Featured in its marketing is a programme that seeks to offset the greenhouse gas emissions of its customers' travel by investing in the installation of natural gas boilers and other practices that reduce these emissions. The Club also attempts to establish connections with environmentally friendly tourism-related businesses (including hybrid and electric cars) and donates 1 per cent of its revenue to environmental clean-up efforts.

European experiences

The European travel agency sector appears to be more proactive than its US counterpart in adopting sustainability principles and practices. A major manifestation of this is the European Travel Agents' and Tour Operators' Association's (ECTAA*) involvement in the VISIT project to unify the continent's ecolabelling schemes. More specifically, ECTAA enhances the availability of consumer information on sustainable European tourism products through its online VISIT holiday guide, which lists hotels, beaches and other products that possess high quality ecolabel recognition.

5.2.2 Disintermediation

Travel agencies are currently faced with the challenge of disintermediation, which Weaver and Lawton (2002a, p. 461) define as 'the removal of intermediaries such as travel agents from the product/consumer connection'. This is primarily a consequence of Internet technologies that allow the consumer to communicate and make bookings directly with tour operators, carriers, car rental agencies and hotels without the intervention of brokers. Travel agencies are responding to the threat of disintermediation by restructuring the services that they offer. Specifically, Internet technologies are being increasingly utilized in routine customer interfacing (see above), while companies such as Travelocity and Expedia have been established as fully online travel agencies. At the same time, many travel agencies are capitalizing on the tradition of face-to-face contact as an opportunity to work in a highly personalized way with clients on more complex specialized purchases such as extended long haul vacations or 'occasion travel' for weddings or anniversaries (Lowengart and Reichel, 1998).

The concurrent and somewhat paradoxical impulses of increased online activity and refocused face-to-face contact both provide excellent opportunities for travel agencies to become more involved with promoting sustainability-related practices. Online interfacing allows travel agencies to incorporate convenient links with green products and organizations, while attention to sustainability-related issues and concerns can be included as a 'value added' component of personalized face-to-face consultations that consider all aspects of the holiday experience. Cultural creatives, with their higher levels of income and education, are a promising market for this re-invented type of travel agency and one that is likely to be receptive to the sustainability add-on.

5.3 Specialized merchandise: guidebooks

Guidebooks, luggage, backpacks, post cards and souvenirs are examples of merchandise intended mainly for tourist consumption. Guidebooks are especially significant, like travel agencies, for their influence on destination image, destination selection and tourist behaviour (Carter, 1998). Green guidebooks are already a well-established component of alternative tourism (see Section 3.4.1), but sustainability-related sensitivities have yet to significantly infiltrate the conventional guidebook market. This is in part because of the incipient nature of the green tourist market (see Chapter 3) and also because some large publishers already provide niche alternative guidebook lines that appeal to green consumers, thereby allowing their conventional publications to focus on concerns (e.g. price, comfort, safety) more pressing to other consumers. An examination by the author of four recent 'conventional' guidebooks on the Caribbean (*Caribbean for Dummies*, *Fodor's 04 Caribbean*, *Footprint Caribbean Islands* and *Frommer's Caribbean 2004*) revealed only one (*Footprint*) that provided even cursory information about responsible or sustainable tourism.

5.4 Outbound tour operators

Arranged travel experiences within the formal tourism industry can involve contact with any combination of (a) outbound tour operators (or wholesalers), (b) inbound tour operators and (c) local tour operators and guides (Higgins, 1996). Outbound tour operators, like travel agencies, are generally large companies situated within origin regions, where they make contracts with airlines and other facilitators (including inbound tour operators), compile package tours, organize travel groups and arrange travel schedules. Because they purchase in bulk at discount prices, these wholesalers are able to offer packages directly or through travel agencies that are substantially cheaper than what it would cost if the components were purchased piece-meal by individual tourists. Outbound tour operators are therefore an extremely influential component of the tourism system because of the linkage they provide between consumers and destinations, the products they choose to become affiliated with and the high volumes of organized tourist activity they generate (Swarbrooke, 1999).

Inbound tour operators are usually based in major gateway cities within destination countries or regions, where they prepare client itineraries, make arrangements with local tour guides, transportation providers and other businesses and market these packages to outbound tour operators. They also hire local staff and pay any fees involved with visiting attractions, etc. These responsibilities position them as a crucial link between the latter and local tourism businesses. Among these businesses are local tour operators and guides who provide 'coalface' mediation between tourists and local attractions and communities (see Chapters 10 and 11).

5.4.1 Implications for sustainability

In contrast to the situation with travel agencies, there is a growing body of research on the sustainability practices of tour operators and on the outbound component in particular, which is attributable mainly to the great influence the latter exerts on destinations. This literature, in general, is highly critical of tour operators. The sector is described as an oligarchy dominated by a small number of large transnational corporations that use their clout to negotiate the lowest possible prices from inbound operators and other suppliers. Revenues for destination-based businesses as a result are reduced, forcing cost cuts that may translate into inadequate wages for local employees, neglect of the environment and other sustainability-related problems (Curtin and Busby, 1999). Even if they are inclined to identify or rectify these problems, outbound tour operators cannot easily act on these inclinations because of the spatial and functional disconnect between their own operations and the destination locales to where their clients are sent.

The inclination to act responsibly, however, is constrained by exceedingly low profit margins, at least in the UK (Forsyth, 1995; Carey et al., 1997), which encourages a high volume of customer turnover and relegates sustainability to a 'luxury' that they cannot afford to pursue in the short term. Outbound operators will therefore be far more sensitive to customer complaints about value for money and service quality (e.g. bad food or uncomfortable accommodations) than to any complaints about labour exploitation or environmental degradation, although the psychocentric nature of the stereotypical mass package tourist makes it questionable whether such issues would even be flagged at a noticeable level in the first place. An additional consideration is that the bulk packages marketed by large outbound tour operators tend to be undifferentiated generic products (e.g. one week at a beach resort) that appeal to the lowest market common denominator, foster homogeneity and send tourists to already overcrowded 'honeypot' destinations in regions such as the Riviera and the Caribbean (Swarbrooke, 1999). The fact, moreover, that they are distinguished mainly by price differentials induces even more cost cutting (Forsyth, 1995).

Ultimately, because they possess few fixed assets outside of the origin regions where they are based, it is very easy for footloose outbound operators to abandon a destination that becomes too socially, politically or environmentally unstable. Hence, they are less likely to be greatly concerned about the implications of life cycle dynamics for particular destinations, or to be swayed by the *in situ* consumption argument (see Section 4.4). This footloose character also provides them with inordinate negotiating clout relative to inbound tour operators and other destination-based suppliers seeking a better deal from the outbound operators (Curtin and Busby, 1999; Swarbrooke, 1999).

5.4.2 Sustainability-related sentiments and practices

Despite the bleak picture painted above, there is evidence of movement in the direction of sustainability among some segments of the outbound tour operator industry. A pioneering initiative was a pilot project of IFTO (the International Federation of Tour Operators) in the early 1990s to engage its members in proactive environmental and social actions. Hjalager (1999) suggested that while the sector had not broadly responded to this effort by the late 1990s, a few exceptional operators did emerge. A leader among these is Germany-based TUI*, which regards sustainability as a core component of product quality and a basis for long-term survival. Swarbrooke (1999) describes how TUI applies pressure on suppliers and destinations to meet designated green standards through an accreditation-based ecolabelling scheme (see Section 7.4.5) and aggressively communicates these policies to potential customers. Short-, medium- and long-term sustainability corporate objectives have also been articulated.

Several empirical studies were conducted in the 1990s on the UK-based outbound operator sector. Forsyth (1995) found evidence of sustainability awareness and practice in a survey of 36 managers. The most prevalent practices cited by respondents included the provision of 'ecotips' in brochures (13 respondents), donating to local charities (13), sponsoring or otherwise supporting research related to sustainability (9), promoting green holidays (8), lobbying in destinations to improve infrastructure (8), recycling brochures (8), selecting tour guides from the local community (7) and promoting codes of conduct (6). Forsyth stresses that the actual coverage given to the ecotips on the brochures was limited, while the lobbying efforts were usually a response to short-term crises such as a disease outbreak that threatened the health or satisfaction of clients.

In terms of constraints to adopting sustainable practices, 18 of the respondents in the Forsyth survey felt that other parties, and government in particular, were primarily responsible for such initiatives. Twelve were reluctant to adopt practices not undertaken by other operators, while a similar number cited the difficulty of educating tourists. Others believed that they were powerless to effect change, felt that there was no demand for change in the UK market, or regarded authorities in destination countries as too corrupt to pursue meaningful sustainability practices (8 each). Seven operators believed that the latter distracted from the need to fill seats on planes, while the same number cited confusion over the meaning of the term 'sustainable tourism'. A majority indicated that they would put priority in the future on increasing the awareness of tourists and/or host governments. Others felt that a more diverse holiday package would reduce price-based competition. Increased staff training and regulation enforcement were each cited by seven respondents as future priorities. Forsyth (1995) concludes that the operators were too concerned with short-term survival to worry seriously about long-term sustainability and hence confined their practices to token gestures or those that cut costs, added value to packages, or were long-term (e.g. consumer awareness). They recognized the need for long-term sustainability, but generally felt that primary responsibility lay with government.

These results were corroborated by Curtin and Busby (1999), who found that senior executives representing UK 'economy mass' tour operators felt that pursuing sustainability would place them at a competitive disadvantage and that the initiative for sustainable tourism had to be imposed by government on all operators. They also believed that their British consumers were more interested in lower prices than sustainability and that the emergence of even less environmentally-aware tourist markets in Asia and Eastern Europe meant that British outbound tour operators had little influence in any case on fostering sustainability in a growing number of destination countries.

Tour Operators Initiative for Sustainable Tourism Development

The UK data described above is from the mid-1990s and given the rapid diffusion of sustainable tourism developments, may not be entirely indicative of sentiments and activity in the sector during the early 2000s. The involvement of ECTAA in the VISIT scheme, as cited in Section 5.2.1, is one important indication of Europe's outbound operator engagement with sustainability. Europe has also played a leadership role in the Tour Operators Initiative (TOI) for Sustainable Tourism Development* that was launched in 2000 to make the sector more environmentally and socioculturally sustainable. The first report of the TOI (UNEP et al., 2002), which includes major operators such as Accor Tours (France), Japan Travel Bureau and TUI, states that members must make a corporate commitment to sustainability. Other evidence of progress includes the pursuit of activities that establish linkages with appropriate suppliers, develop guidelines and indicators and improve communication and cooperation among members as well as with destinations. Case study write-ups of member involvement with sustainable tourism are a major element of this communication. The TOI is also undertaking a pilot project in the Turkish mass tourism destination of Side to promote sustainable tourism through an action plan that emphasizes stakeholder cooperation.

In cooperation with the Global Reporting Initiative* (a collaborating centre of UNEP that monitors progress in achieving sustainable development), the TOI is developing an extensive set of coded indicators that are relevant specifically to the outbound tour operator sector. These indicators are grouped into categories that include 'product management and development', 'supply chain management' (see Figure 5.1) and 'cooperation with destinations'.

5.5 Transportation providers

As discussed in Chapter 1, some sustainability-related issues in tourism arise from the travel component that is inherent to this sector. This component is associated

SCM1. Describe the supply chain management policy, objectives and targets on environmental, social and economic performance. (*State the use of supplier prioritization and screening criteria.*)

SCM2. Describe processes through which suppliers, by type, are consulted during development and implementation of the supply chain management policy, described in SCM1.

SCM3. Describe issues identified through supplier consultation and actions to address them.

SCM4. Describe processes through which suppliers, by type, are engaged in the implementation of the supply chain management policy, described in SCM1. (*Processes include: one way communication (e.g. questionnaires), two-way communication (e.g. information exchange), active cooperation (e.g. supplier training), rewards and recognition for higher performers.*)

SCM5. State joint actions taken with suppliers, by type, to support improvements in suppliers' own environmental and social performance.

SCM6. Describe progress in achieving objectives and targets related to supply chain policy.

SCM7. Indicate percentage of suppliers, by type, subject to supply chain management policy.

SCM8. Indicate percentages of suppliers, by type, subject to supply chain policy that have a published sustainability policy, implemented a sustainability management system and/or have a staff person with management responsibility for corporate sustainability.

SCM9. State types of information requested from suppliers, by type, on their:
(a) Environmental practices and performance. (*Include: materials, water, energy, purchasing, solid waste, hazardous waste, effluents, emissions, transport, land-use and biodiversity.*)
(b) Social practices and performance. (*Include: community and staff development, indigenous and tribal people's rights, formal employment contracts, social security, working conditions according to ILO Convention 172, equal treatment, non-discrimination, recognition of independent trade unions and application of collective bargaining agreements, health and safety committees, policies excluding child labour as defined by ILO, programmes to combat commercial sexual exploitation of children and to combat and mitigate the social impacts of HIV/AIDS.*)

SCM10. Indicate percentage of suppliers, by type, subject of supply chain management policy that provided the requested information.

SCM11. Indicate percentage of suppliers, by type, subject to supply chain management policy whose environmental, social and economic performance has been reported. (*Through, for example, supplier self-declaration, spot checks by reporting organization, environmental and social audits, certification schemes (including eco labels), third party verification (state if verifier is accredited, and by whom).*)

SCM12. State actions taken by the reporting organization in response to suppliers reported performance (as per SCM11), by type of suppliers. (*Include incentives and rewards.*)

SCM13. State actions to inform suppliers of customers' requirements.

SCM14. State contracting policy and how it is communicated to suppliers. (*Include negotiating terms and conditions for payment, cancellation and compensation of contracts with suppliers.*)

SCM15. Describe joint initiatives with suppliers to improve environmental, social and economic conditions in destinations.

SCM16. State benefits for the reporting organization from implementing the sustainable supply chain policy.

Figure 5.1
Global reporting initiative: supply chain management indicators (SCM) for tour operators. Reproduced with permission from GRI (2002).

mainly with transit regions, but also involves travel within destinations and, to a much lesser extent, travel in the origin region (e.g. driving to an airport). Issues related to sustainability include (a) the extraction and production of fossil fuels to meet tourism-related demands, (b) atmospheric and other pollution (e.g. noise, visual), (c) the consumption of fuel and non-fuel natural resources in the production and maintenance of vessels used to transport tourists, (d) the provision of supporting infra-structure, services and facilities such as roads, airports, accommodation concentrations and parking garages and (e) problems of traffic congestion and safety. However, as stressed in Chapter 2, it is difficult especially in the automobile sector to isolate the share of activity that can be related directly to tourism.

The broad historical trend of tourism transportation in the twentieth century has been the supplanting of rail and ship by automobile and aeroplane as primary modes of transit, which in turn have greatly facilitated opportunities for efficient and cost-effective longhaul travel that have made an enormous contribution to the expansion of the pleasure periphery (Middleton and Hawkins, 1998; Weaver and Lawton, 2002a). This section focuses on airlines but also examines the cruise ship industry because of its role as an important and controversial sector in the Caribbean and other pleasure periphery regions.

5.5.1 Airlines

Air travel is regarded as one of the least sustainable forms of transportation (Swarbrooke, 1999), partly because of certain inherent characteristics and also because of dramatic increases in the volume of air traffic during the latter half of the twentieth century. Commercial airlines account for approximately 4 per cent of all atmospheric carbon dioxide and nitrogen oxide emissions, which constitutes a major contribution to anthropogenic global warming that is expected to reach 10 per cent by 2050. The airline industry has also been implicated as a major contributor to stratospheric ozone depletion, while inflight services generate large volumes of solid waste.

Yet, on an individual basis, aircraft have generally become more fuel efficient, lighter, less polluting and less noisy since the early 1970s. Airlines have had a particularly strong commercial incentive to pursue such green practices because the related cost reductions make them more competitive in an era of deregulation and privatization as well as uncertainty due to global instability. Concurrently, the airline industry is especially affected by national and international regulations, such as those enforced through the ICAO's (International Civil Aviation Organization) Committee on Aviation Environmental Protection, that include standards intended to reduce the sector's impacts on the environment.

Airport issues

Increasingly congested airports are a major factor hindering progress towards sustainability in the airline industry. Even without this congestion, environmental problems including noise and elevated pollution levels in the vicinity of airports are often significant because of the concentration of aircraft activity. Increased crowding has exacerbated these problems by adding substantially to the amount of time spent by aircraft 'stacking' in the air as they wait to land and taxiing or idling as they wait to take off. Less obvious is the water pollution resulting from the de-icing of aircraft and the chemical treatment of runways, the impermeable surfaces of which encourage the rapid entry of polluted runoff into local waterways. The popularity of the 'hub and spoke' system of itinerary routing has contributed to environmental problems by diverting additional activity to hub airports, while increasing the mileage flown to travel from one non-hub location to another. The latter, for example, may only be 200 kilometres apart, but diversion to the hub airport (which is done to ensure fuller flights) may result in a 400 kilometre one-way trip between these two locations. Finally, airports themselves require the expropriation of large amounts of land and attract road traffic congestion as well as urban sprawl.

Industry best practice examples: American Airlines and British Airways

Several major airlines, including American Airlines* and British Airways*, have acquired a longstanding reputation as sector leaders in the pursuit of sustainability (Somerville, 1993; Middleton and Hawkins, 1998) and have maintained this reputation despite the problems created by the September 11 attacks and the Iraq war. American Airlines, which made a formal policy commitment to environmental responsibility in 1989 (Middleton and Hawkins, 1998), cites the assignment of about 1000 environmental coordinator positions to employees who have been given the responsibility of ensuring compliance with environmental regulations at its various stations. In addition, an Environmental Management Information System (EMIS) is used to manage and monitor environmental practices, on the basis first of waste reduction, then recycling or re-use, followed by treatment and finally disposal. The company cites among its accomplishments the recycling of enough wastes between 1992 and 2001 to save 51000 trees, 19300000 litres of water, 6.6 million kilowatt hours of electricity and 10600 cubic metres of landfill space. The replacement of older and less fuel-efficient aircraft such as the DC10, DC9 and B727, moreover, resulted in the use of about 360 million less litres of fuel in 2001 compared with 2000, as well as noise reduction. Other initiatives include the use of Zero Emission Vehicles (ZEVs) in its ground equipment and participation in airport and community noise abatement programmes. This attention to sustainable practices accords with the company's adherence to the CERES (Coalition for Environmentally Responsible Economies) Principles, which is a code of ethics (see Section 7.3) that among other obligations requires transparency through the public release of annual progress reports (American Airlines, 2001).

British Airways, similarly, has been releasing a publicly accessible annual Social and Environmental Report since 1990, with recent editions including a third party assessment of the content. Good practices cited in the 2002/03 report include the reduction of domestic carbon dioxide emissions to 16 per cent below the 1998/2000 baseline and an increase from 60 to 78.3 per cent in the proportion of aircraft that meet the highest ICAO noise standards during the 5-year period from 1997 to 2002 (British Airways, 2003). Other indicators include a 4 per cent reduction in water consumption and a 61 per cent reduction in fuel spills over the previous year. The visible image of British Airways as a good corporate citizen is also maintained through its sponsorship of the British Airways Tourism for Tomorrow Awards (see Section 7.5), the British Airways Communities and Conservation (BACC) scheme, which funds conservation projects around the world and the Change for Good programme which, since 1994, has collected more than £15 million in change from passengers to fund development projects in countries such as Nigeria and Zambia. The merit of some of these achievements, however, must be qualified. A government incentive payment of £1.3 million, for example, was provided for the carbon dioxide reduction, while this and other reductions are partly associated with reduced air traffic in the wake of the September 11 attacks. Middleton and Hawkins (1998) also point out that the environmental initiatives of British Airways serves a parallel commercial purpose of distinguishing this carrier from its rivals.

Because it accounts for 40 per cent of the flights originating from Heathrow Airport in London, British Airways is also focusing on improving the environment at this airport and in its vicinity. Achievements include a dramatic reduction in noise violations from 200 in 1998/99 to 19 in 2002/03 and increased monitoring of nitrogen dioxide levels at various locations around the airport. To alleviate road congestion, the company supports a public bus route, is promoting enhanced rail links to the nearby rail network and funds a network of shuttle buses that accounts for an average of 20000 passenger journeys a week. However, the company also supports the construction of a fifth terminal and third runway at Heathrow, which will substantially increase the amount of air traffic and road congestion in the vicinity of the airport.

5.5.2 Cruise ships

The cruise ship industry acquired a reputation for irresponsible environmental and social practices during the latter half of the twentieth century. Several factors have contributed to this image. One reason is the unusual nature of the activity, which amalgamates elements of transportation, accommodation, hospitality and attraction. Passengers therefore spend most of their time on ship during a 3-day or 2-week cruise, producing an enormous per capita amount of direct and indirect waste. According to the Bluewater Network*, an environmental organization, a typical 1-week cruise generates 50 tons of garbage, almost four million litres of greywater (i.e. liquid waste from sinks, showers and laundry), 800000 litres of blackwater (sewage) and 130000 litres of oil-contaminated water. Lesser but more toxic wastes from dry cleaning (20 litres), photographic processing (420 litres) and painting (40 litres) are also produced.

Second, when passengers disembark to visit destination ports, high levels of pollution, congestion and stress on services result from the spatial and temporal concentration of excursionists. Local residents in destinations such as Seychelles, moreover, are often deprived of access to their own bus services when large numbers of cruise excursionists employ the latter to access sites beyond the port of call (Wilson, 1997). Waste and congestion levels in turn are exacerbated by a third factor of 'super sizing', wherein ship size and passenger capacities have been steadily increased to attract market share and increase profits. The 130000-ton *Voyager of the Sea* (Royal Caribbean Line), for example, can accommodate 3840 passengers and a crew of 1181, and is but one example of the new mega-cruise ships that have been described as 'small cities' (GAO, 2000). A sister ship, the *Grand Princess*, is 322 metres long and taller than Niagara Falls (Wood, 2000).

Expenditure monopolization

Fourth, in their desire to capture as much passenger expenditure as possible during land excursions, cruise ship lines encourage their clients to employ ship-designated tour guides and transportation providers as much as possible, thereby reducing economic benefits to the broader local community. An extreme expression of this attempted monopolization is the acquisition of private 'fantasy' islands (e.g. Royal Caribbean Line's CocoCay in the Bahamas) or onshore enclaves (e.g. Labadee in Haiti) where all expenditures on drinks, entertainment, etc. are captured by the cruise lines and passengers are encouraged to avoid the chaos, crime, congestion and poverty of a Caribbean port experience (Showalter, 1994; Wilkinson, 1999; Wood, 2000). Wilkinson (1999) argues that the economic benefits of cruise ship excursionists in the Caribbean, which accounts for about one-half of all cruise ship activity, are low in relation to the actual number of tourists involved or the resulting stress on local infrastructure (see the case study on the Bahamas at the end of Chapter 1). The continuing desire of Caribbean tourism authorities to attract further cruise ship activity, therefore, may at least in part be based on the tenuous hope that these excursionists will return as stayovers.

A globalized phenomenon

Fifth, most cruise ships are registered under 'flags of convenience' such as Liberia, Panama and Bahamas, which allow them to avoid corporate taxes and adhere only to the lax labour (e.g. minimum wage, holiday) and environmental regulations of their host country. Sixthly, adherence to good environmental and social practice is further compromised by the fact that a cruise ship typically spends a substantial amount of time in high seas that are beyond the territorial domain of any country and subject only to fuzzy and still evolving tenets of international law. Both factors contribute to the status of the cruise ship industry as an intensely *laissez-faire* and globalized sector that cannot be easily regulated or policed. Like the outbound tour operators, it is a footloose or 'spatially disembedded' entity that draws on the cheapest possible global labour force and can easily divert its business to locations and suppliers that offer the most favourable opportunities for profit (Wood, 2000, 2004).

Evidence of poor environmental performance

A seventh factor which combines with the previous reasons to foster a bad environmental track record is that underwater actions such as the release of toxic wastes are hard to detect because of their invisibility, the mobility of the ship, the lack of a lasting 'footprint' and their occurrence in relatively remote locations. According to the US General Accounting Office (GAO, 2000), more than 100 instances of illegal discharge by foreign-flagged cruise ships were detected in US coastal waters between 1993 and 1998, resulting in fines of more than $30 million. These, however, likely represent only a small fraction of actual violations, given the amount of time that a cruise ship spends on the high seas. Wood (2004) states that cruise ships produce 77 per cent of all marine pollution, despite accounting for only a small proportion of the world's shipping fleet. Damage to coral reefs from anchor dragging is another common environmental impact that has long been associated with cruise ships but is often not detected (Allen, 1992). Smaller vessels can actually be more of a problem in this regard than their mega-counterparts, which cannot access the shallow coral beds where such damage is most likely to occur.

Sustainability initiatives

The cruising industry is expected to maintain a high growth rate of 8–10 per cent per annum at least during the first decade of the twenty-first century (GAO, 2000; Sweeting and Wayne, 2003) and the issue of cruise ship sustainability is therefore critical in regions such as the Caribbean and Mediterranean that account for most of the world's cruises. During 2001, in the wake of several high profile cases of illegal discharging in US waters and multi-million dollar fines, the ICCL* (International Council of Cruise Lines), which represents the largest cruise line companies and two-thirds of all ships, initiated its Cruise Industry Waste Management Practices and Procedures (CIWMPP) programme. The programme entails compulsory member adherence to environmental standards as defined by the US Environmental Protection Agency (EPA) and in the MARPOL convention that applies to ships engaged in international commerce. Under these provisions, bilge water cannot be discharged unless oil levels are 15 parts per million or less and greywater can only be discharged when the ship is in motion, travelling not less than six knots per hour and is located at least four nautical miles from shore. Similar speed and distance thresholds apply to the discharge of blackwater, which must be first treated using a certified Marine Sanitation Device. Other facets of the programme include environmental awareness training, more aggressive recycling, screening of vendors who offload and process cruise ship wastes and testing of waste treatment technologies.

In 2003, the ICCL formed the Ocean Conservation and Tourism Alliance in partnership with Conservation International to protect the biodiversity of cruising destinations through improved wastewater management, partnerships with destination groups to protect historical and natural resources and promoting environmental awareness among staff and tourists. A major thrust was the creation of a scientific panel under the auspices of Conservation International to review independently core environmental problems and provide advice for their amelioration. Its interim assessment (Sweeting and Wayne, 2003) lauds the industry for responding effectively to environmental problems, but cautions that much more needs to be done, including more research to obtain relevant data. Essentially the same conclusion was drawn by the GAO (2000) with regard to the operation of cruise vessels in US waters.

Other environmental groups, however, are more sceptical. A report sponsored by the Bluewater Network (Klein, 2003) criticizes the industry for attempting to deal with discharges and other problems in US waters through Memorandums of Understanding (MOUs) rather than legislation. Where states such as Alaska have insisted on legislation, industry practices are described as being more responsible than in states such as Florida and Hawaii that have entered into MOU agreements, which are predicated on principles of trust and voluntary compliance. This report contends that the track record of the industry does not inspire confidence in its ability to act as an appropriate self-regulating MOU partner and that legislation is the only effective means of enforcing relevant standards.

5.6 Hospitality providers

Along with some types of attractions, conventional providers of accommodation are the sector of the tourism industry that leaves the most visible and most permanent footprint in the stayover destination region and whose fixed assets are almost wholly concentrated there. Hospitality providers for this reason have an especially strong vested interest in the sustainability of their surrounds and more so because they are more likely than footloose sectors to be held accountable by destination authorities and communities for any perceived environmental or social malpractice. Such malpractice, in any case, is more difficult to disguise than in the case of cruise ship-induced damage.

5.6.1 Major influence on destination and tourism sustainability

Because of its large footprint, the hospitality sector exercises an enormous influence over destination sustainability. The decision to build a particular type and size of hotel in a particular location, for example, will help to shape tourism landscapes by influencing the type and number of tourists in a particular location as well as their spatial activity patterns (Middleton and Hawkins, 1998). Second, hotels often provide the most visible evidence or identity of a tourism region or district and one that can easily overwhelm the local sense of place if designed and situated insensitively (Marin and Jafari, 2002). Third, like cruise ships, the hospitality sector is an enormous consumer of resources and producer of wastes because of the diverse materials that are required to construct and maintain fixed accommodations. In addition, tourists typically spend one-third or more (in the case of all-inclusive packages, for example) of their time in the destination within the confines of accommodation facilities (e.g. while sleeping, eating and relaxing by the swimming pool).

Fourth, large blocks of accommodation are often the centrepiece of integrated resort enclaves that internalize tourist activities and expenditures, thereby constraining the local multiplier effect and potentially alienating local residents through these practices and through informal policies of exclusion (Coles, 2004). Yet, ironically, this same isolation allows the company to implement comprehensive sustainable practices within its own confines, which could potentially stimulate the pursuit of sustainability in the surrounding community. A fifth factor is the concentration of hotel ownership within a few large corporations, with the top 25 chains providing 3.6 million units of accommodation, 75 per cent of which are controlled by the largest eight (Weaver and Lawton, 2002a). As with outbound tour operators and air carriers, this concentration means that the decisions of one or two prominent CEOs to pursue sustainability or not can reverberate profoundly throughout the industry, not least because of the influence that this can have on linked sectors such as tour operators and food producers that rely on the large chains for bulk business.

5.6.2 Pioneering sustainable tourism

The above factors help to account for the hospitality sector's reputation as a pioneer of sustainability within the tourism industry. Another factor is the sector's sensitivity to energy costs, so that some hotel chains implemented comprehensive energy-savings measures as early as the 1970s in response to the so-called 'oil crisis' that emerged from the Yom Kippur War (Knowles et al., 1999). In 1990, two years before the Rio Earth Summit and *Agenda 21*, Inter-Continental Hotels and Resorts formally positioned environmental ethics at the core of its business principles and in 1992 the International Hotels Environment Initiative (IHEI*) was established by CEOs representing many of the largest hotel chains as one of the first formal organization-wide sustainability programmes within tourism. Founded to encourage and fund the adoption of sustainable practices throughout the hospitality industry, the IHEI membership now encompasses 68 brands, 11 200 hotels and two million hotel rooms. Three influential resources that it provides to the hospitality industry are the magazine Green Hotelier, a guide to environmental best practice for hotels (IHEI, 1996) and a web-based benchmarking tool that allows managers to assess and improve their environmental performance.

Otherwise, hotels and other accommodation providers now have at their disposal a growing array of sources and venues focused on environmentally sustainable good practice (e.g. Webster, 2000; Marin and Jafari, 2002; Sweeting and Sweeting, 2003; UNEP, 2003b). There is no lack of anecdotal examples illustrating the adoption of such practices within the hospitality sector, which typically entail energy reduction, recycling, waste minimization, reduced water use, improved water treatment and/or involvement in local environmental and social projects (see also Hawkes and Williams, 1993; Enz and Siguaw, 1999).

Corporate leadership but uncertain permeation

Individual chains such as Marriott, Canadian Pacific Hotels and Resorts (Natural Resources Canada, 1997), Six Continents (which includes Inter-Continental), Accor, Scandic, Starwood (Lembo, 2003), Fairmont (Speck, 2002) and Grecotel (see case study at the end of this chapter) have displayed a level of environmental leadership comparable to American Airlines and British Airways in the transportation sector, or TUI in the outbound tour operator sector. The Marriott initiatives are subsumed under the umbrella of its Environmentally Conscious Hospitality Operations (ECHO) programme, which in turn is part of the broader Spirit to Serve Our Communities corporate citizenship strategy. ECHO is intended to ensure that environmental regulations are adhered to and provides environmental good practice guidelines in the areas of waste management, utility conservation, as well as clean air and water initiatives.

Yet, the actual extent to which such sustainability practices have been adopted within the broader hospitality sector is unclear, with manager surveys indicating mixed results and ambivalence in terms of both motive and practice. As with outbound tour operator surveys, most of this research is focused on the UK and was conducted during the 1990s; hence, it is not necessarily representative of all major destination regions or the situation in the early 2000s. In a survey of 106 hotel general managers, Brown (1994) found that energy-efficiency schemes were implemented by almost all the respondents, but for cost-saving rather than environmental reasons. Recycling of glass, in contrast, was carried out mainly for environmental reasons, but practised only by 60 per cent of respondents. Other measures, such as recycling of aluminium cans and paper, infrequent washing of towels, purchasing from green suppliers and use of water restrictors, were practised only by one-third of the managers or less. It must be also stressed that this survey achieved a response rate of only 35 per cent. Even though managers agreed that the hotel industry has a substantial impact on the environment, the attainment of environmental targets was rated at just 2.62 on a 1–5 scale in terms of its importance, compared with 4.64 for staying within budget and 4.71 for maintaining or improving profitability.

A survey of hotel proprietors in Guernsey (Stabler and Goodall, 1997) revealed that most respondents were aware of environmental problems on the island, but saw tourism's culpability for these problems as being moderate (30 per cent), minimal (47 per cent) or non-existent (12 per cent). To the extent that the hospitality sector shared some responsibility, only one-half believed that hospitality businesses should take their own initiative to rectify the problems. The concepts of 'sustainable tourism' and 'environmental auditing' were each understood by less than one in five respondents and almost no one had heard of the IHEI. Incentives that would induce the proprietors to adopt environmental practices included the availability of 'free advice' (28 per cent), 'evidence of reduced costs' (26 per cent), 'grants to review performance' (21 per cent), opportunities to 'reduce taxes' (19 per cent), 'payments to induce recycling' (14 per cent) and 'operating subsidies' (13 per cent). The authors do not report whether the size of the hotel or other factors influenced the responses.

Ambivalence is also evident in Knowles et al. (1999), who found in a survey of 42 London hotels (which is less than 30 per cent of those solicited) that all except two had by their own admission taken actions to reduce their impact on the natural environment. Two-thirds indicated that they had taken action to reduce consumption of resources, but many did not specify these measures. The same proportion cited recycling, although this mainly involved glass (two-thirds of the sample) and more rarely plastics or cardboard (19 per cent). Only four respondents had implemented any actions to protect or enhance biodiversity. Just 19 per cent indicated that they had an environmental policy, 50 per cent communicated their actions to their guests, 19 per cent had conducted an environmental audit and 17 per cent had negotiated to obtain environmentally friendly goods.

Hotel managers surveyed in Plymouth were similarly confused about the meaning of sustainable tourism (Hobson and Essex, 2001), though one-half of the sample did recognize tourism's deleterious impacts. As in the London survey, most cited the reduction of energy consumption as a measure that they practised. Sixty-seven per cent used low energy light bulbs, 52 per cent purchased recycled products and 52 per cent recycled glass. Small minorities donated to environmental groups (4 per cent), purchased organic produce (13 per cent), monitored waste production (14 per cent) or sought to eliminate disposable packaging (16 per cent). Higher levels of activity were associated with larger hotels. Cited barriers included lack of interest (66 per cent), time and energy required (64 per cent), financial cost (59 per cent) and lack of information or support (53 per cent).

5.7 Summary

Although relevant empirical data on the sustainability aspects of the facilitating tourism sectors is scarce and narrowly focused, it is still possible to speculate on some basic trends. First, the extent to which green awareness and practice is instilled overall in a sector appears related to its tangible footprint in the destination region. Conventional travel agencies, guidebooks, outbound tour operators and cruise ships therefore seem to have the lowest levels of engagement, with the latter two sectors having acquired some notoriety for their alleged unsustainable practices. In contrast, the hospitality sector has a relatively high involvement with sustainability. Airlines have always been intensively regulated and arguably occupy a position closer to the hotels in this respect. Second, all sectors have, however, shown substantial progress toward sustainability compared with the situation in the late 1980s and early 1990s. This progress is reflected in sector-wide formal initiatives such as the CIWMPP, TOI and IHEI and also in the practices undertaken by innovative corporate leaders such as TUI, British Airways and Marriott, which are extremely influential given their size and their high level of vertical as well as horizontal integration.

Third, though progress is evident, it does not appear as if the engagement with sustainability has penetrated deeply into any of these sectors, despite the widespread institutionalization of sustainable tourism both internally and externally. Measures taken even by the corporate leaders are generally those that are not overly expensive to implement (e.g. informational brochures or signage), help to lower costs (e.g. energy use reduction, recycling), foster brand visibility, heighten distinctions with competitors and invite positive consumer response (e.g. through award sponsorship and participation in community projects). More disturbingly, the level of engagement beyond the corporate leaders appears tenuous at best. Tour operators and hoteliers in the UK, where much of the empirical research has been undertaken, reveal not just low effort or minimalist adherence to sustainability, but also high levels of unawareness and non-involvement. Barriers to pursuing sustainability include confusion over the meaning of 'sustainable tourism', lack of knowledge and support, a need to focus on the financial 'bottom line' and the lack of any concerted belief that consumers are actually demanding substantive change. It may therefore be argued that the facilitating sectors of the tourism industry, at least in the UK, currently adhere to a 'veneer' model of sustainability that reflects the dominant veneer environmentalism in the broader consumer market of the more developed regions. The situation may be somewhat brighter in northern European countries such as Sweden and Germany and worse in the pleasure periphery and the less developed regions, though this needs to be investigated empirically. Further analysis will be possible once the attractions sector and quality control issues are addressed in Chapters 6 and 7 respectively.

On the net

American Airlines (environmental position)
http://www.amrcorp.com/facts/2001ceres.pdf

ASTA (American Society of Travel Agents)
http://www.astanet.com/

Better World Travelers Club
http://www.betterworldclub.com/clubtravel/travelhome.html

Bluewater Network (cruise ships)
http://bluewaternetwork.org/campaign_ss_cruises.shtml

British Airways (corporate responsibility)
http://www.britishairways.com/travel/crhome/public/en_us

ECTAA (European Travel Agents' and Tour Operators' Association)
http://www.ectaa.org/ECTAA%20English/Areas_dealt_with/Sustainable.htm

http://www.yourvisit.info/index_gb.html

Global Reporting Initiative (Tour Operators' Sector Supplement, pilot version)
http://www.toinitiative.org/reporting/documents/TourOperatorsSupplementNovember2002.pdf

ICCL (International Council of Cruise Lines)
http://www.iccl.org/whoweare/index.cfm

IHEI (International Hotels Environment Initiative)
http://www.ihei.org/

Tour Operators Initiative for Sustainable Tourism Development
http://www.greenbiz.com/frame/1.cfm?targetsite = http://www.toinitiative.org

TUI (Germany-based tour operator)
http://www.tui.com/en/

For further reading

Speck, E. (2002). The Fairmont Chateau Whistler Resort: moving towards sustainability. In *Sustainable Tourism: A Global Perspective* (R. Harris, T. Griffin and P. Williams, eds) pp. 269–83, Butterworth-Heinemann.
The author provides a detailed case study of a major Canadian resort hotel that is actively pursuing an agenda of sustainability. Processes as well as activities are featured.

Swarbrooke, J. (1999). *Sustainable Tourism Management.* CABI Publishing.
Chapters 25 to 28 respectively address sustainability issues related to attractions, tour operators, transportation providers and the hospitality sector, while Chapter 9 describes the tourism industry in general. Detailed case studies illustrate each of these chapters.

Webster, K. (2000). *Environmental Management in the Hospitality Industry: A Guide for Students and Managers*. Cassell.
From a primarily UK perspective, Webster describes with ample case studies how the hospitality sector is engaging in a wide variety of sustainability-related practices. The book begins with coverage of major environmental issues and ends with a discussion of the green consumer and environmental auditing.

Wood, R. (2000). Caribbean cruise tourism: globalization at sea. *Annals of Tourism Research*, 27, 345–70.
Wood provides an excellent analysis of the cruise ship industry as an intensely globalized phenomenon characterized by serious problems of environmental and social sustainability.

Beyond the book

1. Based on the issues and practices described in this chapter, identify (a) five sustainability indicators that are relevant to individual businesses in all four of the covered industry subsectors and (b) three sustainability indicators that are relevant to individual businesses just in each of these subsectors.
2. (a) Contact the local branch of a major travel agency or outbound tour operator and ask them for sustainability-related information about any of their standard package tours to a beach resort or other conventional destination. (b) Is such information available? (c) Why or why not? (d) How could this business improve its performance?
3. (a) Consult the 2002/2003 Social and Environmental Report of British Airways (see *On the net* for web address link) and identify the indicators used to measure environmental and social sustainability. (b) What does the performance of these indicators say about the environmental and social sustainability of the company? (c) What additional indicators should be added? (d) Do these indicators reflect adherence to a comprehensive or minimalist model of sustainability?

On the ground: Implementing sustainability at Grecotel

Grecotel, which was founded in 1981, is the largest hotel chain in Greece, with 16 four-star and luxury resort hotels containing 9000 rooms. These are concentrated on the islands of the Aegean Sea. The chain is widely regarded as a pioneer in the pursuit of environmentally sustainable practices in conventional resort tourism, having established a separate department for cultural and environmental protection as far back as 1991. An environmental policy statement was formulated in the following year and a policy of incorporating environmental duties in the job descriptions of all employees was implemented in 1993. The statement reflected Grecotel's early intentions to become the environmental leader of the hotel industry and to serve as a positive example to other Mediterranean hospitality providers. A major reason for this emphasis on sustainability is the company's connections with the environmentally conscientious German outbound tour operator TUI, which was a 50 per cent shareholder at the time of the chain's founding and continues to play a dominant role in this component of what may be called TUI's emerging integrated sustainable tourism supply chain.

According to Middleton and Hawkins (1998), partnerships are a key component of Grecotel's environmental strategy. In addition to strong links with TUI (another leading European outbound tour operator), the chain has obtained funding from the European Commission to initiate its programmes. It also participates actively in the IHEI, works closely with the Greek Sea Turtle Protection Society to protect nesting beach habitat and collaborates with local municipalities in a variety of community social and environmental projects. Green practices are standard in Grecotel properties and include the harnessing of solar power to heat water, the use of low-energy light bulbs, the diversion of greywater for garden irrigation and the use of biological wastewater treatment plants. To foster a local sense of place, resort complexes are designed to resemble local traditional architectural styles and special garden areas are reserved for native and endemic plants. The chain is also a pioneer in now-standard industry practices such as recycling and the use of double-glazed windows, towels that are only washed on request and master switches that are respectively activated and de-activated when guests arrive and leave their hotel room.

Other more novel initiatives include the establishment of a farm on the island of Crete that produces organic food for the chain using traditional and innovative farming methods. This farm now provides 80 per cent of the food consumed at Grecotel's eight Crete-based hotels and is an important tourist attraction in its own right as well as an agricultural education facility that encourages improved farming techniques on the island. Other food requirements, to the greatest extent possible, are obtained from local sources. Another Grecotel-owned attraction is the traditional theme park or living museum of Danilia Village on Corfu, which recreates historical Greek streetscapes and artisan activities. For its exemplary sustainability practices, Grecotel has received more than 50 environmental awards and other recognitions.

It is something of a paradox and more than a minor challenge that this paragon of sustainability is located in a mass tourism-intensive region where the overall level of environmental awareness is low relative to Northern Europe or North America. Thus, while Grecotel strives for good environmental practice on its own property, it must contend with widespread practices that negatively affect the tourist experience outside of these properties, such as littering, dumping and burning rubbish in ravines and casual hunting. Suppliers of bottled and canned products are sometimes reluctant to cooperate in recycling programmes. Grecotel educational programmes, for this reason, are designed to inculcate a greater sense of environmental awareness and stewardship among local residents and businesses. Whether the Grecotel innovations will have a broad contagious effect on the tourism industry and local community of the eastern Mediterranean pleasure periphery, however, or will remain relatively isolated, is still unclear.

Exercises

1. (a) What sustainability issues should Grecotel managers be aware of that relate to the insular location of most of the chain's hotels? (b) How can these issues best be resolved?
2. Provide five strategies that will allow Grecotel managers to effectively address the serious environmental problems that occur in the area surrounding their hotels.
3. Design a hypothetical sustainable supply chain focused around the basic link between TUI and Grecotel. Tourism industry sectors, local communities and non-tourism suppliers should all be included.

Chapter 6
Attractions

Chapter objectives

Upon completion of this chapter, the reader should be able to:

■ contextualize attractions as the central element of the tourism system and explain the reasons for this dominant position
■ describe a generic typology of tourist attractions and situate theme parks, casinos, ski resorts and golf courses within this typology
■ evaluate the characteristics of attractions that potentially affect their sustainability
■ discuss the distinct structural and geographical characteristics of theme parks, casinos, ski resorts and golf courses
■ assess the negative environmental and sociocultural impacts associated with each of these four subsectors
■ describe and critically evaluate the extent to which each subsector is pursuing environmentally and socioculturally sustainable practices and
■ articulate the reasons for the sustainability-related progress or lack thereof that has been attained in each subsector.

6.1 Introduction

The facilitating sectors examined in the previous chapter are described as such because they facilitate the interaction between tourists and tourist attractions, which is the core experience of the entire tourism system. This chapter focuses on the attraction component of the conventional tourism industry, specifically by considering the environmental and sociocultural sustainability of four high profile and controversial subsectors that are dominated by the private sector and often found as interrelated components of integrated resort complexes. Section 6.2 begins by discussing in more detail the role of attractions within the tourism system and by presenting a contextual typology of attractions. Characteristics that potentially affect the sustainability of attractions are also considered. Section 6.3 examines theme parks, while Sections 6.4, 6.5 and 6.6 respectively focus on casinos, ski resorts and golf courses. Other types of attractions, because they are mainly within the public domain (e.g. National Parks, bucolic rural landscapes, ethnic neighbourhoods, beaches, scenic highways, special events and historical sites), are considered in Chapters 8, 9 and 10, which focus on tourism destinations. For each of the target subsectors, distinctive structural and geographical characteristics are described and its negative environmental and sociocultural impacts are assessed. The extent to which the subsector has become more environmentally and socioculturally sustainable is then considered and the reasons for this sustainability-related state of affairs, including attraction characteristics, are discussed.

6.2 Role of attractions

There is no consensus on the definition of a 'tourist attraction' (Swarbrooke, 1995), but there is agreement on the centrality of attractions within the tourism system (e.g. Inskeep, 1991; Gunn, 1994; Mill and Morrison, 2002; Goeldner and Ritchie, 2003). Walsh-Heran and Stevens (1990) conveniently regard an attraction as a feature in an area that is a place, venue, or focus of tourist activity. While this definition technically includes business opportunities and people that are the foci of business and VFR tourism respectively, neither of these categories is normally regarded as a tourist attraction *per se*. Hence, they are not included as 'attractions' in this chapter. Construed instead as the focus of recreation and leisure-oriented tourism, attractions are the component of the tourism system that is most intimately connected to the destination and its identity as a location for tourist activity. Attractions, as much or more so than the hospitality sector, influence the type, location and volume of tourist activity in a destination and hence the sustainability of tourism in that area.

6.2.1 Typology of attractions

Weaver and Lawton (2002a) provide a typology that distinguishes between 'natural' attractions and cultural or 'built' attractions, each of which in turn can be divided into sites and events. Natural attractions are further divided on the basis of the focal environmental element (e.g. topographical, climatic, hydrological), which can combine as the raw material for 'semi-built' nature-focused attractions such as scenic highways, lookouts and botanical gardens. Built attractions range from pre-historical and historical sites to specialized, purpose-built sectors such as the theme parks, casinos, golf courses and ski resorts considered below.

6.2.2 Attraction characteristics

As considered below, various interrelated attributes, including ownership, orientation, spatial configuration, situation, authenticity, presentation, image, scarcity, status, carrying capacity, accessibility and market, can influence the environmental and sociocultural sustainability of an attraction.

Ownership and orientation

Ownership, arrayed along a public-to-private continuum, is important because it largely determines primary stakeholder groups and identifies foci of decision-making power. Ownership may also determine *orientation*, that is, whether the attraction is operated primarily to maximize shareholder profit (in the case of private ownership) as opposed to improving the long-term social and economic well-being of the community (in the case of the public sector) (see Section 4.2.1). An intermediate possibility is ownership by a non-governmental organization that may have an explicit mandate to operate an attraction on a non-profit basis to fulfil a specialized mandate such as environmental protection.

Spatial configuration and situation

Wall (1997b) is credited with emphasizing the importance of *spatial configuration* as an attraction attribute. For example, a nodal attraction often draws a high concentration of activity that can create both opportunities and barriers for achieving sustainability. Linear tourist attractions such as canals or hiking trails share lengthy boundaries with external environments that can affect the environmental and historical integrity of the tourism resource. Such a configuration, for example, can facilitate the diffusion of negative impacts (such as exotic plant seeds) into a broad area. Another geographic influence is *situation*, which first of all considers whether the attraction is dependent on a particular setting (e.g. a waterfall or castle) or set of natural/ cultural conditions, or whether it could have been located in a wide variety of site options (e.g. as with a casino, theme park or golf course). Situation also considers the characteristics of the attraction's surroundings. High population density, for example, may increase the probability of negative sociocultural impacts because of noise and congestion. Finally, situation entails relative location, including proximity to markets, competing attractions, or potentially destructive external forces such as hurricanes.

Authenticity, presentation and image

Authenticity is a subjective and contentious attribute that essentially considers if the attraction is genuine or an imitation. Whether imitation is an indicator of unsustainability or not depends in part on the nature of its *presentation* to the visitor. There is usually no problem when a genuine attraction is presented as genuine, or an imitation presented as an imitation (e.g. a fantasy theme park, or a reproduction of the prehistoric Lascaux cave paintings in France). Problems can occur, however, when an imitation is misrepresented as genuine, or vice versa (Weaver and Lawton, 2002a). Presentation in turn affects or is affected by *image*, which can apply to either the tourists or the local residents and can involve familiarity (well known or almost unknown), the perception of authenticity as described above and a broad value judgment as to whether it is regarded positively or negatively. Image can also involve specific and potentially harmful perceptions, such as when a football match is regarded as an excuse for violent behaviour, or the sculpture on a Hindu temple is perceived as pornography. An important issue with image is the absence of the latter, in which case a sustainability-related issue is unlikely to generate public concern or involvement.

Scarcity and status

Scarcity is often linked to image and authenticity and considers whether the attraction is unique or ubiquitous (i.e. found just about anywhere). Ubiquitous attractions such as golf courses or franchise theme parks may contribute to the erosion of a destination's sense of place, but on the positive side can be suitable for an area that requires economic rejuvenation (as with the casinos on Indian Reservations discussed below). The degradation of a unique resource is an especially negative sociocultural cost and is more likely to occur because of the demand to see something singular. The perception of scarcity, however, can also be manipulated through creative marketing. For example, rather than being perceived as just one of one hundred similar sites, a Norman castle in England might be presented as the only one with an intact original dungeon. Scarcity is also related to *status*, which considers whether the attraction has a primary or secondary position within the destination's hierarchy of attractions. Tourists are usually attracted to the better-known primary attractions, especially if they have the iconic or destination defining status of an Eiffel Tower, the Sphinx or the Great Wall of China. Problems can arise when an *iconic attraction* such as Niagara Falls becomes surrounded by a poorly planned cluster of secondary attractions that benefit from their proximity to the magnet primary attraction.

Carrying capacity and accessibility

Carrying capacity is often criticized for its implication of fixed limits. However, it has utility if it is regarded as a variable threshold that can fluctuate depending on the measures, or lack thereof, that are put in place to accommodate visitation (see Section 9.2.3). Thus, at a given point in time, the environmental and sociocultural carrying capacity of a functioning Tibetan monastery may be 50 persons per day on the basis of the actions that have been taken to control noise and tourist movement. Carrying capacity in turn influences *accessibility*, so that tourists may be restricted from visiting certain parts of the monastery and prohibited altogether between sunrise and sunset. Accessibility can also consider the roads, paths and gateways through which the attraction can be reached and the amount of the entry fee.

Market

The *market* for an attraction usually consists of tourists as well as at least some local residents. Attractions that are almost exclusively oriented toward tourists, such as those located within enclave resorts, may engender local resentment, but may also confine direct negative tourist impacts to relatively inaccessible areas away from the local community. In contrast, attractions that rely mainly on local residents may not attract significant amounts of outside revenue. Other potentially influential market parameters from a sustainability perspective are demographic (e.g. mostly older tourists, mostly female, etc.) and geographic (e.g. dominated by Japanese or domestic tourists). Also relevant is whether the attraction is a specialized entity such as battle re-creation or a philatelic museum that draws a niche market, or a diverse attraction such as a theme park that attracts a generic market.

6.3 Theme parks

Camp (1997) defines a theme park as an outdoor attraction, designed around a central theme or themes, which charges a pay-one-price admission fee to access various rides, attractions and shows. Such facilities were first established during the nineteenth century in Europe, but the birth of the modern theme park industry is generally associated with the opening of Disneyland (California) in 1955. The number of large theme parks (over 500 000 annual visits) worldwide has since grown from 225 in 1990 to 240 in 1999, with total visits increasing during that time from 300 million to 545 million (Scheurer, 2004). The continuing primacy of the Disney corporation is evidenced by the 57.1 million visits made to the five US-based Disney parks in 2000 and the status of Disneyland Paris as the leading European theme park with 12 million attendees in that same year (Goeldner and Ritchie, 2003). Theme parks have also become an increasingly common fixture in the rapidly expanding conventional tourism landscapes of Southeast and East Asia (Cartier, 1998).

6.3.1 Sustainability-related issues

Few aspects of the tourism industry have been as subject to critical academic analysis as theme parks, which reflects their imposing presence in certain tourism landscapes, the dominance of large and highly visible corporations such as Disney and their emphasis on highly commercialized fantasy-rooted experiences. Most of this analysis is found in the sociological and anthropological literature, which variably implicates the mega-theme park (and the Disney operations in particular) as a potent symbol of globalization, infantilization, inauthenticity, alienation, stereotyping, technological utopianism, hypersanitization, escapism, decontextualization, standardization, frivolous consumerism, corporatism or some other aspect of the postmodernist sociocultural critique (e.g. Fjellman, 1992; Sorkin, 1992; Rojek, 1993; Bryman, 1995). The not-so-subtle anti-corporatism and anti-Americanism of this literature and the centrality of the Disney theme parks in particular, is evident in Ritzer and Liska (1997), who perceive theme parks as the progenitor and extreme expression of 'McDisneyization', a process that personifies the negative conventional mass tourism ideal type depicted in Table 3.1.

From the perspective of sociocultural sustainability, one broad message of the critics is that people who visit theme parks assimilate the values that these facilities represent. Fjellman (1992), for example, argues that Disney's Future World (a themed section of Orlando-based Disney World) sends the message that technology will solve all environmental issues and that corporations are the best means through which to achieve this. It is further contended that these subliminal and not-so-subliminal messages subsequently influence the visitor's day-to-day patterns of shopping and entertainment, thereby contributing to the McDisneyization of the culture and society as a whole.

Others, of course, argue to the contrary that the theme park offers a fundamentally innocent experience that happens to be carried out through an efficient business model that maximizes the satisfaction of the visitor and the financial gains of the investor (Goeldner and Ritchie, 2003). Complicating this analysis is the difference in domestic reaction to the Disneyland theme parks that opened during the early 1980s and 1990s in Tokyo and Paris respectively, with the latter being regarded far more negatively than the former (Altman, 1995). This included the description of Disneyland Paris as a 'Cultural Chernobyl' by the Culture Minister of France in the early 1990s (Richards and Richards, 1998).

Aside from their participation in selective charitable acts (see below), it is difficult to assess the extent to which theme park managers meaningfully take the sociocultural sensitivities of the local community into account in facility design and operation. Some indication, however, is provided in a survey of North American general managers by Milman (2001), which rated customers as the external factor most likely to impact on future operations, followed by economic forces, employees, demographic forces and competitors. Local communities were regarded as a minor influence, indicating that concerns of sociocultural sustainability may receive only cursory attention by these managers.

Environmental and economic considerations

The debate over the environmental and economic impacts of theme parks is rather less abstract. By their very nature, theme parks are conspicuous, intensely built and enormous generators of waste products such as sewage, greenhouse gases, grey-water, pesticide residue and debris from food products, packaging, etc. The amount of space actually required for a theme park is often surprisingly small, with only 57 of Disneyland Paris' 2000 hectares occupied by the intensively visited core facilities (Camp, 1997). Complementary and facilitating land uses and activities typically account for a much larger amount of space. Camp (1997) estimates that the average European theme park has a 20-hectare parking lot capable of accommodating 5800 vehicles. Theme park companies also tend to establish secondary attractions such as water parks and hotels that complement the theme park and help to extend and internalize tourist expenditures. Land is also often held in reserve for purposes of future expansion.

Beyond the land held by the corporation (Disney World, by way of illustration, consists of an 11100-hectare property), theme parks serve as magnets or unintentional growth poles that attract large amounts of direct, indirect and induced development activity to their vicinity. This activity ranges from clientele-related facilities such as factory outlet malls, mixed-use entertainment centres, restaurants and hotel/motel strips, to motorways, subdivisions and business parks. Because theme parks are usually established in exurban locations that offer an ideal compromise between access to large amounts of relatively cheap land and proximity to urban markets (see Section 8.5.3), the effect of this activity is to exacerbate urban sprawl, often to the extent where the broader urban landscape is significantly shaped by the location of a major theme park (for example, Orlando by Disney World).

Disney World

Major theme park corporations, and Disney in particular, have been accused of sometimes dealing aggressively with local communities in their quest to acquire land of their choosing and to develop it as they see fit (see case study at the end of this chapter). The story of Florida's Disney World is illustrative though not necessarily representative. As described by Foglesong (1999), Disney, after secretly acquiring its 27000-acre property, established an entity called the Reedy Creek Improvement District with essentially the powers of a municipality to control its land use options regardless of state law. This arrangement also enabled the District to issue its own tax-free municipal bonds. Seeking to lure Disney and its economic benefits, pro-development state and municipal authorities provided road improvements and interchanges at public expense.

While enormously beneficial to Disney, the effects on the community have been mixed. There is no question that huge induced economic and environmental impacts were realized, with the theme park being the primary factor in drawing 30 million visitors a year to the Orlando area, resulting in an increase in the number of hotel rooms from 8000 in 1965 to 85000 in 1996. However, Disney has also been accused of fostering a low-wage environment, modest worker benefits and of providing lukewarm support for affordable housing, which exacerbates the additional impact of congestion by forcing workers to make long commutes. Disney's convention centre and shopping complexes, moreover, compete directly with municipal facilities, while bond money has been siphoned off that might have otherwise gone to the city of Orlando. Foglesong (1999) argues that Disney became widely perceived as an arrogant competitor to Orlando rather than a good corporate citizen and concludes that the deregulated model represented by Disney and Reedy Creek stimulates growth and benefits the corporation, but reduces the ability of the public sector to manage the costs and benefits of that growth.

6.3.2 Sustainability initiatives: Disney examples

As with hotels and other built tourism-related facilities, theme park operators practise sustainability at least to the extent that they adhere to environmental and social regulations required by various levels of government in destinations where they operate. Beyond such mandatory compliance, voluntary measures include the allocation of land for environmental purposes. About one-half of the total holdings of Disney World consist of green space or water that is not intended for any future built development. This includes a 3000-hectare Wildlife Management Conservation Area and 485 hectares of restored or enhanced wetlands (Braun, 2003). Disney also purchased a nearby 4850-hectare cattle ranch which it then donated to The Nature Conservancy to be managed as a restorative protected area known as the Disney Wilderness Preserve. The natural appearance of the former initiatives, however, is somewhat misleading in that these lands were part of a massive process of deliberate environmental restructuring involving dredging, rechannelling, infilling and contouring of Disney-owned lands to facilitate the establishment of the constituent theme parks and create an aesthetically pleasing buffer zone (Fjellman, 1992).

Disney's* broader ethos of 'environmentality', launched in 1990, is reflected in the extensive use of native plants in landscaping, measures to prevent the escape of exotic species, the use of organic pesticides and the use of water hyacinths (a noxious exotic weed) and native plants to treat wastewater (Fjellman, 1992). It also led in 1995 to the establishment of the Disney Wildlife Conservation Fund which funds selected projects of non-profit wildlife and conservation organizations. Other measures include various community outreach programmes, recycling and waste minimization activities and reductions in water and energy use. Although the formation of the Reedy Creek Improvement District is cited as a potential problem for sustainability because it concedes planning and land use control to the Disney corporation, it can be argued that this internalization of power is a major factor that has allowed the company to implement new standards of environmental sustainability and to create landscapes that juxtapose heavily built theme park facilities with large areas of relatively undisturbed natural habitat (Murphy, 1997). Disneyland Paris has also been touted for its many environmental and sociocultural innovations both internal and external, but for the very different reason of extensive state intervention (d'Hauteserre, 1999a).

Other initiatives

Similar efforts are undertaken in other large theme parks. Animal-themed entities such as the SeaWorld brand of theme parks are usually involved in activities such as mammal rehabilitation that complement the showcasing of particular charismatic megafauna and generate positive publicity. At an association-wide level, sustainability engagement is not as apparent. The International Association of Amusement Parks and Attractions does feature the involvement of its Charitable Department with three global charities (Give Kids the World, UNICEF and the International Institute for Peace through Tourism) in a recent annual report (IAAPA*, 2003), but the actual level of support appears modest and intended mainly for promotional purposes.

Sustainability in the theme park industry does not appear to be widely manifested in the actual portrayal of environmental or cultural themes. Respondents to the Milman (2001) survey cited interactive adventure, fantasy and mystery, movies and TV shows, science fiction and the future, and outer space as the five most likely themes to be pursued by managers and planners in the future. Nature/ecology, education and sports, and cultural and ethnic diversity were ranked much lower on the list, although theme parks with a cultural or ethnic theme are widespread in Asia (Ah-Keng, 1994; Cartier, 1998).

6.4 Casinos

Casinos are controversial by their very nature, but also because of the rapid diffusion that they experienced since the 1980s when the deregulation of the hitherto tightly controlled gambling industry (the industry prefers the term 'gaming') was initiated. Where legal gambling tourism was once restricted to a few specialized destinations such as Monte Carlo, Macau and Las Vegas, gamblers can now select from a rapidly increasing number of facilities in North America, Australia, southern Africa, Eastern Europe and Southeast Asia (Roehl, 1994). American gamblers, for example, can now access a much larger number of mega-casinos in Las Vegas, but also Vegas-type establishments in Atlantic City and a dizzying array of riverboat, inner city, racetrack and 'Indian' casinos elsewhere. From a tourism perspective, it is important to note that the four latter categories largely consist of 'convenience casinos' catering primarily to local residents rather than tourists. Hence, only a relatively small proportion of the 297 million visits paid to US casinos in 2002 were tourism related (AGA*, 2003a).

6.4.1 Perceived economic benefits

The proliferation of casinos in the USA and elsewhere is the outcome of several forces, including greater public acceptance (Roehl, 1994), increased legitimacy conferred by the involvement of high profile corporations such as Holiday Inn Corporation (Urbanowicz, 2001), cash-strapped municipalities and other levels of government seeking new and reliable sources of revenue and employment and their desire not to raise taxes to obtain this revenue (Volberg, 2001). There is strong empirical evidence, at least in the USA, that casinos do spur economic growth in host communities (Walker and Jackson, 1998). In 2002, non-Indian casinos in the 11 states that host such facilities generated $4 billion in direct gambling taxes and 350 000 jobs (AGA, 2003a).

Indian casinos

The economic impact of Indian casinos is especially dramatic, given the small size of the relevant indigenous communities and their traditionally high levels of poverty and unemployment (Lew and Van Otten, 1998). For the Yavapai-Apache of Arizona, a casino that opened in 1995 and earned $7.4 billion in 1997 first allowed the tribe to provide basic infrastructure and services and then culture language revitalization programmes. Revenue is now being used to establish new sources of revenue, including other tourist attractions, to reduce reliance on the casino and to plan for its possible future closure (Piner and Paradis, 2004). A more extreme and anomalous example of economic benefit from the 'new buffalo' (Hannigan, 1998) is Foxwoods Casino Resort in Connecticut, where revenue from 50 000 visitors each day has converted the 400-member Mashantucket Pequot tribe into a major economic and political force in the state (Carmichael and Peppard, 1998; d'Hauteserre, 1999b). In Canada, Casino Rama in Ontario was projected to generate CAN$200 million in revenue in 1998, of which one-half was to be designated to other Reserves in the province for the construction of schools, community centres and other facilities (Hannigan, 1998).

Other examples

There are other peripheral destinations where casinos have been pursued as an apparently effective vehicle for economic development. Riverboat casinos, for example, have been credited with improving the economic situation in impoverished communities along the Mississippi River such as Tunica County (Mississippi), which was once notoriously referred to as America's Ethiopia, but where unemployment decreased from 19.1 per cent in 1990 to 9.9 per cent in 1992 as a result of this new activity (Hyland, 1997). In apartheid-era South Africa, casinos were used as a geopolitical tool to provide income in the so-called Bantustans, thereby helping to justify their conversion into 'self-reliant' independent states capable of supporting the country's African majority (Crush and Wellings, 1987). Finally, the role of casinos in revitalizing the moribund tourism industry of Atlantic City is well documented (Stansfield, 1978).

6.4.2 Economic and sociocultural costs

Unlike the theme park industry, where criticism has coalesced largely around the Disney operations, the critical literature on casinos is not focused on any particular site or company. Also unlike theme parks, the casino literature has tended to focus more on economic and sociocultural than cultural and environmental costs.

Negative economic impacts

One component of this literature questions whether gambling is the panacea that it is widely perceived to be. The fact that a local clientele dominates most casinos, for example, indicates the internal redistribution of wealth rather than the generation of new revenue from external sources. Research by Hsu (1998) on riverboat casinos in Iowa revealed a limited economic stimulus to local businesses, in part because the proliferation of such facilities has led to market saturation and subsequent reliance on ever more localized market catchment areas. This research also alluded to the ease with which the riverboats (like cruise ships) could literally relocate to other dockside locations if their owners deemed local profits or concessions inadequate. Problems of market saturation and resultant reductions in revenue have also been identified in Australia (Hing et al., 1998).

Negative sociocultural impacts

The expected economic benefits from casinos often lead proponents to downplay accompanying social costs or to argue that the latter are restricted to a few problem gamblers and can be alleviated or avoided through the diversion of gambling revenues to relevant social programmes (see below). Increased crime is one social cost commonly associated with casinos, though Roehl (1994) suggests that this may have as much to do with increased visitation, greater wealth and population growth as with the arrival of opportunistic criminal elements and compulsive gamblers. The presence of casinos, however, may *spawn* compulsive gamblers and other antisocial elements from within the local community as the casino is forced to rely on a shrinking catchment area (Davis and Hudman, 1998).

Reviewing the empirical literature from the 1980s and early 1990s, Roehl (1994) concludes that (a) local residents are often unprepared for the magnitude of change, both positive and negative, that results from the introduction of casinos, (b) the distribution of these costs and benefits is usually not equitable and (c) local residents tend to be ambivalent about casinos, acknowledging significant social costs but also significant economic benefits. This ambivalence is evident in studies of resident attitudes toward casinos in four rural communities in Colorado and South Dakota (Long, 1996) and in Nevada (Roehl, 1999). In a major study of community attitudes in eight midwestern communities (Nichols et al., 2002), most residents indicated that casinos left their quality of life unchanged, though a substantial portion did cite both increased crime and increased economic benefits as outcomes. Interestingly, the tendency by the local community to see both greater economic benefits as well as social costs increased as the size of the casino relative to the local community increased. Internal divisions are indicated by the fact that one-half of all respondents had themselves gambled in their local casinos, while about one-quarter were morally opposed to gambling. These non-gamblers were far more likely to indicate negative effects on quality of life in their communities.

Problems in Indian casinos

The casino issue has had divisive effects within the American Indian community, with the economic success stories of the Pequot and Yavapai-Apache (see above) being offset by many other Reservations that have benefited marginally or not at all, or who like the Navajo, have refused to establish casinos for ethical and cultural reasons (Lew and Van Otten, 1998). Complicating the situation is the dual-host character of many Reservations, wherein the perceptions of adjacent non-indigenous residents must also be taken into account. In the case of Foxwoods, the latter were divided in their attitudes, with recognition of the employment and charitable contribution benefits from the casino being countered by concerns about traffic congestion and attempts by the tribe to purchase non-native owned land with gambling revenues (Carmichael and Peppard, 1998).

6.4.3 Sustainability initiatives

The assessment as to whether casinos are socially sustainable or not depends largely on whether gambling is regarded as an exploitative pathology (as it is by the US-based National Coalition Against Legalized Gambling*) or a mostly benign and entertaining diversion (as it is by the AGA). Proponents concede that casinos sustain and perhaps even create a small number of problem gamblers, but argue that this is outweighed by casino revenues, which directly foster the economic sustainability of communities while concurrently supporting their sociocultural sustainability through the diversion of revenue to social and cultural programmes. Even so, the industry has in recent years contributed extensively to programmes that attempt to identify, treat and pre-empt the problem gambler sector, although there is no evidence that such initiatives are linked to sustainable tourism programmes or policies *per se*. According to Volberg (2001), such efforts are fundamentally an expression of self-interest reflecting the industry's vulnerability to litigation from problem gamblers and anti-gambling activists, especially in the wake of the successful assault by anti-smoking activists on 'Big Tobacco'. Concurrently, they are designed to demonstrate good industry intentions and responsibility in order to pre-empt the imposition of greater government regulation and taxation to mitigate the negative side effects of casinos.

AGA and other programmes

In the USA, the AGA pursues several concurrent initiatives to curtail the problem of compulsive gambling. These include the provision of publications such as the *Responsible Gaming Resource Guide* and the establishment of the *Code of Conduct for Responsible Gaming*, which pledges 'to make responsible gaming an integral part of our daily operations across the United States'. The code states further that 'each AGA member company will implement the code and begin conducting annual reviews of its compliance with this code' 1 year following its adoption in late 2003 (AGA, 2003b). In 1996, the AGA established the National Center for Responsible Gaming to fund scientific research on problem and underage gambling. The Center has an extramural grants programme, but directs most of its funds to a specialized institution within the Harvard Medical School. Funding for problem gambling is also provided by the organizations that oversee riverboat gambling in the Midwest and tribal casinos and by the gambling associations in states such as Illinois and Missouri.

6.5 Ski resorts

Of the four types of attraction featured in this chapter, ski resorts are the most limited in their location by situational requirements. Specifically, a ski resort must have appropriate winter conditions, adequate precipitation (or access to water for making snow) and mountainside slopes that are suitable for the construction of ski runs. The development of skiing as a large-scale form of tourism began in Europe during the early twentieth century and was stimulated by the inclusion of skiing in the 1924 Winter Olympics. Europeans today account for about 43 per cent of the world's 65–70 million skiers, compared with 34 per cent in North America and 20 per cent in Asia (Hudson, 2000).

6.5.1 Expansion and consolidation

According to Hudson (2000), the large-scale establishment and expansion of tourist-oriented ski resorts began in the 1960s and continued through the following decade, giving rise to a significant alpine subregion within the pleasure periphery that includes the western half of North America, the European Alps and northern Japan (Weaver and Lawton, 2002a). Unlike most other tourism products, however, the skiing industry has been consolidating and contracting since the 1980s, with fewer but larger (and more financially viable) ski resorts remaining in operation as the skiing market ages and stagnates. In the USA alone, the number of ski areas has declined from 745 to 509 between 1975 and 2000 (Clifford, 2002). Similar market and restructuring trends have occurred in France (Tuppen, 2000).

6.5.2 Environmental impacts of skiing

The alpine and mountain settings that are most conducive to downhill skiing and snowboarding are also among the world's most scenic and environmentally fragile natural habitats (e.g. Holden, 1999). The most direct detrimental impacts on these habitats include the need to clear and keep cleared all trees and shrubs from designated runs, construct lifts and establish facilities and services at the top and foot of the ski runs. Holden (1999) describes how red grouse and ptarmigan populations at a Scottish ski resort have been reduced by collisions with cable wires. Ski resorts also increasingly employ snowmaking equipment to extend the ski season and improve skiing conditions, a phenomenon that has also allowed the ski industry to expand into new areas such as the southern Appalachian Mountains of the USA. In the early 1990s, 5000 snow cannons were being used in the European Alps, requiring 2.8 million litres of water, usually obtained from local lakes or streams, for each kilometre of ski run (Hudson, 2000). Ecological consequences of artificial snow making include depletion of these local water supplies and reduced recuperation time for alpine vegetation on slopes due to the greater period of snow cover. Furthermore, the enormous amounts of energy that are required to run water pumps and air compressors are often obtained from diesel generators which produce high levels of nitrous oxides and other air pollutants (Clifford, 2002).

Corporatism and real estate

The stagnation in the skier market and the need to remain competitive through the application of expensive technologies such as snow making have combined to drive many of the smaller ski area operators out of business. In their place, control is being invested in a small number of large corporations that are continually expanding and diversifying their ski resort operations to maintain or improve their market share (Loverseed, 2000). Thus, while the number of ski areas in North America declined by 18 per cent between 1980 and 1990, their capacity during the same period has increased by 51 per cent (Hudson, 2000).

The environmental consequences of this localized expansion, however, have not been restricted to the further fragmentation of alpine forests or the construction of ski lifts. Increasingly, the owners of ski resorts, as with golf courses (see Section 6.6), rely on affiliated real estate projects to generate profits, thereby effectively demoting the adjacent ski operations to a secondary product that serves as a hook to attract seasonal or permanent residents. Housing developments are usually situated within narrow riparian valleys, which have the effect of displacing alpine wildlife that depend on these scarce habitats for adequate food and cover during the long winter season. They also require the upgrading and expansion of road networks and other services, including new modes of access such as enhanced airports, thereby inducing a suburbanization effect in formerly remote and relatively undisturbed alpine landscapes. Four well-known North American examples of this phenomenon are Whistler (British Columbia), Mammoth Lakes (California), Vail (Colorado) and Alpine (Colorado). Clifford (2002) cites a number of impending mega-projects, including one in Colorado that, by 2012, will see the construction of 4500 residential units in an area almost 3000 metres above sea level. Clifford (2002) contends that the

US Forest Service, upon whose lands many ski runs have been constructed, is often more sympathetic to the ski corporations than it is to the public or the environment.

Displacement and diminished sense of place

While the critique on ski resorts has focused on the sector's environmental impacts, Clifford (2002) also describes the effects of ski resort suburbanization and gentrification, which has included the displacement of lower income residents to less expensive communities often far removed from their jobs in these resorts. In addition, these processes have eroded the sense of place that distinguished one resort from another, replacing it with a homogeneous monotony inhabited and patronized by the privileged.

6.5.3 Sustainability initiatives

The expansion of energy-intensive ski resorts and associated developments within highly sensitive alpine settings is a scenario tailor made to attract the attention of environmental activists and such has been the case in Europe as well as North America. Tuppen (2000) cites several national and international environmental organizations which have worked together since the early 1990s to oppose the expansion of alpine ski resorts in France, as well as the use of snow cannons and the opening of new runs. Such efforts have been facilitated by the more regulation-friendly governments of the European Union, which among other measures established the Alpine Convention in 1991 to safeguard the region's environmental and cultural integrity, in part through mandatory environmental impact studies of proposed skiing-related developments. Hudson (2000) suggests that the European ski industry is likely to face more restrictions in the future and thus has an incentive to become greener in order to demonstrate its ability to regulate itself in an effective way. Alpine resorts such as Graubünden (Switzerland) are already cited for their proactive implementation of sustainability policies, including the issuance of lift pass tickets coupled with free public transit, the use of solar energy and a programme in which local hotels use only local produce in their breakfast menus (Swarbrooke, 1999).

The situation in North America, and the USA in particular, is somewhat different in that the skiing industry and the idea of growth in general are strongly supported by sympathetic governments at both the state and federal level. The National Ski Areas Association (NSAA*) released *The Environmental Charter for Ski Areas* in 2000 (since endorsed by 72 per cent of all US ski areas), but Clifford (2002) describes this as a greenwashing exercise that was roundly condemned by environmental activists for its qualifiers and absence of commitments. Other actions supported in the Charter were already obligatory. Hudson and Ritchie (2001) offer a contrasting perspective in contending that the skiing industry has made a genuine commitment to protecting the environment through a new management style.

Clifford (2002) and Hudson and Ritchie (2001) do concur that one company in particular, the Aspen Skiing Company*, has made an especially robust commitment to genuine green practice, though Clifford (2002) suggests that this is due to the attachment of the owning family to the resort of Aspen rather than to any deep-seeded environmental ethos. Hudson and Ritchie (2001) cite Heavenly Ski Resort at Lake Tahoe as another exemplary site where environmental actions have included habitat restoration, reseeding of exposed runs, slope stabilization measures and avoidance of development in wildlife foraging areas. Sundance resort in Utah is also cited, with measures such as the removal of parking spaces and the encouraging of car-pools (by offering free skiing to the fourth person in any vehicle) being associated with the environmentalist views of its owner, the actor Robert Redford. Finally, Whistler (British Columbia) is lauded for its assistance in restoring local habitat. As described in Section 4.5.2, Hudson and Ritchie (2001) found environmentalist tendencies among skiers in the USA, Canada and the UK that would support environmental initiatives within the skiing industry, although these attitudes were not especially deep or sophisticated.

6.6 Golf courses

Golf courses are a ubiquitous attraction that has become the *sine qua non* of integrated resorts and a standard attribute of most conventional tourist destinations. Globally, there are an estimated 30000 golf courses, with the USA accounting for about one-half and Europe one-sixth of this total (Markwick, 2000). During the mid-1990s an average of one new golf course opened each day in the USA alone (Terman, 1997), although not all of these facilities rely mainly or even partially on a tourist clientele. This proliferation has resulted in the creation of *golfscapes*, i.e. landscapes dominated by golf courses and affiliated developments, in intensively built pleasure periphery destinations such as the Gold Coast (Australia), greater Orlando (USA) and the Costa del Sol (Spain). In several cases such as St Andrews (Scotland) and Pebble Beach (California), particular golf courses constitute iconic attractions in their own right.

6.6.1 Environmental and sociocultural impacts

With an 18-hole facility occupying an average of 54 hectares (Terman, 1997), golf courses cumulatively are a land-intensive form of built recreational activity. Arguably, the allocation of land for golf courses is environmentally beneficial in so far as it pre-empts the use of this space for higher density and less aesthetically pleasing land uses, while providing habitat and oasis effects for local and migratory wildlife. However, space for golf course development is often obtained at the expense of agricultural and forest land, with an estimated 5000 hectares of woodland in Japan being lost each year for this purpose during the early 1990s (Terman, 1997). Golf courses, moreover, are similar to ski resorts in that they often lose money but attract profitable real estate development. As such, they act as foci of urban sprawl in many exurban and rural settings, including municipalities where such suburban or estate-type housing on its own is prohibited.

Within the actual facility space, various environmental costs are incurred. First, golf course design in the latter half of the twentieth century has largely adhered to a 'scorched earth' philosophy that eradicates and restructures the natural topography, soil, hydrology and biology of the site to meet the alleged needs of the game (Pleumarom, 1992). Second, golf courses require a large amount of water, especially to maintain ideal turf conditions. The turf on an 18-hole course in Thailand uses up to 6500 cubic metres per day, which Pleumarom (2002) describes as sufficient to meet the needs of 60000 villagers. Third, conventional golf courses require enormous inputs of pesticides and fertilizers, which can, among other impacts, contribute to groundwater contamination. Japanese golf courses were estimated to use two tonnes of pesticides per year in the early 1990s, one-third of which is dispersed in the air and 14 per cent of which adheres to or is absorbed by trees and plants (Pleumarom, 1992). Other environmental impacts include the introduction of exotic landscaping species such as Bermuda grass and palms and the suppression or control of wildlife that interferes with golfers.

In the more developed countries, sociocultural impacts from golf are indirect and include opposition to sprawl and the loss of agricultural land. Direct sociocultural costs are more likely to occur in less developed regions such as rural Thailand, where golf course development has been associated with the forced displacement of local residents, land inflation and illness from acute chemical poisoning (Pleumarom, 1992, 2002).

6.6.2 Sustainability initiatives

A movement toward 'green', 'minimalist' or 'naturalistic' facilities is well articulated within the golf industry. One underlying factor is the negative publicity associated with the proliferation and environmentally unfriendly operation of golf courses, especially in countries such as Japan and Thailand (Pleumarom, 1992). Another reason is the potential for a less energy-intensive golf course to provide substantial cost savings through reduced water, pesticide, fertilizer and fossil fuel use. Third, there is growing awareness that naturalized courses can offer golfers an attractive and challenging game, while differentiating an otherwise unremarkable golf course as a unique attraction imbued with its own sense of place. As a result, North American bodies such as the United States Golf Association (USGA*), the Golf Course Superintendents Association of America (GCSAA) and the American Society of Golf Course Architects are all engaged in such initiatives (Terman, 1997), along with the Audubon Cooperative Sanctuary Programme*. European advocacy groups such as the European Golf Association (EGA*) are similarly engaged, with the EGA Ecology Unit serving since 1994 as an information clearing house, drafter of good practice guidelines and disseminator of information and education to operators of member courses. Its successor, the Committed to Green Foundation, operates an accreditation scheme for golf courses that fulfil stipulated sustainability-related criteria (see Section 7.4.5).

There is at present no precise definition of a 'naturalistic' golf course and often such credentials are claimed solely on the basis of reduced energy inputs that serve primarily to improve the profitability of the course. At the other end of the continuum, a small number of courses from their inception have adopted a holistic approach in which sustainable practices pervade all aspects of design and operation. As outlined by Dodson (2000) and the websites of the above-mentioned organizations, these courses retain most of their area in native vegetation and are constructed in harmony with the natural contours and hydrology of the site. Measures are also taken to attract and sustain native wildlife. Terman (1997) describes the Prairie Dunes Country Club in Kansas (USA), where 75 per cent of the course is covered with native prairie vegetation, as a good example of a naturalized golf course and one with a demonstrated capacity to sustain a substantial number of native bird species.

Situation and site considerations

The issue of golf course sustainability, however, must also take into account external factors. The ability to sustain viable wildlife populations, for example, probably depends in large part on the proximity of the course to a higher order protected area. In such a case, the course is more likely to serve as a population 'sink' (or spillover area) that attracts animals from the protected area population 'source', where most reproduction occurs. They may simultaneously serve as buffer zones between the protected area and heavily built environments (Terman, 1997), while contiguously situated golf courses (a common feature of golfscapes) are likely to be more effective as wildlife habitat corridors than isolated facilities.

Finally, the question as to whether a golf course represents a sustainable land use depends in part on how the site was formerly used. An environmentally friendly golf course constructed within a fragile and relatively undisturbed natural area will be widely regarded as an unsustainable intrusion. However, the same golf course constructed on a disused quarry or landfill site is likely to be regarded as a good demonstration of enhancement sustainability. This is illustrated by the Old Works* facility in Anaconda, Montana (USA), which was built on the site of an old copper smelter.

6.7 Summary

The core experience of recreational tourism involves visits to attractions, which from an industry perspective can be divided into natural and built sites or events. Focusing on selected attributes of these attractions, such as ownership and orientation, spatial configuration and situation, authenticity and image, scarcity and status, carrying capacity and accessibility and market, can assist in assessing the opportunities and threats associated with the attainment of environmental, economic and sociocultural sustainability and the parameters of sustainable practice. The relevant indicators and indicator thresholds of a ubiquitous, privately owned, nodal attraction catering to a generic market, for example, would be different than those of a unique, publicly owned, linear attraction catering to a niche market.

Theme parks, casinos, ski resorts and golf courses are four types of specialized built attraction that are prominent within the private sector tourism industry. The eclectic nature of this selection, however, and of attractions more generally, complicates any attempt to identify common sustainability-related patterns. Theme park operators, for example, tend to prefer exurban locations, which have implications for contiguous urban sprawl. Ski resorts, in contrast, require specialized alpine settings that are highly susceptible to environmental degeneration from intensive recreational activity. Casinos in the USA have proliferated on Indian Reservations, a special kind of geopolitical entity and also on the banks of major rivers. In terms of product growth, the proliferation of golf courses contrasts with the maturing and consolidation of ski resorts, while market saturation in the casino industry is increasing the reliance on local customers. With regard to critique, environmental impacts are emphasized in the ski resort and golf course literature, reflecting the energy and land-intensive nature of these attractions and their association with residential development. Cultural and social impacts, in contrast, are emphasized in the theme park and casino literature respectively. Research into community attitudes toward specific types of attractions is focused mostly on casinos and this research reflects the broader tourism literature in finding that local residents tend to associate these facilities with economic benefits but social costs.

In terms of sustainability initiatives, the broader picture in each sector, and in the theme park industry in particular, is obscured by the highly publicized efforts of a few corporate leaders such as Disney and the Aspen Ski Company. This is similar to the situation in several of the facilitating sectors, as discussed in the previous chapter. Also similar is the impression that the sustainability effort, formally endorsed by all the relevant major industry organizations, is concentrated in more superficial areas such as recycling and energy input reductions that are relatively inexpensive to implement but effective in terms of cost recovery and positive public relations outcomes. The casino industry is unique in that its sustainability efforts are focused on the specific and specialized problem of identifying, managing and preventing the expansion of the problem gambler segment. 'Deep' sustainability practices that might affect profitability or customer satisfaction appear to be the exception in all four sectors. Ultimately, the featured sectors, each taken as a whole, adopt a weak and minimalist approach to sustainability, not only as reflected in their sustainability-related practices, but also in the lack of any apparent opposition to the basic premise of continued expansion. Thus, there is some willingness to pursue low risk measures that benefit the local environment and community, but no debate as to whether it might be inappropriate or unsustainable for additional golf courses, theme parks, ski resorts or casinos to be introduced into these settings in the first place. To the contrary, such expansion is usually touted as a vehicle for achieving economic sustainability through the generation of revenues and employment. It is not yet clear whether this pattern indicates a lack of desire to pursue a deeper green path, or simply the early stages of such an effort.

On the net

AGA (American Gaming Association)
http://www.americangaming.org/

Aspen Skiing Company
http://www.aspensnowmass.com/environment/default.cfm?var=1&hasFlash=1

Audubon Cooperative Sanctuary Programme
http://www.audubonintl.org/programmes/acss/golf.htm

Disney environmental initiatives
http://disney.go.com/disneyhand/environmentality/

EGA (European Golf Association) Ecology Unit
http://www.golfecology.com/

IAAPA (International Association of Amusement Parks and Attractions) annual report
http://www.iaapa.org/annualreport.htm

National Coalition Against Legalized Gambling
http://www.ncalg.org

NSAA (The National Ski Areas Association)
http://www.nsaa.org/nsaa2002/_home.asp

Old Works golf course (Montana)
http://www.oldworks.org/

USGA (United States Golf Association) 'Green Section'
http://www.usga.org/green/index.html

For further reading

Dodson, R. (2000). *Managing Wildlife Habitat on Golf Courses*. Ann Arbor Press.
The purpose of Dodson's book is to provide a foundation for managing golf courses as wildlife habitat within a framework of golfer satisfaction and financial viability. Habitat and wildlife management

concepts are examined and much practical advice is provided along with illustrative case studies from the USA.

Fjellman, S. (1992). *Vinyl Leaves: Walt Disney World and America*. Westview Press.
Although dated, this is still one of the most insightful and thorough books written about Disney World, including its formation, management, infrastructure and its effects on the surrounding environment and community.

Hudson, S. (2000). *Snow Business: A Study of the International Ski Industry*. Cassell.
This book offers a detailed description of the international ski business, which has been neglected by tourism academics. Topics include markets, distribution channels, ski resorts, environmental impacts and sustainability strategies.

Lew, A. and Van Otten, G. (eds) (1998). *Tourism and Gaming on American Indian Lands*. Cognizant.
The 15 chapters of this edited volume critically explore the sustainability of gambling activity on American Indian Reservations from both an economic and sociocultural perspective, and within a tourism framework.

Beyond the book

1. (a) Select a major tourist attraction of your choice and assess its status relative to the attributes described in Section 6.2.2. (b) Write a report indicating how each of these assessments can both positively and negatively influence the environmental and sociocultural sustainability of this attraction.
2. The concept of 'authenticity' is highly contentious. Imagine an Aboriginal community that lives in trailer park poverty at the edge of a central Australian city removed from the tourist gaze, but presents only its traditional pre-European culture (i.e. rituals, lifestyle) to tourists in a 'culture centre' on the other side of the town. (a) Is this an 'authentic' tourist attraction? Why or why not? (b) How should the 'culture' of this community be presented so that it is socioculturally sustainable? (c) Would it be compatible and desirable for this community to operate a casino?
3. Download the AGA *Code of Conduct for Responsible Gaming* (see AGA 2003b in References). (a) Does the code, if enforced, provide an acceptable basis for arguing that the US casino industry is seriously pursuing sociocultural sustainability? (b) Prepare a list of ten indicators, four of them related explicitly to tourism, which would allow adherence to the Code to be quantified.
4. Download the 2003 edition of the NSAA Sustainable Slopes report at http://www.nsaa. org/nsaa2002/environ_charter/ss_annual_2003.pdf . Prepare a report which indicates the extent to which this indicates (a) genuine and meaningful initiatives toward sustainable tourism and (b) an exercise in greenwashing.

On the ground: Disney defeated at the third battle of Manassas, Virginia

In 1993, the Walt Disney Company announced plans to build a $625 million, 1215-hectare American heritage theme park ('Disney's America') in Prince William County, Virginia, not far from Manassas National Battlefield Park, the site of two major Civil War battles during the early 1860s. Given the great success of its Disney World operations in Florida, its aggressive expansion into Europe, emphasis on an historical theme and strong support from the local business community and government (including a $163 million incentive package from the Commonwealth of Virginia on terms favourable to Disney), the movement by Disney into the historical and rapidly expanding western exurbs of Washington seemed both logical and desirable. Yet, less than 1 year later, the project was cancelled (Hawkins and Cunningham, 1996).

Disney gathered support for the project during late 1993 and early 1994 by meeting with over 10 000 people representing over 200 organizations and by launching a community outreach campaign. Local business leaders regarded the project as a much needed boost to the local tourism industry and economy more generally and were strongly supportive. Among the alleged benefits was the creation of 2700 permanent jobs at the expected time of opening in 1998, as many as 19 000 by 2007 (the date of completion) and almost $29 million in annual tax revenue by 2010 (Hawkins and Cunningham, 1996).

Despite the apparent inevitability of the project, opposition emerged early in the process and grew steadily. The great secrecy with which Disney assembled its property and planned its proposal was a major factor that spawned broad public suspicion and resentment (Zenzen, 1998). A second factor was the concern over the impacts the theme park would have on urban sprawl and traffic congestion, given the projection of 6.3 million visitors a year. Moreover, 2300 homes, 1300 hotel rooms, a 27-hole public golf course and 185 000 square metres of commercial space would accompany the theme park. A third argument was the deleterious effect that the theme park would have on the Manassas battlefield, which had been periodically subject to a variety of local developmental pressures that threatened its historical and aesthetic integrity (Zenzen, 1998). An adjunct of this argument was the concern that Disney would sanitize, commercialize or otherwise 'imagineer' the historical record as it has done in many of its other facilities (Schaffer, 1996). The offer of public money to Disney and the possibility of increased taxes to offset these concessions was a fourth major area of concern. Other cited problems included its likely effect on local water and air quality and the allegation that most jobs would be low wage and seasonal (Hawkins and Cunningham, 1996).

Gradually, but unexpectedly for Disney, a well-organized and funded coalition of at least 20 local and national organizations, seasoned and inspired by earlier efforts to oppose threats to the battlefield (Zenzen, 1998), emerged to oppose the project. Despite a variety of Disney pledges (e.g. donations to historical preservation groups and the battlefield, build an area visitors centre, commit to environmentally sustainable practices, etc.) and the formation of an advocacy group to support the theme park and counter the arguments of the opponents, the opposition continued to increase. In late September 1994, the project was cancelled because of the damage to the corporation's image from the cumulative negative publicity. Hawkins and Cunningham (1996) argue that the opposition could have been minimized if its 'backroom' approach and arrogance (which worked in Orlando) had been abandoned in favour of transparency and the involvement of a wide spectrum of local residents from the earliest stages of the planning process.

Exercise

1. (a) Do you believe that the Disney theme park proposal for Prince William County was sustainable? (b) Why or why not? (c) How could this project have been made more sustainable? Use the attraction attributes listed in Section 6.2.2 to organize this exercise and consult the online book by J. Zenzen cited in the References.

Chapter 7
Quality control

Chapter objectives

Upon completion of this chapter, the reader should be able to:

- explain the role and importance of quality control in attaining environmental and sociocultural sustainability within the conventional tourism industry
- describe and differentiate the various levels of quality control in tourism
- discuss and compare the positive and negative aspects of codes of conduct, awards and certification-based ecolabel programmes in sustainable tourism
- explain the difference and relation between certification and accreditation
- present and assess examples of best practice quality control in sustainable tourism, especially at the certification and accreditation level and
- assess the factors that increase the likelihood that a quality control initiative in tourism will succeed as a mechanism for fostering sustainable tourism development.

7.1 Introduction

As described in the previous two chapters, the conventional tourism industry, by and large, has formally recognized through its constituent organizations a desire to pursue an environmentally and socioculturally sustainable path of development. The actual extent of this pursuit, however, is a matter of debate, given that most initiatives appear to be of the superficial or 'weak' variety and/or are exemplified by a relatively small number of industry leaders, such as British Airways and the Aspen Ski Company. However far the actual effort within the industry has proceeded, a critical component in achieving sustainability is the implementation of and adherence to quality control mechanisms that guide the process and demonstrate adherence to relevant principles and practices, thereby differentiating the product from those not adhering to these mechanisms. This chapter critically examines the 'state of the art' in sustainable tourism quality control within the conventional tourism industry in particular. The first section discusses the concept and gradations of quality control and its importance within the field of sustainable tourism. Codes of conduct are considered in Section 7.3 and this is followed in Section 7.4 by an examination of ecolabelling schemes associated with certification. Sustainable tourism awards, an intermediate mechanism, are discussed in Section 7.5. The progress of the tourism industry in each of these mechanisms is assessed, along with their strengths and weaknesses as well as the factors that appear to increase the probability of their successful application.

7.2 Quality control

The managers of many tourism-related companies, products and sectors claim to be acting in an environmentally and/or socioculturally sustainable manner and may cite policy statements to that effect as well as anecdotal examples of their exemplary practice. However, a deep green tourist or a government regulator trying to judge for themselves whether this really is the case should ideally have access to mechanisms that indicate, through external recognition or other means, the quality and credibility of the company's sustainability performance. Indeed, the company itself will also usually require such mechanisms to guide its own pursuit of sustainable tourism.

7.2.1 Quality control spectrum

Quality control mechanisms in sustainable tourism are positioned along a continuum ranging from those that are internal and voluntary to those that are increasingly external and obligatory. At the latter extreme of the spectrum are the government laws and regulations that deal for example with waste disposal and noise restrictions, architectural controls, minimum wage and worker benefit regulations and zoning bylaws. The pursuit of sustainable tourism may be assisted by the obligatory nature and external enforcement of such regulations and laws, but also hindered by the fact that the latter are seldom promulgated as part of an integrated and formal programme of achieving sustainable tourism outcomes in cooperation with tourism stakeholder groups. These laws therefore may be either excessive or inadequate in this respect.

The weakest mechanisms in the internal and voluntary end of the spectrum are the above-mentioned statements of policy (usually a vague reference to the environment and/or society in a corporate mission statement) and citations of good practice by the company itself, which provide scant basis for objective assessment. The spectrum continues to codes of conduct and more rigorously to ecolabelling schemes that involve certification. Award schemes constitute an intermediate mechanism.

7.3 Codes of conduct

A code of conduct (also often called codes of ethics) may be defined as a set of guidelines that aims to influence the attitudes and behaviour of those claiming adherence to it. The formulation of such codes was a distinctive feature of the early years of sustainable tourism (UNEP, 1995; MacLellan, 1997) and is related to the call during the Rio Earth Summit in 1992 for various industries to begin the engagement with sustainable development in this way. By the mid-1990s, there were enough sustainable tourism codes in existence to warrant a survey by Genot (1995), who found that they fell into three categories, i.e. those intended for tourists (see Section 10.4.1), host communities, or the tourism industry. The industry-oriented codes include ones that are intended for all facets of the tourism industry (such as the APEC/PATA Environmental Code for Sustainable Tourism depicted in Figure 7.1), those that are sector-specific (e.g. The NSAA Environmental Charter for Ski Areas*) and those that are unique to a particular company.

This code urges PATA Association and Chapter members and APEC Member Economies to:

Conserve the natural environment, ecosystems and biodiversity

- *contribute* to the conservation of any habitat of flora and fauna, affected by tourism
- *encourage* relevant authorities to identify areas worthy of conservation and to determine the level of development, if any, which would be compatible in or adjacent to those areas
- *include* enhancement and corrective actions at tourism sites to conserve wildlife and natural ecosystems.

Respect and support local traditions, cultures and communities

- *ensure* that community attitudes, local customs and cultural values and the role of women and children, are understood in the planning and implementation of all tourism related projects
- *provide* opportunities for the wider community to take part in discussions on tourism planning issues where these affect the tourism industry and the community
- *encourage* relevant authorities to identify cultural heritage worthy of conservation and to determine the level of development if any which would be compatible in or adjacent to those areas
- *contribute* to the identity and pride of local communities through providing quality tourism products and services sensitive to those communities.

Maintain environmental management systems

- *ensure* that environmental assessment is an integral step in planning for a tourism project
- *encourage* regular environmental audits of practices throughout the tourism industry and promote desirable changes to those practices
- *establish* detailed environmental policies and indicators and/or guidelines for the various sectors of the tourism industry
- *incorporate* environmentally sensitive design and construction solutions in any building or landscaping for tourism purposes.

Conserve and reduce energy, waste and pollutants

- *foster* environmentally responsible practices for:
  - reducing pollutants and greenhouse gases
  - conserving water and protecting water quality
  - managing efficiently waste and energy
  - controlling noise levels and
  - promoting the use of recyclable and biodegradable materials.

Encourage a tourism commitment to environments and cultures

- *encourage* those involved in tourism to comply with local, regional and national planning policies and to participate in the planning process
- *foster*, in both management and staff of all tourism projects and activities, an awareness of environmental and cultural values
- *encourage* all those who provide services to tourism enterprises to participate through environmentally and socially responsible actions
- *support* environmental and cultural awareness through tourism marketing.

Educate and inform others about local environments and cultures

- *support* the inclusion of environmental and cultural values in tourism education, training and planning
- *enhance* the appreciation and understanding by tourists of natural environments and cultural sensitivities through the provision of accurate information and appropriate interpretation
- *encourage* and support research on the environmental and cultural impacts of tourism.

Cooperate with others to sustain environments and cultures

- *cooperate* with other individuals and organizations to advance environmental improvements and sustainable development practices, including establishing indicators and monitoring
- *comply* with all international conventions and national, state and local laws which safeguard natural environments and cultural sensitivities.

Figure 7.1
APEC/PATA Environmental Code for Sustainable Tourism. Source: APEC/PATA, 2002.

7.3.1 Characteristics

Genot (1995) contends that the great majority of sustainable tourism codes have in common an expressed commitment to protect the integrity of the natural environment and relevant cultures and an expressed responsibility to take actions to achieve this through environmentally and socioculturally sound planning and management informed by consultation with relevant stakeholder groups. With regard to structure, codes tend to offer general directives rather than specific objectives. For example, the APEC/PATA Code cites the need to 'contribute to the conservation of any habitat of flora and fauna, affected by tourism' but does not say how to achieve this. Second, they do not provide timelines or other indication as to when the directives should be achieved. Third, they are almost always based on the principle of voluntary adherence, as evidenced by the frequent use of conditional terms such as 'encourage', 'urge', 'should', etc. Finally, codes of conduct are usually predicated on the principle of self-regulation, so that the member company is responsible for ensuring its own compliance. The organization under whose auspices the code is issued (e.g. PATA, WTTC, IHEI, etc.), in addition, is implicitly or explicitly responsible for taking some kind of action, such as consultation, reprimand or (in very extreme cases) expulsion, against any member company or individual who is found to be in wilful, serious and/or repeated violation of one or more guidelines.

7.3.2 Weaknesses

All four of these structural characteristics have been cited as major weaknesses that restrict the effectiveness of codes of conduct as quality control mechanisms. Thus, the lack of specific objectives or any timelines to achieve these means that there is no pressure to move expeditiously beyond vague actions. Moreover, vague directives are open to interpretation (e.g. what is a 'quality tourism product' as per the seventh clause of the APEC/PATA Code?). Voluntary adherence allows member companies to pursue these directives at their pleasure and possibly to withdraw if adherence becomes inconvenient or costly. Self-regulation, or internally monitored compliance, appears to provide little reassurance that the company or organization will critically assess its own performance and take appropriate remedial or disciplinary action if necessary. In essence, codes of conduct seem therefore to have little or no power. Yet, the very act of their creation can be presented to the public as an accomplishment in itself, while unscrupulous companies can put this forward as (false) evidence of their green credentials, even though all they sometimes do is restate what is already required by law (Mason and Mowforth, 1996). Adding to this more cynical perspective is the lack of evidence that existing codes of conduct are being monitored and enforced.

Cynicism may also arise when a proviso or disclaimer that appears to undermine the intent of the guidelines qualifies a code of conduct. For example, the CERES Principles, which are supported by American Airlines (see Section 5.5.1), contain a disclaimer that states, among other things, that 'these principles are not intended to create new legal liabilities, expand existing rights or obligations, waive legal defenses, or otherwise affect the legal position of any endorsing company, and are not intended to be used against an endorser in any legal proceeding for any purpose' (American Airlines, 2001, p. 36).

7.3.3 Strengths

There are several strong rationales for codes of conduct that counterbalance the above criticisms, giving credence to Genot's (1995) observation that these codes are neither a panacea nor a soft option. First, codes of conduct are not costly to develop in terms of time or money. Second, the directives are usually easily understood and non-controversial and provide the basis for dialogue and common ground among those who adhere to the code. They are therefore suitable for stakeholders adopting a minimalist approach toward sustainable tourism. Third, the use of general directives is warranted because of the membership diversity of organizations such as the WTTC and PATA, which precludes the citation of specific objectives and timelines that are applicable to all members. Fourth, these general directives provide the basis for the identification of relevant sustainable tourism indicators, from which different members will identify different thresholds.

A 'carrot' rather than 'stick' approach

Fifth, the voluntary and internally regulated nature of codes of conduct – i.e. their non-threatening and minimalist character – makes it far more likely that organization members will sign on and thus commence their engagement with sustainability, hopefully moving toward a more comprehensive approach in the future (see Section 2.5). Bendell and Font (2004) argue that codes of conduct provide a basis for moving towards higher levels of quality control, as the general directives gradually evolve into specific indicators that can be measured and monitored as part of a certification scheme (see below).

Moral suasion

A sixth factor involves the issue of moral suasion. Members are morally and ethically, if not legally, obligated to adhere to codes promulgated by their parent organization. Any lack of adherence, therefore, could potentially result in negative publicity and loss of face for the negligent company. Ryan (2002) describes codes as 'symbols of aspiration' and states that 'those making the statements can be called to account if no progress towards these aims are made' (p. 19).

Pre-emption of external and obligatory regulation

Finally, critics of self-regulation may be ignoring the possibility that government will step in and increase its own (external and obligatory) regulations if industry does not regulate itself in a responsible and credible manner. The potential loss of power over its own affairs is therefore an enormous incentive to adhere to codes of conduct as well as higher forms of internal and voluntary quality control (Mason and Mowforth, 1996).

7.3.4 Elements of success

Based on the above discussion, codes of conduct are more likely to be successful where the individual guidelines or clauses are understandable, reasonable and not too numerous, but also relevant to the ethic of sustainable tourism. The sponsor of the code should also make available examples of tangible practices and objectives that operate the general directives contained in the individual guidelines or clauses.

Moreover, mechanisms should be in place for the sponsor to deal quickly and effectively with members who are violating or neglecting parts of the code and to correct these situations before they escalate into a pattern of serious and repeated violation or neglect that may be imitated by other members. These interventions should be internal at first, but exposed to the public if necessary. Effective self-regulation and the concomitant willingness of the sponsor to use moral suasion on its members and to make this public if necessary, is thus probably the key element to a successful code of conduct, with the first two elements serving to make such violations or neglect less likely.

7.4 Ecolabels

Ecolabels are defined by Font (2001) as 'methods to standardize the promotion of environmental claims by following compliance to set criteria, generally based on third party, impartial verification' (p. 3). As such, they are a type of marketing tool that in principle improves substantially on codes of conduct and awards by providing concise and accurate information indicating that the management and operation of the ecolabelled product is compatible with the principles of environmentally (and sometimes socioculturally) sustainable tourism. These set criteria are directly related to the indicators that were discussed and critiqued in Section 2.6.

Ecolabels are predicated first on the concept of *certification*, which Buckley (2002a) defines as 'a formal process under which a nominally independent body certifies to other interested parties, such as tourists, marketing agencies and regulators, that a tourism provider complies with a specified standard' (p. 179), usually one related to the natural environment. Effective ecolabels in turn require *accreditation*, which is 'a process by which an association or agency evaluates and recognizes a programme of study or an institution [or a certified tourism product] as meeting certain predetermined standards or qualifications' (Morrison et al., 1992, p. 33). These accreditation bodies, which are independent of the certifying agencies, essentially certify the certification schemes (Buckley, 2002a). Certification and accreditation are both clearly relevant to consumers, and green consumers in particular, who wish to make informed purchasing decisions in a service sector environment such as tourism where it is extremely difficult to inspect the product in advance (Royal and Jago, 1998). Ecolabels are also relevant to governments wanting to assess whether the industry can be trusted to regulate some aspects of its own environmental performance in a responsible manner. Hence, 'they are one of the many voluntary instruments that can provide an effective complement to formal regulation by national authorities' (de Larderel, 2001, p. xv).

The growth in the number of tourism ecolabels has paralleled the expanding interest in the sustainable tourism field more generally by tourism and non-tourism institutions, as discussed in Chapter 1. As of 2000, there were between 70 and 100 ecolabelling schemes worldwide, depending on how these are defined (Font and Buckley, 2001; Honey and Rome, 2001), compared with just three in 1988 and approximately 25 in 1992 (Spittler and Haak, 2001). These include those awarded to destinations as well as to tourism products, either for tourism as a whole or by specific sectors such as tour operators or attractions. Ecolabels can also be classified as to whether they apply only to a particular region or country, or to the world as a whole (Buckley, 2001), while an additional classification criterion is whether the eco-label is a single uniform entity or one that is multi-tiered (e.g. provides basic and advanced levels of certification).

7.4.1 Industry incentives for participation

A primary reason for the tourism industry to seek affiliation and certification with ecolabels is to demonstrate external recognition for their sustainability practices and accomplishments (such as those described in Chapters 5 and 6) and to underscore the validity of the claims that they make in this regard. Through the credibility this provides, they are more likely to generate positive publicity that translates into increased business from green consumers, leverage to charge a premium price and a reduced likelihood of government intervention. In addition, the sponsors of ecola-belling schemes often provide advice and assistance to members so that they can meet ecolabel criteria, which is especially important for small and medium-sized businesses that lack the economies of scale to do this on their own (see Section 3.12.2). Participation in ecolabelling also provides opportunities for networking with other member organizations.

7.4.2 Anatomy of ecolabelling schemes

Figure 7.2 depicts the generic structure of ecolabelling schemes in the tourism industry. Non-governmental organizations and government agencies are far more involved as *funding bodies* than tourism industry organizations or companies, because of the credibility that is conferred by third party supervision and because the mandate of such groups often focuses on furthering the attainment of broader social goals such as sustainability. According to Font (2001), the *awarding body* may be a functional arm of the funding body in smaller ecolabels, but often an independent third party entity in larger ones. The awarding body promotes the award to the *tourism market* and potential *applicants*, receives applications from the latter (usually for a fee that may take into account the size of the applicant) and works with an accredited *verifying body* to develop operational criteria on which to base certification and the awarding of the ecolabel. The verifying body receives and analyses evidence from the applicants so that its recommendations can go forward to the awarding body. Once an applicant has been provided with the ecolabel, certification often becomes an important part of promotional efforts aimed at the tourist market.

7.4.3 Attributes of success

A successful ecolabel is one that is widely recognized and patronized by consumers and other stakeholders, thereby conferring the bearer with a competitive advantage over rival products that do not possess the ecolabel. Font and Buckley (2001) empha-size that ecolabelling schemes are far more common in central and northern Europe than North America, indicating perhaps a higher portion of consumers who are aware of and respond to the possession of ecolabels. However, Buckley (2002b) argues that *global* visibility or brand recognition is essential in the long term because of the spatial disconnect between market and product and the increasingly global-ized nature of the tourism industry. Recognition is in part the outcome of effective

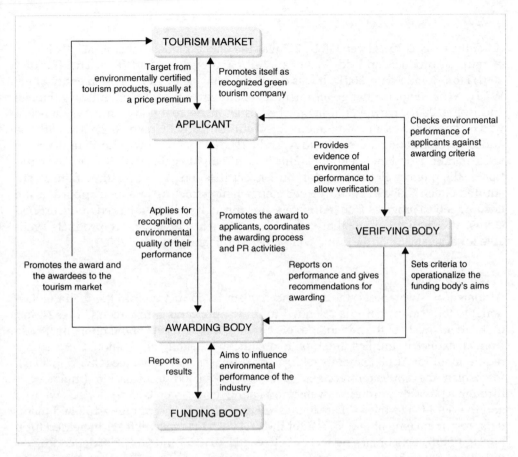

Figure 7.2
The players in tourism ecolabels. Source: Font and Buckley (2001). Tourism ecolabelling: Certification and promotion of sustainable management. CABI Publishing. Reproduced with permission.

logo design and promotion, but mainly derives from the reputability of the funding and accredited certification bodies as they establish and monitor transparent and understandable indicator criteria and, on this basis, make equitable and timely decisions to confer or not confer the ecolabel (Buckley, 2001). Buckley (2002b) is more picturesque in suggesting that a successful ecolabel must have sufficient 'guts', or the substantive criteria that distinguishes products with the ecolabel from those who do not have it, as well as 'teeth', or procedures that ensure the use of the ecolabel only where it is warranted.

Other important criteria include endorsement of the ecolabel by government, consumer advocacy groups and high profile environmental and industry organizations (such as those described in Chapter 1) and the establishment of a multi-tiered ecolabelling structure that distinguishes high achievers while making provision for other applicants to join at a minimalist level (Buckley, 2002b). A global ecolabel should also be flexible in assigning different indicators and benchmarks to different products and regions, as circumstances warrant. To increase its visibility, an ecolabel should be possessed by a relatively large number of companies and/or products.

7.4.4 Green Globe 21

As of the early 2000s, Green Globe 21* was the only ecolabel that embraced all types of tourism products and destinations in all parts of the world (Font and Buckley, 2001; Honey and Rome, 2001). It was originally established in 1994 as an entity of the WTTC to pre-empt further government regulation over the tourism industry (Honey and Rome, 2001). However, it languished as an ineffectual body until 1999 when it was reconstituted as an autonomous for-profit company ('Green Globe 21', with the added '21' indicating adherence to Agenda 21) that placed new-found emphasis on strict standards and independent audits in an attempt to gain credibility and recognition as the premier global body for tourism certification. A core feature of the reconstituted Green Globe 21 is a three-tier membership structure in which applicants are encouraged to progress from Affiliate status through to Benchmarked and Certified status, after indicating whether they want to have just one or more products available for assessment, or the entire company (Griffin and DeLacey, 2002).

Affiliated status

Affiliated or 'Awareness' status is a mechanism for induction into the realm of sustainable tourism in that it is intended to draw applicants into Green Globe 21 and make them aware of the advantages of pursuing higher levels of membership. Aside from an explicit or implicit intention to operate in a sustainable fashion, there is little requirement for Affiliate membership aside from a small annual fee (US$75 in 2003), for which the applicant receives sustainability-related information (much of it through a password-protected website), a listing on the main Green Globe 21 website and the right to use the Affiliate logo (see Figure 7.3). To discourage Affiliated members from remaining at that level after the first year, the renewal fee is increased to 50 per cent of the Benchmarking fee, or between US$112.50 and US$3000 depending on the size of the company.

Benchmarked status

The complexity of the tourism system is initially taken into account through the establishment of different 'Standards' for companies, communities and protected areas. To obtain Benchmarked status within the 'Company Standard', an applicant must maintain a 'Baseline Level' of performance on a selection of indicators specific to the sector

Certified	Benchmarked	Affiliate

Figure 7.3
Green Globe 21 logos. Reproduced with permission of Green Globe 21.

to which the applicant belongs. Twenty-two company-related sectors have been identified as of 2003 (i.e. accommodation, administration office, aerial cableway, airline,
airport, bus company, car hire, convention centre, cruise vessel, ecotourism, exhibition
hall, farmstay, golf course, marina, railway, resort, restaurant, tour company (whole-
saler), tour operator (inbound), trailer park, vineyard and visitor centre). Successful
applicants must also meet the Baseline Level on nine generic indicators that are linked
to 'Key Performance Areas' and specific sustainability objectives (see Figure 7.4).

Applicants are required to supply Green Globe 21 with evidence (e.g. electricity
bills, water bills, etc.) that the Baseline Levels of performance have been met and
must also provide evidence that the company has in place an 'Environmental and
Social Sustainability Policy' as outlined in Figure 7.5. This Policy includes provision
for reporting the company's performance on the Benchmarking indicators and commitment to making annual improvements in indicator performance. The supplied
information is then analysed by Green Globe 21 to produce a 'Green Globe 21
Benchmarking Assessment Report', upon which basis the Benchmarking status is
granted or denied. If the application is denied, advice is provided as to what needs to
be corrected in order for Benchmarked status to be achieved.

The Benchmarking annual fee is graded, with 'micro' companies of four employees or less (or less than ten rooms for accommodation) paying US$225 and 'large
diversified' companies paying a minimum fee of US$6000. In addition to the Affiliate
benefits and Benchmarking Assessment Report described above, the applicant is
allowed to use the Benchmarked logo (see Figure 7.3) and is promoted on a consumer website that includes e-brochure and e-selling access as these are developed.
Successful applicants are also eligible for Green Globe 21 awards. Benchmarked status must be renewed annually by going through the process described above.

Key performance area	Benchmarking indicator	Objective
Greenhouse gas emissions	Greenhouse gas reduction	Reduce greenhouse gas emissions
Energy efficiency, conservation and management	Energy consumption	Minimize overall energy consumption
Management of fresh water resources	Potable water consumption	Minimize consumption of potable water
Ecosystem conservation and management	Resource conservation	Reduce consumption of natural resources and the impact on ecosystem biodiversity
	Biodiversity conservation	Conserve native habitats and biodiversity
Management of social and cultural issues	Social commitment	Develop and maintain positive, productive and sustainable contributions to the local community
Land-use planning and management	na	na
Air quality protection and noise control	Noise nuisance	Minimize noise disturbance from aircraft
	Air quality	Improve air quality through reducing local emissions from energy production
Wastewater management	Storm water management	High quality of surface water discharged off-site
	Cleaning chemicals used	Reduce chemicals discharged into the environment
Waste minimization, reuse and recycling	Solid waste production	Reduce the amount of solid waste generated

Figure 7.4
Green Globe 21 Benchmarking Key Performance Areas and related indicators. Reproduced
by permission of Green Globe 21.

The organization shall:

1.1 Have a written Environmental and Social Sustainability Policy. The Policy shall be appropriate to the scope of the organization's operations and its environmental and local social footprint with respect to its locations and the nature and scale of its activities and the products and services provided. The policy shall contain a:

    1.1.1 framework for regularly recording measures of the relevant Green Globe 21 Sector Benchmarking Indicators, analysing performance, setting targets and supplying annually to Green Globe 21 the measures of the relevant Green Globe 21 Sector Benchmarking Indicators

    1.1.2 commitment to make appropriate year-on-year improvements in relevant Green Globe 21 Sector Benchmarking Indicators that fall below the Green Globe 21 Best Practice Level and maintain all other impacts at, or better than, the Green Globe 21 Best Practice Level

    1.1.3 commitment to comply with relevant environmental, public and occupational health and safety, hygiene and employment legislation, and other requirements to which the organization is obliged to adhere

    1.1.4 commitment to give special consideration to the employment of persons living in nearby communities, for both construction and operational activities

    1.1.5 commitment to give preference to products and services of local origin which do not adversely affect the organization's operational activities, viability and environmental and social impacts.

1.2 Adopt and promote the Policy at the highest managerial level in the organization.

1.3 Communicate the aims of the Green Globe 21 programme to employees, customers and suppliers of products and services to the organization.

1.4 Make the Policy available on request to all interested parties.

1.5 Review the Policy annually.

Figure 7.5
Green Globe 21 Environmental and Social Sustainability Policy (Company Standard). Reproduced by permission of Green Globe 21.

Certified status

Three criteria must be met to achieve Certified status. First, all the indicator criteria must be benchmarked above the Green Globe 21 Baseline Level. Second, all the requirements of the Company Standard must be met. In addition to the indicators and the Policy, these include a commitment to develop a comprehensive Environmental Management System (see Figure 7.6) and a process of 'Consultation and Communication' that allows 'interested parties' (i.e. shareholders, employees, customers, suppliers, local community, government, etc.) to access the Policy and the company's environmental and social performance. Third, the applicant must gain certification as an outcome of an on-site visit by an accredited independent auditor who investigates whether the Company Standard is being adhered to.

In addition to the benefits of Affiliated and Benchmarked status and the sustainability audit report, certified members gain access to the 'check marked' Green Globe 21 logo (Figure 7.3) and receive 'premier' promotion. Certified status must be renewed annually by meeting all three of the criteria described above. The fee structure is identical to that which is in place for Benchmarked status, but does not include the costs of the third party audit.

Membership patterns

The Green Globe 21 website listed 372 members as of April 2004. A bimodal pattern of membership status is evident, with 117 (31 per cent) being Affiliated and 94 (25 per cent) Certified at that time. Eighty-six (23 per cent) were in the process of

The organization shall:

4.1 Develop, implement and maintain a documented Environmental Management System (EMS) that is appropriate to the scope of the organization's operations and its environmental and local social footprint with respect to its locations and the nature and scale of its activities and the products and services provided.

4.2 Nominate a representative from top management to be responsible for the implementation, on-going performance and outcomes of the Environmental Management System.

4.3 Provide where necessary, training for all staff with key responsibilities for actions within the EMS.

4.4 Monitor performance against the organization's Environmental and Social Sustainability Policy and the relevant Green Globe 21 Sector Benchmarking Indicators; Green Globe 21 Baseline performance; improvement targets; relevant legislation and other requirements and on a regular basis review and document progress.

4.5 Maintain records of legal compliance and conformity to requirements and where these are not achieved take appropriate corrective action to return to compliance and/or meet conformity requirements as soon as practicable and to prevent a recurrence.

4.6 Retain for at least 24 months, appropriate records demonstrating legal compliance and conformance with the requirements of this standard, including those related to key performance areas for confidential intra-industry benchmarking, and evidence supporting the measures of the relevant Green Globe 21 Sector Benchmarking Indicators.

4.7 Regularly undertake a review to determine the adequacy and effectiveness of the organization's policy and EMS in fulfilling the requirements of the Green Globe 21 Company Standard. The findings of this review shall be recorded and any necessary actions be implemented effectively.

Figure 7.6
Green Globe 21 Environmental Management System (Company Standard). Reproduced by permission of Green Globe 21.

Table 7.1
Membership of Green Globe 21 by sector, April 2004

Sector	Number
Accommodation	209
Tour operator (inbound)	60
Administration office	29
Community	9
Farmstay, visitor centre	7
Airport, cruise vessel	5
Car hire, ecotourism, protected area, trailer park	4
Activity, airline, bus company, resort, tour company (wholesaler)	3
Aerial cableway, convention centre, exhibition hall, vineyard	2
Attraction, restaurant	1

becoming Benchmarked, while 43 (12 per cent) already held that status. Thirty-two (9 per cent) were in the process of becoming Certified.

Accommodation, with 209 citations, accounted for over one-half (56 per cent) of the membership, followed by inbound tour operators (60, or 16 per cent) and administration offices (29, or 8 per cent) (see Table 7.1). The fact that indicator criteria have only recently been developed, or are still under development for most sectors helps to account for the dominance of the accommodation sector, though the latter may also reflect the pioneering role played by the accommodation sector in the sustainable tourism arena (see Section 5.6). In contrast, major tourism industry sectors such as outbound tour operators and attractions are barely represented,

Table 7.2
Membership of Green Globe 21 by country, April 2004

Country	Number
New Zealand	125
Jamaica	38
Australia	32
Iceland	21
Egypt	17
Indonesia	12
China	10
Fiji, Sri Lanka	9
United Kingdom	8
Barbados, Netherlands Antilles	7
Aruba, Mauritius	6
Dominican Republic, Mexico	5
Cyprus, India, Saint Lucia	4
Maldives, Portugal, USA, Vietnam	3
Chile, Greece, Malaysia, Switzerland, Turkey	2
Antigua & Barbuda, Bahamas, Cambodia, Canada, Costa Rica, Dominica, French Polynesia, Germany, Grenada, Ireland, Italy, Kenya, Laos, Norway, Palau, Peru, Seychelles, Singapore, Suriname, Turks & Caicos Islands	1

while travel agencies are not represented at all. It should be noted, however, that the approximately 200 accommodation providers with Green Globe credentials represent only an infinitesimal proportion of all such entities, while the two aerial cableways account for a relatively large proportion of that sector.

The Green Globe 21 membership structure is also geographically skewed, with Oceania accounting for 168 members (45 per cent) and the Caribbean for a further 72 (19 per cent) (see Table 7.2), even though these two regions collectively account for only about 4 per cent of all international stayover tourist arrivals. In contrast, the European mainland, North America, South America and Africa (except for Egypt) are drastically under-represented. This imbalance is partly explained by the existence of established regional ecolabels in Europe and by the creation of close strategic partnerships between Green Globe 21 and the Caribbean Alliance for Sustainable Tourism (CAST) and the Australia-based Sustainable Tourism Cooperative Research Centre (STCRC). In addition, the restructuring of the organization was accompanied by the relocation of its head office from London to Australia. The large number of New Zealand members is explained by the decision of the Tourism Industry Association of New Zealand to embrace the Green Globe 21 concept. Lagging numbers in other regions are partly accounted for by the organization's focus on establishing rigorous certification procedures rather than marketing and membership recruitment (personal communication, Green Globe 21 management, April 2004).

Critique

In addition to the geographically and sectorally skewed patterns of membership identified above, Green Globe 21 has been criticized for being overly ambitious and stretched too thin in its attempts, with limited resources, to embrace all tourism products at once in all parts of the world. Griffin and DeLacey (2002) concede the resulting lack of consumer awareness, but cite the web-based Green Globe Travel Planner (see Section 4.5.2) as a mechanism that will gradually overcome this limitation. Problems cited by Honey and Rome (2001) include the lack of clear visual differentiation between the Benchmarked and Certified logos, the continued use and abuse of Green Globe logos awarded prior to the reconstitution of the scheme in 1999 and the lack of any differentiation within each of the three levels of membership, so that an exemplary Certified product is not distinguished from one that barely meets the relevant criteria.

7.4.5 Specialized ecolabels

In contrast to the omnibus and global character of Green Globe 21, most tourism ecolabels are regional and/or restricted to a particular sector or, rarely, a single company. The following sample of four specialized ecolabels indicates their diversity, but is not necessarily representative of the entire array of such schemes. See also the case studies at the end of this chapter and Chapter 11.

Blue Flag

The Blue Flag* ecolabel emerged in 1987 as a Europe-wide programme focused on ensuring the maintenance of high quality beaches and marinas. Operated by the non-profit NGO Foundation for Environmental Education in Europe (FEEE), Blue Flag is widely regarded for its rigorous enforcement of 27 beach criteria and 22 marina criteria subsumed under the four areas of water quality, environmental education and information, environmental management, and safety and services. Most of the criteria are designated as obligatory 'imperatives', while others are designated as 'guidelines' that may or may not be adhered to depending on circumstances. Awarded for a 1-year period, Blue Flag certification within Europe was extended to 2264 beaches and 600 marinas in 2004. Expansion of the programme beyond Europe has been a recent priority of the managers, with trials occurring in the Caribbean and South Africa during the early 2000s. A National Jury, consisting of representatives from relevant government agencies and NGOs within the country where the beach is located, initially assesses applications. Those that are successful at this stage are then forwarded to an International Jury consisting of five representatives from the Foundation for Environmental Education (the parent organization of the FEEE) and one each from UNEP, WTO, the European Union for Coastal Conservation and the European Union, which conducts its own assessment and, on this basis, accepts or rejects the application. The ecolabel can be withdrawn at any time if a Blue Flag beach is found to be violation of any of the imperative criteria.

'Green' Hotels Association

The 'Green' Hotels Association*, a private company founded in 1993, 'encourages, promotes and supports the "greening" of the lodging industry' and does so primarily by providing relevant information and products to its membership. Information sources include a 110-page 'Guidelines and Ideas' booklet and a bimonthly newsletter. Products offered for sale at discounted prices include towel rack hangers and sheet changing cards, as well as energy and water-saving devices such as toilet-tank fill diverters, soap dispensers and recycling baskets. The publicity offered by the Association's website, which purports to average 3500 'hits' per day, is cited as a major advantage of membership.

There appears to be no requirement for membership other than the payment of an annual fee of US$1 for every guestroom, with a minimum and maximum fee of US$100 and US$750 respectively. Most of the 240 members (as of April 2004) are 'Partner' hotels 'committed to conserving water and reducing solid waste', but options are also available for 'Ally' vendors offering appropriate products, 'Educator' faculty and government employees and 'Environmentalist' organizations and associations. While the Houston (Texas)-based Association claims to be international, US hotels and individuals account for more than 80 per cent of the membership. Other representation in 2004 was from Canada (12 members, or 5 per cent), the Caribbean (16), Latin America (5), Europe and Asia (3 each) and Africa (one).

Committed to Green Foundation

The UK-based Committed to Green Foundation* was established in 2000 with the support of the Environment Directorate General of the European Commission as an independent charitable trust 'to promote environmental responsibility and sustainability in sport'. Focused primarily on the golf industry within Europe, the Foundation accredits qualifying golf courses through a process that purports to feature good science, independent standards, stakeholder consultation, transparency and independent auditing. Full Committed to Green certification for a period of 3 years is awarded after an expert third party verifies a submitted 'Environmental Statement' that (a) describes the applicant's performance across an array of basic environmental criteria in eight environmental management categories (e.g. water, waste, education and nature conservation), (b) provides a list of achievements that indicate movement beyond the basic criteria and (c) defines specific goals to be achieved over a stipulated time period. At a national level, a National Expert Panel awarding body that normally consists of representatives from the relevant National Golf Federation, National Greenkeepers' Association, environmental NGOs, the relevant Statutory Environmental Agency and academic institutions supervises the certification programme. As of April 2004, 19 European golf courses were fully accredited, including eight in Scotland, three each in England and Portugal, two in Italy and one each in Denmark, Finland and Sweden. Descriptions of these courses are provided on the Foundation's website.

TUI environmental monitoring of contracted hotels*

The European-based outbound tour operator TUI (see Section 5.4.2) is a rare example of a company that awards its own ecolabel, in this case to hotels with which it is contractually affiliated that meet certain environmental criteria. Contracted hotels and other tourism products have been obligated since 1992 to fill out an annual self-assessed environmental checklist that surveys environmental practices, including those associated with sewage treatment, water conservation, recycling, energy savings, policies on purchasing environmentally friendly products, noise protection measures, use of pesticides, environmental communication and possession of environmental certification credentials. Most of these criteria are confined to a 'yes' or 'no' option and the signature of the hotel manager or representative is required to confirm that the information provided is accurate. According to Font and Buckley (2001), about 200 of 10 000 hotels affiliated with TUI were recognized as exemplars of good environmental management in 1999 and this status is acknowledged on some 30 million TUI brochures to assist potential clients in making 'green' purchasing decisions. Unusually, no actual logo accompanies this recognition.

7.4.6 Weaknesses of tourism ecolabels

A major weakness in tourism ecolabelling in general is the continuing lack of consumer recognition, which reduces the incentive for tourism companies to become involved in such schemes and thus leads to a second major problem of lacklustre corporate participation levels. This lack of recognition and participation (at least outside of parts of Europe) is associated with a combination of factors, including the proliferation of ecolabels, their geographically and topically specialized character, the low profile of most funding and certification bodies and the lack of 'guts and teeth' within most of the schemes. Payment of the designated application fee and a simple 'commitment' to become more sustainable, are often all that is required to obtain an ecolabel, thereby making the latter susceptible to greenwashing. Moreover, a company might obtain an ecolabel on the basis of meeting certain criteria (e.g. recycling and energy reduction) while continuing to engage in activities such as habitat clearance that are harmful to the environment but not included in the criteria inventory. Similarly, laudable environmental practices may disguise unethical social and cultural practices. An additional factor impeding the evolution of ecolabels is that corporate leaders such as British Airways may not feel the need to augment their own internal environmental reputation with external ecolabels.

Ultimately, there is still no widespread belief or convincing evidence that products with ecolabels are demonstrably more sustainable than those without. Green Globe 21 appears to be 'pulling ahead of the pack' through its three-tier award structure that culminates in the third party certification of an array of relevant indicators. However, the actual number of participating companies is still negligible relative to the total potential number of companies and its geographic and sectoral scope may be too ambitious relative to its resources. The scheme therefore has a long way to go before it can be regarded as an effective mechanism for attaining sustainable tourism development within the tourism industry.

The Mohonk Agreement

Arguably the greatest impediment to establishing an effective array of credible ecolabels is the absence of an overriding global accreditation body. To address this shortcoming, the Washington-based Institute of Policy Studies (IPS) convened a meeting of certification bodies and other tourism stakeholders in 2000 to explore just such a possibility. The Mohonk Agreement that emerged from this meeting presented a set of guidelines for establishing certification schemes and proposed the establishment of the Sustainable Tourism Stewardship Council* (STSC), a global sustainable tourism accreditation body modelled on the pattern of the Forest Stewardship Council operated by the Rainforest Alliance (Buckley, 2002a). A subsequent survey of the WTO* membership in late 2002 indicated general support for the STSC, although only 26 NTOs (national tourism organizations) completed the questionnaire and expressed the view that the private sector should bear at least part of the associated financial costs. Responding NTOs were also concerned that tour operators and other private enterprises would perceive a global accreditation scheme as a barrier to trade. In 2003, the committee investigating the feasibility of the STSC recommended the establishment of a regional network of bodies that would facilitate the establishment of a global body by promoting and gaining support for the concept, sharing information and discussing criteria for an international accreditation standard (Font et al., 2003). The first of these regional bodies, the Sustainable Tourism Certification Network of the Americas*, was formalized in late 2003.

7.5 Awards

Awards are similar to ecolabels insofar as they involve funding and awarding bodies that use evaluation and verification procedures to recognize, through logos and messages, tourism products deemed to meet specified standards of sustainable environmental and/or sociocultural performance. However, they differ in being available only to a small number of qualifying applicants that become candidates either by application or nomination, usually without having to pay application or other fees. Awards, moreover, are usually made on an annual or biannual basis, are often distributed in a highly publicized ceremony, have a period of duration that lasts between these ceremonies and often involve prize money. Unlike ecolabels, there is no evidence of any attempts at present to establish a global awards accreditation protocol.

Awards are more likely than ecolabels to include overt corporate participation, as demonstrated by high profile examples such as the British Airways Tourism for Tomorrow Awards* (see below), the TUI International Environmental Award* and Marriott's Green Leaves Awards. The latter is unusual in being restricted to the corporation's internal operations. Industry association programmes include the ASTA Environmental Award* and the IH&RA (International Hotel & Restaurant Association) Annual Environmental Award. This category also includes the Sustainable Tourism Awards scheme of the Travelers Conservation Foundation, which was founded by the United States Tour Operators Association (USTOA) to support the conservation and preservation of selected tourist attractions. A smaller number of awards appears to be associated with non-profit environmental organizations such as Conservation International, which jointly sponsors the World Legacy Awards* with National Geographic Traveler Magazine (see below).

Very little research is available on sustainable tourism awards and hence it is unclear whether such recognition actually reflects good environmental and/or sociocultural practice on the part of recipients or translates into increased business from green travellers and other tourists. A perusal of a convenience sample of award winner websites by the author, however, does indicate that award logos are prominently featured. Font and Tribe (2001) describe awards as good opportunities to recognize and publicize purported industry leaders and role models, but they also contend that awards are concurrently intended to serve as public relations exercises for their sponsors. This strong element of self-interest dilutes their integrity and is evident in the inclusion of sponsor names in the award titles and in high profile presentation ceremonies. It is for this reason, and the added factor that only a limited number of qualifying products can obtain awards, that the latter are positioned below ecolabels within the quality control spectrum.

British Airways Tourism for Tomorrow Awards

Originally established in 1989 by a tour operators organization, the Tourism for Tomorrow Awards were taken over in 1992 by British Airways, which extended eligibility to all types and scales of tourism products. Hence, awards are made each year under multiple categories, including National Parks and Protected Areas, Accommodation, Tourism Organization, Environmental Experience, and Large-Scale Tourism. A 'Highly Commended Award' category is also provided for applicants that demonstrate excellence but do not win in the above categories. The application procedure includes a 1500-word description, subject to verification, in which the applicants explain how their product meets the criteria outlined by the sponsors. Funding for the Awards is provided through industry sponsorship and the winners are flown to London to receive their awards in a high profile televised ceremony. Since 2004, the Awards have been co-sponsored by the WTTC and new efforts have been made to increase further their visibility and prestige.

World Legacy Awards

Like the Tourism for Tomorrow programme, the more recently established World Legacy Awards are application-based and divided into categories (i.e. Nature Travel, Heritage Tourism, General Purpose Hotels and Resorts, Destination Stewardship) that reflect the diversity of the global tourism sector. One winner and one Honorable Mention are awarded in each category, assuming that there are suitable candidates. Applicants are required to write no more than 400 words for each of four criteria, including 'contribution to sustainability', 'local benefits and involvement', 'tourist benefits' and 'leadership in sustainable tourism'. An Award Advisory Committee evaluates applications, identifies finalists and makes recommendations to a Judging Panel of seven tourism and/or conservation experts. Verification includes an on-site visit by one or more members of the Panel. Award winners benefit mainly from extensive media exposure, including coverage in the National Geographic Traveler Magazine. The three winners from the 2002 round all feature their World Legacy Award prominently on their websites. Two of the Honorable Mentions also feature the logo, though there is nothing more to indicate that they were runners-up rather than winners.

7.6 Summary

To determine whether claims of sustainable tourism adherence and attainment within the tourism industry are credible, quality control mechanisms must be available that clearly indicate the nature of relevant achievements to anyone wishing to investigate those claims. Codes of conduct have been adopted by many tourism companies and organizations as one such mechanism, but are regarded as a relatively weak form of quality control because their constituent guidelines for behaviour are vague, non-committal, voluntary and self-regulated. Yet, they should not be dismissed out of hand, since well-constructed codes facilitate in a non-threatening way the initial engagement in sustainability (i.e. a minimalist model). They also provide a common ground for networking and a basis for identifying suitable indicators, they exercise moral suasion over adherents and they help to pre-empt further government regulation if they actually support sustainable outcomes.

Ecolabels, which have proliferated since the early 1990s, can be an effective quality control mechanism if they are subject to accreditation and employ rigorous third party verification procedures to ensure compliance with a carefully selected set of relevant indicators. Subsequently, the use of the ecolabel must be restricted to certified tourism products that are broadly recognized, at least by green tourists, as being superior to uncertified competing products. This recognition allows the product to command a price premium and hence serves as a financial incentive for companies to participate in the ecolabel, as long as its acquisition is not too onerous or expensive a process. Unfortunately, most ecolabels (Blue Flag is a notable regional exception) are neither well prescribed nor well recognized and it is not at all clear that ecolabelled products are adequately differentiated from non-ecolabelled products. The Green Globe 21 eco-label demonstrates the weaknesses as well as strengths of contemporary tourism eco-labels. The latter includes a three-tier membership structure that allows participants to move gradually toward the culminating 'Certified' status, which appears to involve rigorous verification procedures. Consumer recognition remains weak, however, and membership is both geographically skewed and representative of only a minute fraction of the global tourism industry. Green Globe 21 therefore does not presently contribute substantially to the attainment of global tourism sustainability, but has the potential to do so. The proposed establishment of the Sustainable Tourism Steward-ship Council, a global accreditation body, represents a major development in the evolution of a credible international network of sustainable tourism certification schemes.

Awards occupy an intermediate position between codes of conduct and ecolabels. Their exclusive nature (i.e. conclusions about sustainability can only be drawn about the small number of awardees), along with their close association with corporate/industry sponsors, limits their effectiveness. However, pending further research into the issue, it may be that this same exclusivity confers more prestige than the possession of an ecolabel, prompting winners to feature such awards more prominently on their websites as compared with the possessors of ecolabels and leading to greater consumer recognition. It may therefore be logical to restructure ecolabels by incorporating an award element that confers these advantages.

On the net

ASTA Environmental Award
http://www.astanet.com/about/environmentalawards.asp

Blue Flag
http://www.blueflag.org/

British Airways Tourism for Tomorrow Awards
http://www.britishairways.com/travel/crt4t/public/en_gb

Certification in Sustainable Tourism Programme (Costa Rica)
http://www.turismo-sostenible.co.cr/EN/home.shtml

Committed to Green Foundation
http://www.committedtogreen.org/index.html

Green Globe 21
http://www.greenglobe21.com/

'Green' Hotels Association
http://www.greenhotels.com/

NSAA Environmental Charter for Ski Areas
http://www.nsaa.org/nsaa/environment/sustainable_slopes/charter2k.pdf

Sustainable Tourism Certification Network of the Americas
http://www.rainforest-alliance.org/programmes/tourism/certification/synopsis-sauipe.pdf

Sustainable Tourism Stewardship Council
http://www.rainforest-alliance.org/programmes/tourism/initiatives/stewardship-council.html

TUI Environment Award
http://www.tui.com/en/konzern/tui_umweltmanagement/umw_dest/uw_auszeichnung.html?darstellung=drucken

TUI environmental checklist for contracting hotels
http://www.tui.com/en/konzern/tui_umweltmanagement/service/monitoring/index.html

World Legacy Awards (Conservation International and National Geographic Traveler)
http://www.wlaward.org/

WTO – Sustainable Tourism Stewardship Council Feasibility: Consultation
http://www.world-tourism.org/sustainable/doc/STSC-eng.pdf

For further reading

Font, X. and Buckley, R. (eds) (2001). *Tourism Ecolabelling: Certification and Promotion of Sustainable Management*. CABI Publishing.
Seventeen individually authored chapters in this book deal with such topics as the purpose and variety of ecolabels, how they are developed, their pitfalls and future trends. A comprehensive list of tourism ecolabels is included.

Honey, M. and Rome, A. (2001). *Protecting Paradise: Certification Programmes for Sustainable Tourism and Ecotourism*. The Institute for Policy Studies. (available on-line at http://www.ips-dc.org/ecotourism/protectingparadise/index.htm)
The authors analyse the process through which tourism ecolabels are developed and examines their types and components. Well-known ecolabels (e.g. GG21, CST, NEAP) are critiqued and suggestions are offered for improving the international certification of sustainable tourism products and companies.

Sasidharan, V., Sirakaya, E. and Kerstetter, D. (2002). Developing countries and tourism eco-labels. *Tourism Management*, 23, 161–74.
The authors consider the issues faced by the tourism products in the less developed world that wish to foster and publicize sustainable practice through the acquisition of ecolabels, but are disadvantaged in doing so relative to their counterparts in the more developed world.

UNEP (1995). *Environmental Codes of Conduct for Tourism*.
This report discusses the need for codes of conduct in the tourism sector and devotes individual chapters to describing and analysing codes for the tourism industry, host communities and tourists and to their implementation and monitoring.

Beyond the book

1. (a) Design a ten-point code of conduct that takes into account the specialized circumstances of the travel agency sector. (b) Prepare a 300-word report that explains why and how this code will help to foster environmental and sociocultural sustainability within this sector.
2. Clause 1.4 of the Green Globe 21 Environmental and Social Sustainability Policy (Company Standard) (see Figure 7.5) states that a Benchmarked or Certified company must have a written Environmental and Social Sustainability Policy which is to be made available to interested parties upon request. Obtain a copy of this Policy from any Certified member (http://www.greenglobe21.com/ViewOperations.aspx?ABCType=3) and assess whether the Policy fulfils the criteria described under clause 1 in Figure 7.5.

3. (a) Enter the 'Green' Hotels Association website and access their membership list (http://www.greenhotels.com/members.htm). Select a random sample of 40 'Partner' members. (b) Enter the Green Globe 21 website and identify all of the Certified members. (c) Prepare a 500-word report that comparatively describes and analyses the extent to which the websites of those members feature their affiliation with these ecolabels on their websites.

On the ground: toward sustainable tourism certification in Costa Rica

Costa Rica has long been recognized as a leader in ecotourism (see Chapter 11), but is less known for its innovative practices in encouraging the sustainability of its rapidly growing conventional tourism industry, which accounts for most of the country's tourism-related expenditures and visitor-nights. Since 1997, the Costa Rican Tourist Board (ICT) as part of the National Strategy for the Development of Sustainable Tourism has been accrediting the country's hotels and guesthouses through the Certification for Sustainable Tourism (CST) programme, which assigns a one- to five-star rating based on environmental and socioeconomic performance. This performance is divided into four categories (i.e. physical-biological parameters, infrastructure and services, external clients and socioeconomic environment), each of which is accompanied by a list of relevant indicator statements to which a 'yes', 'no' or 'not applicable' response is assigned by experts from the programme's National Certification Commission during a no-cost site visit. Each 'yes' response is weighed on a one-to-three point scale depending on the importance attached to that indicator and a score is given to each category based on the cumulative responses.

In the case of the 68-room Palma Real hotel in San Jose, 82 points were assigned out of a possible 101 in the infrastructure and services category, for a score of 81.19 per cent (see Table 7.3). This is based on the response pattern to the statements relevant to this category, each of which is assigned a weighting of between one and three depending on its perceived significance (see Appendix 1). The star rating is awarded according to the lowest score attained on the four categories and therefore three stars were assigned to this hotel on the basis of the 64.71 score (22 out of 34) attained in the 'socioeconomic environment' category (1 star = 20–39.99; 2 stars = 40–59.99; 3 stars = 60–79.99; 4 stars = 80–94.99; 5 stars = 95+).

As of January 2004, 49 Costa Rican accommodation facilities (out of approximately 2000) had been assigned a CST rating. Thirteen of these were assigned one star, 18 had a two-star rating (these were mostly business hotels in the vicinity of San Jose), 12 had a three-star rating, four had a four-star rating and just two had earned the full five-star rating. Thirty-nine were small facilities with less than 50 rooms, while six had 100 rooms or more. The facilities were equally divided between urban, mountain and beach locations.

Table 7.3
2004 CST rating for Palma Real hotel (San Jose)

Criterion	Total potential points	Points awarded	Score
Physical/biological parameters	34	22	64.71
Infrastructure & services	101	82	81.19
External clients	21	15	71.43
Socioeconomic environment	58	45	77.59
Overall score			64.71

Source: http://www.turismo-sostenible.co.cr/EN/home.shtml

The CST programme rewards exemplary performance with a variety of benefits, including greater exposure in international marketing (e.g. trade fairs and brochures) and increased access to training opportunities. A further incentive is indicated by preliminary research that has identified a statistically significant correlation between CST ratings and room rates, suggesting that strong environmental performance, formally recognized through a credible eco-label, may command premium prices in the Costa Rican tourism marketplace (Rivera, 2002). This research, however, was based only on the very small proportion of hotels then participating in the programme. The overall results may be limited within the less developed world to the few countries in addition to Costa Rica that attract a relatively high proportion of international 'green' tourists willing to pay the premium. Nevertheless, versions of the programme are being implemented in other Central American countries, while the WTO has adopted it as a voluntary prototype for hotels worldwide (Rivera, 2002). Honey and Rome (2001) describe the government-run CST programme as one of the most respected ecolabels, but cite several problems that must be addressed. These include the need to generate revenue – perhaps by moving away from the no-cost model, increasing the participation rate while implementing some kind of fee structure, moving towards a more effective marketing model (the website listing certification details of members is hard to locate) and addressing the perception that the indicators are more appropriate for large conventional facilities than for the small alternative tourism operations that form the backbone of the country's ecotourism sector.

Exercises

1. (a) Divide the Appendix 1 statements into three categories, depending on whether they are weighted as one, two or three points. (b) Identify the common characteristics that distinguish statements in each of the three categories from the others. (c) Are these distinctions relevant to the concepts of minimalist and comprehensive sustainable tourism as discussed in Chapter 2?
2. Assess and modify, as necessary, the statements and weightings provided in Appendix 1 so that this checklist provides an even more effective basis for evaluating the sustainability of the accommodation sector.

Chapter 8
Tourist destinations

Chapter objectives

Upon completion of this chapter, the reader should be able to:

■ describe the relationship between the tourism industry and tourist destinations
■ explain the role of place and community in influencing the context and pursuit of sustainable tourism in destinations
■ discuss potential tourism outcomes for tourist destinations using the broad context model of destination development scenarios
■ identify and assess the sustainability contexts and issues that are associated with different types of tourist destinations, including tourism cities, other large urban areas, the urban-rural fringe, protected areas, indigenous territories and small islands
■ assess the distinctive qualities of special events that influence the sustainability issue and
■ evaluate the problems associated with applying quality control mechanisms such as accreditation to destinations and the effectiveness in particular of relevant efforts by Green Globe 21.

8.1 Introduction

Chapters 4 to 7 examined the issue of sustainable tourism within the conventional tourism industry, which has made notable progress toward embracing the ethos and practice of sustainability since the early 1990s. This embrace, however, is not yet pervasive or deep, being apparently motivated for the most part by considerations of self-interest that remain focused on financial sustainability. The extent to which sustainable tourism has been and is being achieved at the destination level is the topic of the following three chapters. In the first two sections of the current chapter, place and community are considered as fundamental characteristics of tourist destinations. Section 8.4 then uses the broad context model of destination development scenarios as a framework to examine potential tourism outcomes. Section 8.5 elaborates on the circumstances in which particular scenarios from this model are more likely to occur by discussing different types of destinations, including specialized tourism cities, other urban areas, the urban-rural fringe, protected areas, indigenous territories and small islands. Section 8.6 considers special events, which are an important component of most destinations, while the final section examines quality control issues, and especially the pursuit of accreditation, as they pertain to destinations.

8.2 Destination and place

Tourist destinations are extremely diverse (see Section 8.4), but they are all spatial entities having in common the characteristic of *place* that fundamentally dictates the way that sustainable tourism is engaged. One implication is the need to perceive the issue of sustainability in geographical terms, as for example through the identification of differential spatial impacts within a destination and through the use of zoning and other mechanisms to manipulate space in order to minimize these negative impacts (see Chapter 9). Characteristics associated with place and described below include cultural landscape, scale, boundaries, absolute and relative location and spatial hierarchies.

8.2.1 Cultural landscapes

A second major and related implication of place is the role of the *cultural landscape* as a tourist attraction in its own right as well as a visible barometer of change. Cultural landscapes with their own unique *sense of place* that support regional tourism activity include the Amish countryside of Lancaster County, (Pennsylvania, USA), the Hunter Valley and Napa Valley wine-producing regions of Australia and California respectively, the Highlands of Scotland, the Cotswold Hills of England and the rice terraces of Luzon* island in the Philippines.

The relationship between these landscapes and the tourism industry is complex and often uneasy, in that the cultural landscape is an amalgam of public and private spaces upon which the tourism industry is often dependent, but over which the latter has little or no control. External decisions to approve a new subdivision or waste disposal site, for example, can undermine the landscape's integrity as a tourist attraction and thereby threaten the viability of a resentful and frustrated tourism industry. The tourism industry, however, benefits from these landscapes on a largely cost-free basis by not having to pay any rent to the owners of the scenery and other tourism resources. This can cause resentment on the part of residents, especially if elements of the tourism industry such as accommodations and built attractions become increasingly visible in the landscape and in their own right contribute to the degradation of its scenic quality.

8.2.2 Scale

As with individual tourism operations (see Section 4.6), the pursuit of sustainable tourism in destinations is also influenced by the spatial quality of *scale*. The indicators that are appropriate for a local municipality, for example, are not necessarily relevant for a destination country. The process of indicator measuring and monitoring is likely to be far more difficult and expensive in the latter, but more resources may be available for the effort. The level of complexity that accompanies increased scale makes it more difficult to identify clear cause-and-effect relationships or to pass confident judgments that the tourism sector is sustainable or not. It is also more difficult to solicit community attitudes or obtain consensus in large destinations that are likely to contain a plethora of interest groups and stakeholder organizations (see below).

Destination hierarchies

A further complication is the positioning of all destinations within a *destination hierarchy* that ranges from the local municipality or sub-municipality to the entire world, with intervening destinations at the provincial, regional, state and continental or hemispheric scale. For the destination country (and especially those with federal systems), this indicates a large number of autonomous internal jurisdictions whose policies and actions will cumulatively influence the sustainability of tourism in the country as a whole. The same applies in reverse to the local municipality, where efforts to implement sustainable tourism may be impeded by contradictory efforts by provincial or national government that (especially in countries with unitary political structures) are often empowered to overrule decisions made by municipalities. The addition of regional scales of engagement is a more recent phenomenon that involves the superimposition of special purpose districts such as tourism regions and associated quasi-governmental authorities such as regional tourism boards and authorities. Concurrently, continental, hemispheric and global bodies such as the EU, PATA and the WTO respectively are seeking to play a broader role in the pursuit of sustainable tourism (see Section 1.4).

8.2.3 Absolute and relative location

Absolute location describes the precise geographical site of a destination. From a sustainability perspective, location on a beach in subtropical latitudes, or in an alpine valley, greatly increases the pressure for and from tourism-related development and hence the likelihood of progression towards the more intensive and unsustainable phases of the destination life cycle. The issue as to whether a destination is experiencing circumstantial or deliberate alternative tourism (see Section 3.5), accordingly, is more critical in such settings. Conversely, a municipality located in the middle of the cold steppe of central Asia or North Dakota, or the industrial Midlands of England, is not likely to experience levels of tourism demand that would induce such an evolution. Another relevant dimension of absolute location is whether the landscape of the destination consists of relatively undisturbed natural habitat or highly modified urban space, in which a strong and weak perspective on sustainable tourism may be respectively warranted.

The Colorado communities that experienced unwelcome tourism growth following the passing of slow-growth regulations in nearby Aspen (see Section 2.4.4) demonstrate the importance of *relative location*, which is an indicator of spatial interdependence. Also illustrative is the Tennessee municipality of Gatlinburg, which has experienced increasing tourism-related sprawl and congestion due to its location as a gateway to Great Smoky Mountains National Park (Howe et al., 1997).

8.2.4 Boundaries

Tourist destinations are all demarcated by formal or informal *boundaries* that separate the destination from other entities in the same level of the hierarchy. Some boundaries, such as those separating countries, are highly stable, while those separating municipalities and regions (which changes absolute location) may be adjusted frequently due, respectively, to annexation and the decision of certain destinations to withdraw from tourism regions or hemispheric associations. Internal boundaries are also important to separate planning zones and various types of spatial activity. Permeability, or the degree to which a boundary resists penetration, is a characteristic that is crucial to sustainable tourism. This is illustrated by the difference between international and municipal boundaries in restricting the influx of tourists. On the other hand, political boundaries at either level are similarly ineffective in resisting the entry of waterborne or airborne pollutants.

8.3 Destination and community

Destinations, with notable exceptions such as Antarctica and higher order protected areas, have permanent resident populations. The notion that the interests and concerns of residents should be given priority when considering tourism outcomes, as they are the stakeholders most affected by unsustainable tourism impacts and the owners of many of the resources that attract and host tourists, was first espoused by the cautionary platform during the 1970s (see Section 1.3.2). Supporters of this platform further argue that community involvement allows local knowledge to inform the planning process, while reducing the likelihood of future conflict between residents and tourists. Subsequently, the democratic principle of community empowerment has been widely accepted as a premise of and precondition for sustainable tourism at the destination level (Swarbrooke, 1999).

8.3.1 Challenges of the community approach

The experience of implementing community empowerment, however, has revealed several serious problems that expose the rift between theory and reality and add to the complexity of tourism systems described in Chapter 2. This is despite the commonly held view that community input is best facilitated and simplified by working through the elected representatives of the population.

Defining the 'community'

A first problem is to define exactly which individuals constitute the 'local community' and hence the group to whom priority consideration should be given. The latter is often equated with those living within a defined place at a given time, but this fails to distinguish between newcomers and long-time residents who may feel alienated and threatened by the former. Other complications include the status of non-resident property holders or seasonal occupants of second homes or cottages. Especially in the case of many indigenous communities, non-residents who have a strong familial and cultural attachment to their ancestral community lands, even though they may have never actually lived there, also have a legitimate claim to be community members. These references to cultural attachments and long-time residents reveal one train of thought that equates 'community' with rootedness in place and that tourism's potential directly or indirectly to disrupt this relationship should be a major consideration in sustainable tourism deliberations. Yet, this does not account for newcomers who may quickly develop a strong sense of attachment and devotion to their new home, or who may have developed this as a result of earlier tourism-related visits.

Apathy and lack of technical knowledge

Even if the issue of definitional ambiguity can be resolved, additional problems will be confronted. Apathy and a lack of technical knowledge are frequently cited impediments to community participation, with most residents being unlikely to learn more about or become involved with a particular proposal or strategy until it is visually tangible and therefore of more immediate relevance to their lives (though perhaps too late to reverse). This makes it difficult for planners to follow the commonly accepted principle that the participation of local residents should be encouraged from the earliest phases of the planning process (Swarbrooke, 1999).

Disproportionate influence of interest groups

The corollary to public apathy is the disproportionate influence of advocacy groups that have a vested interest in particular outcomes. These groups mobilize their activists to write letters to the editor, attend and voice their concerns at public meetings, demonstrate, submit briefs and otherwise convey the impression to decision-makers and other local residents, that their sentiments are representative of the 'community' at large even though they may actually account for only a small minority. Destinations usually contain several competing interest groups and T. Manning (1999) goes so far as to suggest that a 'community' is little more than an agglomeration of competing special interest groups.

Disproportionate allocation of costs and benefits and elusiveness of consensus

The idea that successful advocacy groups are able to fulfil their vested interests reflects the broader truism that the costs and benefits from tourism within a community are not equally distributed, even in cases where alternative tourism is practised (see Section 3.12.4). This complicates efforts to achieve consensus, which can be used as an indicator of sociocultural sustainability. During the era of the cautionary platform, the 'irridex' model of Doxey (1976) proposed that community attitudes progress uniformly from euphoria through to apathy, annoyance and antagonism as tourism evolves through the destination life cycle. However, this notion of an evolving consensus has since been refuted by numerous investigations that reveal conflicting attitudes and community discord at all stages of development in all types of destinations, with those in favour of tourism typically being those who benefit from employment within the sector. An additional complication is that many residents acknowledge positive economic benefits from tourism at the same time that they express concerns about concomitant sociocultural and environmental costs.

8.4 Broad context model of destination development scenarios

Notwithstanding the complications associated with community empowerment, planning for sustainable tourism requires that destinations be periodically assessed

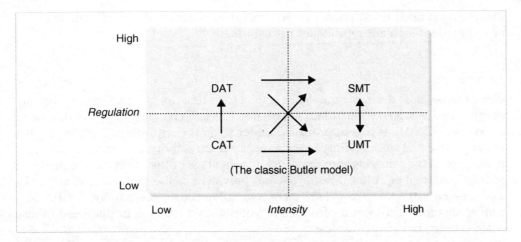

Figure 8.1
Destination development scenarios. Reprinted from Tourism Management 21, Weaver, D. A broad context model of destination development scenarios, pp. 217–24. Copyright 2000, with permission from Elsevier.

in terms of their current sustainability status, where they are headed if current trends are extrapolated and what outcomes are desired (to the extent that the community can reach agreement on this matter). The broad context model of destination development scenarios (Weaver, 2000a) provides a 'big picture' framework for making these assessments. As depicted in Figure 8.1, the scenarios are based on the variables of destination scale or intensity and the extent to which regulations conducive to sustainability are present and enforced. Small-scale destinations where regulations are absent or minimal are experiencing circumstantial alternative tourism or CAT (see Section 3.5). Small-scale destinations having this regulatory environment in place adhere to deliberate alternative tourism or DAT. The line between these two scenarios, as with all the cells in this matrix, is dotted to reflect the transitional nature of the division. The third possibility is the unsustainable mass tourism (UMT) experienced by large-scale destinations lacking regulations, which contrasts with the sustainable mass tourism (SMT) that theoretically exists when these regulations are implemented and enforced. The broad context model is consistent with the knowledge-based platform in that 'positive' and 'negative' scenarios are associated with both large- and small-scale destinations (see Section 1.3.4).

8.4.1 CAT to UMT

At least seven one-step scenarios emerge from the broad context model, one of which involves the progression of a destination from CAT to UMT. Most places in the world at the present time are CAT destinations where modest amounts of tourism-related activity do not warrant the imposition of sophisticated tourism regulations. However, where demand results in increased levels of tourism activity, these places are likely to evolve into UMT destinations if no such regulations are implemented. Essentially this is the classic unsustainable destination life cycle described in the Butler sequence (see Section 1.3.2). Since destinations experience variable levels of tourism-related demand, it is necessary to identify the CAT places that are most likely to experience such demand so that more desirable outcomes can be attained through appropriate tourism strategies.

8.4.2 CAT to DAT

One of these more desirable outcomes is the DAT scenario, in which regulations are enacted and enforced to maintain alternative tourism characteristics. As described by Weaver (2000a), this is appropriate under several circumstances, including the above-mentioned susceptibility to increased tourism activity, evidence that the destination is already moving into the development stage of the life cycle, the presence of fragile natural or cultural resources and prevalent desire within the community against large-scale tourism. Where there is doubt or confusion as to the desired outcomes, this may also be a useful 'default' option that remains in place until those desired outcomes are made clear.

8.4.3 CAT to SMT

Less common is the option of moving directly from CAT to SMT, which occurred at least temporarily in Mexico when governments initially developed well-planned tourism-based growth poles in favourable coastal locations such as Cancún and Ixtapa in order to induce regional economic development. A controversial aspect of this option is whether it is desirable for small coastal fishing villages in pristine natural settings to embark on a radical transition to a highly urbanized setting, given that a strong case can be made in the former for a 'strong' model of sustainability that precludes such models of rapid tourism intensification.

8.4.4 DAT to SMT

Stakeholders in a DAT destination may sometimes decide that intensification is desirable for economic or other reasons as well as feasible from an environmental perspective and subsequently take actions that will result in SMT. As described in Chapters 9 and 10, these actions can focus on site hardening, visitor education and other strategies that increase the destination's carrying capacity. If, however, these actions are not carried out properly, undesirable UMT outcomes may result, as has arguably occurred in some high profile protected areas (see Section 8.5.4 below).

8.4.5 UMT to SMT

A situation that urgently requires redress is the UMT destination, which is likely to experience decline as crime and congestion levels become unacceptably high for both residents and visitors. Since it is unrealistic to revert to DAT-type dynamics, the SMT scenario is the appropriate outcome for these situations. This is not to imply that the transition is an easy one, since great difficulties will be encountered in undoing the damage already done to the physical and cultural environment, as well as to market image and the attitudes of residents. And yet, somewhat perversely, the UMT destination may have certain advantages in working toward sustainability, such as the reduced cost of acquiring degraded land and facilities and the positive effect this has in facilitating the re-entry of local investors. They may also in some countries be eligible for government funds to assist with the enhancement of the environment. The Mediterranean resort of Calviá is a good illustration of the UMT to SMT scenario (see case study at the end of Chapter 9).

8.4.6 SMT to UMT

A final and undesirable possibility is the SMT destination that moves towards UMT. Arguably, this occurred in Cancún once the critical threshold of self-propelled growth was reached, at which point the government moved away from a public regulation model towards one based more on *laissez-faire* market forces. Parts of some US National Parks, such as Great Smoky Mountains and Shenandoah, also appear to illustrate this scenario, as escalating visitor numbers place undue stress on local infrastructure, services and habitat.

8.5 Destination types

A theme that emerged in the earlier chapters of this book is that the assumptions and approaches associated with sustainable tourism will vary in accordance with the type of destination. This is demonstrated in the distinction between weak and strong models of sustainability, wherein the former is regarded as appropriate for heavily developed urban areas and the latter for relatively undisturbed natural environments. Each type of destination, moreover, will have its own specialized indicators, as recognized by the WTO in its indicator trials (see Table 2.2). The following subsections focus on selected tourism environments, including tourism cities, other large urban areas, the urban-rural fringe, indigenous territories, protected areas and small islands. These profiles recognize that all destinations are ultimately unique, but that certain commonalities can be identified among destinations in similar settings.

8.5.1 Tourism cities

Tourism cities (or sometimes 'tourist cities') are the outcome of *tourism urbanization*, which Mullins (1992, p. 188) defines as 'the process whereby urban areas, particularly large cities, are specially developed for the production, sale, and consumption of goods and services providing pleasure'. As illustrated by Orlando, Las Vegas, Atlantic City, Nice-Cannes, Pattaya (Thailand), Acapulco, Mar del Plata (Argentina) and the Gold Coast of Australia (see case study at the end of this chapter), tourism is both directly and indirectly the driver of economic activity in such urban destinations, assisted by complementary economic activity such as high technology, call centres, movie making and wholesaling (Judd and Fainstein, 1999). Not surprisingly, most tourism cities are located within the pleasure periphery, although smaller-scale versions are also found near large cities in other regions (see Section 8.5.3 below).

Spatial and symbolic distinctiveness

Because of their emphasis on the production and consumption of leisure-related activities, tourism cities may be described as the consummate spatial expression of post-modernism. According to Mullins (1991, 1992), tourism cities are spatially distinct in that the dynamics of urban expansion are mostly influenced by the location of primary tourism resources such as the beach or major theme parks. Moreover, dual commercial districts usually exist in the form of the central business district, which serves the local population and the *recreational business district*, which serves a mainly tourist clientele (Stansfield and Rickert, 1970). They are also symbolically distinct in that their identity is inextricably linked to their emphasis on tourism and leisure. This is extremely significant from a sustainability perspective in that tourism is more of a basis for the destination's sense of place than an activity that has usurped a pre-existing identity. Theme parks and casinos, often castigated as placeless intruders in other urban areas, are very much part of the identity of tourism cities such as Las Vegas, rather than necessarily a negative indicator.

Demographic distinctiveness

Tourism cities tend to be characterized by very rapid rates of migration-centred population growth, as illustrated by the status of Las Vegas and Orlando as among the fastest growing major metropolitan areas in the USA. Similarly, the resident population of the Gold Coast of Australia increased from an estimated 9000 in 1947 (Stimson and Minnery, 1998) to about 500000 in 2004. This has several important implications for sustainable tourism, aside from the observation that a weak approach towards sustainability is warranted and SMT is the only long-term desired outcome that is realistic. First, the issue must be approached in the context of the rapid and dramatic – and possibly unsustainable – environmental changes that accompany this population growth, most of which is at least indirectly associated with tourism. Second, most of the migrants who constitute a very high proportion of the resident population are relatively recent arrivals who moved to the tourism city fully aware of, and presumably attracted by, its identity as a tourism city. Such individuals are not as likely to experience the antagonism towards tourism that is anticipated in the late development stages of the destination life cycle, as per Doxey's irridex. This is corroborated by Lawton (2001a), who found that the residents of the Gold Coast regard highly contrived and commercial specialized built attractions as contributing in a very positive way to their personal quality of life.

Third, the resident population of tourism cities tends to be transient and a sense of community that could be undermined by rapid growth therefore does not often characterize such urban environments. Out-migration, in addition, is perceived as a 'normal' and 'natural' option for residents and especially those who are dissatisfied with the results of this growth. This outflow of residents provides a safety valve that helps to pre-empt negative community responses to continued tourism growth. The pattern of in- and out-migration, along with the arrival of temporary residents (i.e. tourists) from across the country and around the world, gives rise to a cosmopolitan atmosphere in many tourism cities in which no particular ethnic or cultural group is regarded as indigenous or dominant and hence vulnerable to dilution or dissolution as a result of rapid growth. Lawton (2001a) describes the Gold Coast as an expression of the forces of globalization, which implies the normality of diversity and resilience to the consequences of rapid change.

8.5.2 Other large urban areas

Major urban tourist destinations such as London, Paris, Sydney, Prague and Washington often receive visitation levels well in excess of those experienced by tourism cities and, like the latter, are therefore suited to SMT outcomes. However, the main structural characteristic that distinguishes these urban places from tourism cities is the fact the tourism accounts for only a small component of all economic activity within the city. Their spatial and symbolic distinctiveness, moreover, is not primarily influenced by tourism, which has a less visible impact on the cultural landscape or community composition. In districts where tourism is dominant, something akin to destination life cycle dynamics may occur, but this would not be the case throughout all parts of the city. Hence, the concept of applying the destination life cycle to London or Paris as a whole is untenable and also because multiple factors and environments external to tourism will substantially influence the physical landscape and the attitudes of residents. Among other effects, the urban economy is not as likely to be universally depressed by seasonal fluctuations in the tourism sector.

The higher proportion of business and VFR (visiting friends and relatives) tourists, whose motives and behaviour differ substantially from the leisure tourists upon which the destination life cycle model is predicated, is another factor that distinguishes such urban tourism from tourism cities and further affects the engagement with sustainability. The tourism industry, in addition, will probably not have the same influence in shaping public policy and actions as it does in a tourism city. Whatever the extent of this influence, the industry has a vested interest in supporting the resources that sustain visitation in such cities, including the historical buildings, ethnic neighbourhoods, green space and cultural and sport facilities that contribute to overall cultural and environmental sustainability. Alliances between industry and community and cultural advocacy groups to achieve sustainable outcomes are therefore commonplace and tourism often serves as a vehicle for urban renewal, as demonstrated by the Shaw neighbourhood case study profiled at the conclusion of Chapter 3.

8.5.3 Urban-rural fringe

The *urban-rural fringe*, or 'exurbs', is a transitional space between clearly urban and rural landscapes that attracts residents and commercial activity because it offers a trade-off in relative location between cheaper rural land and proximity to urban markets (Beesley and Russwurm, 1981). It has been neglected in the traditional fields of urban and rural studies, even though the urban-rural fringe is estimated to account for one-third of the land and one-quarter of the population in the lower 48 states of the USA (Wolf, 1999). Not surprisingly, a large and increasing amount of tourism activity is accommodated in such areas, even though the fringe has been similarly neglected as a destination venue within the field of tourism studies. Attractions that benefit from access to extensive amounts of relatively cheap land and access to large nearby urban markets and hence may be described as typical components in the exurban tourism product amalgam, include theme parks, golf courses and factory outlet malls.

The role of theme parks and golf courses in facilitating urban sprawl, noted in Chapter 6, has distinctively exurban implications for sustainable tourism. Other characteristically exurban implications stem from the fact that exurban tourism is dominated by day-only excursionists, which means that such venues do not possess large numbers of accommodation units, or generate substantial revenue through the patronage of such facilities. However, high volumes of excursionist traffic increase the need for parking lots, roads and related infrastructure used by buses and cars.

Destination and residential life cycle dynamics

Finally, the urban-rural fringe is inherently unstable due to its transitional nature and fluid boundaries, wherein the urban zone is continually encroaching on the inner fringe while the outer fringe expands into rural areas. One significant implication for sustainable tourism is that the destination life cycle is accompanied if not necessarily paralleled by a very similar residential life cycle, in which the first urban migrants (i.e. the 'explorers') are eventually followed by an influx of new residents in what is equivalent to the development stage in tourism. As the area literally fills with residents and the potential for new growth in an area declines dramatically, something akin to consolidation and stagnation is evident. If the two life cycles do in fact coincide, then the most volatile phases of both tourism and residential development will be concurrent, thereby dramatically increasing uncertainty and the potential for conflict and chaos within a rapidly changing cultural landscape. This might entail, for example, dramatically greater traffic congestion along a major artery that serves a new residential subdivision as well as an expanded theme park. The demand from these two new activities, moreover, may cause an overload in the local water and sewage treatment systems. In any case, the sustainability of any tourism activity in the exurbs cannot be divorced from the activity that occurs in the residential sector and other external environments. From the perspective of the broad context model, it may be that destinations in the urban-rural fringe should initially aim toward DAT, but anticipate that encroaching urban pressures will eventually necessitate a transition to SMT.

Tourist shopping villages

Tourist shopping villages are defined by Getz (1993) as villages or towns with a well demarcated commercial strip that offers specialized retail shopping and eating opportunities to a clientele consisting mainly of tourists. Typically located in the urban-rural fringe, tourist shopping villages may tentatively be described as a type of miniature tourism city to the extent that tourism is the dominant economic activity. However, the high level of tourism activity is often a relatively recent phenomenon associated with the incorporation of the area into the urban-rural fringe. It may therefore conflict with the town's existing identity as a local or regional service centre. Long-time residents who embody this existing identity may come into conflict with newcomers who are seen as agents and symbols of change and uncertainty. Weaver and Lawton (2001) identified such a relationship at Tamborine Mountain, a settlement of 7000 located in the exurbs of the Gold Coast (Australia). Moreover, newcomers tended to be far more positive about tourism than the long-time residents (see case study at the end of this chapter).

An interesting feature of some tourist shopping villages is their status as 'hyper-destinations' in which the number of annual visitors far exceeds the number of local residents, often by several orders of magnitude. For example, at least 500 000 tourist visits are made annually to Tamborine Mountain, while the southern Ontario village of St Jacobs (Canada), with 1500 permanent residents, hosts an estimated 1–2 million visitors per year. Given the fixation in much of the cautionary platform literature with visitation levels, it may be useful to investigate how some hyper-destinations cope with the disparity in scale between the local community (i.e. small scale) and the tourist influx (i.e. large scale) without experiencing a UMT-type breakdown in community cohesion or destruction of the local landscape and sense of place.

8.5.4 Protected areas

Public protected areas are by definition places, usually in a non-urban setting, where constituent cultural and natural resources are given a defined level of legal protection by a national, state or municipal government. In theory, protected area status is therefore to a greater or lesser extent an indicator of sustainability. The highest level of protection is provided by Category Ia (Strict Nature Reserves) and Ib (Wilderness Areas) protected areas under the World Conservation Union's standard classification system. In contrast, Managed Resource Protected Areas (Category VI) are managed as relatively unmodified natural habitats that provide a sustainable yield of natural resources. Other categories include National Parks (II), Natural Monuments (III), Habitat/Species Management Areas (IV) and Protected Landscapes/Seascapes (V). In 2003, it was estimated that 11.5 per cent of the world's land area, or 17.1 million square kilometres, fell under these six categories, compared with about 6 per cent in 1997 (Chape et al., 2003).

Public protected areas are becoming increasingly important as tourism venues, in part because the resources they contain are attractive to nature-based tourists and ecotourists in particular (see Chapter 11). They also account for a growing proportion of the world's remaining relatively undisturbed natural habitats. Moreover, all protected area categories with the exception of Strict Nature Reserves are intended to accommodate complementary forms of recreational tourism activity, ranging from non-mechanized, non-serviced experiences in Wilderness Areas to motorized recreation and hunting in Managed Resource Protected Areas. Many protected areas, and especially Category II National Parks such as Yellowstone, Banff, Kruger and Kakadu, experience high levels of visitation because they have attained the status of iconic tourist attractions in their respective countries. An added factor underlying the growing importance of tourism in protected areas is the worldwide problem of chronic funding shortfalls, which has forced protected area managers to rely increasingly on tourism-related forms of revenue such as entry and licensing fees to maintain their ability to operate (Goodwin, 2000).

The relationship between protected areas and tourism is an ambivalent one. Managers are not only becoming more dependent on revenues derived from tourism, but it is increasingly argued that the ability to generate these revenues is a major incentive for maintaining the existence of many protected areas that would otherwise be used more profitably in the short term for farmland or tree plantations (Lawton, 2001b). Public interaction with protected areas also helps to mobilize support for protected area systems. On the other hand, the need to manage growing tourist numbers and provide appropriate services and facilities may divert attention and resources away from the preservationist mandate, without necessarily reducing the likelihood that these tourism activities will have deliberate or inadvertent negative impacts on the natural environment.

In contrast to the other types of destination profiled in this section, the absence of a permanent resident human population is an important and distinctive characteristic of higher order protected areas such as National Parks, although local communities in the surrounding area may perceive a strong vested interest in such areas (see Section 8.5.5). Unlike urban destinations, a strong model of sustainability is warranted in these same higher order entities because of the paramount importance of the preservationist mandate.

8.5.5 Indigenous territories

Approximately 400 million people, or 7 per cent of the world's population, are considered 'indigenous' insofar as they are recognized as the original inhabitants of a particular area or the people who occupied that area prior to colonization by the current residents (Zeppel, 2001). Despite their relatively small numbers, however, they constitute a majority or substantial minority within as much as one-half of the earth's land area, including northern Canada, the Amazon basin, eastern Africa, the Sahara, eastern Russia, central and northern Australia, New Zealand and western China. Indigenous groups are becoming increasingly involved with tourism, as evidenced by experience of the Aborigines in Australia, Maori in New Zealand, Melanesians in Fiji and Vanuatu, Navajo, Cherokee, Seminole and Sioux in the USA, Maasai in East Africa, San in southern Africa, Inuit and Haida in Canada and Yi in China's Yunnan province. Several factors influence the sustainable tourism issue as it applies to indigenous cultures.

Economic and cultural deprivation

With notable exceptions, indigenous people are economically disadvantaged in relation to their non-indigenous counterparts and have experienced substantial erosion of their traditional culture due to acculturation and conflict. The embrace by many (though by no means all) indigenous people of tourism is usually part of a strategy to overcome economic deprivation and initiate a cultural revival, as per the advocacy platform. This appears to be the case, for example, with the Maori of New Zealand (Hall, 1996). Whether tourism-related efforts are sustainable or not must be assessed in the context of this cultural and economic situation, which for most indigenous people would not be considered sustainable to begin with. This suggests that indicator benchmarks using the status quo (e.g. 50 per cent unemployment) are normally inappropriate, since this would involve sustaining the unsustainable. More appropriate in most cases is an enhancement sustainability approach that seeks minimally to position indigenous people on par with the non-indigenous people of their country.

Blurred cultural/natural distinctions

By occupying and adapting to particular places for long periods of time, indigenous people have had profound ecological impacts on these areas, to the point where distinctions between the 'natural' and 'cultural' landscape are extremely problematic. An indicator such as 'percentage of land in relatively undisturbed natural habitat', accordingly, may not be relevant in an area where fire has been used for millennia to suppress the natural forest cover, or where a large variety of food-producing plants have been seeded in a rainforest. Moreover, 'percentage of land in Category II (National Park) protected areas', which is widely regarded as a good indicator of environmental quality for most destinations, may have negative connotations to indigenous communities who are normally excluded from engaging in traditional economic activities such as hunting in such areas. Conversely, lower order protected areas that accommodate such activities are more clearly associated with sustainable economic and cultural outcomes for indigenous people. Robinson (1999) regards this issue as indicative of the conflict between indigenous tradition and the Eurocentric concept of environmentalism that has largely informed the sustainability debate. Eurocentrism is also evident in the assumption of Urlich Cloher (1999) and others that DAT is the option most sympathetic with indigenous communities. Another implication of the blurred distinction is that 'ecotourism' may be infused with a much higher cultural component than that which is usually encountered in high order protected areas.

Alleged harmony with community approach

Rightly or wrongly, it is commonly assumed that indigenous people are attuned to a communal or community approach toward making decisions, so that the problems described in Section 8.3 are less likely to occur and consensus reached more readily on issues such as appropriate indicators and benchmarks as well as desired modes of tourism development. This assumption, however, must be reassessed, since some indigenous communities have also been associated with nepotism, clan rivalries (see Section 3.12.4), undemocratic decision-making procedures and other problems, based on tradition or not, that have negative implications for the sustainability of certain groups or individuals within those groups (Smith, 1996).

Increased power

A trend that has profound implications for all communities is the growing empower-ment and assertiveness of indigenous people, which can be likened to an indigen-ous 'renaissance' (Weaver, 2001b). In the USA and Canada, this is first of all evident in the movement toward self-government on native-controlled Reserves and Reservations, which includes recognition from the wider society that such entities possess a high degree of autonomy and even sovereignty. This self-determination allows indigenous communities to circumvent the influence that the relevant municipal, provincial or national government would normally exercise in tourism planning and management. It has facilitated, for example, the establishment of casi-nos on indigenous land (see Section 6.4.1). One implication may be reluctance to participate in accreditation schemes that cede some control to outside interests. Another implication is the desirability for individuals within the wider society to be affiliated with an indigenous community, which may lead to problems in determin-ing membership within a given community.

An additional aspect of this renaissance is the willingness to assert at least some degree of control over traditionally occupied lands and resources outside of their Reserves and Reservations. Formal land claims that effectively freeze tourism-related investment are an extreme manifestation of this influence. 'Co-management' (or 'joint management') strategies that impose a layer of indigenous decision-making over the existing non-indigenous policy/management structure are somewhat less controversial (Notzke, 1999). Australia's Uluru National Park illustrates the trend toward extended indigenous control by the fact that it has reverted to Aboriginal ownership and is being leased back to the federal government for 99 years. In addi-tion, Aborigines form a majority on the park's management board, which has resulted in a much stronger Aboriginal 'flavour' to the interpretation and manage-ment of park resources (Hall, 2000; Wearing and Huyskens, 2001). Notable is the increased Aboriginal resistance to tourist activities deemed harmful or inappropri-ate to indigenous culture, such as the 'must do' climb of the Uluru monolith. As of the early 2000s, the climb was not formally prohibited, but actively discouraged (Weaver, 2001b).

This is an example of what Robinson (1999) refers to as an emerging 'permission to gaze' model in which indigenous people decide what is made available for tourist consumption and under what terms, so that their own version of an 'authen-tic' and 'sustainable' tourist experience is featured. Johnston (2003), however, notes that the global tourism industry in general, as well as many indigenous commu-nities, still remains largely ignorant about the implications that inherent indigenous rights such as self-determination, under international law, have for all aspects of tourism, including the pursuit of sustainable tourism and the basic meaning for terms such as 'sustainable development'.

8.5.6 Small islands

Small islands are substantially over-represented as tourist destinations, with SISODs (small island states or dependencies) accounting in 1998 for just 0.3 per cent of the world's population, but 4.6 per cent of all international stayover arrivals (Weaver and Lawton, 2002a). As illustrated by the Bahamas (see case study at the end of Chapter 1), this often leads to a state of hyper-dependency, wherein tourism, dominated by resort-related activity, can account for as much as 70 per cent or more of the economy, particularly given that islands otherwise tend to have a very limited array of economic activity. Like tourist cities and tourist shopping villages and as recognized in a growing body of specialized literature (e.g. Ionnides et al., 2001; Gössling, 2003), the issue of tourism sustainability is therefore of particular significance to small island destinations of the pleasure periphery, not least because of the scale disparity between the small local community and mass tourism development.

Isolation and endemism

All destinations are open systems in that they are influenced by a host of external forces, but islands are less open due to the fact that they are isolated and clearly bounded by water from other terrestrial destinations. One advantage of this limited accessibility for sustainable tourism is the enhanced ability to control the arrival of tourists, who normally arrive and depart through just a small number of airports or seaports (see Section 10.2.3). However, even small fluctuations in tourist numbers can cause significant economic and social reverberations due to layoffs or overtaxed infrastructure (Conlin and Baum, 1995). Isolation has also given rise to ecological distinctiveness through time as a result of genetic drift. Accordingly, SISODs such as Mauritius, Seychelles and St Helena and other small island entities such as the Galapagos Islands and Easter Island, possess a high number of sensitive endemic species that are threatened by the growth of tourism. Indeed, the question of sustainability-related environmental indicator benchmarks is already confounded by the extent to which many insular ecosystems (e.g. Mauritius) have been irrevocably damaged by human activity. One external factor that is especially germane to small islands is global warming, which threatens to inundate large areas of coastline and increase the incidence of hurricanes, high tides and other severe weather events.

Individual weakness but collective power

The limited human and financial resources that accompany smallness hamper the pursuit of sustainable tourism in most SISODs, with sovereign states such as Maldives, Tuvalu and Barbados effectively functioning as modestly sized municipalities. However, paradoxically, the 30 independent small island entities cumulatively project inordinate potential power in international bodies such as the United Nations, where they account for about 15 per cent of all members. Hence, they are well positioned to influence issues such as global warming and sustainable tourism. This influence, moreover, is likely to increase in the future given the numerous small island entities that have the potential to become independent through decolonization (e.g. Aruba, Cook Islands, Falkland Islands, New Caledonia, Turks and Caicos Islands) or separation from existing countries (e.g. Bougainville from Papua

New Guinea, Madeira from Portugal, Nevis from St Kitts/Nevis, Tobago from Trinidad and Tobago, Zanzibar from Tanzania).

8.6 Special events

Special events, which can range from small local heritage or food festivals to global 'mega-events' such as the Olympics or football World Cup, are a critical part of the tourism equation in most destinations. It is therefore surprising that remarkably little has been written on the subject of sustainability in special events and that negligible consideration has been given to the issue of sustainable event accreditation. An exception to the literature dearth is Bramwell (1997), who examined whether the 1991 World Student Games promoted sustainable tourism in the host city of Sheffield, UK. One finding in the affirmative was the legacy of infrastructure (e.g. Olympic standard swimming facilities) that contributed to residents' quality of life and offered ongoing potential for revenue generation through the accommodation of subsequent sporting events. The author also notes the mobilization of volunteers and other members of the local community as a positive social outcome, as well as the revitalization of older neighbourhoods, the environmental restoration of derelict industrial sites and increased community interest in sports.

Smaller events, while not likely to entail the scale of construction and exposure that induces the above benefits, can still serve to mobilize the local community and foster a positive sense of place. Smaller events are also more amenable to cultural, historical or environmental themes that focus on a sustainability component. One example of the latter is the annual Toronto-based International Environmental Film and Video Festival*, which promotes films and videos as catalysts for raising awareness of environmental issues from a diversity of perspectives. Earthday-related festivals and events are another example.

Other advantages of special events from a sustainability perspective include the availability of extensive preparation and recovery time and greater flexibility relative to fixed attractions in choosing economically, socially and environmentally optimum event locations and times. Many advantages and disadvantages derive from the fact that special events, by definition, occur within compressed spatial and temporal parameters, creating in effect a temporary hyper-destination. The potential for congestion and service overload is considerable, but most of the negative effects are confined to a brief period of time within a constricted area (Fredline and Faulkner, 2000). This compressed focus can result in extensive on-site degradation, but also provides many opportunities for innovative visitor and event management strategies that are conducive to sustainable outcomes (see Chapters 9 and 10).

8.7 Quality control and destinations

The previous chapter illustrated the extent to which the tourism industry is becoming increasingly involved with quality control mechanisms such as codes of conduct and accreditation schemes to provide some degree of assurance to consumers and government regulators that sustainable tourism is actually being practised. Unfortunately, due to several factors, similar initiatives are lacking at the destination level, even though these could have the similar effect of improving a place's competitiveness, at least among green consumers. One reason is the complexity issue. As has been described in this chapter, destinations are a complicated amalgam of public and private sector components represented by numerous stakeholders ranging in their awareness and pursuit of sustainability from highly active to apathetic and even hostile. As the scale of the destination increases, so too does the complexity and range of responses. And even if the government of the moment can be likened to the management of a corporation as a policy- and decision-making body empowered amidst this complexity to pursue sustainable tourism, it is less clear how the former can enforce policy and implement the actions to achieve a goal as amorphous and subjective as sustainable tourism.

8.7.1 Green Globe 21 Community Standard*

The Community Standard is one of four Green Globe 21 foci of sustainable tourism (the Company Standard was featured in Chapter 7) and represents the most ambitious international effort to extend the idea of sustainability accreditation to destinations. As with the Company Standard, the Community Standard is based on a trajectory of involvement that begins with Affiliate (or Awareness) status and progresses to Benchmarked and Certified status. The actual body receiving accreditation is the relevant municipal council or 'Community Authority'. Community Standard criteria for certification are similar in many respects to the Company Standard, with both for example having similarly worded sections on environmental and social policy and performance. However, the former differs in placing greater emphasis on community consultation and participation and in formulating a sustainable tourism destination master plan. As of mid-2004, there were no Certified communities, although three (Douglas and Redland Shire Councils in Australia, Kaikoura District Council in New Zealand) were Benchmarked.

8.8 Summary

Destinations are inherently complex places in which the pursuit of sustainability is critically influenced by factors such as cultural landscape, scale, boundaries, absolute and relative location and the fact that all destinations are positioned within and influenced by a nested hierarchy of other destinations. The presence of permanent resident populations, or communities, is another distinctive characteristic of most destinations that fundamentally affects the prioritization of outcomes and the decision-making process. The subsequent incorporation of a community-based approach into sustainable tourism planning, however, while desirable, is impeded by problems of definition, widespread apathy and lack of technical knowledge, the disproportionate influence of interest groups, the unequal distribution of costs and benefits and the difficulty in obtaining consensus.

The broad context model of destination development scenarios provides a framework for identifying the current status of a destination as well as possible future scenarios with regard to sustainability. Four basic options within this framework are circumstantial alternative tourism (CAT), deliberate alternative tourism (DAT), sustainable mass tourism (SMT) and unsustainable mass tourism (UMT). The model accommodates movement between these options, so that the CAT-to-UMT scenario is essentially the classic destination life cycle, while CAT-to-SMT is illustrated by the 'instant resort' phenomenon. An important consideration for destination decision-makers is whether DAT or SMT is the most appropriate outcome and at what point in the future. This decision depends largely on the type of destination under consideration, which also influences other aspects of the sustainability equation. Tourism cities, for example, should strive for SMT but are vulnerable to the destination life cycle despite a high level of tolerance for tourism and a sense of place that is shaped by the latter. Other urban areas are also suited to SMT outcomes, though the applicability of the destination life cycle model is diminished by the relatively small contribution of tourism to the overall economy. The urban-rural fringe is an increasingly important tourism environment where instability and conflict is normative and where contingencies for a CAT-to-DAT-to-SMT trajectory are therefore advisable.

High order protected areas are distinctive because of their lack of permanent resident population and because of the need to balance the mandate of environmental preservation with the need to accommodate visitation. Indigenous communities are interesting in the context of growing empowerment, which extends to increasing influence on tourism through co-management to large parts of countries such as Canada and Australia. DAT outcomes are commonly assumed to be appropriate for indigenous territories, although the growth of casinos on US Reservations indicates the possibility for SMT outcomes. A final type of destination examined in this chapter is the small island, which is disproportionately affected by tourism yet ill equipped because of scale limitations to cope with this growth. Special events are an important component of destinations whose sustainability is influenced both positively and negatively by the compression of activity within a narrow spatial and temporal framework.

The complex and diverse nature of destinations makes it difficult to pursue sustainability-related quality control mechanisms such as accreditation. The Green Globe 21 Community Standard represents the highest profile attempt thus far to do so, although it is too soon to assess whether this is effective as a mechanism for achieving sustainable tourism.

On the net

Gold Coast Visioning Project (GCV)
http://www.goldcoast.qld.gov.au/t_std.asp?PID=3609

Green Globe 21 Community Standard
http://www.greenglobe21.com/Documents/General/CommunityStandard.pdf

International Environmental Film and Video Festival
http://www.planetinfocus.org/index.html

Luzon rice terraces (Philippines)
http://www.philippines.hvu.nl/Luzon2.htm

For further reading

Gössling, S. (ed.) (2003). *Tourism and Development in Tropical Islands: Political Ecology Perspectives*. Edward Elgar.

This excellent volume contains 11 chapters that explore the linkages between tourism, politics and environmental sustainability in island settings such as Zanzibar, Cayman Islands, Seychelles, Dominica, Hainan (China) and the Bay Islands of Honduras.

Judd, D. and Fainstein, S. (eds) (1999). *The Tourist City.* Yale University Press.
The authors explore the sociopolitical and economic foundations of the tourism city, featuring Las Vegas, Orlando and Cancún as case studies. The broader role of tourism as a dominant activity in other kinds of urban areas is also considered.

Weaver, D. (2000a). A broad context model of destination development scenarios. *Tourism Management*, 21, 217–24.
This article describes the broad context model using numerous destination examples and places it in the context of Jafari's four platforms. The Gold Coast of Australia is used as an example of how the model can be used to outline the broad contours of sustainable tourism planning in a diverse coastal resort.

Zeppel, H. (2006). *Indigenous Ecotourism: Sustainable Development and Management.* CABI Publishing.
While focusing on ecotourism, this book discusses a range of issues that is relevant to indigenous tourism more generally. These include empowerment and self-determination, involvement with protected areas, wildlife and cultural representation through tourism.

Beyond the book

1. (a) Identify the local tourist destination that includes your hometown and construct a hierarchy of destinations in which this local place is a component. (b) Identify the sustainable tourism policy and actions of each component in this hierarchy, including your hometown. (c) To what extent are these policies contradictory or complementary with respect to the efforts being made by your hometown to achieve sustainable tourism?
2. (a) Where is your hometown located in the broad context model of destination development scenarios? (b) Where is it likely to be situated ten years from now based on an extrapolation of current trends? (c) Where would you like to see your hometown situated ten years from now? (d) Why?
3. (a) For each of the destination types profiled in Section 8.5.1, identify a broad context model scenario, or amalgam of scenarios, that would represent an optimal long-term outcome. (b) Rationalize your selection in each case.
4. (a) Using the Green Globe 21 Community Standard for assistance (access the website address provided above), devise a list of ten core indicators that are applicable to any populated destination but not to companies. (b) Describe how each of these indicators could be measured and monitored.

On the ground: tourism options for Australia's Gold Coast

The Gold Coast, in the southeastern Queensland pleasure periphery, is Australia's best example of tourism urbanization and a good case study for examining sustainable tourism scenarios and outcomes at a regional scale. The Gold Coast region consists of the urbanized tourism city known as the 'Gold Coast' and an extensive urban-rural fringe, or 'hinterland', that extends inland for a distance of approximately 40 kilometres and includes at least one tourism shopping village, Tamborine Mountain, and high profile protected areas at Lamington and Springbrook. While the Gold Coast is known primarily for its 3S tourism opportunities, deliberate efforts have been made in recent years to diversify and reinvigorate the Gold Coast tourism 'brand' by incorporating the hinterland into the destination's marketing mix and sense of place identity. This is evident in recent promotional campaigns extolling the 'Green Behind the Gold' and the 'Coast with the Most', in which scenes of pristine

- Market dominated by mass tourists arriving on high-volume, low-yield package tours
- Decline in average visitor length of stay (usually only 2 or 3 nights)
- Growing market perception that destination is becoming over-commercialized, crowded and tacky
- Decline in appeal to international tourists
- Destination is no longer fashionable
- Competition from emerging newer destinations in Australia and elsewhere in the Asia-Pacific region
- Over-capacity within the tourism industry
- Declining profits of major tourism businesses
- Diversification into conventions and conferences to maintain visitor numbers and
- Growing number of built and contrived attractions, which start to outnumber the natural attractions (and especially the beach) that made the destination popular in the first place.

Figure 8.2
Indicators of UMT on the Gold Coast. Source: Faulkner, 2003.

rainforest are juxtaposed with beaches and high-rise resorts as iconic tourism images of the Gold Coast.

The incorporation of the hinterland into the Gold Coast tourism product, however, while logical from a marketing perspective, complicates the pursuit of sustainable tourism outcomes. The Gold Coast tourism city by itself is widely regarded as a 'mature' destination in which resort life cycle indicators of stagnation are increasingly evident, especially in tourism-intensive coastline neighbourhoods such as Surfers Paradise (Faulkner, 2003) (see Figure 8.2). Even the generally tourism-tolerant residents of the Gold Coast express negative views about the congestion, crime and tackiness of Surfers Paradise (Lawton, 2001a), indicating that much of the ageing high-rise tourism plant along the beach has moved toward UMT. Rapid urbanization, much of which is indirectly related to tourism, also affects the overall sustainability equation by contributing to environmental problems in the Gold Coast region.

While CAT-type tourism dynamics characterize almost all of the hinterland, nodes of mass tourism activity at Tamborine Mountain, Lamington and Springbrook attest to the incorporation of non-urban hinterland attractions into the regional tourism product. Here too, periodic problems of congestion, litter, aesthetically displeasing construction and resident disconnect are evidence of localized UMT-type problems. The worst-case scenario for the Gold Coast region is that UMT will become more pervasive in these nodes and that growing visitor numbers will result in the diffusion of mass tourism to other local rural areas, while the high-rise coastal strip of the tourism city will become increasingly intensive, unsustainable and dysfunctional. Environmentalists and others, for example, expressed concern in 2004 over the impacts of an 80-storey residential apartment complex, billed as the tallest such facility in the world, under construction in Surfers Paradise.

To avert this worst-case scenario, a coalition of tourism stakeholders embarked on a Gold Coast Visioning Project (GCV)* in the early 2000s to apply the principles of sustainable tourism in a collaborative and holistic way to the planning of regional tourism (Faulkner, 2003). In effect, the broad strategic vision of the GCV is to foster SMT in the tourism city and hinterland nodes where mass tourism is already dominant and DAT in the remainder of the hinterland as well as within some of the inland residential suburbs (Weaver, 2000a) (see Figure 8.3). Numerous obstacles, however, impede the ability of the Gold Coast City Council to adapt to a new strategic vision based on a sustainability-oriented planning model. These include the unremitting arrival of new residents, a strong business community supportive of the status quo pro-growth philosophy, the strong potential for cyclones and other major natural disasters and a state boundary that effectively removes an important part of the Gold Coast functional region (i.e. the Tweed district of New South Wales) from involvement in the GCV.

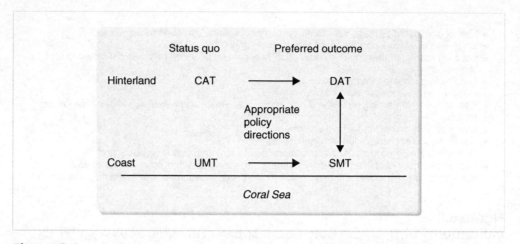

Figure 8.3
Application of the Broad Context Model to the Gold Coast of Australia.
Reprinted from Tourism Management 21, Weaver, D. A broad context
model of destination development scenarios, pp. 217–24. Copyright 2000,
with permission from Elsevier.

Exercise

Download the final report of the Gold Coast Visioning Project, which outlines the 'preferred
tourism future' of the Gold Coast (http://www.goldcoast.qld.gov.au/attachment/Tourism_
Final_Report.pdf). Note the vision statement on page 19 and the values on pages 18–19 that
underlie this vision. Is the implementation strategy outlined on subsequent pages a viable
means of implementing this vision?

Chapter 9
Spatial strategies for destinations

Chapter objectives

Upon completion of this chapter, the reader should be able to:

■ employ the concepts of frontstage and backstage as a framework for assigning tourism of different intensities to suitable areas within a destination
■ assess the circumstances under which assumptions of flexible and fixed carrying capacity, respectively, should be adopted by destination planners
■ describe the utility of development standards as a means of ensuring the quality of tourism-related landscape modifications and
■ evaluate the role of zoning, districting, redevelopment, purchase of development rights (PDR) agreements and trade-offs as spatial strategies that can be implemented by destination managers and planners to achieve sustainable tourism.

9.1 Introduction

The type and circumstances of any given destination dictate whether SMT or DAT outcomes, or some combination of the two, are appropriate for that particular place. Although accreditation and other quality control mechanisms for implementing either mode of sustainable tourism are not yet well articulated at the destination level, it is still possible to identify specific types of strategies that contribute to this goal. The purpose of this chapter is to outline sustainable tourism strategies that are broadly spatial or geographic in character. Section 9.2 differentiates between the concepts of frontstage and backstage and discusses the principles of flexible and fixed carrying capacity that respectively dictate whether a more or less intensive mode of tourism development should be pursued in a particular area within a destination. Section 9.3 then considers the role of development standards in ensuring that new construction and other landscape modifications adhere to the intent of backstage and frontstage designations. Subsequent sections examine spatial strategies related to zoning and districting, purchase of development rights (PDR) agreements and trade-offs. The role of government incentives is also briefly considered.

9.2 Frontstage and backstage

The concepts of *frontstage* and *backstage* emerge from the work of Goffman (1959), who distinguished between 'front regions' where performances in social establishments are made in front of customers and 'back regions', where performers retire to recuperate and prepare for future performances. MacCannell (1976) subsequently applied the concept specifically to tourism in differentiating between spaces manipulated and managed to accommodate tourists (the frontstage) and those where the private, everyday lives of the local residents are given priority (the backstage). The difference, however, can be transitional rather than dichotomous, with a distinction being made by MacCannell (1976) between unapologetically contrived performance areas such as the casinos of Las Vegas (stage one), frontstages decorated with artifacts from the backstage, such as those often found in the boutiques and restaurants of tourist shopping villages (stage two), frontstages such as the Polynesian Cultural Center in Hawaii (Stanton, 1989) that are organized to appear like backstages (stage three) and backstages such as the cultural villages of Senegal's Casamance region (see Section 3.2) and the Iban longhouses of Borneo (Zeppel, 1998) that are regularly opened to tourists (stage four; essentially a backstage/frontstage hybrid). Alternative tourism activities generally fall into this category. Moving even farther from the frontstage are backstages such as the Russian scientific bases in Antarctica or Strict Nature Reserves (IUCN Category I protected areas) where tourists are allowed only occasional and privileged access (stage five) and true backstages, where the only tourists normally encountered are VFR or business-related (stage six).

While the above distinctions apply mainly to different spaces, it is also possible for the same space to be used as different types of stage at different times. For example, a certain beach may function as a local backstage on Sunday mornings and every evening after dusk, but serve as a tourist frontstage at all other times. This beach may therefore be referred to as a *periodic frontstage*. There is also a dimension of mobility to the frontstage/backstage distinction, as illustrated by the difference between a tour bus or tourist taxi (i.e. mobile frontstage) and local transportation (i.e. mobile backstage). The roads that these vehicles occupy may variably qualify as a frontstage, backstage, or hybrid, depending on location and other factors.

9.2.1 Formal and informal designations

Many of the strategies described below, including zoning and districting, imply a formal designation of space and/or time to accommodate frontstage or backstage dynamics. However, the distinctions may also be implemented in an informal, temporary or spontaneous manner, especially during the informal early stages of the destination life cycle. Smith (1989), for example, describes how the Eskimo (Inuit) residents of Kotzebue, Alaska, erected sealskin barricades to shield their seal butchering from the prying eyes of tourist photographers during the early years of the tourism industry there. Weaver (the author of this book) had a personal experience with the informal backstage during a fieldtrip to Antigua in 1983 when an older local woman armed with a machete stepped into the road at the boundaries of a local village and menacingly stated that tourists from the nearby resort hotel were not allowed beyond that point. This example demonstrates how unclearly designated backstage demarcations increase the risk of cross-cultural misunderstanding, confrontation and vigilantism.

9.2.2 Implications for sustainability

The frontstage/backstage distinction has important implications for the realization of sustainable tourism outcomes. It can be argued that local residents are better able to cope with the demands and impacts of tourism if the brunt of such activity is confined to designated frontstage locations where, ideally, various strategies (see below) are implemented to moderate the impacts of this activity so that DAT or SMT outcomes are achieved. Elements of the local culture are offered to tourists in commodified form within the frontstage, leaving the backstage as an area where the traditional and 'authentic' culture can be practised and preserved beyond the conventional tourist gaze and where local residents can retreat and recuperate after their exposure to tourists in the frontstage. It is because of this 'sanctuary factor' that the intrusion of even well meaning alternative tourists holds such a high potential for negative sociocultural consequences, as described in Section 3.12.4.

As demonstrated by the experience of Egypt's Giza Plateau, the potential for serious conflict increases where the backstage/frontstage distinction is not clearly made or understood. The Egyptian government, aware of the site's value as an iconic tourist attraction, wishes to establish a controlled frontstage where activities and land uses not conducive to heritage preservation and visitor satisfaction are prohibited (Evans, 1998). However, this conflicts with the status of the area as an informal shantytown populated by an increasing number of poor Cairo residents, many of whom operate informal tourist-oriented businesses. Complicating the situation is the presence of middle-class Cairo visitors who perceive the site as an urban park that satisfies their own leisure and recreation needs. Mutual antagonism apparently characterizes relationships among all three groups, thereby jeopardizing the likelihood of sustainable tourism outcomes.

Implications for indicators

The frontstage/backstage distinction is relevant to the sustainable management of destinations and should therefore be taken into consideration when identifying the indicators of sustainable tourism and their critical thresholds. These indicators should include the percentage of the destination occupied by frontstage and backstage (and their sub-stages) and the stability of these distributions, as measured for example by the change in the area occupied by each category. A measure of the distribution and adjacency of the stages should also be included, since there is a higher potential for conflict in situations where a high intensity stage one frontstage shares a boundary with a 'pure' stage six backstage. The relevant indicator could therefore measure the length of such boundaries within a destination and the degree to which this has increased or decreased over a stipulated period of time. The physical nature of the boundary should also be documented as an indicator, since these can significantly influence the sustainability equation. A large concrete wall, for example, may effectively bar the intrusion of tourists and hide obtrusive built tourist attractions, but itself constitute an intrusive eyesore. Conversely, a buffer zone of dense tree cover may serve the former objectives without being intrusive or aesthetically displeasing.

Another implication is that frontstage spaces may require a different set of indicators and indicator benchmarks than those used in the backstage, in keeping with the weaker approach toward sustainability that is warranted if the former is already experiencing intensive levels of tourism activity. For example, a high tourist-to-resident ratio and high rate of annual growth may be sustainable in a tourism frontstage site hardened to cope with such patterns, but unsustainable in a residential backstage area.

9.2.3 Flexible and fixed carrying capacity assumptions

In designating an area as frontstage or backstage, assumptions are made implicitly or explicitly about the amount of tourism activity that is desirable in that area and the idea of flexible and fixed approaches to the *carrying capacity* of an area is therefore relevant. Weaver and Lawton (2002a) define carrying capacity as 'the amount of tourism activity that can be accommodated without incurring serious harm to a destination' (p. 460). Distinctions, moreover, can be made between ecological, economic and social carrying capacity (Page and Dowling, 2002), in keeping with the three dimensions of sustainability used throughout this book.

Limits of acceptable change (LAC) and carrying capacity

In recent years, models such as the LAC (limits of acceptable change) have been proposed as replacements for carrying capacity because of contentions that the latter is too difficult and subjective to identify, too negative and constraining, or too deterministic. The LAC, in contrast, starts by emphasizing the values that are deemed worthy of protection and then focuses on ways of providing this protection (McCool and Moisey, 2001). These might for example involve visitor education or improvements to infrastructure so that more visits can be accommodated without compromising the integrity of the natural environment. As described by Newsome et al. (2002), the basic question in carrying capacity is 'how much use is too much?' while the LAC asks 'how much change is acceptable?' It can be argued, however, that the idea of carrying capacity is still implicit in and compatible with the LAC, given that the former was originally intended to be employed as a variable threshold open to manipulation through the kinds of management techniques just described (Manning, R., 1999). Hence, once the LAC or a similar model is used to identify the amount and type of change that is acceptable, the question of 'how much use is *therefore* too much' must still be asked. It is for this reason that R. Manning (1999) refers to the LAC and allied models as 'carrying capacity frameworks' (p. 74).

Fixed carrying capacity assumption

A basic premise in designating an area as backstage is that anything more than minimal tourism-related change in this area is undesirable. Accordingly, as depicted in Figure 9.1a, fixed carrying capacity assumptions are warranted. That is, the level and mode of tourism activity are maintained below the critical carrying capacity threshold range of the destination, regardless of the actual level of tourism demand. This can be described as a supply-side approach, in that the decision to accept this assumption of fixed carrying capacities is based on what the destination (i.e. the supply) is deemed to be capable of supporting under these circumstances. Such an assumption may be warranted under several circumstances, including: (a) the area where the designation is being considered is known to be occupied by a fragile, relatively undisturbed natural environment or culture; (b) its carrying capacity is unknown (in which case the precautionary principle is invoked); (c) resources are not available to accommodate the intensification or expansion of tourism; and/or

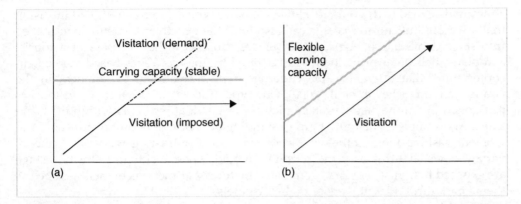

Figure 9.1
Stable and flexible carrying capacity thresholds. Source: Lawton, L.J. (2001). Encyclopedia of Ecotourism, D.B. Weaver (ed.), CABI Publishing. Reproduced with permission.

(d) residents are opposed to intensification. More generally, the decision is underpinned by the assumption that a strong sustainability approach is appropriate.

Flexible carrying capacity assumption

Because frontstage spaces are intended primarily to accommodate tourism-related activity and land uses, increases in the level of tourism in those areas are often considered desirable. Accordingly, strategies are implemented to allow for a gradual increase in the critical carrying capacity threshold range so that higher levels of tourism activity can follow (Figure 9.1b). Even though this approach is basically demand-driven, it is important to stress that the visitation or intensification curve should ideally *follow* the threshold curve so that the conditions are already in place to cope with increased demand at the time that more visitors arrive. The risky alternative to this proactive approach is to raise the threshold range *in response* to increased visitation, in which case the coping mechanisms might not be in place. However, this reactive approach might be adopted because of the understandable unwillingness of managers to invest in coping mechanisms intended to address visitation levels that may not actually be realized.

The assumption of flexible carrying capacities is appropriate when (a) the area in question is already heavily modified or urbanized and a weak sustainability approach is taken, (b) there is confidence in the projected carrying capacity thresholds associated with a given level of intensification, (c) resources are available to invest in the appropriate coping mechanisms, and/or (d) local residents and other stakeholders support intensification that leads toward SMT.

9.2.4 Violations of the backstage/frontstage demarcation

As mentioned above, negative social impacts are possible when tourists deliberately or inadvertently intrude by foot or vehicle into the 'pure' (or stage six) backstage of a destination, which measures such as the construction of a fence or forest buffer zone are designed to discourage. However, other types of tourism-related intrusion that are more difficult to manage can also limit the effectiveness of the backstage/ frontstage demarcation. *Aerial intrusions* are caused by the overpass of a tourist aeroplane, helicopter or balloon, as illustrated by the Las Vegas-based scenic helicopter tours that often disrupt wilderness-type recreational experiences in the Grand Canyon (Schewer et al., 2000). One type of *visual intrusion* involves tourists positioned in a frontstage who take pictures or gawk at residents within the backstage. An example is the tourist group standing on a bridge taking pictures of local women washing their clothes in the river below. Contrasting with this 'gaze-in' variant of visual intrusion is the 'gaze-out' model, where residents in the backstage are exposed to frontstage vistas dominated by tourist attractions or facilities such as theme park thrill rides, towers or high-rise hotels.

Aural intrusions are associated with unwelcome noises from theme parks, festivals, idling tour buses or other tourism-related activities carried out in the frontstage. The 2002 Washington DC Grand Prix auto race, for example, was tainted by complaints from residents of the neighbourhood adjacent to the track about excessive noise, where recorded decibel levels of 100–105 far exceeded the 60-decibel limit permitted in the city's residential areas (Kovaleski and Fallis, 2002). Finally, odours and fumes such as those generated by auto races, food festivals or idling buses are examples of *olfactory intrusions*.

9.3 Development standards

According to Bosselman et al. (1999), *development* or *performance standards* are 'legal restrictions that regulate a physical or measurable aspect of development. They are a means by which a community can mandate that the physical characteristics of a development meet certain standards and also that a development does not generate certain measurable impacts' (p. 70). Development standards are directly relevant to the discussion of sustainability since in principle they ensure that a particular area visually and functionally adheres to the spirit and intent of its frontstage or backstage designation and hence help to realize DAT or SMT outcomes. Accordingly, they represent one of the main ways in which the public sector can enforce sustainable tourism practices within the private sector (Middleton and Hawkins, 1998). Development standards are usually derived from the broad goals and related policy directives that are ideally identified through a process of stakeholder consultation. For example, the preservation of the traditional cultural landscape is a commonly sought goal in many backstages and low-density frontstages, from which a policy requiring new construction to adhere to traditional architectural norms may be adopted. Development standards are then articulated to provide the legal technical specifications that allow builders and renovators to adhere to these norms. Various types of development standards are described below.

9.3.1 Development density controls

Density, as commonly measured by the number of accommodation units per hectare or square kilometre, is one of the most objective ways of differentiating between frontstage and backstage, as well as between DAT and SMT tourism outcomes. According to Inskeep (1991), densities of 12–25 per hectare are 'very low' and indicate either cottage-type development or low-rise multiple unit structures surrounded by a large amount of open space. 'Low to medium' density of 25–75 per hectare suggests two-storey block buildings or multi-storey structures surrounded by open space. 'Higher' density of 75–150 units per hectare usually consists of four-storey block buildings, while 'high' density areas above 150 units per hectare are indicative of the high-rise strips that characterize intensively developed tourism cities such as Miami Beach and the Gold Coast.

Height restrictions

Increased height indicates increased obtrusiveness in the cultural landscape, but this may not necessarily be an indicator of unsustainability in tourism cities such as Miami Beach and the Gold Coast where the sense of place is closely related to signature high-rise beachfront strips. However, in rural resort settings, the negative impact of high-rise on the viewscape is more evident because of their discordance with the natural features of the landscape. For this reason, many Caribbean destinations have regulations that restrict the height of beachfront hotels to three storeys, thus effectively allowing mature coconut palms to hide the hotel skyline. In urban settings such as Oxford or Prague, height restrictions are implemented to preserve the medieval skyline of towers and spires. In other situations, the motivation is not so much landscape-related as based on the lack of infrastructural or road capacity to cope with the volume of use associated with a high-rise hotel tower.

Size and configuration of building 'footprint'

Another indicator of density in an area is the cumulative 'footprint' of all buildings, which can be expressed by the floor area ratio (FAR) (or floor space ratio – FSR), i.e. the area of all floors of all buildings on a site divided by the area of that site (Inskeep, 1991). A floor area of 2000 square metres on a 10 000 square metre property would yield a FAR of 0.2, or 20 per cent. The FAR, however, should not be used as an indicator without taking into account the actual configuration of the floor space. For example, four sprawling one-storey buildings occupying 20 per cent of the property may be less preferable from an ecological and aesthetic perspective than one ten-storey building occupying just two per cent of that site. The latter percentages, which measure the amount of a parcel occupied by buildings as seen from the air, is a footprint indicator known as *site coverage*. Low site coverage means that the property could retain a large amount of open space that could be used as a park or for natural habitat preservation.

Setbacks

Setbacks, or minimum distances required between landscape features, play a critical role in sustainable landscaping design. In 3S tourism, these are commonly manifested in the amount of open space that must be maintained between hotel buildings and the beach, as often defined by the high tide mark. The setback threshold in the Indian state of Goa is 500 metres, but just 12 metres in Hawaii (Inskeep, 1991). Notably, beach setbacks not only reduce the likelihood of erosion and light pollution (which can disrupt nesting sea turtles), but also improve the long-term financial sustainability of resorts by reducing the probability of serious damage from storms, high tides or salt-laden air. They also provide beach-goers with a greater sense of seclusion, but can also lead to inconvenience and dissatisfaction for hotel customers if the hotels are too far from the beach. Setbacks are also commonly used to protect watersheds and water quality and the quality of aquatic recreational experiences, by maintaining distance between buildings and streams or lakes. In urban settings, setbacks are often used to create adequate buffer zones between buildings and public roads or sidewalks, to the advantage of residents as well as visitors.

9.3.2 Building standards

Building standards that influence the pursuit of environmentally sustainable tourism include those related to energy efficiency, storing and disposing of liquid wastes in a non-polluting way and reducing glare from light pollution. Cultural sustainability is fostered by standards that require conformity to vernacular architectural norms and use of complementary paint colours and building materials, although it may not be desirable to obtain these from local sources if the relevant resources are endangered or cause environmental damage if removed. This is illustrated by Bermuda, where new tourism-related and other construction is required to mimic vernacular architectural styles characterized by distinctive pastel colours. However, new construction no longer uses the rare endemic Bermuda cedar or local coral-derived limestone traditionally used on the island.

9.3.3 Landscaping

Spaces that are kept open through setbacks, footprint minimization and zoning strategies (see Section 9.4) can be landscaped in ways that foster environmental and social sustainability. These include the maintenance of natural contours, drainage networks and wetlands; the retention of tree cover or other natural vegetation on open spaces and especially on sensitive sites such as steep slopes and floodplains; the avoidance or minimization of pesticide, herbicide and fertilizer applications; and preference for native trees, shrubs and grasses. Such standards typically form the basis of a *naturalization* strategy for selected public and private open areas that replaces the conventional emphasis on energy and chemical-intensive exotic vegetation, including large areas of heavily irrigated and manicured turf. The expansion of naturalization practices on golf courses was discussed in Section 6.6.2. Landscaping standards also include the construction of berms, or earthen embankments, to provide sound and visual barriers between potentially incompatible land uses such as parking lots and promenades, or a concert venue and a residential neighbourhood. Elevated wooden walkways in sensitive wetland areas are another example. The term *site softening* describes a type of development standard whereby heavily degraded open spaces left over from the construction of parking lots, roads, buildings, etc. are naturalized and restored through re-contouring and the planting of native flora.

9.3.4 Signage and above ground utility controls

Garish signs are an intrinsic part of the identity and attractiveness of intensively developed commercial tourist districts in Hong Kong (Hollywood Road), Tokyo (Ginza), Bangkok (Sukhumvit Road), New York (Times Square) and Las Vegas (the Strip) and thus are not necessarily indicative of unsustainable tourism. Signs more generally can facilitate sustainability by providing information that fosters appropriate tourist behaviour, including the identification of backstage and frontstage areas. Inappropriate signage, however, is distracting and substantially degrades the aesthetics of smaller communities and rural areas in particular. This creates a need for standards that reduce their visual impact through regulations that govern size, number, colour, shape, location, content, illumination and height. The paradox faced in such efforts is that while discrete signage may be preferable from a sustainability perspective, they may increase the probability that tourists will not be exposed to the information they contain. Hence, the above restrictions must be undertaken while preserving the effectiveness of signs as conveyers of strategically important information. Above ground utility structures such as telephone poles and wires also diminish the aesthetic qualities of the landscape and interrupt scenic viewscapes, leading to the widespread application of standards that require these to be buried.

9.3.5 Noise regulation

As mentioned above, aural intrusions into a backstage area can generate community dissatisfaction with the tourism sector. In addition to sound-muffling landscaping measures, standards which restrict decibel levels and the hours in which given levels of noise can be produced are therefore commonly applied to attractions such as theme parks, festivals, concerts and auto races that generate large volumes of noise. An added consideration is noise generated by tourism-related aircraft and vehicles, including personal recreational vehicles such as snowmobiles and jet skis and commercial vehicles such as tour buses. Because of the number of residents affected, considerable progress to reduce aircraft-related noise has been made by federal, state and local government. Less progress is evident with regard to personal recreation vehicles and buses, since even if technical standards are in place to reduce the noise volume from individual machines, it is more difficult to prohibit concentrations of machines that collectively violate local noise standards.

9.3.6 Public access

Sustainable development strategies may require that the public be effectively denied access to certain highly sensitive public places. Yet, as private tourism development occupies an increasing amount of space within a destination, it is also vital to preserve and facilitate community access to other strategic public spaces in order to maintain the goodwill of residents towards tourism. For example, most Caribbean destinations require public access corridors to the beach (which is usually regarded as public domain below the high water mark) to be provided at regular intervals (e.g. every 500 metres) from roadways. Strategically located private resorts may therefore be obligated to provide such access in an unencumbered and visible way.

In the UK, access to the network of rural Public Rights of Way is emerging as a major political and social issue and one made increasingly complex by the composition of those seeking greater restrictions. These include not only rural property owners on whose land the walkways are located, but also urban middle-class walkers who do not want these walkways to be 'overwhelmed' by other users. Whether such mass demand exists or not, however, is unclear, as is therefore the portion of the 'community' that is disadvantaged or advantaged by greater or reduced access to the public walkways (Kay and Moxham, 1996). An extreme example of a public access standard is the Swedish traditional concept of *Allemannsrätt* (literally 'everyman's right'), which opens up privately owned land to many different types of public recreation, including camping and berry picking, as long as these are undertaken in a responsible manner (Mortazavi, 1997).

9.4 Zoning and districting

Inskeep (1991) defines *zoning* as 'regulations [that] demarcate specific areas for different types of land uses and the development standards to be applied within each land use zone' (p. 432). In essence, zoning confines certain types of land use and activity to specified areas and thus formally recognizes spaces that fulfil backstage or frontstage-type functions at the municipal, regional, provincial or national level. Backstage areas are often identifiable because of zoning designations such as 'residential' or 'industrial' that preclude or restrict tourism-related land uses and activities. Stage four backstage/frontstage hybrids are evident in 'residential' zones that allow for the establishment of guesthouses, bed and breakfast establishments, or the renting of residential space to visitors on a short-term basis. Frontstage tourism-related zoning designations are extremely diverse, but normally combine a type of use (e.g. accommodation, recreation or attraction, retail) with an intensity of use as per a desired development standard (high density, medium density, low density), yielding for example a 'medium density accommodation' zoning option.

9.4.1 Sample application

The Resort Municipality of Whistler*, in the Canadian province of British Columbia, is a well-known ski resort widely regarded as an exemplar of sustainable destination planning and management (Bosselman et al., 1999; Waldron and Williams, 2002). Included in its practices is an elaborate and detailed zoning bylaw that attempts to minimize the environmental and sociocultural impacts of tourism on the community. Table 9.1 illustrates the complexity of this bylaw by providing an abbreviated description of six tourist accommodation zones and relevant selected development standards that apply to each. An additional zone, Tourist Bed and Breakfast One (TB1), facilitates the establishment of DAT-type accommodations in single-family residential areas. TB1 development standards include a 325 square metre limitation on B&B size, a 70 square metre limitation on auxiliary parking space, a height limit of 7.6 metres, a maximum site coverage of 35 per cent, minimum front and rear setbacks of 7.6 metres and a maximum of three guest rooms occupying no more than 74 square metres.

9.4.2 Protected area zoning

Land use within an individual protected area is largely determined by its IUCN designation, as outlined in Section 8.5.4. However, because most of these designations entail multiple mandates, zoning systems are commonly implemented by protected area authorities in order to minimize negative environmental impacts and stakeholder conflicts that potentially arise from these diverse demands. The zoning system used in the Canadian National Parks network by Parks Canada, which provides 'a framework for the area-specific application of policy directions' (Eagles and McCool, 2002, p. 90) is illustrative. As described in Table 9.2, Special Preservation and

Table 9.1
Zoning bylaw, Resort Municipality of Whistler, British Columbia

Zone	Intent	FSR	Max. height	Site coverage (%)	Setback
TA1	Provide for commercial tourist accommodation that complements the scale & density of surrounding development	0.20	11.0 m; 3 storeys	35	7.5 m from all boundaries
TA2	Provide for commercial tourist accommodation that complements the scale & density of surrounding development	0.30	8.0 m; 2 storeys	30	7.5 m from all boundaries
TA3	Provide for commercial tourist accommodation facilities outside in the principal commercial areas in the Resort Munic. of Whistler	0.58	12.0 m	30	7.5 m from all boundaries
TA4	Provide for commercial tourist accommodation facilities within the principal commercial areas in the Resort Munic. of Whistler	0.79	12.0 m; 4 storeys	30	9.0 m from all boundaries
TA7	Provide for commercial tourist accommodation facilities within the principal commercial areas in the Resort Munic. of Whistler	0.45	10.7 m; 3 storeys	35	7.6 m from all boundaries
TA8	Provide for commercial tourist accommodation facilities in the area peripheral to the Town Centre & to Lands North	na	23.0 m; 7 storeys	na	2.5 m if height <10 m; 5.0 m if height = 10–15 m; 15.0 m if height >15 m

Source: http://www.whistler.ca/reading/index.php?id=28

Table 9.2
Zoning system summary for Parks Canada

Zone class	Purpose	Boundary criteria	Resources	Public opportunity
Special Preservation	Specific areas or features that deserve special preservation because they contain or support unique, rare or endangered features or the best examples of features	The natural extent and buffer requirements of designated features	Strict resource preservation	Usually no internal access. Only strictly controlled and non-motorized access
Wilderness	Extensive areas that are good representations of each of the natural history themes of the park and which will be maintained in a wilderness state	The natural extent and buffer requirements of natural history themes and environments in areas 2000 ha and greater	Oriented to preservation of natural environment setting	Internal access by non-motorized means. Dispersed activities providing experiences consistent with resource preservation. Primitive camping areas. Primitive, roofed accommodation including emergency shelters
Natural Environment	Areas that are maintained as natural environments and which can be sustained with a minimum of low-density outdoor activities and a minimum of related facilities	The extent of natural environments providing outdoor opportunities and required buffer areas	Oriented to preservation of natural environment setting	Internal access by non-motorized and limited motorized means, including in the north, authorized air charter access to rivers/lakes, usually dispersed activities, with more concentrated activities associated with limited motorized access. Rustic, small-scale, permanent, fixed-roof accommodation for

		The extent of outdoor opportunities and facilities and their area of immediate impact	Oriented to minimizing impact of activities and facilities on the natural landscape	...visitor use and operational use. Camping facilities are to be at the semi-primitive level
Recreation	Limited areas that can accommodate a broad range of education, outdoor recreation opportunities and related facilities in ways that respect the natural landscape and are safe and convenient	The extent of outdoor opportunities and facilities and their area of immediate impact	Oriented to minimizing impact of activities and facilities on the natural landscape	Outdoor opportunities in natural landscapes or supported by facility development and landscape alteration. Camping facilities will be to the basic serviced category. Small and decentralized accommodation facilities
Park Services	Towns and visitor centres in certain existing national parks that contain a concentration of visitor services and support facilities as well as park administration functions	The extent of services and facilities and their area of immediate impact	Oriented to emphasizing the national park setting and values in the location, design and operation of visitor support services and park administration functions	Internal access by non-motorized and motorized means. Centralized visitor support services and park administration activities. Facility-based opportunities. Major camping areas adjacent to, or within, a town or visitor centre to the basic serviced category. Town or visitor centre

Source: Eagles, P. and McCool, S. (2002). Tourism in National Parks and Protected Areas: Planning and Management. pp. 91–2, CABI Publishing. Reproduced with permission.

Wilderness zones are respectively comparable in intent to the Strict Nature Reserves and Wilderness Areas of the IUCN classification scheme. These two zones allow for the delineation of what might be called the *environmental backstage*, where intrusions by tourists and other visitors are minimized. Natural Environment zones, because they accommodate compatible recreation-related structures such as rustic fixed-roof shelters, represent a backstage/frontstage hybrid. In contrast, sustainable recreational uses and related support activities are emphasized in Recreation and Park Services zones, which therefore reveal frontstage intentions potentially at an SMT level. Unlike municipalities or other populated political units, the implementation of a zoning system in the Canadian National Parks and similar networks is simplified by the fact that the relevant authority owns most or all of the area, although the interests of local indigenous groups may have to be taken into consideration (see Section 8.5.5).

A less conventional zoning system – and one that is especially relevant to a less developed country or areas where indigenous people are a significant factor – is used in the management of the protected area network of the Philippines (Eagles and McCool, 2002). Among its innovative options is a Sustainable Use Zone that emphasizes the maintenance of biodiversity but potentially allows for the sustainable harvesting of natural resources by indigenous people. Areas where priority is given to the proactive long-term rehabilitation of natural habitat may be designated as Restoration Zones, while Buffer Zones can be established in adjoining areas as a 'social fence' to minimize encroachment into the protected area. Cultural Zones protect areas where traditional cultural rights or ceremonies are exercised.

9.4.3 Districting

Districting involves the formal delineation of an area with special attributes, such as a historical urban neighbourhood or a scenic rural landscape. As such, it can be managed as a coherent and focused spatial unit to achieve specified goals such as historical preservation, urban renewal, protection of culture, environmental remediation and/or encouragement and containment of tourism. The resulting districts are superimposed over the existing structure of zones and generally conform in their management and planning to the latter. However, specially designated districts usually have their own administration structure and may be eligible for special funding and other provisions that help to meet the goals for which they were designated. For example, the 'Chinatown' districts that have been established in many large North American cities often accommodate street market stalls and highly obtrusive storefront signs that would not normally be allowed in other downtown commercial areas, but which lend an aura of cultural authenticity to the district that is attractive to tourists and other visitors. The sex or 'redlight' areas of Amsterdam and Hamburg are another example of a tourism-oriented urban district where special provisions prevail (Ashworth et al., 1988).

Control of access is a major issue in many urban historical districts. Vehicular traffic is prohibited or severely restricted in medieval town centres of European cities such as Rothenburg ob der Tauber (Germany), where traffic is prohibited in the Old Town each day from 11:00 to 16:00 hours and from 19:00 to 06:00 hours. Additional restrictions apply to the area within the town walls, which may have the perverse effect of increasing congestion in areas beyond the town walls (see Section 2.4.4). Similar traffic restrictions apply to the Old City of Krakow (Poland), where the authorities have banned the entry of tourist coaches but compensate for the inconvenience with a 'park and ride' scheme (see Chapter 10). The government of

Poland also established a special fund to restore the district's monuments following its designation as a World Heritage Site in 1978 (Airey, 2000).

Redevelopment

Districting strategies provide a convenient framework for undertaking neighbourhood redevelopment (or 'revitalization', 'renewal', 'regeneration', etc.), which epitomizes the enhancement approach to sustainable development and is necessary if an area is to be transformed from a UMT to an SMT situation. Ideally, redevelopment involves the removal or renovation of environmentally or socioculturally unsustainable structures and features and their replacement by land uses that embody the principles of sustainable tourism. Redevelopment also embraces the notion of public/private partnerships, since reconstruction activity is usually undertaken by the private sector. Major ongoing redevelopment projects in Canada that have been credited with improving the local quality of life and stimulating inner city tourism include Vancouver's Gastown, Old Montreal and the Toronto waterfront (Broadway, 1997). Even more dramatic is the role of redevelopment in addressing the rapid decline of the industrial sector in Birmingham, UK during the 1970s and 1980s. The International Convention Centre and related developments within the Broad Street Redevelopment district that were constructed during this time on the edge of the central business district have been credited with stimulating tourism, revitalizing the downtown area, providing a significant amount of direct and indirect employment and providing more cultural and recreational activities for local residents (Lutz and Ryan, 1997).

Vieux Carré (New Orleans)

Bosselman et al. (1999) describe the 90-block Vieux Carré (Old Quarter) of New Orleans (USA) as a classic example of inner city tourism-related districting. Any renovations or new construction must be approved by the Vieux Carré Commission*, a body appointed by the mayor to safeguard the district's colonial French architectural heritage. Detailed development standards govern such aspects as building materials and design, paint type and colour, height, sidewalks and signage. The actual application of these standards, as well as options for redevelopment, are influenced by a 'micro-zoning' classification system that assigns a rating to every structure based on its assessed historical and architectural significance (see Table 9.3).

Table 9.3
Ratings of architectural and historical importance, Vieux Carré

Rating	Description
Purple	National architectural or historical importance
Blue	Major architectural or historical importance
Green	Local architectural or historical importance
Pink	Local or major architectural or historical importance that has been detrimentally altered but, if properly restored, could be upgraded to blue or green
Yellow	Contributes to the character of the district
Orange	Unrated 20th century construction
Brown	Objectionable or of no architectural or historical importance

Source: http://www.new-orleans.la.us/home/vcc/ratings.php

As with many nature-based national parks, Bosselman et al. (1999) contend that the need to balance the preservationist mandate with increased tourist demand, especially during the annual Mardi Gras, is the greatest overall challenge facing the Commission. To this, however, must be added the site and situational characteristics of New Orleans, which is largely below sea level and positioned in the potential path of Caribbean hurricanes.

9.5 Purchase of development rights (PDR) agreements

The purchase of environmentally or culturally sensitive property and its subsequent designation as a public protected area, is one very effective way in which various levels of government can pursue an agenda of environmental sustainability. However, this option is frequently precluded by the absence of funds to carry out the purchase or manage the acquired property, or by the unwillingness of some or all property holders to sell their land. Expropriation of property is one means by which government can overcome this resistance, but its controversial nature and the likelihood that it will create animosity within the community limits its use, especially if the acquisition is not seen to be in the vital public interest.

Purchase of development rights or *PDR agreements* represent a compromise between the private property status quo and the acquisition of that property by government. PDR agreements in essence involve the payment of a negotiated sum to a landowner in exchange for permanent deed restrictions on the land uses and activities that are allowed on that land, which is retained as the private property of the existing landowner (Wright and Skaggs, 2002). The operative principle of these strictly voluntary arrangements is that the payment represents compensation for the decline in property value that is caused by the stipulated restrictions, which are usually intended to remain in effect for perpetuity. A property, for example, might be worth $100 000 in its present condition as a single lot mature forest, but $1 000 000 as a subdivision zoned for single family dwellings, assuming that such a zoning can currently be obtained by the landowner. A PDR agreement in this hypothetical case could involve a $900 000 payment to the landowner in exchange for retaining the property as an undivided mature forest. If the landowner sells this property to another individual, the PDR agreement remains in effect, so presumably the landowner will only obtain $100 000 for this land or whatever else market forces dictate for a single-lot mature forest with no development potential. Variations in this principle are possible, so that a smaller payment might be involved in exchange for increasing the minimum allowable lot size from 1 acre to 10 acres, for example.

PDR agreements are especially common in the USA and are commonly referred to as *conservation* or *agricultural easements* when they involve rural land that is retained as natural habitat or farmland. In such cases, land trusts are often established as non-governmental bodies empowered to accumulate and disseminate funds and otherwise monitor and manage PDR agreements within a given jurisdiction. Funds are often acquired through tax-deductible donations, although some municipalities raise funds through special voter-approved taxes. The American Farmland Trust* is among the largest US-based land trusts, having preserved about 400 000 hectares of farmland since 1980. While support for tourism is not explicitly cited as a motive of farmland protection by such land trusts, loss of farmland to urban sprawl has negative implications for the pursuit of sustainable tourism in destinations such as Lancaster County (Pennsylvania) and the Napa Valley (California) that depend upon the rural amenity of the cultural landscape (see Section 8.2.1).

9.5.1 Boulder County, Colorado

Boulder County, a rapidly growing municipality north of Denver, is often touted along with the City of Boulder as a case study of exemplary PDR agreements, having entered such arrangements on more than 8000 hectares of farmland and 245 properties since the mid-1970s. Another 10 000 hectares have been acquired by the County and are leased back to farmers. PDR agreements have also been undertaken on non-agricultural land as part of an overall attempt to contain urban sprawl and preserve the rural character of the local landscape. More than $135 million has been spent on all PDR agreements in Boulder County, with the monies coming primarily from voter-approved increases in the County sales tax.

9.6 Trade-offs

A trade-off is a catch-all term that describes *quid pro quo* arrangements in which the mutual interests of the relevant public and private sectors are advanced through compromise agreements that deviate from the strict interpretation of existing regulations and other laws. For example, a developer might be allowed a higher-than-allowed density of construction in one area – the 'receiving area' (presumably one that can cope with this higher density) – in exchange for allowing another parcel – the 'sending area' (presumably an environmentally sensitive site) – to be set aside as a conservation easement. Formal arrangements of this nature are known as *transfer of development rights (TDR) agreements*.

An advantage of the TDR over the PDR is that no-payment options are possible, since the developer recoups the loss of revenue from the conservation easement area through the higher revenues gained from the greater number of units allowed in the higher density area. Alternately, the developer can pay for the higher density concession in the receiving area and the government can use this money to obtain conservation easements in the sending area. This can even be effected through a competitive bidding process if several developers are interested in the same receiving area site. The probability that TDR schemes will help to achieve the goal of environmental and financial sustainability is increased when government effectively delimits sending and receiving areas between which the TDR exchanges can be made. In many cases these will involve areas where backstage and frontstage intentions respectively pertain. Other traits necessary for success include ease of understanding (since they tend to be complex in nature) and the provision of adequate incentives for property owners in sending areas to sell their development rights. From the public sector perspective, it is also important that the sending areas are areas subject to real development pressure, since to make TDR arrangements (or PDR arrangements for that matter) in areas where there is no reasonable prospect of such pressure is to make needless concessions to developers or needless outlays of revenue (Lawrence, nd).

Mitigation strategies

Another type of trade-off occurs when an agency agrees to or is required to make compensation for development-related damages incurred in one site by engaging in environmental or cultural restoration at another site. A recent example of such a mitigation strategy involved the Washington DC-based Smithsonian Institute*, which in 2003 funded the restoration of 44 hectares of the Manassas battlefield to its Civil War-era condition, in order to compensate for a bog destroyed in the construction of its National Air and Space Museum annex at a nearby location (Weiss, 2004).

9.7 Government incentives

Although not a spatial strategy as such, destination governments can facilitate destination sustainability by offering incentives to individuals, companies and organizations for adopting green practices that are not already strictly required. For example, capital gains and income tax deductions are provided by many US states to landowners who donate land to the government, while inheritance taxes are commonly reduced for landowners who enter into PDR agreements (Crompton, 1996). Since 1983, the state of North Carolina has provided a tax credit that allows landowners to deduct 25 per cent of the fair market value of their 'conservation gift' from the donor's state income or estate taxes. The Montana Department of Environmental Quality* offers an array of tax exemptions, credits and reductions for property owners who install renewable energy systems. Among the relatively small number of incentive programmes that specifically target the tourism industry is the Barbados Tourism Development Act of 2002 which, among other sustainability-related measures, allows hotel operators to claim a 150 per cent tax deduction on expenses resulting from the pursuit of Green Globe 21 certification.

9.8 Summary

Various spatial strategies can facilitate the sustainable development of tourism in different kinds of destinations. A fundamental concept that underlies these strategies is the frontstage/backstage continuum, wherein the frontstage is an area where sustainable tourism, including either SMT or DAT, is concentrated and fostered. The backstage is in essence an area where local residents can seek refuge from the tourism sector, although a limited amount of DAT might be tolerated under some circumstances. The sustainable tourism indicators and thresholds that are relevant in each type of area, accordingly, will differ, as different assumptions about their respective carrying capacities are adopted. Backstages tend to be managed on the assumption of fixed carrying capacities for tourism, while frontstages are often based on flexible capacity assumptions in order to accommodate channelled tourism growth. To be effective, opportunities for tourists and other frontstage activities to intrude into the backstage must be minimized by effective boundary maintenance and other measures, though this is complicated by the possibility of aerial, visual, aural and olfactory violations that can cause dissatisfaction among local residents.

Development standards are a more specific category of strategy that facilitate frontstage and backstage distinctions. These include development density controls, height controls, the size and configuration of a structure's footprint, setbacks, building standards that conform to vernacular architectural norms and/or that foster energy conservation, landscaping protocols, signage and above ground utility controls, noise regulation and maintenance of public access to strategic public space. Zoning systems, as exemplified by the Canadian ski resort of Whistler and some higher order protected areas, provide a spatial framework for designating areas where different standards are applicable and where incompatible land uses and activities are therefore prohibited. These systems, in turn, may be complemented by the designation of districts such as the Vieux Carré of New Orleans where sustainability efforts based on historical or environmental preservation, or other modes of redevelopment, are focused. Many destinations, and especially those in North America, do not wish to purchase land to establish protected areas, but have the option of pursuing purchase of development rights (PDR) agreements in which landowners in essence are paid to forego development options on their land that would increase its market value. A related trade-off option is a transfer of development rights (TDR) agreement, in which the development rights on a particular parcel of land are transferred to another parcel so that the environmental and cultural sustainability objectives of the public and the financial sustainability objectives of the private landowners and developers are both satisfied. Mitigation strategies represent another type of trade-off strategy. Governments in many destinations offer incentives to encourage the adoption of sustainability-related practices.

On the net

American Farmland Trust
http://www.farmland.org/what/index.htm

Calviá, City Council
http://www.calvia.com/Pages/Idiomas/Ingles/iindex.htm

Montana Department of Environmental Quality
http://www.deq.state.mt.us/energy/Renewable/TaxIncentRenew.asp

Smithsonian Institute (Manassas battlefield restoration)
http://www.nasm.si.edu/museum/udvarhazy/bts/bts_wetlands.cfm

Vieux Carré Commission
http://www.new-orleans.la.us/home/vcc/index.php

Whistler, Resort Municipality (Canada) Zoning bylaw
http://www.whistler.ca/reading/index.php?id=28

For further reading

Bosselman, F., Peterson, C. and McCarthy, C. (1999). *Managing Tourism Growth: Issues and Applications*. Island Press.
A range of global case study destinations is used in this book to illustrate sustainable tourism strategies such as districting, performance standards and PDR agreements, as well as carrying capacity and related concepts such as limits of acceptable change (LAC).

Inskeep, E. (1991). *Tourism Planning: An Integrated and Sustainable Development Approach.* Van Nostrand Reinhold.
Chapter 11 provides a detailed discussion of development standards and Chapter 15 examines the role of zoning, in a classic textbook that emphasizes tourism planning from a sustainability perspective.

Beyond the book

1. (a) Draft a map of your local community that demarcates backstage and frontstage spaces according to the six stages identified by MacCannell (1976). (b) Indicate whether these spaces are formally or informally demarcated and describe the boundaries that separate them. Note any characteristics (e.g. juxtaposition of incompatible spaces, inadequate boundary separation, etc.) that may impede the quest for sustainable tourism.
2. Table 9.1 provides a simplified description of the Whistler Bylaw as it relates to hotels and other frontstage tourist accommodations. (Further detail can be accessed from the listed website.) Write a 500-word report that describes how the zones attempt sequentially to accommodate sustainable development, both environmental/sociocultural and financial, within zones that are increasingly frontstage in character as they progress from TA1 to TA8. Comment on any improvements that you think could be made to these designated development standards.
3. The Vieux Carré Commission ratings of architectural and historical importance include a 'brown' rating that can be applied to structures judged to be 'Objectionable or of no Architectural or Historical Importance' (Table 9.3). However, it can be argued that *any* construction is a legitimate and authentic expression of the diversity of human values and norms and hence should be considered for protection in the interests of preserving a cultural landscape that truly reflects this diversity and its evolution. Do you agree or disagree? What does this say about the role of redevelopment in promoting cultural sustainability?

On the ground: attempting to rejuvenate the mature tourism resort of Calviá, Spain

Calviá*, on the island of Mallorca in the Spanish Mediterranean pleasure periphery, is an illustrative example of a mature tourism city that is attempting to move from UMT to SMT. The 143-square kilometre municipality, which includes 55 kilometres of coastline, 120 000 units of tourist accommodation and 50 000 permanent residents, attracted 1.2 million visitors in 1997 and 1.6 million in 2000. Twenty per cent of the area, mostly adjacent to the coast, is urbanized, while a Gold Coast-type rural hinterland occupies the interior. Tourism in Calviá began to accelerate following World War II and by 1960 there were almost 7000 units of accommodation catering to the clients of cheap northern Europe-based package tours. This and subsequent tourism-related development has been characterized as spontaneous and haphazard, so that Calviá showed evidence by the late 1980s of the stagnation and decline stages of the destination life cycle model (Essex et al., 2004).

In response to this situation, municipal leaders in the early 1990s embarked on a comprehensive attempt to implement sustainable tourism in Calviá. This was carried out as part of the Local Agenda 21 initiative, which encourages the grassroots pursuit of the sustainable development agenda that emerged from the Rio Earth Summit in 1992. After several years of community consultation involving about one-third of Calviá's adult population, a strategy of radical rehabilitation was selected and subsequently articulated by 1998 in a Comprehensive Rehabilitation Scenario consisting of ten 'lines of action' and 40 specific initiatives related to these lines.

The first of these actions expresses the intent 'to contain the human pressure, to limit the growth and favour the comprehensive restoration of the territory and its littoral'. Related initiatives include the declassification of 1350 hectares of land that had been zoned for urban development, the prohibition of new buildings on rural land and the introduction of 'ecofriendly' building standards that take into account bioclimatic adaptation. The third action, 'to maintain the land and sea natural heritage and promote the creation of a tourist and regional eco-tax with environmental purpose', has proven controversial. The ecotax was introduced into the Balearic Islands in 2000 on the 'user pay' principle and entailed a progressive tax on tourist accommodation, the proceeds of which were to be allocated for environmental remediation. Thus, visitors in five-star accommodation were charged 2 euros per day, while those staying in DAT-type rural tourism facilities were charged just 0.25 euros per day (Palmer and Riera, 2003). Problems included high administrative costs and differences in interpretation as to what constitutes environmental remediation as well as in determining how the money should be allocated. However, it was aggressive opposition from the tourism industry (local hotel operators as well as overseas outbound tour operators) and a decline in visitor numbers, that resulted in the repeal of the ecotax in November 2003 (Essex et al., 2004).

Action five intends 'to promote the comprehensive restoration of the residential and tourist population centres' of Calviá. A related initiative is the establishment of Environmental Renovation Areas where restoration efforts are focused. This builds on innovative efforts, commencing in 1993, to demolish poorly situated and designed beachfront hotels that were constructed in the 1960s and 1970s. Through the Beach Clearance Plan, over 30 building clearance action plans have been undertaken, involving the reclamation of 51 000 square metres of land. Most of this newly acquired land has been converted to green space, or used for the establishment of a Maritime Esplanade. Other relevant initiatives include the introduction of the Ecotur ecolabel, which is used to rate the environmental performance of hotels and other accommodation in the Balearic Islands. As part of efforts to improve public transportation and public access, it is also the intent to restore a network of ancient public footpaths that had been neglected due to the decline of the agrarian economy and the acquisition by non-residents of the estates where these paths are located. The ability to carry out this and other actions, however, has been impeded by the repeal of the ecotax and by continued pressure from increasing numbers of tourists and migrants from other parts of Spain and Europe.

Exercise

1. Prepare a 500-word report that considers the positive and negative aspects of introducing an ecotax to a destination similar to the one that was implemented briefly in the Balearic Islands. Include a plan of implementation that reduces the negative impacts while maximizing its positive effects.

Chapter 10
Visitor management strategies for destinations

Chapter objectives

Upon completion of this chapter, the reader should be able to:

- assess the circumstances under which visitation capping strategies such as quotas, entry fees and infrastructure limitations are warranted in a destination to prevent negative tourism impacts
- describe how spatial and temporal channelling strategies can be employed to obtain sustainable tourism outcomes
- apply the recreation opportunity spectrum (ROS) as a framework for matching visitor expectations with available tourism resources
- evaluate the strategies by which visitor behaviour can be positively modified through effective education, including persuasion and interpretation and
- explain how destination managers can use target marketing and demarketing to attract desired visitors and discourage those that are unwanted.

10.1 Introduction

To be truly effective, the spatial strategies outlined in the previous chapter must be accompanied by a parallel set of strategies that focus on the management of visitors and visitation flows within a given destination. The first section in this chapter (Section 10.2) considers the option of capping visitor numbers through the implementation of formal quotas, user fees and deliberate limitations on tourism-related infrastructure and other services. Micro-scale capping strategies such as group size limits are also considered. Section 10.3 focuses on the redistribution and channelling of tourists both spatially as well as temporally and examines the recreation opportunity spectrum (ROS) as a framework for matching tourist expectations with spaces and resources that are capable of meeting those expectations in a sustainable way. This is followed in Section 10.4 with a discussion of visitor education strategies. The broader issues of effective persuasion and interpretation are discussed in the context of guidebooks and other pre-experiential settings and in experiential contexts such as those provided by tour guides and signage. Finally, Section 10.5 considers the option of target marketing desired tourist segments, as well as the possibility of destination 'demarketing' as a way of discouraging the presence of unwanted tourist segments or tourists more generally.

10.2 Visitation caps

Strategies to cap visitor numbers at a given level are consistent with the fixed carrying capacity approach to destination management (see Section 9.2.3), wherein it is assumed that additional visitor numbers, all else being equal, will result in an unsustainable tourism sector within a given area over a given period of time. If, however, the caps involve a restriction on the annual *growth* of visitors (e.g. no more than a 2 per cent increase per year), then this is indicative of a flexible carrying capacity approach that allows for increased visitor numbers in concert with the implementation of measures that accommodate these increases. Formal quotas, group size limits, entry and other user fees, as well as infrastructure controls, are all vehicles through which visitation caps can be achieved within the context of the spatial strategies described in the previous chapter.

10.2.1 Quotas

Quotas entail formal restrictions on rates of visitation increase or in the number of visitors allowed into a certain area, over a specified period of time (e.g. annual, monthly, seasonal, daily, etc.). Private sector facilities such as theme parks and ski resorts frequently use quotas as a means of ensuring quality of visitor experience and avoiding over-capacity, though rarely to fulfil the goal of environmental or socio-cultural sustainability. In contrast, the latter is a major consideration for the application of quotas to higher order protected areas, where managers are mandated to preserve habitat integrity and where access may already be controlled through entrance fees and a small number of entry points (see below).

Galapagos National Park is an iconic high order protected area off the coast of Ecuador that was declared a World Heritage Site in 1978. Its managers have employed a strategy wherein visitor caps are established and periodically raised, thus indicating a fluctuation between fixed and flexible carrying capacity approaches. The 1973 Master Plan established a ceiling of 12 000 annual visitors, which was subsequently raised to 25 000 in 1981 and 50 000 in the early 1990s. There is evidence to suggest that these ceilings have been frequently and deliberately violated, although it is unclear in the first instance whether such exponential increases were viable from a sustainability perspective (Wallace, 1993; Weaver, 2000b). Visitor caps are also becoming increasingly prevalent at high demand linear recreational resources such as the West Coast Trail in British Columbia, Canada and the wilderness trails of Yosemite National Park in California, where numbers are regulated through a free permit system. In the former case, no more than 60 hikers are permitted to begin the hike each day and an annual quota of 8000 users has been imposed.

Political jurisdictions

In a democratic society, formal visitor quotas are only rarely applied to municipality-level political units due to issues such as freedom of access rights, political opposition and enforceability (e.g. easy physical access, cost). At the national level, countries with border controls in place are in a better position to levy quotas on foreign visitors, though they seldom do so because of the desire to increase revenue from international tourism. There are, however, several notable exceptions to this generalization, some of which are motivated more by political considerations (e.g. North Korea, Himalayan states of India) and others ostensibly more by sustainability considerations. In the latter category, Bhutan is noted for its policy of rigorously restricting international tourist flows, despite high demand, to a few thousand individuals per year in the interests of increasing its 'gross national happiness' (Brunet et al., 2001). At the opposite end of the tourism continuum, Bermuda, already long faced with the problems of product 'maturity', introduced a policy in 1988 to limit cruise ship excursionists to 120 000 during the May–October high season. This was subsequently raised to 150 000 in the early 1990s after excursionist arrivals fell to just 113 000 in 1990. The local hospitality industry supported these restrictions, indicating a political motivation behind Bermuda's excursionist cap (Conlin, 1996).

Group size limits

Limitations on group size can be regarded as micro-scale quotas imposed within specific attractions or sites. A classic example is Antarctica, where the strict bylaws of the International Association of Antarctica Tour Operators (IAATO) provide for a maximum of 400 ship passengers. No more than 100 of these are allowed ashore at any given time and one expert guide must be provided for every 15–20 tourists (Weaver, 2001b). At Nefertari's tomb in Luxor, Egypt, a visitor limit of 150 per day was imposed in the mid-1990s following the release of research showing that 125 people staying in the tomb for one hour would expose the walls to the equivalent of three gallons of water. In addition, only small groups were allowed into the tomb for stays that could not exceed 16 minutes (Rivers, 2000). The management of British Columbia's West Coast Trail does not allow hiker group size to exceed ten individuals except in the case of qualifying school and non-profit organization groups.

Quotas are often used to reinforce zoning systems. For example, Zone 1 areas (the most pristine) within Saba Marine Park in the Netherlands Antilles allow for no more than 20 individuals in a diver group 90 per cent of the time. This is lowered to 75 per cent in the less pristine Zones 2–4 (Halpenny, 2002).

10.2.2 User fees

In lieu of or in addition to formal quotas, a popular management tool in protected areas and many other types of attraction is the manipulation of *user fees* to regulate demand (Lindberg, 1998). Managers ideally can increase prices until the desired level of visitation reduction is achieved, without incurring any concomitant decrease in revenue. For example, 10 000 visitors paying $10 each produces the same revenue as 20 000 visitors paying $5 each, but incur lower management costs. In addition to entry costs, other areas where user fees can potentially be implemented include recreation service fees, accommodation, equipment rental, food sales, parking, merchandise, permits and licenses (Eagles and McCool, 2002).

The case of entry fees in the Costa Rican national park system illustrates the potential and problems of user fee manipulation. Long set at $1.25 per entry despite chronic revenue shortfalls, the entry fee was raised to $15 in 1994 but lowered to about $6 in 1996 in response to opposition from inbound tour operators who felt that they would be absorbing the extra costs and others who claimed that this would foster an elitist form of tourism (Mowforth and Munt, 1998). To address the latter charge, a *differential fee policy* was implemented wherein Costa Rican nationals continued to pay the original $1.25 entry fee. The elasticity of the entry fee for international tourists is substantial, since even this increase of almost 400 per cent (i.e. from $1.25 to $6) represents only a negligible increase in the overall cost of a trip to Costa Rica from Europe or North America and hence is not likely to affect demand. Menkhaus and Lober (1996) argue that this fee could be increased to $40 without significantly affecting demand, thereby indicating the potential of user fees to fund the management and expansion of protected areas in Costa Rica, while providing an even greater incentive for their preservation. Evidence from Australia appears supportive, with Knapman and Stoeckl (1995) estimating that an increase in entry fee to Kakadu National Park from AU$4 to AU$16 would only nominally reduce estimated visitation from 239 000 to 227 000, while an AU$80 fee would still produce 173 000 visits.

In the case of Indonesia's Bunaken National Park, a survey dominated by back-packer visitors revealed a willingness to pay an entry fee of at least $12.50. For most respondents, however, this was conditional upon having assurance that the fee would be put toward conservation programmes within the park. As with Costa Rica, a differential fee structure was implemented whereby Indonesian citizens pay a nominal fee while international visitors pay $8. The decision to opt for a lower fee than yielded by the survey was based on the desire to minimize opposition from tour operators, prevent the government from appropriating a more attractive pool of funds and demonstrate that the funds will actually be used for conservation purposes before asking for an even larger fee. Park managers apparently hope to raise the entry fee gradually to $25 (Halpenny, 2002).

10.2.3 Infrastructure and service limitations

As with user fees, a *de facto* quota effect on visitors is produced when government controls infrastructure and other services to restrict the number of visitors who can access a particular area. Demand is thus limited by constraining supply rather than by raising prices. An example is provided by Bermuda, which limits the number of available bed-spaces to 10 000. When new spaces come available due to closures or downsizing, reallocation priority is given to hotels that maintain the highest operational standards (Conlin, 1996). In 1993, the Italian island of Capri temporarily abolished ferryboats to reduce congestion from tourist vehicles, though the problem actually became worse when private fishermen subsequently stepped in to provide ferry services to tourists (Van der Borg, 1998). This particular case suggests the need for a holistic planning approach that takes such exigencies into consideration, but also points to the limited powers of a municipal-level government to exercise control over such external forces.

It has been argued that the expansion of two small international airports on the Caribbean island of Dominica has been delayed or discouraged in the interests of maintaining visitation to levels consistent with a DAT-type policy (Weaver, 1991). However, this delay may also have as much to do with the government's inability to secure the necessary funding. At an urban municipal level, many European towns (e.g. Brugge in Belgium and Rothenburg ob der Tauber in Germany) prohibit parking lots or parking spaces in order to discourage the presence of private vehicles in historical core areas. Such infrastructure limitation policies, notably, contradict the advocacy platform, which posits that one of government's fundamental roles is the provision of infrastructure to accommodate market demand.

10.3 Redistribution

An alternative to restricting visitation numbers is to redistribute, channel or otherwise divert visitor flows so that problems of congestion and over-capacity (and also under-capacity) are avoided. Such strategies can be usefully divided between those that disperse and concentrate tourism activity (Bosselman et al., 1999).

10.3.1 Dispersal

Dispersal strategies that 'dilute' tourism-related activity and in theory distribute its employment and revenue benefits more equitably can be enacted at the national, regional, local and site-specific level. Nepal and the Maldives both illustrate this at the nationwide scale through their policies of opening new regions and locations to tourism in order to disperse benefits while preventing over-crowding in existing tourism locations (Brown et al., 1997). In the case of the Maldives, there is an added deliberate attempt to scatter resorts among remote and uninhabited atolls so as to minimize contacts between tourists and local residents and thereby preserve the residential backstage while keeping the resorts widely separated from one another. The Canterbury City Centre Initiative (CCCI) in the UK is an example of a municipal-level dispersal strategy that was implemented in the late 1990s to relieve congestion at Canterbury Cathedral, the city's iconic tourist attraction. The intent of the Initiative is to convert the nodal pattern of concentration (i.e. the Cathedral) into a linear one in which the Cathedral is positioned as just one of several pilgrimage-themed historical attractions along a new walking trail in the city core (Queen Bertha's Walk). Tourists are encouraged to walk the entire trail in order to gain a better appreciation of the medieval pilgrimage experience (Bosselman et al., 1999).

10.3.2 Concentration

Unregulated tourism development, as depicted in the destination life cycle model, tends toward spatial and temporal concentration, which in turn is commonly regarded as both a cause and symptom of unsustainability (Butler, 1980). Yet, with appropriate regulation and management, spatial concentration can actually serve as an effective strategy contributing to the attainment of sustainable tourism within the destination as a whole. This contention is based in part on the premise that concentrated tourism activity serves to confine negative impacts such as congestion to a small portion of the destination, thereby leaving most of the latter as a backstage relatively unscathed by these direct negative impacts while still receiving benefits from employment and revenue disbursements. The Gold Coast of Australia illustrates this phenomenon, wherein the vast majority of tourism activity occurs along a narrow coastal strip occupying less than 2 per cent of the City Council area.

Strategies focused on concentration are also justified by the economies of scale they generate that allow otherwise uneconomical site hardening and visitor management measures to be pursued within confined frontstage spaces. For example, the sophisticated and environmentally friendly facility development that is being carried out at the South Rim area of Grand Canyon National Park* is only feasible because of the expectation of four million or more visitors per year at the site. Central to this development is the introduction of mass transit shuttle options that will largely eliminate the need for private vehicles and parking lots in the South

Rim area. In addition, the construction of the Canyon View Information Plaza serves as a transit hub and a centre for focused visitor orientation, education and retail activity. Located only a few hundred metres from the canyon rim, the Centre when fully operational is designed to accommodate 4200 visitors per hour in a way that is efficient, sustainable and satisfying to visitors (National Park Service, 2001). Seen in this light, the confined frontstages that are generated through concentration strategies can be described as nodes of sustainable mass tourism rather than 'sacrificial spaces' in which negative environmental or sociocultural impacts are assumed.

10.3.3 Dispersal/concentration hybrids

Heavily visited high order protected areas, in practice, tend to pursue a combination of dispersal- and concentration-based strategies. Together, they consciously or unconsciously represent some variant of the so-called *95/5 rule*, wherein 95 per cent of visitor-related activity, or a similarly dominant portion of visitation, is deliberately channelled to 5 per cent of the park's area, or a similarly subordinate portion of space (Lawton, 2001b). In the nomenclature of the Parks Canada zoning system (see Table 9.2), a small part of a park's area would be zoned for 'Recreation' or 'Parks Service' and would be designed to accommodate large numbers of mainly day-only visitors engaging in a wide variety of facility and service-intensive nature-based activities. In contrast, the remainder of the park would be zoned as 'Wilderness' or 'Natural Environment', attracting a relatively small number of visitors engaged in physically challenging activities requiring few if any services or facilities. Essentially, the 5 per cent 'confinement zone' is a recreational frontstage accommodating SMT, while the 95 per cent 'dispersal zone' is a recreational backstage accommodating DAT.

Beyond protected area networks, hybrid planning strategies are also sometimes pursued at the regional and national scale. A classic example of the former is the Languedoc-Roussillon region of the French Riviera, where central planners since the 1960s have strived to avoid continuous ribbon development by channelling tourism activity into five intensively developed areas along the coast while leaving intermediate areas in a largely undeveloped condition (Pearce, 1989). At the national level, the Mexican government policy of dispersing 3S resort development through the establishment of tourism growth poles at Cancún, Ixtapa, Huatulco, Los Cabos and Loreto (see Section 8.4.3) is illustrative. These five sites were selected as the result of a 2-year scientific analysis of potential sites that attempted to increase the probability of success by taking into account such factors as the quality of the scenery and beaches, the need for economic development, the scope for alternative economic activity, the availability of infrastructure and water and travel times from major potential market regions (Collins, 1979).

Recreation opportunity spectrum (ROS)

The recreation opportunity spectrum, or ROS, is an organizational framework that facilitates concentration and dispersal strategies by matching various types of recreational expectations and desired experiences with areas where these experiences are compatible and where satisfying as well as environmentally sustainable experiences can be subsequently undertaken (Sofield and Li, 2003). Hence, it is closely related to the concepts of carrying capacity and LAC as discussed in Section 9.2.3. As employed by the US Forest Service, the ROS allows for six categories or 'opportunity classes', ranging from 'primitive' spaces that emphasize isolation and close contact with nature to 'urban' spaces that are heavily serviced to accommodate large numbers of visitors pursuing a wide range of activities. Intermediate categories include 'semi-primitive non-motorized', 'semi-primitive motorized', 'roaded natural' and 'rural' (Forest Service, 1986).

Proper application of the ROS would mean that areas within a protected area or elsewhere are designated according to the degree to which they can sustainably accommodate certain activities and tourists and other visitors would be directed towards or would select areas where their desired activities can be undertaken. A four-wheel drive enthusiast, for example, would be channelled to a 'semi-primitive motorized' area where trails and other facilities are presumably in place to accommodate this kind of activity in an environmentally responsible manner and where encounters with incompatible activities are minimized.

The accommodation and encouragement of a diverse array of recreational activities within compatible areas is a major strength of the ROS, as is its ability to provide the basis for formal zoning and management structures. It is alleged that 30 per cent of the USA's land area had been classified through the ROS by the early 1980s and it has also been extensively applied within Australian and New Zealand protected areas (Newsome et al., 2002). Weaknesses, however, include the potential for disagreement as to how certain areas should be designated and the lack of any mechanism to ensure that excessive amounts of space are not zoned for more intensive or invasive types of activity, thereby creating an overall situation that is unsustainable. A novel critique is offered by R. Manning (1999), who criticizes the ROS for adhering to rigid linear alignments of environmental, social and managerial criteria (i.e. 'natural' environmental conditions are aligned with 'low-density' social conditions and 'undeveloped' managerial conditions) when there is no inherent basis for precluding the possibility, for example, of high density use in natural areas under intensely managed circumstances.

10.3.4 Temporal considerations

The dispersal or concentration of visitors through *time*, in conjunction with or in lieu of spatial management strategies, is another option to consider in the pursuit of sustainable tourism outcomes. The periodic closure of camping areas and sections of beach to facilitate natural recovery is one illustration of a temporal component to a redistribution strategy, as is the above-mentioned time limit on group visits to Nefertari's tomb in Egypt. Many destinations, hotels and attractions offer direct (i.e. to tourists) and indirect (i.e. to travel agents and tour operators) incentives such as reduced prices and meal vouchers to encourage visitation during the off-season, although this is usually done with the specific goal of improving financial performance rather than environmental or sociocultural sustainability. There is no reason, however, why such strategies cannot be utilized specifically for sustainability purposes. This similarly applies to the option of raising user fees or instituting quotas only during periods of high anticipated demand.

10.4 Education

Travellers who seek educational experiences constitute a well-established segment of the tourist market (Ritchie, 2003). However, this concept of 'educational tourism' is distinct from the contention that *all* tourists should be exposed to education that promotes sustainable behaviour. The same, of course, might also be said about local residents and all other stakeholders in the tourism system, though the need for sustainability education is most often directed towards the tourist. The ROS, outlined in Section 10.3.3 above, is an example of a visitor-oriented education tool insofar as one purpose is to match visitor expectations with areas in which these expectations and their associated activities are environmentally compatible. Well-publicized tourism awards and accreditation programmes (see Chapter 7), as well as advisory websites (see Section 4.5.2) also serve an educational purpose by directing environmentally and socially conscientious tourists towards products and destinations that fulfil a variety of sustainability criteria.

10.4.1 Persuasion

McKercher (1993), in his exposition of the 'fundamental truths' about tourism, reminds us that tourists are not anthropologists, but consumers who are primarily concerned with being entertained. This assertion fails to recognize that tourist motivations are extremely diverse, but it does suggest that desired sustainability outcomes are unlikely to be achieved in a destination if mass tourists are exposed to education that is too pedantic or heavy-handed. It is therefore relevant in the interests of effective tourist-oriented education and communication to emphasize *persuasion*, which is an 'indirect' educational approach that influences rather than directly regulates or forces desired behaviour (Marion and Farrell, 1998). Persuasion is a form of *soft intervention* that contrasts with *hard interventions* such as physical barriers and policing (Van der Borg, 1998).

In practice, direct and indirect strategies as well as hard and soft intervention must all be incorporated into visitor management strategies, given the diversity of tourists that are likely to visit a given destination. According to R. Manning (1999), direct and hard interventions are necessary to minimize problems created by the relatively small number of tourists engaging in maliciously illegal behaviour such as vandalism and disturbing the peace (see Figure 10.1). Persuasive messages, in contrast, are moderately effective in curtailing careless actions such as littering and

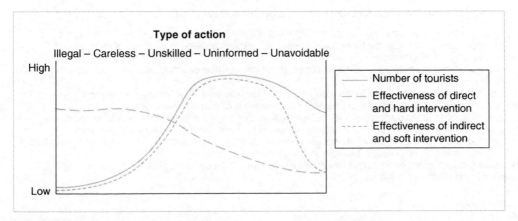

Figure 10.1
Effectiveness of intervention strategies by type of action.

trespassing undertaken by a larger number of tourists and most effective in reducing the incidence of unskilled actions (e.g. selecting an improper camping site) and uninformed actions (e.g. camping too close to another camping party) carried out by large numbers of tourists. However, they are relatively ineffective in curtailing unavoidable but non-malicious actions such as the elimination of bodily wastes and the trampling of vegetation at the site of a tent.

Tourist codes of conduct

In concordance with the priorities and concerns of the cautionary platform, codes of conduct aimed directly at the tourist are authored mainly by non-profit NGOs such as Tourism Concern and focused on destinations in the developing world. They are also especially prevalent in the ecotourism sector (see Chapter 11). A good example is the Himalayan Tourist Code (see Figure 10.2), which features simple guidelines to convey the idea that the tourist's cooperation will help to protect the environment and culture of the area while conferring the respect and warm welcome of local residents.

THE HIMALAYAN TOURIST CODE – TOURISM CONCERN, UK

The Himalayan Tourist Code – Tourism Concern, UK

By following these simple guidelines, you can help preserve the unique environment and ancient cultures of the Himalayas:

Protect the natural environment

* Limit deforestation – make no open fires and discourage others from doing so on your behalf. Where water is heated by scarce firewood, use as little as possible. When possible choose accommodation that uses kerosene or fuel efficient wood stoves.
* Remove litter, burn or bury paper and carry out all non-degradable litter. Graffiti are permanent examples of environmental pollution.
* Keep local water clean and avoid using pollutants such as detergents in streams or springs. If no toilet facilities are available, make sure you are at least 30 metres away from water sources, and bury or cover wastes.
* Plants should be left to flourish in their natural environment – taking cuttings, seeds and roots is illegal in many parts of the Himalayas.
* Help your guides and porters to follow conservation measures.

As a guest, respect local traditions, protect local cultures, maintain local pride

* When taking photographs, respect privacy – ask permission and use restraint.
* Respect Holy places – preserve what you have come to see, never touch or remove religious objects. Shoes should be removed when visiting temples.
* Giving to children encourages begging. A donation to a project, health centre or school is a more constructive way to help.
* You will be accepted and welcomed if you follow local customs. Use only your right hand for eating and greeting. Do not share cutlery or cups, etc. It is polite to use both hands when giving or receiving gifts.
* Respect for local etiquette earns you respect – loose, light weight clothes are preferable to revealing shorts, skimpy tops and tight fitting 'action wear'. Hand holding or kissing in public are disliked by local people.
* Observe standard food and bed charges but do not condone overcharging. Remember when you're shopping that the bargains you buy may only be possible because of low income to others.
* Visitors who value local traditions encourage local pride and maintain local cultures, please help local people gain a realistic view of life in Western Countries.

Figure 10.2
Himalayan Tourist Code. Source: Tourism Concern (tel: +44(0)2071333330; fax: +44(0)2071333331; www.tourismconcern.org.uk).

Instructions to the tourist in this code are direct, but the reasons why one should act in a particular way are also provided in order to increase the Code's persuasive effect.

The Green Guide Series*, developed by Professor Ralf Buckley of Griffith University, Australia, is a more recent example of a tourist-oriented code of conduct. Issued for four-wheel drive operators, small boat operators, whitewater rafters, kayakers and other sectors, each Green Guide contains a large number of specialized guidelines. Whether this or any other code (or any other sustainability message) is actually effective, however, depends on how widely the message is disseminated, absorbed, received, interpreted, integrated and acted upon in the desired way (Petty et al., 1992). As indicated in Figure 10.3, the erosion occurring at each stage of this process means that only a small portion of the intended audience is likely to change their behaviour in response to the production of a particular code. Therefore, the more the sponsoring agency understands each of these stages and the factors that influence them, the greater the 'mindful' assimilation of the message and its translation into positive action (Christie and Mason, 2003).

Influences on persuasion

At least five overlapping sets of factors must be taken into account when designing and disseminating persuasive tourist-oriented information that educates the audience into behaving in a sustainable way, as depicted in Figure 10.3 (Petty et al., 1992).

Channel factors

Channel factors consider how the message is delivered. The above-mentioned Green Guides are available as brochures, but can also be downloaded from the website of Green Globe 21. The Himalayan Tourist Code can be obtained from many different

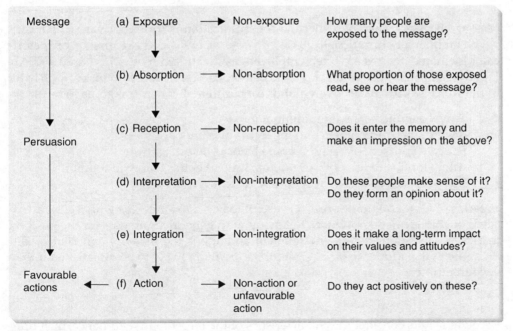

Figure 10.3
Steps for effective persuasion. Source: adapted from Petty et al., 1992.

online sites, though one would need to have heard of the Code to know which term to search under. The Code is also reprinted in many alternative tourism guidebooks, though this is perhaps akin to preaching to the converted. A general problem with all tourist codes and other tourist-oriented education, at least in the pre-trip phase, is that those most in need of such information are the ones least likely to be exposed to it. This is in part due to the expense of channelling such information through mass media such as television, radio or high circulation national newspapers and magazines. There is rather more potential to reach a mass audience during the actual tourism experience, through effective signage and other means (see below).

Source factors

Even if effective exposure is achieved through the efficient utilization of the appropriate channel factors, success in subsequent stages requires successful manipulation of the *source factors* or conveyer(s) of the message. This largely considers the type of power that is exerted by the latter. Legitimacy or *ex officio* power derives from the position or status of the conveyer, so that a uniformed tour guide or well-known director of a large environmental organization is likely to elicit more attention and respect than one dressed casually. Reward and coercion power, respectively, consider the degree to which the conveyer can project advantages and penalties to the tourist as a consequence of particular actions. Thus, the ranger can impose a monetary fine, while a parent can provide a well-behaved child with a piece of candy. Expert power is exemplified in a conveyer who holds a PhD in the relevant field, or by a university that sponsors a code. Finally, referent power involves associations or references that the conveyer makes with the audience, thereby positively influencing behaviour. Positive referent factors include celebrity, confidence, humour and commonalities in age, gender, ethnic group, etc.

Message factors

Message factors include whether the communication is formal or vernacular, conveyed emotionally or rationally, based on one- or two-sided arguments, or rhetorical. Mnemonic devices are often employed, as illustrated by the US-based TREAD Lightly! campaign directed toward users of motorized recreational vehicles. Each letter of the word TREAD respectively stands for a different core message, as follows:

> **T**ravel and recreate with minimum impact
> **R**espect the environment and the rights of others
> **E**ducate yourself, plan and prepare before you go
> **A**llow for future use of the outdoors, leave it better than you found it
> **D**iscover the rewards of responsible recreation

In terms of a general framework, it is useful to begin the message with a clear advocated position (e.g. do not litter), follow up with general arguments for the position (e.g. litter contaminates the environment and spoils the reader's experience) and illustrate with supportive facts (e.g. tourists are more likely to be dissatisfied if they encounter litter).

Receiver factors

Receiver factors consider the characteristics of the target tourist audience, including culture, national origin, sex, gender orientation, age, income, level of educational attainment, religious affiliation, life cycle stage (e.g. young families, unattached young singles, solitary survivors, etc.) and disability. Also relevant is the alleged proclivity of certain markets to engage in the illegal, careless, unskilled or unintentional actions described above. Groups at 'high risk' of committing illegal acts might include English football 'lager louts' travelling to competitions in Europe, students engaged in spring break (USA) (Josiam et al., 1998) or 'schoolies week' (Australia) and 'sex tourists' travelling to developing world destinations such as Cambodia (Leiper, 1998). Destination managers sometimes choose deliberately to discourage the arrival of such segments (see Section 10.5). It remains to be investigated whether the cultural creatives described in Section 4.5.1 are more receptive to 'green' education and less likely to engage in careless or uninformed actions, than traditionals or moderns.

Situational factors

Finally, the propensity of any given tourist to respond positively to a persuasion attempt is influenced by idiosyncratic situational factors such as weather and the presence of annoying insects. For example, a tourist seeking to escape uncomfortable heat or mosquitoes during a hike may not be focused on minimizing their impact on the natural environment. This category also includes the state of one's emotions and the impact of broader events such as the September 11, 2001 terrorist attacks in the USA, which may have distracted attention away from sustainability issues among some Americans. Others, however, may have been imbued with a stronger sense of community service and obligation as well as greater sensitivity toward environmental issues.

10.4.2 Interpretation

Interpretation is a distinctive form of education that goes beyond the simple conveyance of factual information to reveal meanings and relationships through firsthand exposure to the real world and through illustrative media (Knudson et al., 1995). According to Ham (1992), effective interpretation must be enjoyable and entertaining, bearing in mind that tourists are non-captive recipients who can walk away from or otherwise tune out messages that are not satisfying. Second, it must be made personally relevant to the audience through the use of analogies and metaphors and by referring to their values and convictions and to issues and impacts that directly affect the listener. A third characteristic is good organization, whereby a commentary is delivered around five or fewer main ideas. Finally, the revelation of meanings and relationships requires that effective interpretation be thematic, i.e. be based on overriding messages about selected topics (Weiler and Ham, 2001).

Overriding messages that are relevant to sustainable tourism include the deliberate and unintended direct and indirect environmental and social costs of Western lifestyles, the links between those lifestyles and resource exploitation, the sustainability of traditional indigenous lifestyles and the role that individuals can play in contributing to environmental and cultural rehabilitation. Effective conveyance of these messages can have transformational consequences, making people more environmentally and socially conscientious and thereby helping to achieve an enhancement-oriented, comprehensive model of sustainable tourism (see Section 2.3). Evidence for this possibility is provided by Orams (1997), who conducted exit interviews with participants and non-participants in an environmental education programme at the Tangalooma Dolphin Feeding Programme in Queensland, Australia. Of the participants, 32 per cent indicated that they had become more involved in environmental issues as a direct result of this participation, compared with 6.4 per cent of non-participants. Results of 20.4 and 8.3 per cent, respectively, were obtained in response to the question of whether they had become more environmentally aware as a result of their visit to Tangalooma. Such statistics constitute significant indicators of sustainable tourism and should be regularly collected at sites where interpretation with transformational intentions is offered.

Tour guides

Tour guiding is a facilitating tourism sector that is often described as a 'coalface' or 'frontline' activity because of the role played by the guide in directly mediating the contact between the tourist and the attraction. While the tour guide is therefore well positioned to provide effective interpretation, the ability to do so is complicated by the multiple roles that must be played by the guide and the multiple masters that must be served (Weiler and Ham, 2001). In addition to offering quality interpretation on request, the tour guide is expected to provide group leadership and coordination of logistics, ensure the safety of clients, prevent inappropriate behaviour, deal with emergencies, mediate interactions between clients and the host community and otherwise fulfil the expectations (which may not be environmentally or socially sustainable) of the clients, tour operators, attraction managers and host communities to whom they are accountable. Hence, tour guides, assuming that they are motivated to do so, may only be able to devote a small portion of time and energy to the development and presentation of persuasive interpretation that promotes positive behaviour in the tourist.

Various advantages and disadvantages are associated with tour guides as conduits of persuasive interpretation. Unlike static modes of interpretation such as signs, experienced tour guides are able to adjust message factors and content in response to the demographic and psychological characteristics of their audience as well as relevant situational factors. They can also respond to and pose questions and otherwise engage in dialogue with the audience, utilizing enthusiasm, bonding and personalization to increase the persuasive power of their interpretation. A basic problem is that effectiveness tends to diminish as group size increases, creating problems in particular at mass tourism attractions. Expert and referent power are often conferred when long-time local residents and members of local indigenous groups are employed as tour guides. However, local residents may also be more likely to lack professionalism, or to comprehend adequately the language, culture and values of the audience. In general, the perception that tour guiding is a low-paying occupation without strong professional underpinnings may dissuade tour guides from developing and disseminating top quality interpretation imbued with an ethos of sustainability (Ap and Wong, 2001; Christie and Mason, 2003).

Static interpretation

Static interpretation includes signage, displays, brochures, videos, web cams, audiotapes and other technologies that do not rely on the presence of an actual tour guide or interpreter. Cost effectiveness is therefore a major advantage, along with the ability to carefully control the content so as to provide the greatest positive impact on audience behaviour. However, as pointed out above, static interpretation, even if it utilizes interactive technologies, cannot effectively take into account specific or obscure inquiries and cannot bond with visitors, personalize interactions, or adjust to ever changing situational factors. Exposure is negatively affected by the vandalism of displays and signage and by the fact that many visitors (and younger visitors in particular) lack sufficient motivation, patience, or literacy skills to read (much less assimilate) extensive amounts of information in brochures or on display signs. For most attractions, it is sensible to have available effectively designed and interactive static interpretation that complements professionally trained and highly motivated local tour guides.

10.5 Target marketing

Target marketing is the attempt to attract specified market segments that are believed to provide particular advantages for a product or destination. Destinations such as Bermuda, Bhutan and Vail (Colorado), for example, try to cultivate a 'quality', 'high end' or 'upscale' tourism sector by attracting relatively small numbers of high-spending, older and well-educated tourists who generate large revenue flows but are perceived as being less likely to behave inappropriately or cause congestion and overcrowding. More explicitly related to sustainability is the desire by a growing number of destinations to attract ecotourists (see Chapter 11).

10.5.1 Demarketing

The concept of *demarketing* was introduced in the early 1970s by Kotler and Levy (1971), who defined it as 'that aspect of marketing that deals with discouraging customers in general or a certain class of customers in particular on a temporary or permanent basis' (p. 75). Demarketing is evident in the tourism strategies of Bermuda and other 'high end' destinations described above, wherein mass tourists are actively discouraged at the same time as high spending visitors are encouraged. Hence, demarketing can be regarded as the opposite of target marketing. Indirect demarketing strategies include reductions in overall promotion, price increases and the elimination of products that attract the undesirable markets.

Beeton and Benfield (2002) regard promotional efforts as one of the most influential modes of demarketing, but one that has not been used widely by destination managers to dissuade visits from some or all potential visitor groups. An exception involves sex tourism destinations such as Thailand, where TAT*, the national tourism organization, uses its official website and other media to publicize the increasingly severe penalties that await paedophiles and other undesirable sex tourists. One of the few demarketing case studies featured in the tourism literature examines attempts by the government of Cyprus to discourage the arrival of rowdy young tourists by discouraging nightclubs and discounted package tours and by clearly identifying desirable and undesirable market segments in its promotional campaigns (Clements, 1989). In either example, however, an unintended consequence of successful policy might be the displacement of these segments to other destinations. Many paedophiles dissuaded from visiting Thailand, for example, are now seeking sexual opportunities in the African country of The Gambia (Smith, 2004).

10.6 Summary

Destination managers can employ visitor management strategies in conjunction with the spatial strategies outlined in Chapter 9 to effect positive sustainability outcomes. Visitation caps facilitate strategies based on fixed or flexible carrying capacities, depending on whether they apply to absolute numbers or rates of growth. Quotas, most commonly used in high order protected areas as well as in a small number of countries, are the most formal type of visitation cap and are often used to abet the objectives of zoning systems. User fee increases, also commonly employed in protected areas, provide an informal capping effect by reducing the number of potential tourists who can afford to visit the affected site. Restrictions on services and infrastructure have a similar capping effect and are more frequently used by municipal governments that do not have the option of controlling access to their communities through quotas or user fees.

Redistribution strategies do not involve changes in the number of visitors to a destination, but rather the redirecting of this traffic to spaces and times within the destination that are best suited to accommodating portions of the visitor flow. Dispersal strategies are based on the premise of dilution, wherein tourism-related activity does not overwhelm any particular area. In contrast, concentration strategies attempt to minimize impacts by confining tourism-related activity to a small area that is carefully managed to cope with this activity in an environmentally and socioculturally sustainable way. Such strategies often take advantage of the economies of scale created by intensive visitation to employ sophisticated site hardening and other management measures. In many destinations, redistribution strategies include both dispersal and concentration elements, as for example in protected areas managed in line with the 95/5 principle. The Recreation Opportunity Spectrum or ROS is a technique that facilitates these hybrid strategies by matching the expectations of various types of tourists with areas within a destination that sustainably fulfil these expectations.

Education, which is implicit in the ROS, is a third major way in which visitor behaviour can be positively influenced. The extent to which visitors can be persuaded to behave sustainably depends on whether the target activity is unavoidable, illegal, careless, unskilled, or uninformed. Persuasive messages that employ a 'soft' or 'indirect' approach are more effective in addressing the latter types of activity. Tourist-oriented codes of conduct are one frequently employed type of education, although their effectiveness may be impeded by their limited exposure to target audiences requiring this education and by erosion through subsequent stages of absorption, reception, interpretation, integration and, ultimately, conversion into desirable action. As with all persuasive messages, this conversion factor may be increased through the careful consideration of channel, source, message, receiver and situational factors. This is especially true for interpretation, which seeks to educate and transform behaviour through the transmission of meanings and relationships about the world. Tour guides are influential agents of transformational interpretation because of their personal contact with tourists at the attraction interface, although this influence is often under-realized due to the low pay and lack of professionalism that characterizes this facilitating sector. Static means of interpretation are also often employed, but lack the flexibility to adapt to specific audiences, inquiries and situational factors.

Finally, managers can increase the likelihood of positive tourism outcomes by controlling the type of tourist that visits the destination. Target marketing is employed to attract segments such as high spending and well-educated tourists who are associated with high expenditures, low levels of congestion and other positive impacts. Conversely, demarketing strategies such as negative publicity and pricing adjustments are used to dissuade segments regarded in some places as undesirable, such as sex tourists, football hooligans and backpackers. In theory, the cultivation of visitor flows dominated by desirable market segments reduces the need for persuasive messages and 'hard' policing measures and increases receptivity to education in general.

On the net

Grand Canyon National Park (park management)
http://www.nps.gov/grca/mgmt/

Green Guide series (CRC Sustainable Tourism, Australia)
http://www.crctourism.com.au/CRCBookshop/page.aspx?page_id=1&CatID=4

TAT (advisories to potential visitors)
http://www.tatnews.org/tat_news/1571.asp#10

Tourist Board of Venice (tourist card)
http://www.turismovenezia.it/eng/dynalay.asp?PAGINA=853

For further reading

Lindberg, K. (1998). Economic aspects of ecotourism. In *Ecotourism: A Guide for Planners and Managers*. Volume 2 (K. Lindberg, M. Epler Wood and D. Engeldrum, eds) pp. 87–117, The Ecotourism Society.
Lindberg provides a short but succinct discussion of protected area user fees in this chapter, including the issue of whether fees should be charged and how they can be set. The issues are illustrated by a variety of international case studies.

Manning, R. (1999). *Studies in Outdoor Recreation: Search and Research for Satisfaction.* 2nd edn. Oregon State University Press.
Although focused on outdoor recreation specifically, the coverage in this text of the ROS and other visitor management strategies such as persuasion is relevant to all facets of tourism.

Shackley, M. (ed.) (2000). *Visitor Management: Case Studies from World Heritage Sites.* Butterworth-Heinemann.
Visitor management is examined in this book from the context of ten cultural World Heritage Sites in different parts of the world, including Easter Island, Giza (Egypt), Hadrian's Wall (UK) and Bukhara (Uzbekistan). Relevant problems are featured along with actual and proposed solutions.

Beyond the book

1. For your own home community, list the advantages and disadvantages, respectively, of strategies that would concentrate and disperse tourism-related activity within the destination. Which type of strategy, or combination of strategies, would be likely to attain the most environmentally, socioculturally and financially sustainable outcomes for your community?
2. Download the Green Guide for 4WD Tours from the above-listed website. Prepare a 500-word report that describes the positive and negative features of this code as a device for achieving more environmentally sustainable behaviour from its target audience. Indicate how you would modify this Code so that it can more effectively serve this purpose.

On the ground: coping with the tourist hordes in Venice

Venice is a medium-sized 'tourist-historic city' that is becoming increasingly inundated with visitors as a result of its status as an iconic Italian hyper-destination (Ashworth and Tunbridge, 1990). With just 70 000 permanent residents, the island-city of Venice hosts more than seven million tourist visits per year. Tourist/resident ratios rise to as much as 175:1 in the central city during the peak summer season, with 100 000 visits per day not being uncommon. Russo (2002) alludes to a 'vicious circle' in Venice whereby increased congestion and breeching of the city's visitor carrying capacity has led to the gradual deterioration of its tourism product as a result of overcrowding, pollution, litter, crime and price-gouging. This has prompted tourists to seek accommodations on the mainland rather than in Venice itself. Most visitors to Venice, as a result, are now day-only excursionists who generate very little revenue for the municipality but contribute to the problems of congestion and pollution through their reliance on tour buses. Because excursionists spend a large amount of time commuting into Venice on these tour buses, they have less time to retrieve and assimilate information and are therefore regarded as being more naïve, less responsive to persuasive education and more likely to congregate in the most intensively visited parts of the city where they are dropped off by their drivers. Their sensitivity to weather conditions also means that they are more likely to visit during the peak summer season. This all leads to further product deterioration and the loss of even more accommodation to the mainland, which in turn produces even more day-only excursionists and concomitant problems.

Various strategies have been proposed to deal with the deterioration of Venetian tourism (which is reminiscent of the consolidation and stagnation phases of Butler's (1980) destination life cycle model), but little has actually been done so far. A radical one-day response occurred in 1987 when municipal authorities closed the causeway that links Venice to the mainland to incoming traffic due to extremely high levels of crowding in the central city. However, a more regular policy of access limitation has never been seriously regarded as a feasible strategy due to the difficulty it would cause in maintaining legitimate access for residents, commuters and VFR as well as business stayover tourists (Van der Borg, 1998). In 1990, rumours that Venice was planning to introduce visitor quotas led to outcries from tour operators and hotel owners who saw this as an unfair assault on their rights as an industry. However, these rumours were false, with Venice's options for pursuing formal visitor caps being similarly constrained by its status as an open municipality within Italy rather than a separate country.

Recognizing that most of the tourism-related problems are associated with excursionists, the Venetian government has commissioned a series of advertisements described by Beeton and Benfield (2002) as 'irreverent and cynical' that try to discourage potential visitors by featuring scenes of dead pigeons, rats and garbage-infested lagoons (Specter, 1999). There has also been talk of placing a web cam on the official tourism authority website so that potential tourists could see for themselves real time scenes of overcrowding at St Mark's Square and other intensely visited frontstage sites. To augment such demarketing efforts, the Tourist Board of Venice* has introduced a tourist code of conduct that offers 'ten suggestions for a pleasant stay'. One of the suggestions appeals to tourists to obtain a 'Venice card' by booking their visit in advance. The Venice Card provides substantial discounts on a variety of goods and services, including entry fees to peripheral attractions outside the city core and to iconic attractions during off-peak times. The introduction of the Card represents an attempt to regulate visitation levels and positively influence visitor behaviour through attractive incentives denied to spontaneous arrivals. It also raises revenue to help mitigate the negative impacts of tourism-related activity. At a broader scale, however, efforts to foster sustainable mass tourism (SMT) in Venice may be ultimately undermined by the impacts of acid rain, industrial pollution in the lagoon and increased and more severe flooding. Since 1900, the water level has increased by more than 100 millimetres due to global warming, while the land base has concurrently subsided by 400 millimetres. As a result, the number of times that St Mark's Square has been flooded has increased from six in 1900 to 99 in 1996 (Specter, 1999).

Exercise

Download the Venice Card information from the website of the Tourist Board of Venice (see above). Do the indicated discounts and privileges appear effective in promoting sustainable tourism in Venice? How could the card be enhanced better to achieve the objective of environmentally and socioculturally sustainable tourism?

Chapter 11

Ecotourism: the conscience of sustainable tourism

Chapter objectives

Upon completion of this chapter, the reader should be able to:

- explain the three criteria that constitute an ecotourism product and show how the variance within these criteria gives rise to comprehensive and minimalist interpretations of ecotourism
- differentiate the concepts of hard and soft ecotourism and demonstrate how this typology relates to the comprehensive/minimalist distinction and affects estimates of the magnitude of the ecotourism sector
- assess the strengths and weaknesses of specialized components within the ecotourism industry
- describe the spatial distribution of ecotourism both globally and within protected areas as well as modified spaces
- assess the potential environmental costs and benefits of ecotourism and discuss how these vary within hard and soft ecotourism
- explain the extent to which quality control and credibility within ecotourism are being positively and negatively affected by certification initiatives such as Australia's EcoCertification Programme and
- critically assess the importance of a comprehensive ecotourism model that incorporates soft as well as hard ecotourism dimensions.

11.1 Introduction

An increasing number of destinations and businesses are aggressively pursuing ecotourism as a specialized part of their sustainable tourism development strategies. This chapter critically assesses this growing involvement with ecotourism, initially in Section 11.2 by defining the sector and analysing its three core criteria. One outcome of this analysis is the identification of comprehensive and minimalist ideal types. Section 11.3 continues this discourse by discussing the widely recognized distinction between hard and soft ecotourism that significantly influences further considerations of the sector. These include the emergence of specialized components such as tour operators, ecolodges and mediating attractions (Section 11.4) as well as the spatial distribution of ecotourism by region as well as in terms of its focus on high order protected areas (Section 11.5). The role of ecotourism within highly modified spaces is also considered. The potential environmental costs and benefits of the sector are analysed in Section 11.6 and this is followed in Section 11.7 by a discussion of the quality control mechanisms that are being implemented to ensure that optimal benefits are obtained. The final section presents a broad model of ecotourism that would help this sector to achieve its potential as an effective agent of environmental and community enhancement.

11.2 Definitions and criteria

The emergence of ecotourism in the mid-1980s is closely associated with the Mexican consultant Hector Ceballos-Lascuráin, who defined the sector as involving travel 'to relatively undisturbed or uncontaminated natural areas with the specific object of studying, admiring and enjoying the scenery and its wild plants and animals, as well as any existing cultural aspects (both past and present) found in these areas' (1988, p. 13). This oft-quoted definition captures two criteria – nature-based attractions and educational or appreciative motivations – that have since become almost universally recognized as two of the three core prerequisites of an ecotourism experience (Blamey, 1997, 2001; Wearing and Neil, 1999; Page and Dowling, 2002). The third criterion, environmental and sociocultural sustainability, is implicit in most of the definitions that have been subsequently put forward. Epler Wood, for example, defines ecotourism as 'purposeful travel to natural areas to understand the cultural and natural history of the environment, taking care not to alter the integrity of the ecosystem while producing economic opportunities that make the conservation of natural resources financially beneficial to local citizens' (1991, p. 200). Fennell regards ecotourism as 'a sustainable form of natural resource-based tourism that focuses primarily on experiencing and learning about nature and which is ethically managed to be low-impact, non-consumptive and locally oriented' (1999, p. 43). Each of these three criteria will now be considered in more detail.

11.2.1 Nature-based attractions

The nature-based or ecological attractions that are the focus of ecotourism can range from an emphasis on an entire ecosystem such as a rainforest or coral reef to selected components of the ecosystem. In the latter scenario, which may be described as an elemental approach, ecotourism destinations focus on non-captive *charismatic megafauna* such as giant pandas (Sichuan province, China), quetzals (Central America) or mountain gorillas (Rwanda, Uganda and Congo DR) that are especially attractive to ecotourists. More rarely, *charismatic megaflora* such as redwood trees (California) or the giant *Rafflesia* flower (Indonesia and Malaysia) are featured. The former scenario, in contrast, can be described as a holistic approach in which these megafauna and megaflora are contextualized within their ecosystem, but are given no more weight than any other interdependent element of that ecosystem.

Role of cultural attractions

Many ecotourism definitions, including that of Ceballos-Lascuráin (see above), recognize the role of associated cultural influences as secondary ecotourism attractions. This role may be cursory in the elemental approach, but central in the holistic approach, given the argument that direct and indirect human influences critically affect the dynamics of any contemporary ecosystem and therefore form a vital part of ecosystems' interpretation and understanding. This is especially relevant in the case of indigenous territories. Section 8.5.5 described how the distinction between 'natural' and 'cultural' in areas occupied by the same culture for millennia is especially blurred. Hence, the cultural component is an essential and not just secondary part of the ecotourism product in destinations such as Uluru (Australia) and the Queen Charlotte Islands (Canada). The incorporation of the cultural element more broadly also implies that ecotourism venues are not restricted to 'relatively undisturbed' settings as argued by Ceballos-Lascuráin, but can potentially be located within substantially modified environments as well (see Section 11.5.3).

11.2.2 Educational interaction

Motivations of education and learning about the natural environment distinguish ecotourism from other nature-based tourism products such as beach resorts, where the natural environment provides a convenient setting for the fulfilment of hedonistic or similar impulses (Weaver, 2001b). As with nature-based attractions, educational opportunities and experiences can be ranged along a continuum. At one pole, these attempt to foster deep understanding through interpretation that conveys complex messages and seeks to transform the attitudes and behaviour of the audience along a more environmentalist-oriented trajectory (see Section 10.4.2). This model, which is evident in the whale watching tours at Kaikoura, New Zealand (Curtin, 2003), aligns with the holistic approach to nature-based attractions described above. At the other pole, shallow understanding is conveyed through relatively simple and basic messages that focus on charismatic megafauna. In either case, ecotourism product managers should provide appropriate interpretation, or at least maintain conditions (e.g. peacefulness, non-interference) that allow ecotourists to pursue a more self-directed or contemplative path of learning.

11.2.3 Environmental and sociocultural sustainability

Ecotourism is the only high profile tourism sector where environmentally and socioeconomically sustainable practices, or at least the credible attempt to engage in such practices, are widely regarded as a prerequisite. It is because of this explicit accountability and the issues of credibility it raises, that ecotourism is referred to in the title of this chapter as the conscience of sustainable tourism. The reference to credible attempts is from Weaver (2001b), who regards as unrealistic any definition that *requires* the ecotourism product to be sustainable, given the challenges and issues of sustainability discussed in Chapter 2. These render it effectively impossible to say that any particular ecotourism product or destination is, without doubt, sustainable, especially if these products and destinations involve high order protected areas or similar venues that merit a strong approach to sustainability. Rather, the litmus test of ecotourism according to Weaver (2001b) is the application of best practice strategies to attain optimal sustainability outcomes and the timely remediation of any inadvertent negative impacts that become apparent to management (see Section 11.6).

As with other sectors, the engagement with sustainability within ecotourism can range from a 'basic' model that focuses on sustaining the on-site direct impact status quo, to a deeper approach that focuses on the enhancement of the site and its surroundings (potentially at a global level), while also taking into account the amelioration of indirect impacts and the effects of external forces and systems (see Figure 2.1).

11.2.4 Comprehensive and minimalist ideal types

Variations in the above three core criteria give rise to two distinctive ecotourism ideal types. The first can be characterized as a comprehensive model that entails a holistic approach to nature-based attractions, fosters deep understanding and adheres to the traits of the comprehensive sustainable tourism ideal type depicted in Figure 2.1. The minimalist model, in contrast, adheres to the minimalist sustainability outlined in Figure 2.1 while adopting an elemental approach to the product that focuses on shallow understanding (Weaver, 2005a). Both models recognize the need for financial sustainability and customer satisfaction. As with sustainable tourism more broadly, the comprehensive model is the preferred model because it pursues more universal and deeper sustainability outcomes and is less likely to produce inadvertent negative impacts. However, it is more difficult and expensive to operate. The minimalist model is less difficult and offers an entry-level framework for ecotourism stakeholders, though at the risk of producing negative outcomes, both deliberate and inadvertent, that could erode the credibility of ecotourism as a sustainability-focused sector.

11.3 Hard and soft manifestations

While recognition of the comprehensive/minimalist distinction is a recent development in the literature, a distinction between 'hard' and 'soft' dimensions of the sector is long established as both a theoretical (see for example Laarman and Durst, 1987; Lindberg, 1991; Weaver, 1998) and empirical (Chapman, 1995; Palacio and McCool, 1997; Weaver and Lawton, 2002b) construct. As depicted in Figure 11.1, *hard ecotourism* is essentially a form of alternative tourism involving small groups of ecotourists who take relatively long specialized trips into relatively undisturbed settings where opportunities for physically and mentally challenging experiences are available. Hard ecotourists typically do not rely on facilitating sectors such as travel agencies and tour operators, or services at the destination. *Soft ecotourists* are associated with a more conventional tourist market that engages in mentally and physically unchallenging ecotourism experiences as a short duration component of a multi-purpose trip. They generally prefer a high level of comfort and facilitation during these experiences.

The comprehensive/minimalist and hard/soft typologies are superficially similar, but differ crucially in that the former is based mainly on broad sector outcomes and philosophies (holistic or elemental approach, enhancement or status quo sustainability, global or local spatial scope, etc.) while the latter is based more on market and experience characteristics (specialized or diversionary focus, few or many services,

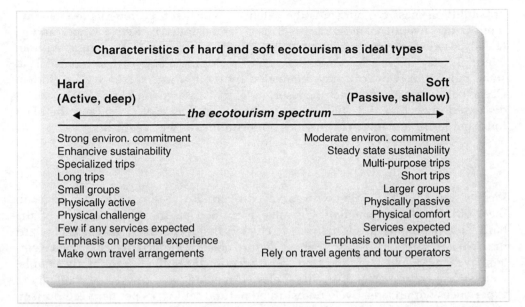

Characteristics of hard and soft ecotourism as ideal types

Hard (Active, deep)	Soft (Passive, shallow)
◄———— *the ecotourism spectrum* ————►	
Strong environ. commitment	Moderate environ. commitment
Enhancive sustainability	Steady state sustainability
Specialized trips	Multi-purpose trips
Long trips	Short trips
Small groups	Larger groups
Physically active	Physically passive
Physical challenge	Physical comfort
Few if any services expected	Services expected
Emphasis on personal experience	Emphasis on interpretation
Make own travel arrangements	Rely on travel agents and tour operators

Figure 11.1

Characteristics of hard and soft ecotourism as ideal types. Source: Weaver, D. Journal of Travel Research 40 (3) p. 272, copyright 2002. Reprinted by permission of Sage Publications, Inc.

remote or well serviced sites, small or large groups, etc.). Comprehensive/hard and minimalist/soft alignments emerge logically from a comparative analysis of the two typologies and may reflect the dominant ecotourism pattern in the real world. Soft ecotourists in their diversionary mode, for example, are not expected to seek out experiences that are troubling or physically uncomfortable, while the more ethereal motives of hard ecotourists often include strong ethical considerations and a desire to improve the world. Such alignments, however, which imply that hard ecotourism is superior to soft ecotourism, are not inevitable or even desirable in terms of realizing the potential of this sector to achieve sustainability outcomes. The case for a comprehensive model of ecotourism that encompasses the hard *and* soft dimensions is made in Section 11.8 rather than here, since the following sections provide further insight into the differential impacts of hard and soft ecotourism and thus inform this line of argument.

11.3.1 Mass ecotourism

One important implication that arises from the recognition of the soft dimension as a legitimate form of ecotourism is the concomitant recognition of *mass ecotourism*, or the possibility that ecotourism can occur as a form of mass tourism. As mentioned in Section 1.3.3, ecotourism first emerged as a formal concept in the mid-1980s as a nature-based form of alternative tourism, an identity that is retained in the hard ecotourism dimension. However, the emergence of nature-based tourism sites such as Grand Canyon National Park that can accommodate millions of visitors each year in an apparently sustainable manner invalidates the argument that only the harder manifestations of ecotourism legitimately qualify as such. Further confirming the possibility of mass ecotourism is the extent to which soft ecotourists are synonymous with conventional mass tourists. This is demonstrated by Kenya, where Sindiga (1996) describes the typical international tourist experience as beginning with an overnight stay in Nairobi or Mombassa and including a one- or two-day safari at some point in a two-week stay dominated by the tourists' presence at an Indian Ocean beach resort. Often, it is the resort hotel that arranges and hosts the safari. As discussed in Section 11.8, this close association between ecotourism and the mass tourism market and industry provides opportunities as well as threats.

11.3.2   Structured ecotourists

Weaver and Lawton (2002b), who surveyed overnight visitors at two ecolodges in the Gold Coast hinterland of Australia, identified an intriguing variant of the hard/soft dichotomy. In addition to two clusters that respectively gravitated toward the hard and soft poles described above, a third cluster emerged that combined elements of each. Members of this group, who accounted for 40 per cent of the sample, were strong environmentalists who preferred mentally and physically challenging experiences within a relatively undisturbed natural setting, as per hard ecotourism. However, they also prefer interpretation, escorted tours and pre-arranged travel planning, as well as comfortable accommodations and opportunities for social interaction with other ecotourists, as per soft ecotourism. The authors refer to members of this cluster as *structured ecotourists* in recognition of the desire for structure and organization to mediate the ecotourism experience. The broader implication for the tourism industry is the extent to which incongruent tendencies align, necessitating marketing and management strategies that amalgamate hard and soft tendencies. It also indicates common ground between strong environmentalist sentiments and mediating sectors such as tour operators and travel agencies that are associated with the conventional tourism industry.

11.4 Ecotourism industry

The distinction between hard and soft ecotourism helps to account for the variability in estimates of the ecotourism sector's size. For example, the WTO's declaration in the late 1990s that ecotourism accounted for about 20 per cent of the global tourism market (in Wight, 2001) clearly embraces the soft side of the ecotourism continuum, as does the finding of the Bureau of Tourism Research (BTR, 2000) that almost one-half of international visitors to Australia visit National Parks, go bush walking, or participate in rainforest walks. In contrast, the hard side of the spectrum is apparently evoked by the US-based Specialty Travel Index, which estimated that ecotourists accounted for between 1.5 and 2.5 per cent of all travel undertaken by Americans in the late 1980s (in Whelan, 1991).

The ecotourism *sector*, however, is not the same as the ecotourism *industry*. McKercher (2001) cites the problem of phantom demand, i.e. the erroneous assumption that all ecotourism experiences are mediated through the specialized ecotourism industry, as a major reason for business failure in the latter. At least three factors contribute to this phantom demand. First, many actual ecotourism experiences (e.g. National Park visits) can be purchased at little or no cost and therefore provide few opportunities for business intervention. Second, the vast majority of soft ecotourism experiences are mediated through the conventional tourism industry, as illustrated by the National Park visitor in the USA who stays in a motel at the edge of the park rather than a specialized ecolodge. Third, while the consumption of specialized ecotourism products may be most evident among the small proportion of the market qualifying as hard ecotourists, this proclivity is eroded by the tendency of hard ecotourists, like other alternative tourists, to make their own travel arrangements and to minimize their reliance on mediating services. These three factors help to account for the discrepancy between the 50 per cent participation rate in ecotourism among international visitors to Australia and the estimate that the specialized industry in that country consisted of just 600 operations employing approximately 6500 full-time, part-time and casual staff during the mid-1990s, a very small proportion of the overall tourism industry (Cotterill, 1996).

11.4.1 Tour operators

The tour operator sector is one area where the emergence of a significant specialized ecotourism component is discernable. In the mid-1990s, 155 outbound US tour operators were identified that offered at least one 'nature tour' within Latin America during the mid-1990s (Higgins, 1996). Extrapolating from 82 of these operators who responded to a survey, it was estimated that approximately 230 000 ecotourists were served by this sector during 1993–94. A broader and more recent analysis of ecotour operators is provided by Higgins (2001), who describes the growing role of non-profit organizations and university travel groups in offering outbound ecotours and of community-based inbound and local tour operators, often controlled by indigenous groups, within LDC ecotourism destinations.

11.4.2 Ecolodges

The *ecolodge* has emerged since the early 1990s as perhaps the most distinctive component of the specialized ecotourism industry. There is no universally accepted definition of such facilities, although they are generally perceived as small lodges located within or adjacent to higher order protected areas and designed to blend into the local natural and cultural environment and to utilize extensively green building and energy technologies (Gardner, 2001). They typically are oriented to providing accommodation, food, interpretation and tour guide services for a hard ecotourist clientele at the luxury end of the market (Hawkins et al., 1995), making them especially attractive to the structured ecotourist. Based on a perusal and extrapolation of the literature as well as relevant certification programmes and the membership lists of organizations such as the International Ecotourism Society (TIES) and Ecotourism Australia, there are perhaps 500–1000 facilities worldwide that can reasonably be classified as ecolodges, recognizing that only a few fulfil all of the above requirements.

While most ecolodges appear to be owned and operated by local communities or small entrepreneurs both domestic and expatriate, a corporatization trend is evident, according to Weaver (2001b). Conservation Corporation Africa, which operates more than 20 ecolodges in six African countries, is a prime example of this trend, as is P&O Australian resorts, which operates seven ecolodges in Australia (Buckley, 2003).

11.4.3 Mediating attractions

A *mediating attraction* is a mobile or fixed structure that not only facilitates inter-action with another attraction, but also constitutes an attraction in its own right. An example of a mobile/fixed mediating attraction in ecotourism is the growing array of cable cars that ferry tourists over a forest or water body. One of the best known and allegedly most sustainable of these is the Skyrail* facility that carries tourists over the canopy of the World Heritage rainforests in the hinterland of Cairns, Australia (Moscardo, 1998). Rainforests and other wooded areas are also popular settings for fixed canopy walkways such as the Tree Top Walk located within Western Australia's Valley of the Giants. The Atlantis submarine fleet that trans-ports ecotourists to Caribbean coral reefs is perhaps the best current example of a mobile mediating attraction.

Unlike ecolodges or specialized ecotour operators, mediating attractions tend to cater to large numbers of soft ecotourists, which is not surprising considering that such facilities tend to provide convenient and comfortable access to relatively inaccess-ible settings that are otherwise likely to be visited only by hard ecotourists. It was estimated, for example, that the Atlantis fleet in its first 10 years of operation (early 1980s to early 1990s) hosted 4.5 million customers on 200 000 dives (Orams, 1999). Also unsurprising is the corporate nature of such businesses, which is necessitated not only by the high visitor numbers, but also the high costs of construction and operation. Skyrail, according to the product website, incurred initial construction costs of AUS$35 million and has since been subject to several multi-million dollar upgrades. The Atlantis fleet produced an annual turnover of $75 million in the mid-1990s and had more than 500 employees (Orams, 1999). These mediating attractions, then, exemplify the concept of specialized mass ecotourism.

11.5 Spatial distribution

Although ecotourism is rapidly attaining the status of a ubiquitous tourism sector, certain countries and regions have gained reputations as ecotourism 'hotspots'. In terms of biotic regions, this sector is probably most closely associated with rainforests and, in particular, those of the Amazon basin, Central America and Southeast Asia (Evans, 2000; Frost, 2001). A theme of alpine ecotourism is also discernable (Williams et al., 2001; Nepal, 2002), while virtually all tourism in Antarctica arguably falls under the ecotourism rubric (Stonehouse, 2001; Bauer and Dowling, 2003). Coral reefs are another biotic region where ecotourism is well established, although there is controversy as to the extent to which scuba diving and snorkelling qualify as such (Cater and Cater, 2001; Garrod and Wilson, 2003). In contrast, there is relatively little evidence of extensive ecotourism activity in desert or grassland settings.

At a national level, Australia has perhaps the strongest reputation as an ecotourism destination, not just because of its diverse array of charismatic endemic species, but also because of its active and influential peak ecotourism body (Ecotourism Australia*) and its pioneering EcoCertification initiative (Dowling, 2001, 2002) (see Section 11.7.1). Other countries closely associated with ecotourism include Costa Rica, Belize, New Zealand, Iceland and Peru, although in each case (and in Australia as well), conventional tourism activity remains dominant with regard to markets and revenue (Weaver, 2001b). This arguably holds true even for the small number of microstates, including Dominica, Montserrat, Samoa and Tonga that are some-times touted as being dominated by ecotourism in its harder manifestations (Weaver, 1998).

11.5.1 Concentration in public protected areas

Within the above regions and countries, most ecotourism activity occurs within public protected areas and especially higher order entities such as National Parks that offer a combination of characteristics conducive to ecotourism. These include outstanding natural attractions, legislation and regulations that ensure the preser-vation of these attractions, an increasing tendency to include compatible forms of tourism in the mandate of such areas (in part because of the need to diversify rev-enue sources), an emphasis on educational and other sustainable interactions between visitors and the natural environment and in some parks a well-established image in the tourist market (e.g. National Parks such as Kruger, Uluru and Grand Canyon have iconic status in their respective countries) (Lawton, 2001b). A broader issue is what Weaver (2001b) terms the convergence between protected and natural landscapes, wherein unprotected natural settings are being destroyed and degraded at an unprecedented pace and it is increasingly only in high order protected areas that such environments can be experienced by the ecotourist. This convergence has already occurred in Costa Rica, where the proportion of land that is protected (about 25 per cent) coincides with the proportion of the country still occupied by relatively undisturbed natural habitat (about 25 per cent) (Weaver, 1998).

Concentration of ecotourism activity is apparent not only in the extent to which such activity is focused on protected areas, but also in the degree to which only a few high profile protected areas within a given country accommodate a dispropor-tionate share of the sector. For example, just four of Costa Rica's 21 high order pro-tected areas in the late 1990s accounted for two-thirds of all visitation, while the comparable figure for Kenya's protected area system was 54 per cent (Weaver, 1999). Within these intensely visited protected areas, the 95/5 rule (see Section 10.3.3) indicates further concentration, with the hard ecotourists constituting the small minority of visitors dispersed over the great majority of the park where services and facilities are minimal.

Private protected areas

Although public protected areas overwhelmingly dominate the ecotourism sector, their private counterparts are increasing rapidly in number and cumulative size. Langholz and Brandon (2001) attribute this phenomenon to several factors, includ-ing the failure of government to adequately safeguard biodiversity through the public systems, rising public awareness of environmental issues (see Section 4.5) and the growth of ecotourism. These varied motivations have produced a diverse array of private protected areas, ranging from relatively obscure networks estab-lished by non-profit organizations primarily for preservation purposes, to commer-cial nature reserves and game parks that aggressively attract tourists in order to realize a profit. The former scenario is represented by The Nature Conservancy which, in 2004, controlled a network of 1400 preserves covering 47 million hectares. While this organization is becoming increasingly involved with ecotourism, these efforts to date are focused mainly on public protected area systems. The growing number of commercial game parks in sub-Saharan Africa exemplifies the latter scenario, wherein tourism provides the primary source of income and often includes profitable activities such as big game hunting that may conflict with ecotourism.

11.5.2 Modified spaces

Most definitions of ecotourism, including that of Ceballos-Lascuráin (see above), emphasize the importance of relatively undisturbed natural environments as ecotourism venues. This has the advantage of focusing the potentially positive aspects of ecotourism on settings that desperately require protection. However, it also creates a dilemma by concentrating ecotourism, and its potentially negative impacts, in a shrinking amount of vulnerable space with the highest conservation value that is least capable of withstanding these impacts (see Section 11.6). Given this situation, the possibilities for accommodating ecotourism in highly modified spaces such as farmland and landfill sites, which have been neglected in the literature, need to be considered more seriously (Lawton and Weaver, 2001). With regard to nature-based attractions, many charismatic species have adapted to modified landscapes or structures on a permanent or periodic basis. Examples include migrating whooping cranes grazing on stubble in the croplands of Saskatchewan (Canada), polar bears feeding at the town rubbish tip in Churchill, Manitoba (Canada) and storks nesting in the chimneys of medieval buildings in central Europe. The capacity of naturalized golf courses to accommodate native wildlife was noted in Section 6.6.2.

In addition to being conducive to an elemental approach to ecotourism attractions, modified spaces offer excellent opportunities for deep learning and sophisticated interpretation because of the complex landscape influences and effects that they feature. The juxtaposition of remnant natural habitat with intensive arable land, for example, can be used to illustrate concepts such as edge and oasis effect, while succession can be featured in areas where rehabilitation is being undertaken. With regard to the third core criterion of sustainability, modified spaces have the advantage of having a high carrying capacity compared to relatively undisturbed natural venues, thereby meriting a weaker approach to sustainability. Ecotourism is therefore not only less likely to generate serious negative environmental impacts, but may serve as an effective agent of enhancement sustainability because of the opportunities for rehabilitation. From the perspective of sociocultural sustainability, modified spaces are more accessible to the 'masses' and hence avoid the problem of elitism that characterizes the visitation of hard ecotourists to remote wilderness locations.

Urban ecotourism

Urban areas are an extreme version of modified space and therefore seem at first to be especially unsuited to ecotourism. However, the apparently oxymoronic concept of *urban ecotourism* is now receiving considerable attention in the literature (Lawton and Weaver, 2001; Higham and Lück, 2002; Dodds and Joppe, 2003). Weaver (2005b) argues that within the urban area proper, ecotourism settings can range from remnant natural habitats in river valleys and hills, through to derelict and reclaimed sites, manicured green spaces such as municipal parks and golf courses, and built sites. The preserved forests in the centre of densely urbanized Singapore are a good illustration of the first scenario (Henderson et al., 2001), while the latter scenario is represented by the above-mentioned storks of Europe as well as the peregrine falcons reintroduced into high-rise buildings in some North American central business districts. The city of Austin, Texas, is noted for a colony of 1.5 million Mexican free-tailed bats that roosts beneath the Congress Avenue Bridge*. Perhaps the best articulated example of urban ecotourism centred on a built structure, the bridge attracts an estimated 100 000 visitors per year and approximately $8 million in revenue (Moreno, 2004).

11.6 Potential costs and benefits

All tourism entails costs as well as benefits and ecotourism is no exception. What distinguishes ecotourism from other forms of tourism in this respect, however, is that to qualify as such, every effort must be made to ensure that environmentally and socioculturally sustainable practices are undertaken. Hence, most of the negative impacts that *do* arise from ecotourism are inadvertent, while the positive impacts are generally deliberate (Weaver, 2002). The sub-sections below adopt this perspective and do *not* consider negative impacts associated with products that are deliberately or inadvertently labelled as ecotourism but do not meet any or all of the three core criteria.

11.6.1 Environmental benefits

In potential perhaps more than practice, ecotourism's greatest environmental benefit is its role in providing a direct financial incentive for the preservation of relatively undisturbed natural habitats that would otherwise be exposed to more exploitative and profitable (at least in the short term) activities. This effect can also be indirect, as demonstrated by efforts to protect terrestrial watersheds in parts of the Philippines from logging in order to protect the clarity and quality of water in an area used for marine ecotourism (Sherman and Dixon, 1991). Ecotourism revenues, additionally, are a critical source of the funding required to undertake basic protected area management as well as park system expansion and enhancement. The potential of these revenues to increase is demonstrated by the observation that a $1 increase to a $4 park entry fee will likely have no dissuasive effect on a potential inbound visitor spending $2000 on the trip to that park, but represents a very large growth in revenue flow for a heavily visited park and one that is amenable to further increases of similar magnitude. All of these effects, it should be noted, are more likely to be realized from the economies of scale generated by soft rather than hard ecotourism, although the individual hard ecotourist may be willing to pay more in terms of entry fees, licences, etc. for their experience.

Other potential environmental benefits derive from the capacity of ecotourism to foster the rehabilitation of modified spaces (see above) and to mobilize ecotourists as volunteers (e.g. to plant trees, maintain trails and serve as informal auxiliary police) and a potent source of on-site and ongoing donations (Barnes, 1996; Laarman and Gregersen, 1996; Weaver and Lawton, 2002b). The potential for effective interpretation and participation to transform the attitudes and behaviour of ecotourists was noted earlier in the context of the Tangalooma dolphin facility in Australia (see Section 10.4.2). This tendency may also extend to local residents who take on the role of environmental advocates and stewards in order to maintain the economic benefits of ecotourism. Lindberg et al. (1996), for example, noted that ecotourism was the major factor given by the residents of three villages in Belize to account for their elevated levels of support for local protected areas.

11.6.2 Environmental costs

Deliberate environmental costs from ecotourism, incurred mainly by the removal of native vegetation in the construction of ecolodges, mediating attractions, trails and other footprint facilities, are usually regarded as negligible and acceptable because of the small area affected and the possibilities that exist for site softening and rehabilitation. Inadvertent costs are mainly associated with the effects of wildlife viewing and the hiking, driving, riding, flying, boating or swimming that is carried out in order to access wildlife. A large and growing body of empirical evidence supports the first assertion. For example, ecotourists are alleged to have spread human diseases to mountain gorillas in east Africa (Nowak, 2001), while whale watching has been linked to a wide variety of behavioural changes in targeted cetaceans (Higham and Lusseau, 2004). Thorough reviews of the literature pertaining to birds and terrestrial wildlife are provided respectively by Buckley (2004b,c). The second assertion is also well supported, as for example in research by Buckley et al. (2004) demonstrating the role of ecotourists in facilitating the spread of dieback disease in Australian vegetation and in Warnken and Buckley (2004), who found increased *E. coli* bacteria levels in a remote swimming hole in Lamington National Park, Australia. Notably, it is the harder ecotourist segment that is most likely to be inadvertently culpable for the spread of such exotic pathogens into relatively remote areas, although it can be counter-argued that soft ecotourists account for a much larger proportion of all wildlife–human interactions and hence stresses arising from such contact.

With regard to the elemental approach toward natural attractions, Weaver (2002) cites the dangers that could emerge from constructing implicit or explicit hierarchies of wildlife species. If for example a giant panda is deemed to be more attractive and hence more valuable than a particular species of fungus or slime mould, then managerial priority may be given to the former even though the latter play an equally important role in the local ecosystem.

11.7 Quality control

The ecotourism industry has assumed a prominent role in the introduction of quality control mechanisms, which is not surprising given the sector's explicit emphasis on achieving sustainability-related outcomes. Notably proactive sub-sectors within ecotourism include the whale watching industry (see case study at the end of this chapter) and Antarctic tourism. The latter situation is accounted for in large part by exclusivity, wherein the 30 members of IAATO* (International Association of Antarctic Tourism Operators) constitute an elite collection of businesses who monopolize the continent's tourism industry and whose reputation for enlightened self-regulation derives from the rigorous and unique provisions of the Antarctic Treaty System (Bauer and Dowling, 2003). Included in the IAATO regulations are strict guidelines as to group size and the number of required qualified tour guides per group (see Section 10.2.1).

11.7.1 EcoCertification Programme

Australia's EcoCertification Programme, operated under the auspices of Ecotourism Australia, is widely regarded as the world's leading national ecotourism certification initiative. Originally established in 1996 under the banner of NEAP (National Ecotourism Accreditation Programme), the programme extends certification eligibility to ecotourism products (accommodations, tours and attractions) that adhere to eight core principles. These include the need to focus on a personal experience with nature that leads to increased understanding and appreciation, the integration of opportunities to understand the natural environment into each experience and the pursuit of best practice. Positive contributions to conservation and local communities are also emphasized, as are sensitivity to local cultures in product interpretation, accurate marketing and meeting client expectations on a consistent basis. Each principle is in turn associated with an array of core and advanced indicators, which cumulatively fill more than 120 pages of the application document.

To achieve Ecotourism Certification, a product must meet 100 per cent of the core criteria, while Advanced Ecotourism Certification additionally requires that at least 75 per cent of the advanced criteria be met. Certification is valid for 3 years and requires an annual report (and annual fee) that advises of any operational changes that might affect the product's status. Certification is based initially on a self-assessed application that is scored by an independent Assessor who liaises with referees identified by the applicant to confirm the information on the application. An independent on-site audit of all criteria is undertaken at some pre-determined time during the 3-year period of certification. As of late 2004, 337 Australian ecotourism products were certified, 58 per cent under the Advanced Ecotourism Certification rubric. More than three-quarters (257) of the products were tours, followed by accommodations (52) and attractions (28). One hundred and fifty-five operators were represented, indicating that each operator had on average 2.2 certified products.

11.8 Hard and soft ecotourism within a comprehensive framework

Despite the progress indicated through initiatives such as the EcoCertification Programme, the credibility of ecotourism has been widely questioned by academics and practitioners (Honey, 1999; Fennell, 2002; Page and Dowling, 2002; Mader, 2003), especially since ecotourism was placed under the spotlight during the UN-declared International Year of Ecotourism in 2002. This questioning has occurred in part because of the extent to which the term is applied inappropriately to products that do not meet the three core criteria and also because products that do qualify usually adopt a minimalist approach that increases the probability of negative impacts. The comprehensive approach is therefore preferable, as discussed in Section 11.2.4. However, it is argued here that this comprehensive approach must be applied to both hard and soft ecotourism (see Figure 11.2), since it is allegedly the latter that produces the economies of scale necessary to operationalize the incentive and funding effects described in Section 11.6.1. Through such accommodation, the model embraces all the opportunity classes of the Recreation Opportunity Spectrum, as well as both weak and strong approaches to sustainability, depending on the setting. In this way, the model in theory has a universal application that embraces ecotourism both as locally focused alternative tourism as well as corporation-focused mass tourism.

11.8.1 Ecotouriums

A basic challenge of this model is to make the comprehensive approach attractive to and suitable for the giant soft ecotourist market, whose characteristics suggest an inclination toward the minimalist end of the spectrum. Fennell and Weaver (in

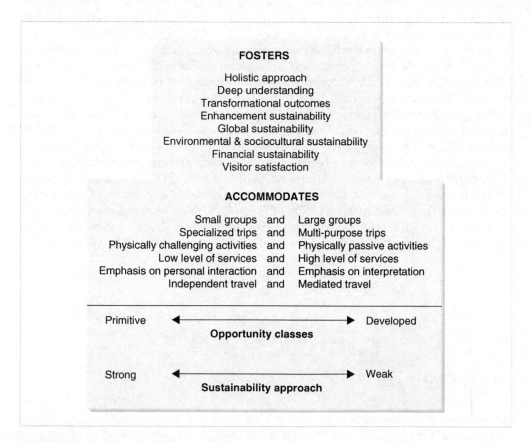

Figure 11.2
Modified Comprehensive Ecotourism Model. Source: adapted from Weaver (2005a). Reprinted from Annals of Tourism Research, Weaver, D. Comprehensive and minimalist dimensions of ecotourism, in press. Copyright 2005, with permission from Elsevier.

press) propose to operationalize the modified comprehensive ecotourism model through the concept of the *ecotourium*, which they define as a protected area where all types of ecotourist are mobilized in conjunction with the tourism industry, local communities, government and NGOs to participate in activities consistent with the principles of comprehensive ecotourism that protect and enhance these places, thereby generating symbiosis between tourism and conservation. Ecotourists, then, are regarded in this model as active agents of positive environmental and social change. Relevant activities can include tree-planting (suitable in modified and degraded areas), removal of invasive exotic species, trail maintenance, assistance with scientific research (e.g. plant identification surveys), participation in community-based projects and donations. Crucial to the concept is the formation of an accredited global network of such areas in which all types of environments and ecosystems are represented and results from the activities are shared.

11.9 Summary

It is now widely accepted that ecotourism involves an emphasis on nature-based attractions, educational interactions with these attractions and management practices that make every reasonable effort to achieve environmentally and socioculturally sustainable outcomes. However, a closer analysis of these three core criteria reveals the existence of comprehensive and minimalist ideal types, which suggest different expectations and outcomes. A parallel typology, based more on market and experience characteristics, differentiates between hard and soft ecotourists, although a combination of hard and soft traits characterizes the structured ecotourist market. Hard ecotourism is essentially a form of alternative tourism, while soft ecotourism suggests mass tourism or even 'mass ecotourism' and it is this distinction that helps to account for large variations in the estimated size of the ecotourism industry. The tour operators and ecolodges of the specialized ecotourism industry itself cater mainly to the hard ecotourist market, while mediating attractions such as cableways and submarines have a broader soft ecotourist market orientation.

Although ecotourism has become ubiquitous, places such as rainforests, mountains, Antarctica, coral reefs, Australia, Costa Rica and Belize have achieved reputations as prominent ecotourism destinations. Within these places, soft ecotourism tends to be concentrated within a small area of a few higher order protected areas, while hard ecotourism is more broadly dispersed. Substantially modified spaces, including urban areas, have the potential to accommodate ecotourism and this may be a useful directive for the sector given the stress that the growing ecotourism sector could place on the relatively undisturbed natural settings found in higher order protected areas. The same logic pertains to the growing network of private protected areas. The inadvertent costs that may result from ecotourism are associated mainly with the act of wildlife observation and the travel required to access such opportunities and, in this regard, hard ecotourism may affect a larger area while soft ecotourism accounts for most of the actual wildlife–human interactions. In contrast, the benefits associated with the incentive and funding effects of ecotourism are more likely to be realized from soft ecotourism because of the economies of scale it entails. In any case, the likelihood of negative environmental and social outcomes is reduced through stringent certification initiatives that ensure compliance to core ecotourism criteria. The IAATO guidelines and Australia's EcoCertification

Programme are 'works in progress' that embody industry best practice in this regard. However, for the credibility of ecotourism as the conscience of sustainable tourism to be established and maintained, it is necessary to implement a modified comprehensive ecotourism model that embraces both hard and soft ecotourism. This can potentially be realized through a network of accredited ecotouriums where ecotourists are mobilized through relevant activities to function as effective agents of environmental protection and enhancement.

On the net

Congress Avenue Bridge bat colony, Austin (Texas, USA)
http://www.batcon.org/discover/congress.html

EcoCertification Programme (Australia)
http://www.ecotourism.org.au/EcoCertification3.pdf

Ecotourism Australia
http://www.ecotourism.org.au/

IAATO (International Association of Antarctic Tourism Operators)
http://www.iaato.org

Skyrail (Queensland, Australia)
http://www.skyrail.com.au/

Whale Watch (Kaikoura, New Zealand)
http://www.whalewatch.co.nz/

For further reading

Buckley, R. (ed.) (2004a). *Environmental Impacts of Ecotourism*. CABI Publishing.
The 25 chapters in this collation address a diverse array of contemporary environmental impact issues associated with ecotourism, illustrated by a global array of case studies. The editor provides a good synopsis and critique of these issues.

Hawkins, D., Epler Wood, M. and Bittman, S. (eds) (1995). *The Ecolodge Sourcebook for Planners & Developers*. The Ecotourism Society.
Though now somewhat dated, the Sourcebook provides practical advice for the sustainable planning, design and management of ecolodges, as well as sections on resource interpretation and case studies.

Weaver, D. (2001b). *Ecotourism*. John Wiley & Sons, Australia.
Designed for specialized senior level courses in ecotourism, this text covers definitions, markets, venues, impacts, business considerations, external environments and organizational issues. A world survey is also provided and special venues such as Antarctica, indigenous territories and small islands are featured.

Weaver, D. (ed.) (2001c). *The Encyclopedia of Ecotourism*. CABI Publishing.
This compilation of 41 individually authored chapters provides a state-of-the-art review of major ecotourism topics, divided into eight sections, as follows: introduction; regional survey by continent; regional survey by biome; venues; impacts; planning, management and institutions; business issues; and methodologies, research and resources.

Beyond the book

1. Most ecotourism experts would agree that a large Category II National Park is an ecotourism venue, while an urban zoo is not. However, within this captive/non-captive setting spectrum, there are transitional facilities such as wildlife parks and rehabilitation

centres that may be described as semi-captive. Prepare a report in which you outline the case for and against including these two types of attraction as ecotourism products.

2. It can be argued that hard ecotourism cannot exist as a form of circumstantial alternative tourism. Why not, and what does this say about the existence of ecotourism products within a destination that is in the exploration stage of the resort cycle?

3. In Section 11.4.3, mediating attractions are described as exemplifying mass ecotourism. Since mass tourism is associated with a weak approach to sustainability, does it therefore follow that such an approach is warranted in the rainforest and coral reef settings where mediating attractions are commonly situated?

4. Why is it argued in this chapter that the modified comprehensive model of ecotourism must accommodate soft as well as hard ecotourism? What are the risks associated with this approach and how could those be overcome?

On the ground: quality control in the whale watching industry of Kaikoura, New Zealand

Whale watching (which includes porpoises and dolphins) is a rapidly growing sub-sector within ecotourism, with an estimated annual revenue growth rate of 12.1 per cent during the late 1990s (Berrow, 2003). Whale Watch, based in the small town of Kaikoura on the northeastern coast of New Zealand's South Island, is widely regarded as one of the best illustrations of a financially and environmentally sustainable whale watching enterprise. Also distinguishing this case study is the maintenance of control by the local indigenous Maori community and its transformation during a 10-year period from an alternative tourism operation with 3500 clients in 1988 to a mass ecotourism operation hosting 60 000 clients in 1998 (Cater and Cater, 2001).

A comprehensive operator certification system comparable to Australia's EcoCertification Programme is not currently in place in Kaikoura, in large part because sustainable interactions with cetaceans are perceived as being effectively governed through the provisions of the Marine Mammals Protection Act 1978 and later additions that pertain specifically to whale watching. These regulations, which are premised on the key principles that whale watching should cause no harm to the mammals and should have an educational component, are mainly concerned with maintaining appropriate distances and positions relative to the whales. For example, vessels may approach no closer than 50 metres from a whale, cannot block its path and must travel at a 'no wake' speed. No more than three vessels (including aircraft) can be positioned within 300 metres of a whale at any given time and vessels must approach from a direction parallel to the whales and slightly to their rear (Cater and Cater, 2001). The Department of Conservation (DOC) of New Zealand enforces these regulations through spot checks, follow-ups on complaints from the public and by placing staff members incognito on board a certain number of trips as observers. The DOC also issues permits, though has currently imposed a 10-year moratorium on the issuance of new permits in recognition of the precautionary principle (Curtin, 2003).

For its own part, Whale Watch customers are shown a safety and introductory video prior to their tours, which lasts about 3 hours. Sensibly, no guarantees are made that whales will be seen, but provision is made to reimburse most of the tour's expenses to customers if no whales are viewed, in order to minimize dissatisfaction. The enterprise currently operates four vessels with a capacity of 50 passengers each, with no more than four trips allowed per vessel per day. Water-jet-powered boats are used because they generate less underwater noise (Curtin, 2003). Whale Watch has won several sustainable tourism awards, including the British Airways Tourism for Tomorrow Award in 1994, a Green Globe Achievement Award with Distinction in 1997 and a PATA Gold Award in 1999.

The whale watching activity associated with Whale Watch and Kaikoura more generally has not been without controversy. A major point of contention is the monopoly over whale watching provided to local Maori under the provisions of the 1840 Treaty of Waitangi, which gives the Maori broad rights over their natural, cultural and spiritual treasures, including whales. This monopoly has had the positive environmental result of restricting the number of whale watching operators in the town, but has also had the negative sociocultural outcome of generating resentment among local non-Maoris (Orams, 2002). But even without this competition, research has indicated the potential for whale watching to alter the behaviour of cetaceans in potentially unsustainable ways (Orams, 2002; Curtin, 2003), an effect that may be exacerbated by the fact that the four vessels have the potential to make 112 trips per week, involving at full capacity more than 5000 passengers and crew. Moreover, the monopoly does not apply to seal swimming or dolphin watching tours, which are undertaken by 11 other local enterprises.

Exercise

Discuss the pros and cons of allowing an indigenous group to monopolize a component of a community's ecotourism industry. In what ways could the non-indigenous residents of Kaikoura be accommodated without offending or violating the rights of the local Maori?

References

Ackerstein, D. and Lemon, K. (1999). Greening the brand: environmental marketing strategies and the American consumer. In *Greener Marketing: A Global Perspective on Greening Marketing Practice* (M. Charter and M. Polonsky, eds) pp. 233–54, Greenleaf.

AGA (2003a). *2003 State of the States: the AGA Survey of Casino Entertainment*. American Gaming Association. http://www.americangaming.org/assets/files/AGA_survey_2003.pdf

AGA (2003b). *Code of Conduct for Responsible Gaming*. http://www.americangaming.org/assets/files/Code_with_bookmarks.pdf

Ah-Keng, K. (1994). Assessing the market receptivity of a new theme park in Singapore: An exploratory study. *Journal of Travel Research*, 32 (3), 44–50.

Airey, D. (2000). Cracow (Poland): the former capital and 'national shrine'. In *Visitor Management: Case Studies from World Heritage Sites* (M. Shackley, ed.) pp. 46–65, Butterworth-Heinemann.

Akama, J. (1996). Western environmental values and nature-based tourism in Kenya. *Tourism Management*, 17, 567–74.

Allen, W. (1992). Increased dangers to Caribbean marine ecosystems: cruise ship anchors and intensified tourism threaten reefs. *BioScience*, 42, 330–5.

Altman, Y. (1995). A theme park in a cultural straitjacket: the case of Disneyland Paris, France. *Managing Leisure*, 1, 43–56.

American Airlines (2001). *Environmental Leadership and Stewardship in a Changing World*. 2001 CERES Report. http://www.amrcorp.com/facts/2001ceres.pdf (visited 18 November 2003).

Ap, J. and Wong, K. (2001). Case study on tour guiding: professionalism, issues and problems. *Tourism Management*, 22, 551–63.

APEC (2000). *Seoul Declaration on an APEC Tourism Charter*.

Archer, B. (1981). *The Tourist Dollar: Its Impact on Incomes and Employment in the Bahamas*. Ministry of Tourism, Government of the Bahamas.

Ashworth, G. and Tunbridge, J. (1990). *The Tourist-historic City*. Belhaven Press.

Ashworth, G., White, P. and Winchester, H. (1988). The redlight districts of the West European city. *Geoforum*, 19, 201–12.

Ateljevic, I. and Doorne, S. (2004). Theoretical encounters: a review of backpacker literature. In *The Global Nomad: Backpacker Travel in Theory and Practice* (G. Richards and J. Wilson, eds) pp. 60–76, Channel View.

Aziz, H. (1995). Understanding attacks on tourists in Egypt. *Tourism Management*, 16, 91–5.

Barnes, J. (1996). Economic characteristics of the demand for wildlife-viewing tourism in Botswana. *Development Southern Africa*, 13, 377–97.

Bauer, T. and Dowling, R. (2003). Ecotourism policies and issues in Antarctica. In *Ecotourism Policy and Planning* (D. Fennell and R. Dowling, eds) pp. 309–29, CABI Publishing.

Beesley, K. and Russwurm, L. (eds) (1981). *The Rural-Urban Fringe: Canadian Perspectives*. York University/Atkinson College Geographical Monographs no. 10.

Beeton, S. and Benfield, R. (2002). Demand control: the case for demarketing as a visitor and environmental management tool. *Journal of Sustainable Tourism*, 10, 497–513.

Beirman, D. (2003). *Restoring Tourism Destinations in Crisis: a Strategic Marketing Approach*. CABI Publishing.

Bendell, J. and Font, X. (2004). Which tourism rules? Green standards and GATS. *Annals of Tourism Research*, 31, 139–56.

Berrow, S. (2003). An assessment of the framework, legislation and monitoring required to develop genuinely sustainable whalewatching. In *Marine Ecotourism: Issues and Experiences* (B. Garrod and J. Wilson, eds) pp. 66–78, Channel View.

Blake, A. and Sinclair, M. (2003). Tourism crisis management: US response to September 11. *Annals of Tourism Research*, 30, 813–32.

Blamey, R. (1997). Ecotourism: the search for an operational definition. *Journal of Sustainable Tourism*, 5, 109–30.

Blamey, R. (2001). Principles of ecotourism. In *The Encyclopedia of Ecotourism* (D. Weaver, ed.) pp. 5–22, CABI Publishing.

Blangy, S. and Vautier, S. (2001). Europe. In *The Encyclopedia of Ecotourism* (D. Weaver, ed.) pp. 155–71, CABI Publishing.

Bossel, H. (1999). *Indicators for Sustainable Development: Theory, Method, Applications.* International Institute for Sustainable Development.

Bosselman, F., Peterson, C. and McCarthy, C. (1999). *Managing Tourism Growth: Issues and Applications.* Island Press.

Boyd, M. (2000). Reconstructing Bronzeville: racial nostalgia and neighborhood redevelopment. *Journal of Urban Affairs*, 22, 107–22.

Bramwell, B. (1997). A sport mega-event as a sustainable tourism development strategy. *Tourism Recreation Research*, 22 (2), 13–19.

Bramwell, B. and Lane, B. (1993). Sustainable tourism: an evolving global approach. *Journal of Sustainable Tourism*, 1, 1–5.

Braun, D. (2003). *Inside Disney World's landscaping army.* National Geographic News. August 28. http://news.nationalgeographic.com/news/2003/08/0827_030828_greendisney.html

British Airways (2003). *2002/2003 Social and Environmental Report.* http://www.britishairways.com/cms/masterEN/content/company_information/community_and_environmental/social_and_environ_report_03.pdf (visited 10 December 2004).

Britton, S. (1982). The political economy of tourism in the Third World. *Annals of Tourism Research*, 9, 331–58.

Broad, S. (2003). Living the Thai life – a case study of volunteer tourism at the Gibbon Rehabilitation Project, Thailand. *Tourism Recreation Research*, 28 (3), 63–72.

Broadway, M. (1997). Urban tourism development in the modern Canadian city: a review. In *Quality Management in Urban Tourism* (P. Murphy, ed.) pp. 25–40, Wiley.

Brown, K., Turner, R., Hameed, H. and Bateman, I. (1997). Environmental carrying capacity and tourism development in the Maldives and Nepal. *Environmental Conservation*, 24, 316–25.

Brown, M. (1994). Environmental auditing and the hotel industry: an accountant's perspective. In *Tourism: State of the Art* (A. Seaton et al., eds) pp. 675–81, Wiley.

Brunet, S., Bauer, J., DeLacey, T. et al. (2001). Tourism development in Bhutan: tensions between tradition and modernity. *Journal of Sustainable Tourism*, 9, 243–63.

Bryman, A. (1995). *Disney and His Worlds.* Routledge.

BTR (2000). *International Visitors to Australia, 1999.* Bureau of Tourism Research.

Buchanan, I. and Rossetto, A. (1997). *With my Swag upon my Shoulder: a Comprehensive Study of International Backpackers to Australia.* Bureau of Tourism Research, Occasional Paper No. 24.

Buckley, R. (2001). Major issues in tourism ecolabelling. In *Tourism Ecolabelling: Certification and Promotion of Sustainable Management* (X. Font and R. Buckley, eds) pp. 19–26, CABI Publishing.

Buckley, R. (2002a). Tourism ecocertification in the International Year of Ecotourism. *Journal of Ecotourism*, 1, 197–203.

Buckley, R. (2002b). Tourism ecolabels. *Annals of Tourism Research*, 29, 183–208.

Buckley, R. (2003). *Case Studies in Ecotourism.* CABI Publishing.

Buckley, R. (ed.) (2004a). *Environmental Impacts of Ecotourism.* CABI Publishing.

Buckley, R. (ed.) (2004b). Impacts of ecotourism on birds. In *Environmental Impacts of Ecotourism* pp. 187–209, CABI Publishing.

Buckley, R. (ed.) (2004c). Impacts of ecotourism on terrestrial wildlife. In *Environmental Impacts of Ecotourism* pp. 211–28, CABI Publishing.

Buckley, R., King, N. and Zubrinich, T. (2004). The role of tourism in spreading dieback disease in Australian vegetation. In *Environmental Impacts of Ecotourism* (R. Buckley, ed.) pp. 317–24, CABI Publishing.

Budowski, G. (1976). Tourism and environmental conservation: conflict, coexistence, or symbiosis? *Environmental Conservation*, 3, 27–31.

Buhalis, D. and Cooper, C. (1998). Competition or co-operation? Small and medium sized tourism enterprises at the destination. In *Embracing and Managing Change in Tourism: International Case Studies* (E. Laws, B. Faulkner and G. Moscardo, eds) pp. 324–46, Routledge.

Bull, C. (1992). Tourism in Australia Part II – Sustainable tourism in Australia. *Landscape Australia*, 14, 105–8.

Busby, G. and Rendle, S. (2000). The transition from tourism on farms to farm tourism. *Tourism Management*, 21, 635–42.

Butler, R. (1980). The concept of a tourist area cycle of evolution: implications for management of resources. *Canadian Geographer*, 24, 5–12.

Butler, R. (1990). Alternative tourism: pious hope or Trojan horse? *Journal of Travel Research*, 28 (3), 40–5.

Butler, R. and Boyd, S. (eds) (2000). *Tourism and National Parks: Issues and Implications*. Wiley.

Camp, D. (1997). Theme parks in Europe. *Travel and Tourism Analyst*, 5, 4–21.

Carey, S., Gountas, Y. and Gilbert, D. (1997). Tour operators and destination sustainability. *Tourism Management*, 18, 425–31.

Carmichael, B. and Peppard, D. (1998). The impacts of Foxwoods Resort Casino on its dual host community: Southeastern Connecticut and the Mashantucket Pequot tribe. In *Tourism and Gaming on American Indian Lands* (A. Lew and G. Van Otten, eds) pp. 128–44, Cognizant.

Carroll, A. (1989). *Business and Society: Ethics and Stakeholder Management*. South-Western Publishing.

Carson, R. (1962). *Silent Spring*. Houghton Mifflin.

Carter, S. (1998). Tourists' and travellers' social construction of Africa and Asia as risky locations. *Tourism Management*, 19, 349–58.

Cartier, C. (1998). Megadevelopment in Malaysia: from heritage landscapes to 'leisurescapes' in Melaka's tourism sector. *Singapore Journal of Tropical Geography*, 19, 151–76.

Cater, C. and Cater, E. (2001). Marine environments. In *The Encyclopedia of Ecotourism* (D. Weaver, ed.) pp. 265–82, CABI Publishing.

Cazes, G. (1989). Alternative tourism: reflections on an ambiguous concept. In *Towards Appropriate Tourism: The Case of Developing Countries* (T.V. Singh, H.L Theuns and F.M. Go, eds) pp. 117–26, Peter Lang.

CDOT (1995). *National Backpacker Tourism Strategy*. Commonwealth Department of Tourism, Australia.

Ceballos-Lascuráin, H. (1988). The future of 'ecotourism'. *Mexico Journal*, January 27, 13–14.

Chan, R. (2001). Determinants of Chinese consumers' green purchase behavior. *Psychology and Marketing*, 18, 389–413.

Chape, S., Blyth, S., Fish, L. et al. (2003). *2003 United Nations List of Protected Areas*. IUCN – The World Conservation Union, UNEP – World Conservation Monitoring Centre.

Chapman, D. (1995). *Ecotourism in State Forests of New South Wales: Who Visits and Why?* State Forests of New South Wales and the University of Sydney.

Christie, M. and Mason, P. (2003). Transformative tour guiding: training tour guides to be critically reflective practitioners. *Journal of Ecotourism*, 2, 1–16.

Clarke, J. (1996). Farm accommodation and the communication mix. *Tourism Management*, 17, 611–16.

Clements, M. (1989). Selecting tourist traffic by demarketing. *Tourism Management*, 10 (2), 89–94.

Clifford, H. (2002). *Downhill Slide: Why the Corporate Ski Industry is Bad for Skiing, Ski Towns, and the Environment*. Sierra Club Books.

Cohen, E. (1988). Authenticity and commodification in tourism. *Annals of Tourism Research*, 15, 371–86.

Cohen, E. (1989). 'Primitive and remote': hill tribe trekking in Thailand. *Annals of Tourism Research*, 16, 30–61.

Coles, T. (2004). What makes a resort complex? Reflections on the production of tourism space in a Caribbean resort complex. In *Tourism in the Caribbean: Trends, Development, Prospects* (D. Duval, ed.) pp. 235–56, Routledge.

Collins, C. (1979). Site and situation strategy in tourism planning: a Mexican case study. *Annals of Tourism Research*, 6, 351–66.

Conlin, M. (1996). Revitalizing Bermuda: tourism policy planning in a mature island destination. In *Practicing Responsible Tourism: International Case Studies in Tourism Planning, Policy, and Development* (L. Harrison and W. Husbands, eds) pp. 80–102, John Wiley & Sons.

Conlin, M. and Baum, T. (1995). Island tourism: an introduction. In *Island Tourism: Management Principles and Practice* (M. Conlin and T. Baum, eds) pp. 3–13, John Wiley & Sons.

Cotterill, D. (1996). Developing a sustainable ecotourism business. In *Taking the Next Steps* (H. Richins, J. Richardson and A. Crabtree, eds) pp. 135–40, Ecotourism Association of Australia.

Crane, A. (2000). *Marketing, Morality and the Natural Environment*. Routledge.

Crittendon, A. (1975). *Tourism's terrible toll. International Wildlife*, 5 (2), 4–12.

Crompton, J. (1996). Tax incentives for making donations to park and recreation agencies. *Journal of Park and Recreation Administration*, 14 (4), 65–81.

Crush, J. and Wellings, P. (1987). Forbidden fruit and the export of vice. In *Ambiguous Alternative: Tourism in Small Developing Countries* (S. Britton and W. Clarke, eds) pp. 91–112, University of the South Pacific.

Curtin, S. (2003). Whale-watching in Kaikoura: sustainable destination development? *Journal of Ecotourism*, 2, 173–95.

Curtin, S. and Busby, G. (1999). Sustainable destination development: the tour operator perspective. *International Journal of Tourism Research*, 1, 135–47.

Dahl, A. (1997). The big picture: comprehensive approaches. In *Sustainability Indicators: Report of the Project on Indicators of Sustainable Development* (B. Moddan and S. Bilharz, eds) pp. 69–83, Wiley.

D'Amore, L. (1988). Tourism – a vital force for peace. *Tourism Management*, 9, 151–4.

D'Amore, L. (1992). Promoting sustainable tourism – The Canadian approach. *Tourism Management*, 3, 258–62.

Daniel, J. (ed.) (1993). *The Buzzworm Magazine Guide to Ecotravel*. Buzzworm Books.

Davies, J. (2002). Exploring open spaces and protecting natural places. *Journal of Ecotourism*, 1, 173–80.

Davis, J. and Hudman, L. (1998). The history of Indian gaming law and casino development in the western United States. In *Tourism and Gaming on American Indian Lands* (A. Lew and G. Van Otten, eds) pp. 82–92, Cognizant.

Davis, K. and Fredrick, W. (1984). *Business and Society*, 5th edn. McGraw Hill.

Dearden, P. (1991). Tourism and sustainable development in Northern Thailand. *Geographical Review*, 81, 400–13.

de Larderel, J. (2001). Foreword. In *Tourism Ecolabelling: Certification and Promotion of Sustainable Management* (X. Font and R. Buckley, eds) pp. xv–xvii, CABI Publishing.

Dernoi, L. (1981). Alternative tourism: Towards a new style in North–South relations. *Tourism Management*, 2, 253–64.

Dernoi, L. (1991). Canadian country vacations: the farm and rural tourism in Canada. *Tourism Recreation Research*, 16, 15–20.

d'Hauteserre, A. (1999a). The French mode of social regulation and sustainable tourism development: the case of Disneyland Paris. *Tourism Geographies*, 1, 86–107.

d'Hauteserre, A. (1999b). Lessons in managed destination competitiveness: the case of Foxwoods Casino Resort. *Tourism Management*, 21, 23–32.

Dodds, R. and Joppe, M. (2001). Promoting urban green tourism: the development of the *other* map of Toronto. *Journal of Vacation Marketing*, 7, 261–7.

Dodds, R. and Joppe, M. (2003). The application of ecotourism to urban environments. *Tourism*, 51, 157–64.

Dodson, R. (2000). *Managing Wildlife Habitat on Golf Courses*. Ann Arbor Press.

Doxey, G. (1976). When enough's enough: the natives are restless in Old Niagara. *Heritage Canada*, 2 (2), 26–7.

Dowling, R. (2001). Oceania (Australia, New Zealand and South Pacific). In *The Encyclopedia of Ecotourism* (D. Weaver, ed.) pp. 139–54, CABI Publishing.

Dowling, R. (2002). Australian ecotourism – leading the way. *Journal of Ecotourism*, 1, 89–92.

Dunlap, R. and Van Liere, K. (1978). The new environmental paradigm. *Journal of Environmental Education*, 9 (4), 10–19.

Duska, R. (ed.) (1998). *Education, Leadership and Business Ethics: Essays on the Work of Clarence Walton*. Kluwer.

Eagles, P. and McCool, S. (2002). *Tourism in National Parks and Protected Areas: Planning and Management*. CABI Publishing.

Eber, S. (ed.) (1992). *Beyond the Green Horizon: A Discussion Paper on Principles for Sustainable Tourism*. Tourism Concern & World Wildlife Fund.

EC (2003). *Consultation Document: Basic Orientations for the Sustainability of European Tourism: An Invitation to Comment*. European Commission Directorate-General.

Echtner, C. (1999). Tourism in sensitive environments: three African success stories. In *Tourism Development in Critical Environments* (T.V. Singh and S. Singh, eds) pp. 149–62, Cognizant.

Elander, M. and Widstrand, S. (1998). *Eco-touring: the Ultimate Guide*. Firefly Books.

Elliott, G., Mitchell, B., Wiltshire, B. et al. (2001). Community participation in marine protected area management: Wakatobi National Park, Sulawesi, Indonesia. *Coastal Management*, 29, 295–316.

English, E. (1986). *The Great Escape? An Examination of North–South Tourism*. The North–South Institute.

Enz, C. and Siguaw, J. (1999). Best hotel environmental practices. *Cornell Hotel and Restaurant Administration Quarterly*, 40 (5), 72–7.

Epler Wood, M. (1991). Global solutions: an ecotourism society. In *Nature Tourism: Managing for the Environment* (T. Whelan, ed.) pp. 200–6, Island Press.

Essex, S., Kent, M. and Newnham, R. (2004). Tourism development in Mallorca: is water supply a constraint? *Journal of Sustainable Tourism*, 12, 4–24.

Evans, K. (1998). Competition for heritage space: Cairo's resident/tourist conflict. In *Managing Tourism in Cities: Policy, Process and Practice* (D. Tyler, Y. Guerrier and M. Robertson, eds) pp. 179–92, John Wiley & Sons.

Evans, S. (2000). Ecotourism in tropical rainforests: an environmental management option for threatened resources? In *Forest Tourism and Recreation: Case Studies in Environmental Management* (X. Font and J. Tribe, eds) pp. 127–42, CABI Publishing.

Faulkner, B. (2003). Rejuvenating a maturing tourist destination: the case of the Gold Coast. In *Progressing Tourism Research – Bill Faulkner* (L. Fredline, L. Jago and C. Cooper, eds) pp. 34–86, Channel View.

Faulkner, B. and Russell, R. (1997). Chaos and complexity in tourism: in search of a new paradigm. *Pacific Tourism Review*, 1, 93–102.

Faulkner, B. and Vikulov, S. (2001). Katherine, washed out one day, back on track the next: a post-mortem of a tourism disaster. *Tourism Management*, 22, 331–44.

Fennell, D. (1999). *Ecotourism: an Introduction*. Routledge.

Fennell, D. (2002). *Ecotourism Programme Planning*. CABI Publishing.

Fennell, D. and Malloy, D. (1995). Ethics and ecotourism: a comprehensive ethical model. *Journal of Applied Recreation Research*, 20 (3), 163–83.

Fennell, D. and Weaver, D. (in press). The Ecotourium Concept and Tourism-Conservation Symbiosis. *Journal of Sustainable Tourism*.

Finney, B. and Watson, K. (eds) (1975). *A New Kind of Sugar: Tourism in the Pacific*. East–West Centre.

Fjellman, S. (1992). *Vinyl Leaves: Walt Disney World and America*. Westview Press.

Fleischer, A. and Buccola, S. (2003). War, terror, and the tourism market in Israel. *Applied Economics*, 34, 1335–43.

Foglesong, R. (1999). Walt Disney World and Orlando: deregulation as a strategy for tourism. In *The Tourist City* (D. Judd and S. Fainstein, eds) pp. 89–106, Yale University Press.

Font, X. (2001). Regulating the green message: the players in ecolabelling. In *Tourism Ecolabelling: Certification and Promotion of Sustainable Management* (X. Font and R. Buckley, eds) pp. 1–17, CABI Publishing.

Font, X. and Buckley, R. (eds) (2001). *Tourism Ecolabelling: Certification and Promotion of Sustainable Management*. CABI Publishing.

Font, X., Sanabria, R. and Skinner, E. (2003). Sustainable tourism and ecotourism certification: raising standards and benefits. *Journal of Ecotourism*, 2, 213–18.

Font, X. and Tribe, J. (2001). Promoting green tourism: the future of environmental awards. *International Journal of Tourism Research*, 3, 9–21.

Forest Service (1986). *ROS Users Guide*. United States Department of Agriculture.

Forsyth, T. (1995). Business attitudes to sustainable tourism: self-regulation in the UK outgoing tourism industry. *Journal of Sustainable Tourism*, 3, 210–31.

Frater, J. (1983). Farm tourism in England: planning, funding, promotion and some lessons from Europe. *Tourism Management*, 4, 155–66.

Frazier, J. (1997). Sustainable development: modern elixir or sack dress? *Environmental Conservation*, 24, 182–93.

Fredline, L. and Faulkner, B. (2000). Host community reactions: a cluster analysis. *Annals of Tourism Research*, 27, 763–84.

Frost, W. (2001). Rainforests. In *The Encyclopedia of Ecotourism* (D. Weaver, ed.) pp. 193–204, CABI Publishing.

Fuller, D. (1999). *Sustainable Marketing: Managerial-Ecological Issues*. Sage.

Gaillard, F. (1996). *If I were a carpenter: twenty years of Habitat for Humanity*. J.F. Blair.

GAO (2000). *Marine Pollution: Progress Made to Reduce Marine Pollution by Cruise Ships, but Important Issues Remain*. United States General Accounting Office. February.

Gardner, J. (2001). Accommodations. In *The Encyclopedia of Ecotourism* (D. Weaver, ed.) pp. 525–34, CABI Publishing.

Garrod, B. and Wilson, J. eds. (2003). *Marine Ecotourism: Issues and Experiences*. Channel View.

Genot, H. (1995). Voluntary environmental codes of conduct in the tourism sector. *Journal of Sustainable Tourism*, 3, 166–72.

Getz, D. (1993). Tourist shopping villages: development and planning strategies. *Tourism Management*, 14, 15–26.

Gill, A. and Williams, P. (1994). Managing growth in mountain tourism communities. *Tourism Management*, 15, 212–20.

Goeldner, C. and Ritchie, J. (2003). *Tourism: Principles, Practices, Philosophies, 9th edn*. John Wiley & Sons.

Goffman, E. (1959). *The Presentation of Self in Everyday Life*. Doubleday.

Gonsalves, P. (1987). Alternative tourism: The evolution of a concept and establishment of a network. *Tourism Recreation Research*, 12 (2), 9–12.

Goodwin, H. (2000). Tourism, national parks and partnerships. In *Tourism and National Parks: Issues and Implications* (R. Butler and W. Boyd, eds) pp. 245–62, John Wiley & Sons.

Gössling, S. ed. (2003). *Tourism and Development in Tropical Islands: Political Ecology Perspectives*. Edward Elgar.

Green Tourism Association (2000). *The Other Guide to Toronto: Opening the Door to Green Tourism*.

Griffin, T. and Boele, N. (1997). Alternative paths to sustainable tourism: problems, prospects, panaceas and pipe-dreams. In *Tourism and Economic Development in Asia and Australasia* (F. Go and C. Jenkins, eds) pp. 321–37, Pinter.

Griffin, T. and DeLacey, T. (2002). Green Globe: sustainability accreditation for tourism. In *Sustainable Tourism: A Global Perspective* (R. Harris, T. Griffin and P. Williams, eds) pp. 58–83, Butterworth-Heinemann.

Gunn, C. (1994). *Tourism Planning: Basics, Concepts, Cases, 3rd edn*. Taylor & Francis.

Gurung, C. and De Coursey, M. (1994). The Annapurna Conservation Area Project: a pioneering example of sustainable tourism? In *Ecotourism: A Sustainable Option?* (E. Cater and G. Lowman, eds) pp. 177–94, Wiley.

Hall, C. (1996). Tourism and the Maori of Aotearoa, New Zealand. In *Tourism and Indigenous Peoples* (R. Butler and T. Hinch, eds) pp. 155–75, International Thomson Business Press.

Hall, C. (1998). Historical antecedents on sustainable development: new labels on old bottles? In *Sustainable Tourism: A Geographical Perspective* (C.M. Hall and A.A. Lew, eds) pp. 13–24, Longman.

Hall, C. (2000). Tourism, National Parks and Aboriginal people. In *Tourism and National Parks* (R. Butler and S. Boyd, eds) pp. 29–38, John Wiley & Sons.

Halpenny, E. (2002). Tourism in marine protected areas. In *Tourism in National Parks and Protected Areas: Planning and Management* (P. Eagles and S. McCool, eds) pp. 211–32, CABI Publishing.

Halpenny, E. and Caissie, L. (2003). Volunteering on nature conservation projects: volunteer experience, attitudes and values. *Tourism Recreation Research*, 28 (3), 25–33.

Ham, S. (1992). *Environmental Interpretation: A Practical Guide for People with Big Ideas and Small Budgets*. Fulcrum/North American Press.

Hampton, M. (1998). Backpacker tourism and economic development. *Annals of Tourism Research*, 25, 639–60.

Hannigan, J. (1998). *Fantasy City: Pleasure and Profit in the Postmodern Metropolis*. Routledge.

Harrigan, N. (1974). The legacy of Caribbean history and tourism. *Annals of Tourism Research*, 2, 13–25.

Hawkes, S. and Williams, P. (eds) (1993). *The Greening of Tourism: From Principles to Practice*. Simon Fraser University.

Hawkins, D. and Cunningham, J. (1996). It is 'never-never land' when interest groups prevail: Disney's America project, Prince William County, Virginia, USA. In *Practicing Responsible Tourism: International Case Studies in Tourism Planning, Policy, and Development* (L. Harrison and W. Husbands, eds) pp. 350–65, Wiley.

Hawkins, D., Epler Wood, M. and Bittman, S. (eds) (1995). *The Ecolodge Sourcebook for Planners & Developers*. The Ecotourism Society.

Henderson, J., Koh, A., Soh, S. et al. (2001). Urban environments and nature-based attractions: green tourism in Singapore. *Tourism Recreation Research*, 26 (3), 71–8.

Higgins, B. (1996). The global structure of the nature tourism industry: ecotourists, tour operators, and local businesses. *Journal of Travel Research*, 35 (2), 11–18.

Higgins, B. (2001). Tour operators. In *The Encyclopedia of Ecotourism* (D. Weaver, ed.) pp. 235–48, CABI Publishing.

Higham, J. and Lück, M. (2002). Urban ecotourism: a contradiction in terms? *Journal of Ecotourism*, 1, 36–51.

Higham, J. and Lusseau, D. (2004). Ecological impacts and management of tourist engagements with cetaceans. In *Environmental Impacts of Ecotourism* (R. Buckley, ed.) pp. 171–86, CABI Publishing.

Hills, T. and Lundgren, J. (1977). The impact of tourism in the Caribbean: a methodological study. *Annals of Tourism Research*, 4, 248–67.

Hing, N., McCabe, V., Lewis, P. et al. (1998). Hospitality trends in the Asia-Pacific: a discussion of five key sectors. *International Journal of Contemporary Hospitality Management*, 10, 264–71.

Hjalager, A. (1999). Consumerism and sustainable tourism. *Journal of Travel & Tourism Marketing*, 8 (3), 1–20.

Hobson, K. and Essex, S. (2001). Sustainable tourism: a view from accommodation businesses. *The Service Industries Journal*, 21, 133–46.

Hobson, P. and Mak, B. (1995). Home visit and community-based tourism: Hong Kong's Family Insight Tour. *Journal of Sustainable Tourism*, 3, 179–90.

Holden, A. (1999). High impact tourism: a suitable component of sustainable policy? The case of downhill skiing development at Cairngorm, Scotland. *Journal of Sustainable Tourism*, 7, 97–107.

Holden, P. (ed.) (1984). *Alternative Tourism: Report of the Workshop on Alternative Tourism with a Focus on Asia*. Ecumenical Coalition on Third World Tourism.

Holing, D. (1991). *A Guide to Earthtrips: Nature Travel on a Fragile Planet*. Living Planet Press.

Honey, M. (1999). *Ecotourism and Sustainable Development: Who Owns Paradise?* Island Press.

Honey, M. and Rome, A. (2001). *Protecting Paradise: Certification Programs for Sustainable Tourism and Ecotourism*. The Institute for Policy Studies.

Horneman, L., Beeton, R. and Huie, J. (1997). Environmental quality assurance: are consumers of hospitality and tourism services willing to pay? *Australian Journal of Hospitality Management*, 4, 42–6.

Howe, J., McMahon, E. and Propst, L. (1997). *Balancing Nature and Commerce in Gateway Communities*. Island Press.

Hsu, C. (1998). Gaming as an economic development tool: a case study of two Iowa communities. *Pacific Tourism Review*, 1, 211–24.

Hudson, B. and Ritchie, J. (2001). Cross-cultural tourist behavior: an analysis of tourist attitudes towards the environment. *Journal of Travel & Tourism Marketing*, 10 (2/3), 1–22.

Hudson, S. (2000). *Snow Business: A Study of the International Ski Industry*. Cassell.

Hunter, C. (1997). Sustainable tourism as an adaptive paradigm. *Annals of Tourism Research*, 24, 850–67.

Hyland, S. (1997). Tourism in the Lower Mississippi Delta: whose field of Dreams? The struggle among the landed aristocracy, the grass-roots indigenous and the gaming industry. In *Tourism and Culture: An Applied Perspective* (E. Chambers, ed.) pp. 147–62, State University of New York Press.

IAAPA (2003). *Progress. 2003 Annual Report*. International Association of Amusement Parks and Attractions.

IHEI (1996). *Environmental Management for Hotels: the Industry Guide to Best Practice*. Butterworth-Heinemann.

Ilbery, B., Bowler, I., Clark, G. et al. (1998). *Farm-based tourism as an alternative farm enterprise: a case study from the Northern Pennines, England*. Regional Studies, 32, 355–64.

Inskeep, E. (1991). *Tourism Planning: An Integrated and Sustainable Development Approach*. Van Nostrand Reinhold.

Ioannides, D., Apostolopoulos, Y. and Sonmez, S. (eds) (2001). *Mediterranean Islands and Sustainable Tourism Development*. Continuum.

Ioannides, D. and Petersen, T. (2003). Tourism 'non-entrepreneurship' in peripheral destinations: a case study of small and medium tourism enterprises on Bornholm, Denmark. *Tourism Geographies*, 5, 408–35.

IUCN, UNEP and WWF (1980). *World Conservation Strategy: Living Resource Conservation for Sustainable Development*. International Union for Conservation of Nature and Natural Resources, United Nations Environment Programme, and World Wildlife Fund.

Jaakson, R. (1997). Exploring the epistemology of ecotourism. *Journal of Applied Recreation Research*, 22 (1), 33–47.

Jafari, J. (1989). An English language literature review. In *Tourism as a Factor of Change: A Sociocultural Study* (J. Bystrzanowski, ed.) pp. 17–60, Centre for Research and Documentation in Social Sciences.

Jafari, J. (2001). The scientification of tourism. In *Hosts and Guests Revisited: Tourism Issues of the 21st Century* (V.L. Smith and M. Brent, eds) pp. 28–41, Cognizant.

Johnston, A. (2003). Exercising indigenous rights in tourism. In *Tourism in Destination Communities* (S. Singh, D. Timothy and R. Dowling, eds) pp.115–34, CABI Publishing.

Jones, A. (1992). Is there a real 'alternative' tourism? Introduction. *Tourism Management*, 13, 102–3.

Josiam, B., Hobson, P., Dietrich, U. et al. (1998). An analysis of the sexual, alcohol and drug related behavioral patterns of students on spring break. *Tourism Management*, 19, 501–13.

Judd, D. and Fainstein, S. eds. (1999). *The Tourist City*. Yale University Press.

Kay, G. and Moxham, N. (1996). Paths for whom? Countryside access for recreational walking. *Leisure Studies*, 15, 171–83.

Klein, R. (2003). *The Cruise Industry and Environmental History and Practice: Is a Memorandum of Understanding Effective for Protecting the Environment?* Bluewater Network and Ocean Advocates. http://bluewaternetwork.org/reports/rep_ss_kleinrep.pdf (visited 7 March 2004).

Knapman, B. and Stoeckl, N. (1995). Recreation user fees: an Australian empirical investigation. *Tourism Economics*, 1, 5–15.

Knill, G. (1991). Towards the green paradigm. *South African Geographical Journal*, 73, 52–9.

Knowles, T., Macmillan, S., Palmer, J. et al. (1999). The development of environmental initiatives in tourism: responses from the London hotel sector. *International Journal of Tourism Research*, 1, 255–65.

Knudson, D., Cable, T. and Beck, L. (1995). *Interpretation of Cultural and Natural Resources*. Venture Publishing.

Kotler, P. and Levy, S. (1971). Demarketing? Yes, demarketing! *Harvard Business Review*, 49 (6), 74–80.

Kovaleski, S. and Fallis, D. (2002). *Noise imperils 2003 Grand Prix*. Washington Post, 22 July. http://student-voices.org/news/index.php3?NewsID=3009

Krippendorf, J. (1987). *The Holiday Makers: Understanding the Impact of Leisure and Travel*. Heinemann.

Kuhn, T. (1970). *The Structure of Scientific Revolutions*, 2nd edn. University of Chicago Press.

Laarman, J. and Durst, P. (1987). *Nature Travel and Tropical Forests*. FREI Working Paper Series, Southeastern Center for Forest Economics Research.

Laarman, J. and Gregersen, H. (1996). Pricing policy in nature-based tourism. *Tourism Management*, 17, 247–54.

Lane, B. (1991). Sustainable tourism: A new concept for the interpreter. *Interpretation Journal*, 49, 2–4.

Langholz, J. and Brandon, K. (2001). Privately owned protected areas. In *The Encyclopedia of Ecotourism* (D. Weaver, ed.) pp. 303–14, CABI Publishing.

LaPlanche, S. (1995). *Stepping Lightly on Australia: a Traveller's Guide to Ecotourism*. Angus & Robertson.

Lawrence, T. (2004). *Transfer of Development Rights*. Ohio State University, Land Use Series CDFS-1264-98. http://ohioline.osu.edu/cd-fact/1264.html (visited June 7, 2004).

Lawton, L. (2001a). *Resident Perceptions of Tourist Attractions on the Gold Coast of Australia*. Unpublished PhD thesis, School of Tourism and Hotel Management, Griffith University, Gold Coast, Australia.

Lawton, L. (2001b). Public protected areas. In *The Encyclopedia of Ecotourism* (D. Weaver, ed.) pp. 287–302, CABI Publishing.

Lawton, L. and Weaver, D. (2001). Modified spaces. In *The Encyclopedia of Ecotourism* (D. Weaver, ed.) pp. 315–26, CABI Publishing.

Lea, J. (1988). *Tourism and Development in the Third World*. Routledge.

Leiper, N. (1998). Cambodian tourism: potential, problems, and illusions. *Pacific Tourism Review*, 1, 285–97.

Leiper, N. and Hunt, S. (1998). A proposed strategic alliance: why tourism commissions should promote universities and why universities should be represented on commission's boards. *Pacific Tourism Review*, 2, 191–7.

Lembo, J. (2003). Starwood's strategic energy management initiative. *HPAC Engineering*, February, 18–26.

Lew, A. (2001). Tourism development in China: the dilemma of bureaucratic decentralization and economic liberalization. In *Tourism and the Less Developed World: Issues and Case Studies* (D. Harrison, ed.) pp. 109–20, CABI Publishing.

Lew, A. and Van Otten, G. eds. (1998). *Tourism and Gaming on American Indian Lands*. Cognizant.

Lindberg, K. (1991). *Policies for Maximizing Nature Tourism's Ecological and Economic Benefits*. World Resources Institute.

Lindberg, K. (1998). Economic aspects of ecotourism. In *Ecotourism: A Guide for Planners and Managers*. Volume 2 (K. Lindberg, M. Epler Wood and D. Engeldrum, eds) pp. 87–117, The Ecotourism Society.

Lindberg, K., Enriquez, J. and Sproule, K. (1996). Ecotourism questioned: case studies from Belize. *Annals of Tourism Research*, 23, 543–62.

Loker-Murphy, L. and Pearce, P. (1995). Young budget travelers: backpackers in Australia. *Annals of Tourism Research*, 22, 819–43.

Long, P. (1996). Early impacts of limited stakes casino gambling on rural community life. *Tourism Management*, 17, 341–53.

Lovelock, J. (1979). *Gaia: A New Look at Life on Earth*. Oxford University Press.

Loverseed, H. (2000). Winter sports in North America. *Travel & Tourism Analyst*, no. 6, 45–62.

Lowengart, O. and Reichel, A. (1998). Defining opportunities and threats in a changing information technology environment: the case of the travel agent. *Journal of Hospitality & Leisure Marketing*, 5 (4), 57–71.

Lund, E. (2004). 'This is my history and my city'. Christian Science Monitor. February 04 http://www.csmonitor.com/2004/0204/p11s02-lihc.html (visited February 4, 2004).

Lutz, J. and Ryan, C. (1997). Impacts of inner city tourism projects: the case of the International Convention Centre, Birmingham, UK. In *Quality Management in Urban Tourism* (P. Murphy, ed.) pp. 41–54, Wiley.

MacCannell, D. (1976). *The Tourist: A New Theory of the Leisure Class*. Schocken Books.

MacGregor, J. (1995). *Sustainable Tourism Policy and Guidelines: Out Islands of the Bahamas*. Ecoplan:net Ltd.

MacLellan, L. (1997). The tourism and the environmental debate: from idealism to cynicism. In *Hospitality, Tourism and Leisure Management: Issues in Strategy and Culture* (M. Foley, J. Lennon and G. Maxwell, eds) pp.177–94, Cassell.

Macleod, D. (1998). Alternative tourism: a comparative analysis of meaning and impact. In *Global Tourism, 2nd edn* (W. Theobald, ed.) pp. 150–67, Butterworth-Heinemann.

Mader, R. (2003). Latin American ecotourism: what is it? In *Global Ecotourism Policies and Case Studies: Perspectives and Constraints* (M. Lück and T. Kirstges, eds) pp. 100–7, Channel View.

Mann, M. (2002). *The Good Alternative Travel Guide*. Tourism Concern & Earthscan.

Manning, R. (1991). Sustainable tourism. In *Tourism and Leisure: Dynamics and Diversity* (J. Zeiger and L. Caneday, eds) pp. 107–15, National Recreation and Park Association.

Manning, R. (1999). *Studies in Outdoor Recreation: Search and Research for Satisfaction, 2nd edn*. Oregon State University Press.

Manning, T. (1999). Indicators of tourism sustainability. *Tourism Management*, 20, 179–81.

Marin, C. and Jafari, J. (2002). Sustainable hotels for sustainable destinations. *Annals of Tourism Research*, 29, 266–8.

Marion, J. and Farrell, T. (1998). Managing ecotourism visitation in protected areas. In *Ecotourism: A Guide for Planners and Managers*. Volume 2 (K. Lindberg, M. Epler Wood and D. Engeldrum, eds) pp. 155–81, The Ecotourism Society.

Marklein, M. (2002). *Report suggests 9/11 hasn't derailed overseas study programs*. USA Today, 7D.

Markwick, M. (2000). Golf tourism development, stakeholders, differing discourses and alternative agendas: the case of Malta. *Tourism Management* 21, 515–24.

Mason, P. and Mowforth, M. (1996). Codes of conduct in tourism. *Progress in Tourism and Hospitality Research*, 2, 151–67.

McCool, S. and Moisey, N. (eds) (2001). *Tourism, Recreation and Sustainability: Linking Culture and the Environment*. CABI Publishing.

McGehee, N. (2002). Alternative tourism and social movements. *Annals of Tourism Research*, 29, 124–43.

McKercher, B. (1993). Some fundamental truths about tourism: understanding tourism's social and environmental impacts. *Journal of Sustainable Tourism*, 1, 6–16.

McKercher, B. (1998). *The Business of Nature-Based Tourism*. Hospitality Press.

McKercher, B. (1999). A chaos approach to tourism. *Tourism Management*, 20, 425–34.

McKercher, B. (2001). The business of ecotourism. In *The Encyclopedia of Ecotourism* (D. Weaver, ed.) pp. 565–77, CABI Publishing.

McMillan, B., Cutchins, D. and Geissinger, A. (2003). *Volunteer Vacations: Short-term Adventures that will Benefit You and Others, 8th edn*. Chicago Review Press.

McNulty, R. (1985). Revitalizing industrial cities through cultural tourism. *International Journal of Environmental Studies*, 25, 225–28.

Medlik, S. (2003). *Dictionary of Travel, Tourism and Hospitality, 3rd edn*. Butterworth-Heinemann.

Menkhaus, S. and Lober, D. (1996). International ecotourism and the valuation of tropical rainforests in Costa Rica. *Journal of Environmental Management*, 47, 1–10.

Middleton, V. and Hawkins, R. (1998). *Sustainable Tourism: A Marketing Perspective*. Butterworth-Heinemann.

Mill, R. and Morrison, A. (2002). *The Tourism System, 4th edn*. Kendall/Hunt.

Miller, G. (2001). The development of indicators for sustainable tourism: results of a Delphi survey of tourism researchers. *Tourism Management*, 22, 351–62.

Miller, G. (2003). Consumerism in sustainable tourism: a survey of UK consumers. *Journal of Sustainable Tourism*, 11, 17–39.

Milman, A. (2001). The future of the theme park and attraction industry: a management perspective. *Journal of Travel Research*, 40, 139–47.

Mings, R. (1969). Tourism's potential for contributing to economic development in the Caribbean. *Journal of Geography*, (March), 173–7.

Mohsin, A. and Ryan, C. (2003). Backpackers in the Northern Territory of Australia – motives, behaviours and satisfactions. *International Journal of Tourism Research*, 5, 113–31.

Moreno, S. (2004). *City embraces the bats who came home to roost*. Washington Post, 19 July, A3.

Morrison, A., Hsieh, S. and Wang, C. (1992). Certification in the travel and tourism industry: the North American experience. *Journal of Tourism Studies*, 3 (2), 32–40.

Mortazavi, R. (1997). The right of public access in Sweden. *Annals of Tourism Research*, 24, 609–23.

Moscardo, G. (1998). Interpretation and sustainable tourism: Functions, examples and principles. *Journal of Sustainable Tourism*, 9, 2–13.

Mowforth, M. and Munt, I. (1998). *Tourism and Sustainability: New Tourism in the Third World*. Routledge.

Mullins, P. (1991). Tourism urbanization. *International Journal of Urban and Regional Research*, 15, 326–42.

Mullins, P. (1992). Cities for pleasure: the emergence of tourism urbanization in Australia. *Built Environment*, 18 (3), 187–98.

Murphy, L. (2001). Exploring social interactions of backpackers. *Annals of Tourism Research*, 28, 50–67.

Murphy, P. (1985). *Tourism: A Community Approach*. Methuen.

Murphy, P. (1997). Attraction land use management in Disney theme parks: balancing business and environment. In *Quality Management in Urban Tourism* (P. Murphy, ed.) pp. 221–34, Wiley.

National Park Service (2001). *Canyon View Information Plaza*. http://www.nps.gov/grca/publications/cvip.pdf (visited 26 June 2004).

Natural Resources Canada (1997). *Canadian Pacific Hotels: Hospitality, Tradition and Good Environmental Stewardship*. Energy Efficiency Case Studies.

Nepal, S. (2002). Mountain ecotourism and sustainable development: ecology, economics, and ethics. *Mountain Research and Development*, 22, 104–9.

Newsome, D., Moore, S. and Dowling, R. (2002). *Natural Area Tourism: Ecology, Impacts and Management*. Channel View.

Nichols, M., Stitt, G. and Giacopassi, D. (2002). Community assessment of the effects of casinos on quality of life. *Social Indicators Research*, 57, 229–62.

Nickerson, N., Black, R. and McCool, S. (2001). Agritourism: Motivations behind farm/ranch business diversification. *Journal of Travel Research*, 40, 19–26.

Nilsson, P. (2002). Staying on farms: an ideological background. *Annals of Tourism Research*, 29, 7–24.

Notzke, C. (1999). Indigenous tourism development in the Arctic. *Annals of Tourism Research*, 26, 55–76.

Nowak, R. (2001). Tourists in the mist endanger gorillas. *New Scientist*, 169, 18.

Ocko, S. (1990). *Environmental Vacations: Volunteer Projects to Save the Planet*. John Muir Publications.

OECD (2003). *About Tourism*. http://www.oecd.org/about/0,2337,en_2649_34389_1_1_1_1_1, 00.html (visited 19 January 2004).

Oppermann, M. (1997). Rural tourism in Germany: farm and rural tourism operators. In *The Business of Rural Tourism: International Perspectives* (S. Page and D. Getz, eds) pp. 108–19, International Thomson Business Press.

Oppermann, M. (1998). Service attributes of travel agencies: a comparative perspective of users and providers. *Journal of Vacation Marketing*, 4, 265–81.

Orams, M. (1997). The effectiveness of environmental education: can we turn tourists into 'greenies'? *Progress in Tourism and Hospitality Research*, 3, 295–306.

Orams, M. (1999). *Marine Tourism: Development, Impacts and Management*. Routledge.

Orams, M. (2002). Marine ecotourism as a potential agent for sustainable development in Kaikoura, New Zealand. *International Journal of Sustainable Development*, 5, 338–52.

Ottman, J. (1998). *Green Marketing: Opportunity for Innovation, 2nd edn*. NTC Business Books.

Page, S. and Dowling, R. (2002). *Ecotourism*. Prentice Hall.

Palacio, V. and McCool, S. (1997). Identifying ecotourists in Belize through benefit segmentation: a preliminary analysis. *Journal of Sustainable Tourism*, 5, 234–43.

Palmer, T. and Riera, A. (2003). Tourism and environmental taxes. With special reference to the 'Balearic ecotax'. *Tourism Management*, 24, 665–74.

Pearce, D. (1989). *Tourist Development*, 2nd edn. Longman.

Pearce, D. (1992). Alternative tourism: concepts, classifications, and questions. In *Tourism Alternatives: Potentials and Problems in the Development of Tourism* (V. Smith and W. Eadington, eds) pp. 15–30, University of Pennsylvania Press.

Peckham, V. (2003). *BEST Community Profile: The Shaw Heritage Tours*. The Conference Board and WTTC.

Petry, J. (1996). *Northern exposure: touring the less travelled areas of northern Thailand no longer means roughing it*. PATA Travel News, May, p. 10.

Petty, R., McMichael, S. and Brannon, L. (1992). The elaboration likelihood model of persuasion: applications in recreation and tourism. In *Influencing Human Behavior: Theory and Applications in Recreation, Tourism, and Natural Resources Management* (M. Manfredo, ed.) pp. 77–101, Sagamore.

Pigram, J. (1990). Sustainable tourism: Policy considerations. *Journal of Tourism Studies*, 1 (2), 2–9.

Piner, J. and Paradis, T. (2004). Beyond the casino: sustainable tourism and cultural development on Native American lands. *Tourism Geographies*, 6, 80–98.

Pleumarom, A. (1992). Course and effect: golf tourism in Thailand. *The Ecologist*, 22 (3), 104–10.

Pleumarom, A. (2002). How sustainable is Mekong tourism? In *Sustainable Tourism: A Global Perspective* (R. Harris, T. Griffin and P. Williams, eds) pp. 140–66, Butterworth-Heinemann.

Plog, S. (1998). Why destination preservation makes economic sense. In *Global Tourism, 2nd edn* (W. Theobold, ed.) pp. 251–66, Butterworth Heinemann.

Poon, A. (1993). *Tourism, Technology and Competitive Strategies*. CAB International.

Prideaux, B. and Dunn, A. (1995). Tourism and crime – how can the tourism industry respond? The Gold Coast experience. *Australian Journal of Hospitality Management*, 2 (1), 7–15.

Ranck, S. (1987). An attempt at autonomous development: the case of the Tufi guest houses, Papua New Guinea. In *Ambiguous Alternative: Tourism in Small Developing Countries* (S. Britton and W. Clarke, eds) pp. 154–65, University of the South Pacific.

Ray, P. and Anderson, S. (2000). *The Cultural Creatives: How 50 Million People are Changing the World*. Three Rivers Press.

Richards, G. and Richards, B. (1998). A globalised theme park market? The case of Disney in Europe. In *Embracing and Managing Change in Tourism: International Case Studies* (E. Laws, B. Faulkner and G. Moscardo, eds) pp. 365–78, Routledge.

Richards, G. and Wilson, J. (eds) (2004). *The Global Nomad: Backpacker Travel in Theory and Practice*. Channel View.

Richter, L. and Waugh, W. (1986). Terrorism and tourism as logical companions. *Tourism Management*, 7, 230–8.

Ritchie, B. (ed.) (2003). *Managing Educational Tourism*. Channel View.

Ritzer, G. and Liska, A. (1997). 'McDisneyization' and 'post-tourism': complementary perspectives on contemporary tourism. In *Touring Cultures: Transformations of Travel and Theory* (C. Rojek and J. Urry, eds) pp. 96–109, Routledge.

Rivera, J. (2002). Assessing a voluntary environmental initiative in the developing world: the Costa Rican Certification for Sustainable Tourism. *Policy Sciences*, 35, 333–60.

Rivers, J. (2000). Traffic and visitor flow management in the West Bank Necropolis. In *Visitor Management: Case Studies from World Heritage Sites* (M. Shackley, ed.) pp. 161–81, Butterworth-Heinemann.

Roberts, J. (1996). Green consumers in the 1990s: profile and implications for advertising. *Journal of Business Research*, 26, 217–31.

Roberts, L. (2002). Farm tourism – its contribution to the economic sustainability of Europe's countryside. In *Sustainable Tourism: A Global Perspective* (R. Harris, T. Griffin and P. Williams, eds) pp. 195–208, Butterworth-Heinemann.

Robinson, M. (1999). Collaboration and cultural consent: refocusing sustainable tourism. *Journal of Sustainable Tourism*, 7, 379–97.

Roehl, W. (1994). Gambling as a tourist attraction: trends and issues for the 21st century. In *Tourism: The State of the Art* (A. Seaton, ed.) pp. 156–68, Wiley.

Roehl, W. (1999). Quality of life issues in a casino destination. *Journal of Business Research*, 44, 223–9.

Roekaerts, M. and Savat, K. (1989). Mass tourism in South and Southeast Asia – a challenge to Christians and the churches. In *Towards Appropriate Tourism: The Case of Developing Countries* (T.V. Singh, H.L Theuns and F.M. Go, eds) pp. 35–69, Peter Lang.

Rojek, C. (1993). Disney culture. *Leisure Studies*, 12, 121–35.

Romeril, M. (1994). Alternative tourism: the real tourism alternative? In *Progress in Tourism, Recreation and Hospitality Management*. Vol. 6 (C. Cooper and A. Lockwood, eds) pp. 22–9, Wiley.

Rostow, W.W. (1960). *The Stages of Economic Growth*. Cambridge University Press.

Royal, C. and Jago, L. (1998). Special event accreditation: the practitioners' perspective. *Festival Management and Event Tourism*, 5, 221–30.

Russo, A. (2002). The 'vicious circle' of tourism development in heritage cities. *Annals of Tourism Research*, 29, 165–82.

Ryan, C. (2002). Equity, management, power sharing and sustainability – issues of the 'new tourism'. *Tourism Management*, 23, 17–26.

Sasidharan, V., Sirakaya, E. and Kerstetter, D. (2002). Developing countries and tourism eco-labels. *Tourism Management*, 23, 161–74.

Schaffer, S. (1996). Disney and the imagineering of histories. *Postmodern Culture*, 6 (3), e-journal: http://muse.jhu.edu/journals/postmodern_culture/toc/pmc6.3.html

Scheurer, R. (2004). Theme park tourist destinations: creating an experience setting in traditional tourist destinations with staging strategies of theme parks. In *The Tourism and Leisure Industry: Shaping the Future* (K. Weiermair and C. Mathies, eds) pp. 227–36, Haworth Hospitality Press.

Schewer, R., Gazel, R. and Daneshavary, R. (2000). Air-tour impacts: the Grand Canyon case. *Annals of Tourism Research*, 27, 611–23.

Scheyvens, R. (2002). Backpacker tourism and third world development. *Annals of Tourism Research*, 29, 144–64.

Schumacher, E. (1973). *Small is Beautiful*. Abacus.

Shackley, M. (1993). Guest farms in Namibia: an emerging accommodation sector in Africa's hottest destination. *International Journal of Hospitality Management*, 12, 253–65.

Shackley, M. (1996). Too much room at the inn? *Annals of Tourism Research*, 23, 449–62.

Shackley, M. (ed.) (2000). *Visitor Management: Case Studies from World Heritage Sites*. Butterworth-Heinemann.

Sherman, P. and Dixon, J. (1991). The economics of nature tourism: determining if it pays. In *Nature Tourism: Managing for the Environment* (T. Whelan, ed.) pp. 89–131, Island Press.

Showalter, G. (1994). Cruise ships and private islands in the Caribbean. *Journal of Travel and Tourism Marketing*, 3 (4), 107–18.

Silver, I. (1992). Alternative tourism isn't always responsible tourism. *Cultural Survival Quarterly*, 16 (2), 54–9.

Sindiga, I. (1996). Domestic tourism in Kenya. *Annals of Tourism Research*, 23, 19–31.

Singh, S. (2001). Indian tourism: policy, performance and pitfalls. In *Tourism and the Less Developed World: Issues and Case Studies* (D. Harrison, ed.) pp. 137–49, CABI Publishing.

Smith, A. (2004). European paedophiles flock to Gambian 'Smiling Coast'. *The Guardian*, July 4. http://www.guardian.co.uk/print/0,3858,4963030-105248,00.html (visited 4 July 2004).

Smith, V. (1989). Eskimo tourism: micro-models and marginal men. In *Hosts and Guests: the Anthropology of Tourism* (V. Smith, ed.) pp.55–82, University of Pennsylvania Press.

Smith, V. (1996). Indigenous tourism: the four Hs. In *Tourism and Indigenous Peoples*. (R. Butler and T. Hinch, eds) pp. 283–307, International Thomson Business Press.

Social Investment Forum (2003). *2003 Report on Socially Responsible Investing Trends in the United States*. http://www.socialinvest.org/areas/research/trends/sri_trends_report_2003.pdf (visited 27 February 2004).

Soemodinoto, A., Wong, P. and Saleh, M. (2001). Effect of prolonged political unrest on tourism. *Annals of Tourism Research*, 28, 1056–60.

Sofield, H. and Li. F. (2003). Processes in formulating an ecotourism policy for Nature Reserves in Yunnan Province, China. In *Ecotourism Policy and Planning*. (D. Fennell and R. Dowling, eds) pp. 141–67, CABI Publishing.

Somerville, H. (1993). British Airways: airlines, tourism and environment. In *The Greening of Tourism: From Principles to Practice* (S. Hawkes and P. Williams, eds) pp. 3–8, Simon Fraser University.

Sorensen, A. (2003). Backpacker ethnography. *Annals of Tourism Research*, 30, 847–67.

Sorkin, M. (ed.) (1992). *Variations on a Theme Park: The New American City and the End of Public Space*. Hill and Wang.

Speck, E. (2002). The Fairmont Chateau Whistler Resort: moving towards sustainability. In *Sustainable Tourism: A Global Perspective* (R. Harris, T. Griffin and P. Williams, eds) pp. 269–83, Butterworth-Heinemann.

Specter, M. (1999). A sinking feeling: doesn't Venice want to be saved? *The New Yorker*, July 12, 40–3.

Spittler, R. and Haak, U. (2001). Quality analysis of tourism ecolabels. In *Tourism Ecolabelling: Certification and Promotion of Sustainable Management* (X. Font and R. Buckley, eds) pp. 213–45, CABI Publishing.

Spreitzhofer, G. (1998). Backpacking tourism in South-East Asia. *Annals of Tourism Research*, 25, 979–83.

Stabler, M. and Goodall, B. (1997). Environmental awareness, action and performance in the Guernsey hospitality sector. *Tourism Management*, 18, 19–33.

Stansfield, C. (1978). Atlantic City and the resort cycle: background to the legalization of gambling. *Annals of Tourism Research*, 5, 238–51.

Stansfield, C. and Rickert, J. (1970). The recreational business district. *Journal of Leisure Research*, 2, 213–25.

Stanton, M. (1989). The Polynesian Cultural Center: a multi-ethnic model of seven Pacific cultures. In *Hosts and Guests: the Anthropology of Tourism* (V. Smith, ed.) pp. 247–62, University of Pennsylvania Press.

Stimson, R. and Minnery, J. (1998). Why people move to the 'sun-belt': a case study of long-distance migration to the Gold Coast, Australia. *Urban Studies*, 35, 193–214.

Stonehouse, B. (2001). Polar environments. In *The Encyclopedia of Ecotourism* (D. Weaver, ed.) pp. 219–34, CABI Publishing.

Swarbrooke, J. (1995). *The Development and Management of Visitor Attractions*. Butterworth-Heinemann.

Swarbrooke, J. (1999). *Sustainable Tourism Management*. CABI Publishing.

Swarbrooke, J. and Horner, S. (eds) (1999). *Consumer Behaviour in Tourism*. Butterworth-Heinemann.

Sweeting, J. and Sweeting, A. (2003). *A Practical Guide to Good Practice: Managing Environmental and Social Issues in the Accommodations Sector*. http://www.toinitiative.org/about/documents/HotelBooklet.pdf (visited 8 February 2004).

Sweeting, J. and Wayne, S. (2003). *A Shifting Tide: Environmental Challenges and Cruise Industry Responses*. Conservation International Center for Environmental Leadership in Business. http://www.iccl.org/pressroom/cruise.pdf (visited 2 March 2004).

Terman, M. (1997). Natural links: naturalistic golf courses as wildlife habitat. *Landscape and Urban Planning*, 38, 183–97.

TIA (2003). *Tourism Works for America, 12th edn*. Travel Industry Association of America.

Timothy, D. and Wall, G. (1997). Selling to tourists: Indonesian street vendors. *Annals of Tourism Research*, 24, 322–40.

Tourism Concern (2003). *Tourism Concern: Annual Report & Accounts*.

Tourism Concern (2004). *Tourism Concern: Campaigning for ethical and fairly traded tourism*. http://www.tourismconcern.org.uk/ (visited 29 February 2004).

Townsend, M. (1999). *Partnerships with the Australian Trust for Conservation Volunteers*. Proceedings of the Ecotourism Association of Australia annual meeting, 1999, pp. 171–4.

Truett, L.J. and Truett, D.B. (1982). Public policy and the growth of the Mexican Tourism Industry, 1970–1979. *Journal of Travel Research*, 20 (3), 11–19.

Tuppen, J. (2000). The restructuring of winter sports resorts in the French Alps: problems, processes and policies. *International Journal of Tourism Research*, 2, 327–44.

Turner, L. and Ash, J. (1975). *The Golden Hordes: International Tourism and the Pleasure Periphery*. Constable.

Turner, R., Miller, G. and Gilbert, D. (2001). The role of UK charities and the tourism industry. *Tourism Management*, 22, 463–72.

UNCED (1992). *Agenda 21*. United Nations Conference on Environment and Development.

UNDP (2003). *Human Development Reports*. http://www.undp.org/hdr2003/indicator/index.html (visited 3 February 2004).

UNEP (1995). *Environmental Codes of Conduct for Tourism*.

UNEP (2002). *UNEP Tourism Programme*. http://www.uneptie.org/pc/tourism/about-us/why-tourism.htm (visited 16 January 2004).

UNEP (2003a). *Tourism and Local Agenda 21: The Role of Local Authorities in Sustainable Tourism*.

UNEP (2003b). *Switched On: Renewable Energy Opportunities in the Tourism Industry*.

UNEP, UNESCO and WTO (2002). *Work in Progress: Tour Operators Initiative for Sustainable Tourism Development*. http://www.greenbiz.com/frame/1.cfm?targetsite=http://www.toinitiative.org (visited 5 March 2004).

Urbanowicz, C. (2001). Gambling into the 21st century. In *Hosts and Guests Revisited: Tourism Issues of the 21st Century* (V.L. Smith and M. Brent, eds) pp. 69–79, Cognizant.

Urlich Cloher, D. (1999). The sustainability of indigenous tourism. In *Geodiversity: readings in Australian Geography at the Close of the 20th Century* (J. Kesby, J. Stanley, R. McLean and L. Olive, eds) pp. 491–6, Institute of Australian Geographers.

Van der Borg, J. (1998). Tourism management in Venice, or how to deal with success. In *Managing Tourism in Cities: Policy, Process and Practice* (D. Tyler, Y. Guerrier and M. Robertson, eds) pp. 125–35, John Wiley & Sons.

Volberg, R. (2001). *When the Chips are Down: Problem Gambling in America*. Century Foundation Press.

Waldron, D. and Williams, P. (2002). Steps towards sustainability monitoring: the case of the Resort Municipality of Whistler. In *Sustainable Tourism: A Global Perspective* (R. Harris, T. Griffin and P. Williams, eds) pp. 180–94, Butterworth-Heinemann.

Walker, D. and Jackson, J. (1998). New goods and economic growth: evidence from legalized gambling. *Review of Regional Studies*, 28 (2), 47–69.

Wall, G. (1997a). Rethinking impacts of tourism. In *Tourism Development: Environmental and Community Issues* (C. Cooper and S. Wanhill, eds) pp. 1–9, John Wiley & Sons.

Wall, G. (1997b). Tourism attractions: points, lines, and areas. *Annals of Tourism Research*, 24, 240–3.

Wallace, G. (1993). Visitor management: lessons from Galápagos National Park. In *Ecotourism: A Guide for Planners and Managers* (K. Lindberg and D. Hawkins, eds) pp. 55–81, The Ecotourism Society.

Walle, A. (1995). Business ethics and tourism: from micro to macro perspectives. *Tourism Management*, 16, 263–8.

Walsh-Heran, J. and Stevens, T. (1990). *The Management of Visitor Attractions and Events*. Prentice-Hall.

Walton, C. (1998). Corporate social responsibilities: the debate revisited. In *Education, Leadership and Business Ethics: Essays on the Work of Clarence Walton* (R. Duska, ed.) pp. 135–50, Kluwer.

Warnken, W. and Buckley, R. (2004). Instream bacteria as a low-threshold management indicator of tourist impacts in conservation reserves. In *Environmental Impacts of Ecotourism* (R. Buckley, ed.) pp. 325–37, CABI Publishing.

WCED (1987). *Our Common Future*. The World Commission on Environment and Development.

Wearing, S. (2001). *Volunteer Tourism: Experiences that Make a Difference*. CABI Publishing.

Wearing, S. and Huyskens, M. (2001). Moving on from joint management policy regimes in Australian National Parks. *Current Issues in Tourism*, 4, 182–209.

Wearing, S. and Neil, J. (1999). *Ecotourism: Impacts, Potentials and Possibilities*. Butterworth-Heinemann.

Weaver, D. (1991). Alternative to mass tourism in Dominica. *Annals of Tourism Research*, 18, 414–32.

Weaver, D. (1993). Model of urban tourism for small Caribbean islands. *Geographical Review*, 83, 134–40.

Weaver, D. (1998). *Ecotourism in the Less Developed World*. CAB International.

Weaver, D. (1999). Magnitude of ecotourism in Costa Rica and Kenya. *Annals of Tourism Research*, 26, 792–816.

Weaver, D. (2000a). A broad context model of destination development scenarios. *Tourism Management*, 21, 217–24.

Weaver, D. (2000b). Tourism and national parks in ecologically vulnerable areas. In *Tourism and National Parks: Issues and Implications* (R. Butler and S. Boyd, eds) pp. 107–24, John Wiley & Sons.

Weaver, D. (2001a). Mass tourism and alternative tourism in the Caribbean. In *Tourism and the Less Developed World: Issues and Case Studies* (D. Harrison, ed.) pp. 161–74, CABI Publishing.

Weaver, D. (2001b). *Ecotourism*. John Wiley & Sons, Australia.

Weaver, D. (ed.) (2001c). *The Encyclopedia of Ecotourism*. CABI Publishing.

Weaver, D. (2002). The evolving concept of ecotourism and its potential impacts. *International Journal of Sustainable Development*, 5, 251–64.

Weaver, D. (2004). The contribution of international students to tourism beyond the core educational experience: evidence form Australia. *Tourism Review International*, 7, 95–105.

Weaver, D. (2005a). Comprehensive and minimalist dimensions of ecotourism. *Annals of Tourism Research*, 32, 439–55.

Weaver, D. (2005b). Mass and urban ecotourism: new manifestations of an old concept. *Tourism Recreation Review*, 30 (2), 19–26.

Weaver, D. (2005c). The 'Plantation' variant of the TALC in the small island Caribbean. In *The Tourism Area Life Cycle: Applications and Modifications* (R. Butler, ed.), Channel View.

Weaver, D. and Fennell, D. (1997). The vacation farm sector in Saskatchewan: a profile of operations. *Tourism Management*, 18, 357–65.

Weaver, D. and Lawton, L. (2001). Resident perceptions in the urban-rural fringe. *Annals of Tourism Research*, 28, 439–58.

Weaver, D. and Lawton, L. (2002a). *Tourism Management, 2nd edn*. John Wiley & Sons, Australia.

Weaver, D. and Lawton, L. (2002b). Overnight ecotourist market segmentation in the Gold Coast hinterland of Australia. *Journal of Travel Research*, 40, 270–80.

Webster, K. (2000). *Environmental Management in the Hospitality Industry: A Guide for Students and Managers*. Cassell.

Weiler, B. and Ham, S. (2001). Tour guides and interpretation. In *The Encyclopedia of Ecotourism*. (D. Weaver, ed.) pp. 549–63, CABI Publishing.

Weiss, E. (2004). Project wins back Manassas battlefield. *Washington Post*, June 18, B1, B4.

Welk, P. (2004). The beaten track: anti-tourism as an element of backpacker identity construction. In *The Global Nomad: Backpacker Travel in Theory and Practice* (G. Richards and J. Wilson, eds) pp. 77–91, Channel View.

Westerhausen, K. and Macbeth, J. (2003). Backpackers and empowered local communities: natural allies in the struggle for sustainability and local control? *Tourism Geographies*, 5, 71–86.

Wheeler, M. (1994). The emergence of ethics in tourism and hospitality. In *Progress in Tourism, Recreation and Hospitality Management*. Vol. 6 (C. Cooper and A. Lockwood, eds) pp. 46–56, Wiley.

Wheeller, B. (1993). Sustaining the ego. *Journal of Sustainable Tourism*, 1, 121–9.

Whelan, T. (ed.) (1991). Ecotourism and its role in sustainable development. In *Nature Tourism: Managing for the Environment* pp. 3–22, Island Press.

Wight, P. (2001). Ecotourists: not a homogeneous market segment. In *The Encyclopedia of Ecotourism* (D. Weaver, ed.) pp. 37–62, CABI Publishing.

Wilkinson, P. (1997). *Tourism Policy and Planning: Case Studies from the Commonwealth Caribbean*. Cognizant.

Wilkinson, P. (1999). Caribbean cruise tourism: delusion? illusion? *Tourism Geographies*, 1, 261–82.

Williams, P., Singh, T. and Schlüter, R. (2001). Mountain ecotourism: creating a sustainable future. In *The Encyclopedia of Ecotourism* (D. Weaver, ed.) pp. 205–18, CABI Publishing.

Wilson, D. (1997). Strategies for sustainability: lessons from Goa and the Seychelles. In *Tourism and Sustainability: Principles to Practice* (M. Stabler, ed.) pp. 173–97, CAB International.

Wolf, P. (1999). *Hot Towns: The Future of the Fastest Growing Communities in America.* Rutgers University Press.

Wood, K. and House, S. (1991). *The Good Tourist: a Worldwide Guide to the Green Traveller.* Mandarin.

Wood, R. (2000). Caribbean cruise tourism: globalization at sea. *Annals of Tourism Research*, 27, 345–70.

Wood, R. (2004). Global currents: cruise ships in the Caribbean Sea. In *Tourism in the Caribbean: Trends, Development, Prospects* (D. Duval, ed.) pp. 152–71, Routledge.

Wright, J. and Skaggs, R. (2002). *Purchase of Development Rights and Conservation Easements: Frequently Asked Questions.* New Mexico State University College of Agriculture and Home Economics. Technical Report 34. http://www.cahe.nmsu.edu/pubs/research/economics/TR34.pdf (visited June 7, 2004).

WTO (1980). *Manila Declaration on World Tourism.*

WTO (1985). *The State's Role in Encouraging the Development of New Destinations and Ensuring Balanced Distribution of Tourist Flows.*

WTO (1989). *The Hague Declaration on Tourism.*

WTO (1996). *What Tourism Managers Need to Know: A Practical Guide to the Development and Use of Indicators of Sustainable Tourism.*

WTO (2003a). *Tourism Highlights: Edition 2003.*

WTO (2003b). *Chinese Outbound Tourism.*

WTO and UNEP (1982). *Joint Declaration Between World Tourism Organization and United Nations Environment Programme.*

WTO and UNEP (1983). *Workshop on Environmental Aspects of Tourism.*

WTTC (2003a). *World Travel & Tourism: A World of Opportunity.* World Travel & Tourism Council.

WTTC (2003b). *Blueprint for New Tourism.*

Yu, D., Hendrickson, T. and Castillo, A. (1997). Ecotourism and conservation in Amazonian Peru: short-term and long-term challenges. *Environmental Conservation*, 24, 130–8.

Zenzen, J. (1998). *Battling for Manassas: The Fifty-year Preservation Struggle at Manassas National Battlefield Park.* Pennsylvania State University Press. (on-line book) http://www.cr.nps.gov/history/online_books/mana/adhi.htm

Zeppel, H. (1998). Entertainers or entrepreneurs: Iban involvement in longhouse tourism (Sarawak, Borneo). *Tourism Recreation Research*, 23 (1), 39–45.

Zeppel, H. (2001). Aboriginal cultures and indigenous tourism. In *Special Interest Tourism* (N. Douglas, N. Douglas and R. Derrett, eds) pp. 232–59, John Wiley and Sons, Australia.

Zeppel, H. (2006). *Indigenous Ecotourism: Sustainable Development and Management.* CABI Publishing.

Zhang, G., Pine, R. and Zhang, H. (2000). China's international tourism development: present and future. *International Journal of Contemporary Hospitality Management*, 12, 282–90.

Zurick, D. (1992). Adventure travel and sustainable tourism in the peripheral economy of Nepal. *Annals of the Association of American Geographers*, 82, 608–28.

Appendix 1
Hotel facilities

1 Formulation of policies

1.1 The hotel has established a sustainability mission and policies.
Weight: 1   [×]yes   [ ]no   ?

1.2 The hotel has prepared a brochure to publish the goals of its sustainability policies.
Weight: 1   [×]yes   [ ]no   ?

1.3 The employees know the goals of the hotel's sustainability mission and policies.
Weight: 2   [×]yes   [ ]no   ?

1.4 The hotel has designed a manual that defines the goal of its sustainability plan and describes its sustainability programs.
Weight: 1   [×]yes   [ ]no   ?

1.5 The hotel keeps a record of efforts implemented in order to achieve its sustainability goals.
Weight: 1   [×]yes   [ ]no   ?

2 Water consumption

2.1 The water consumption is periodically monitored.
Weight: 1   [×]yes   [ ]no   ?

2.2 The hotel keeps a record of total water consumption.
Weight: 1   [×]yes   [ ]no   ?

2.3 The hotel has a water usage plan with specific saving goals.
Weight: 1   [×]yes   [ ]no   ?

2.4 A person is responsible for the execution of scheduled water saving activities. This schedule is known by all employees.
Weight: 2   [×]yes   [ ]no   ?

2.5 Water saving by employees and customers is encouraged by a permanent promotion program.
Weight: 2   [×]yes   [ ]no   ?

2.6 Water leakage problems are periodically monitored and the hotel keeps a record of location and repairs.
Weight: 1   [×]yes   [ ]no   ?

2.7 The hotel uses faucet water-saving devices.
Weight: 2   [×]yes   [ ]no   ?

2.8   At least every two months, an independent laboratory monitors the quality of drinking water quality and ice used by the hotel.
Weight: 3   [✕]yes   [ ]no   ?

2.9   The swimming pool water quality is periodically monitored. The hotel keeps record of this process.
Weight: 3   [ ]yes   [ ]no   [✕]n/a ?

2.10 The swimming pool has a system to obtain chloride daily.
Weight: 1   [ ]yes   [ ]no   [✕]n/a ?

2.11 The swimming pool water is treated using a chloride-free process.
Weight: 2   [ ]yes   [ ]no   [✕]n/a ?

3 Energy consumption

3.1   The water consumption is periodically monitored.
Weight: 1   [✕]yes   [ ]no   ?

3.2   The hotel keeps a record of monthly total energy consumption. The energy usage is statistically analyzed.
Weight: 1   [✕]yes   [ ]no   ?

3.3   The hotel has an energy usage plan with specific saving goals.
Weight: 1   [✕]yes   [ ]no   ?

3.4   A person is responsible for the execution of scheduled energy saving activities. All the employees know this schedule.
Weight: 1   [✕]yes   [ ]no   ?

3.5   Natural illumination systems are used wherever possible.
Weight: 1   [✕]yes   [ ]no   ?

3.6   The hotel has a program of preventive maintenance for all electric installations and equipment.
Weight: 2   [ ]yes   [✕]no   ?

3.7   The hotel promotes turning off illumination systems whenever they are not necessary.
Weight: 1   [✕]yes   [ ]no   ?

3.8   An energy-efficient illumination system is used in at least 80 per cent of the hotel facilities.
Weight: 2   [✕]yes   [ ]no   ?

3.9   The hotel uses new technologies for energy saving. For instance, automatic switches for illumination systems and electric/electronic equipment.
Weight: 2   [✕]yes   [ ]no   ?

3.10 The hotel is using alternative energy systems (i.e. solar energy) for illumination.
Weight: 3   [ ]yes   [✕]no   ?

3.11 The hotel is using alternative energy systems (i.e. solar energy) for water heating or other energy needs.
Weight: 3   [✕]yes   [ ]no   ?

3.12 The hot water deposits and pipes are covered with insulated material to prevent heat loss.
Weight: 1   [×]yes   [ ]no   ?

3.13 The hotel uses natural ventilation, shading and other alternative air conditioning systems.
Weight: 1   [×]yes   [ ]no   ?

3.14 The hotel uses new technologies to increase the energy efficiency of the refrigeration and air conditioning systems.
Weight: 2   [×]yes   [ ]no   [ ]n/a   ?

3.15 The hotel has a program to control the leakage of air and other gases from the refrigeration and air conditioning systems.
Weight: 1   [×]yes   [ ]no   [ ]n/a   ?

3.16 Energy efficient electric equipment is used to cover at least 50 per cent of the hotel's needs.
Weight: 2   [×]yes   [ ]no   ?

3.17 The laundry takes advantage of solar heat to dry clothes, sheets and towels.
Weight: 2   [ ]yes   [×]no   [ ]n/a   ?

4 General supplies consumption

4.1 The hotel has a supplies buying and consumption policy that incorporates environmental and social aspects.
Weight: 1   [×]yes   [ ]no   ?

4.2 The employees know the standards established by the buying policy.
Weight: 2   [×]yes   [ ]no   ?

4.3 The hotel has a suppliers' manual to guarantee their compliance with the buying policy's social and environmental standards.
Weight: 1   [×]yes   [ ]no   ?

4.4 The hotel does not use or sell products that are harmful for the environment.
Weight: 1   [×]yes   [ ]no   ?

4.5 At least 50 per cent of printed material used by the hotel is made with chloride-free recycled paper.
Weight: 2   [ ]yes   [×]no   ?

Food and beverages

4.6 The food is prepared using preferably fresh products.
Weight: 1   [×]yes   [ ]no   ?

4.7 The hotel has certified the use of organic food products.
Weight: 3   [×]yes   [ ]no   [ ]n/a   ?

4.8 The hotel menu offers national or regional dishes.
Weight: 2   [×]yes   [ ]no   ?

4.9 The canned food bought by the hotel is acquired in full, industrial-sized containers that are preferable made of glass or recyclable steel.
Weight: 1   [×]yes   [ ]no   ?

4.10 The reuse or recycling of containers is a standard practice. The hotel also has specific suppliers of recycling services.
Weight: 2   [×]yes   [ ]no   ?

4.11 Butter, sauces, sugar, honey and fruit jelly are served on reusable containers.
Weight: 2   [×]yes   [ ]no   [ ]n/a   ?

4.12 The kitchen, restaurant and bar of the hotel use reusable dishes, glasses, cups, etc.
Weight: 2   [×]yes   [ ]no   [ ]n/a   ?

Cleaning and cosmetic products

4.13 The hotel uses non-toxic, non-corrosive biodegradable cleaning products.
Weight: 1   [×]yes   [ ]no   ?

4.14 The detergents used by the laundry and kitchen are phosphate- and bleach-free.
Weight: 1   [×]yes   [ ]no   ?

4.15 The soap and other cosmetic products given to customers and employees are biodegradable.
Weight: 1   [×]yes   [ ]no   ?

4.16 The cleaning and cosmetic products come in biodegradable, recyclable or reusable packaging.
Weight: 1   [ ]yes   [×]no   ?

4.17 The cosmetics in customer rooms and toilets are supplied using dispensers.
Weight: 2   [ ]yes   [×]no   ?

4.18 The cosmetic product wastes are appropriately recycled or reused.
Weight: 2   [×]yes   [ ]no   [ ]n/a   ?

5 Management of solid wastes

5.1 The quantity and quality of solid wastes is continuously monitored.
Weight: 1   [×]yes   [ ]no   ?

5.2 There are records of the production of waste by room or hotel section.
Weight: 1   [ ]yes   [×]no   ?

5.3 The hotel has a solid waste reduction plan with specific goals.
Weight: 1   [ ]yes   [×]no   ?

5.4 A person is responsible for the execution of scheduled solid waste reduction activities. All the employees know this schedule.
Weight: 1   [×]yes   [ ]no   ?

Organic wastes

5.5   Organic wastes are deposited in separated containers.
Weight: 1   [×]yes   [ ]no   ?

5.6   The organic wastes generated are composted or recycled.
Weight: 2   [ ]yes   [×]no   [ ]n/a   ?

Inorganic wastes

5.7   The hotel has separated containers for classifying different kinds of inorganic solid wastes (i.e. glass, paper, plastic and steel).
Weight: 2   [×]yes   [ ]no   ?

5.8   The room service employees classify the inorganic solid waste not classified by the customers.
Weight: 2   [×]yes   [ ]no   ?

5.9   The hotel has a specific area where the final classification of inorganic solid waste is performed.
Weight: 1   [ ]yes   [×]no   ?

5.10 The hotel participates in a recycling program.
Weight: 3   [×]yes   [ ]no   ?

Final destiny of wastes

5.11 The solid waste generated is appropriately stored before its final disposal.
Weight: 2   [×]yes   [ ]no   ?

5.12 The hotel verifies and guarantees the final disposal of waste is efficiently done.
Weight: 1   [ ]yes   [×]no   ?

6 Training

6.1   All employees are informed about the sustainability policies of the hotel.
Weight: 2   [×]yes   [ ]no   ?

6.2   The hotel maintains a training program for employees according to its responsibilities.
Weight: 1   [×]yes   [ ]no   ?

6.3   The employees actively participate in the design of environmental activities and policies of the hotel.
Weight: 2   [×]yes   [ ]no   ?

6.4 The employees periodically participate in meetings that deal with hotel sustainability issues.
Weight: 1   [X]yes   [ ]no   ?

6.5 The hotel has a strategy providing incentives to employees who suggest improvements to the hotel's sustainability program.
Weight: 2   [X]yes   [ ]no   ?

6.6 The hotel periodically evaluates and controls the results of its employee training program.
Weight: 1   [ ]yes   [X]no ?

Index

Acapulco (Mexico), 139
Accommodation *see* Mass tourism
    industry, conventional
Accor, 86
  Tours, 78
Adaptancy platform, 4, 8–9, 19, 51
Advocacy platform, 4, 5–6, 9,
    19, 177
  economic benefits of tourism,
    5–6
  sociocultural and
    environmental benefits
    of tourism, 6
African Union, 12
*Agenda 21 for the Travel and
    Tourism Industry*, 13
Airlines *see* Mass tourism
    industry, conventional,
    transportation
Airports *see* Mass tourism
    industry, conventional,
    transportation
Alaska
  cruise ships, impacts, 84
Allocentric tourists, 42
Alpine Convention, 103
Alpine ski resort (Colorado,
    USA), 102
Alps, European
  ski resorts, use of snow
    cannons, 102
Alternative tourism, 9, 17, 19, 20,
    38–57, 68
  accommodations, 42, 84–7
  attractions, 42
  deliberate and circumstantial
    alternative tourism, 43,
    137–9
  economic status, 42–3
  elitism and ecoimperialism, 53
  guidebooks, 42
  history, 38–9
    role of ecumenical church
      groups, 39
  homestay, 39
  ideal type, 40–43

problems, potential, 51–4
  community disruption, 53–4
  limitations of scale, 52–3
  links to mass tourism, 51–2
  Trojan Horse effect, 52
regulation, 43
typology, 39–40
  alternative cruises and tall
    ships, 40
  backpacking, 40, 47–9,
    53, 177
  ecotourism, 40
  education tourism, 40, 50–51
  educational tours, 40
  Elderhostel, 40
  farm-based tourism, 40,
    43–5, 52
  feminist travel, 40
  freighters, 40
  guesthouses, 40, 46–7
  historical re-enactments, 40
  homestay, 40
  New Age sites, 40
  political tourism, 40
  religious and spiritual
    retreats, 40
  urban heritage tourism,
    40, 49
  volunteer tourism, 40, 45–6
American Airlines, 81
American Farmland Trust,
    168–9
American Gaming Association,
    100–101
American Society of Golf Course
    Architects, 105
American Society of Travel
    Agents (ASTA), 74
  Environmental Award, 126
Amsterdam
  districting, sex industry, 166
Antarctica, 154
  ecotourism, 198
  quotas on group size, 176
Antigua, 4
  frontstage and backstage, 154

Green Globe 21 membership,
    122
APEC/PATA Environmental
    Code for Sustainable
    Tourism, 13, 14, 111–12,
    113
Argentina, 29
Aruba
  Green Globe 21 membership,
    122
Asia-Pacific Economic
    Cooperation (APEC)
    region, 12
Aspen ski resort, Colorado, 23
Aspen Skiing Company,
    103
Association of Caribbean States,
    12, 14
Association of South-East Asian
    Nations (ASEAN), 12
Atlantic City (New Jersey, USA),
    33, 99, 139
Atlantis submarine fleet, 198
Attractions *see* Mass tourism
    industry, conventional
Audubon Cooperative Sanctuary
    Programme, 105
Austin (Texas)
  Ecotourism, 201
Australia, 3, 4, 14
  casinos, 99
  ecotourism, 197, 198
    EcoCertification Programme,
    203
  education tourism, 50–51
  farm-based tourism, 44
  green consumers, 66
  Green Globe 21 membership,
    122
  National Backpacker Tourism
    Strategy, 48
  Northern Territory, 48
  Queensland, 14
Austria, 3
  farm-based tourism, 44
  green tourists, 66

Backpacking *see* Alternative
    tourism, typology
Backstage *see* Strategies for
    sustainable tourism,
    spatial
Bahamas, 4, 16–17
    Green Globe 21 membership,
        122
Banff National Park (Alberta,
    Canada), 143
Bangkok (Thailand)
    signage and place identity, 160
Barbados, 4, 146
    government incentives for
        sustainability, 170
    Green Globe 21 membership,
        122
Belize
    ecotourism, 198, 202
Bellagio Principles, 31, 32–3
Bermuda
    building standards, 160
    demarketing, 187
    infrastructure and service
        limitations, 177
    quotas, 176
    target marketing of high-end
        tourists, 187
Better World Travelers Club, 74
Bhutan, 48
    quotas, 176
    target marketing of high-end
        tourists, 187
Birmingham (United Kingdom)
    redevelopment, urban, 167
Blue Flag ecolabel, 123
Bluewater Network, 82, 84
Borneo, 154
Boston, Massachusetts, 49
Boulder County (Colorado, USA)
    purchase of development rights
        (PDR) agreements, 169
British Airways, 28, 69, 81–2, 125
British Airways Tourism for
    Tomorrow Awards,
    126–7
British Trust for Conservation
    Volunteers, 45
Broad context model of
    destination development
    scenarios, 136–9
    CAT to DAT, 138
    CAT to SMT, 138
    CAT to UMT, 137–8

DAT to SMT, 138
UMT to SMT, 138–9, 167, 172–3
Bronzeville neighbourhood
    (Chicago), 49
Brunei, 14
Bulgaria, 39
Bunaken National Park
    (Indonesia)
    user fees, 177
Burma, 72

Calvía (Spain)
    rejuvenation, 139
    strategies for sustainable
        tourism, spatial, 172–3
Cambodia, 8
    Green Globe 21 membership, 122
Canada, 3, 29
    farm-based tourism, 44
    Green Globe 21 membership,
        122
    Green Hotels Association
        ecolabel membership, 124
    indigenous people, reassertion
        of rights, 145
    Newfoundland and Labrador,
        14
    redevelopment, urban, 167
    Saskatchewan, 44
    ski resorts, environmentalist
        tendencies among
        skiers, 104
    zoning, National Parks, 162–6,
        179
Canadian Pacific Hotels and
    Resorts, 86
Cancún, Mexico, 6, 138, 139
Canterbury City Centre Initiative,
    178
Capri (Italy)
    infrastructure and service
        limitations, 177
Caribbean, 6, 12, 47
    Blue Flag ecolabel trials, 123
    development standards, height
        restrictions, 159
    Green Hotels Association
        ecolabel membership, 124
    public access to beach, 161
Caribbean Alliance for
    Sustainable Tourism
    (CAST), 122
Carrying capacity, 94, 156–7, 179
    limits of acceptable change, 156

Casino Rama (Ontario,
    Canada), 99
Casinos *see* Mass tourism
    industry, conventional,
    attractions
Cautionary platform, 4, 6–8,
    19, 135
    economic costs of tourism, 5, 7
    sociocultural and
        environmental costs of
        tourism, 5, 7–8
CERES Principles, 81, 113
Certification for Sustainable
    Tourism programme,
    130–31
Chiangmai Workshop on
    Alternative Tourism,
    39
Chile, 14
    Green Globe 21 membership,
        122
China, 3, 60
    domestic tourism, 4
    green consumers, 65
    Green Globe 21 membership,
        122
Codes of conduct, 77, 111–15
    characteristics, 113
    definition, 111
    strengths, 114
    success, elements of, 114–15
    tourist-oriented, 182–3
    weaknesses, 113
    see also APEC/PATA Code for
        Sustainable Tourism,
        Green Guide Series
Co-generation technology, 69
Committed to Green Foundation
    ecolabel, 124
Conservation Corporation
    Africa, 197
Conservation International,
    12, 84
    World Legacy Awards, 126, 127
Conservation Volunteers
    Australia, 45
Costa Rica
    convergence of natural habitat
        and protected area
        land, 199
    ecotourism, 198
    Green Globe 21 membership,
        122
    National Parks, 199

user fees, National Parks, 176–7
    see also Certification for
        Sustainable Tourism
        programme
Council of Europe, 11–12, 14
Croatia, 29
Cruise ships *see* Mass tourism
        industry, conventional,
        transportation
Cuba, 16
Cyprus, 4, 29
    demarketing, 187
    Green Globe 21 membership,
        122

Demarketing, 48
Denmark
    golf courses, membership in
        Committed to Green
        Foundation, 124
    importance of environmental
        factors in destination
        selection, 65
    Meet the Danes programme, 39
Dependency theory, 7
Destination life cycle model, 8, 33,
        43, 137, 140, 141–2, 178,
        190
Destinations, 132–52
    absolute and relative location,
        134
    boundaries, 134–5
    community, 135–6
        apathy, 136
        costs and benefits of tourism,
            disproportionate
            distribution, 136
        definition, 135
        interest groups, influence,
            136
    cultural landscapes, 133
    hierarchy, 134
    place, 133–5
    quality control, 147–8
        Green Globe 21 Community
            Standard, 148
    scale, 133–4
    types, 139–47
        indigenous territories, 143–6
        protected areas, 142–3
        small islands, 146–7
        tourism cities, 139–40, 159
        tourist shopping villages, 142
        urban areas, large, 140–41

urban-rural fringe, 141–2
    see also Broad context model
        of destination
        development scenarios
Disneyland (Anaheim), 94
Disneyland (Paris), 95, 96, 97
Disney World, 95, 96–8
Dominant Western Environmental
        Paradigm, 67–8
Dominica
    ecotourism, 199
    Green Globe 21 membership,
        122
    infrastructure and service
        limitations, 177
Dominican Republic
    Green Globe 21 membership,
        122
Douglas Shire Council
        (Queensland, Australia),
        148

Earthwatch Institute, 45–6
Easter Island (Chile)
    isolation and endemism, 146
Ecolabels, 115–26
    accreditation, 115
    anatomy, 116, 117
    certification, 115
    classification, 115–16
    definition, 115
    incentives to participate, 116
    number, 115
    success, attributes of, 116–17
    weaknesses, 125
    see also Green Globe 21
Economies of scale, advantages,
        68–9
Ecotourism, 9, 12, 40, 191–208
    comprehensive and minimalist
        ideal types, 194
    costs and benefits, potential,
        201–202
    criteria, 192–4
        cultural component, 144, 193
        educational interaction, 193
        environmental and
            sociocultural
            sustainability, 193–4
        nature-based, 192–3
    definitions, 192
    hard and soft, 194–6
    industry, 196–8
        ecolodges, 197

mediating attractions, 198
        tour operators, 197
    magnitude, 196–7
    quality control, 202–203
    spatial distribution, 198–201
        modified spaces, 200–201
        private protected areas,
            199–200
        public protected areas,
            143, 199
        urban areas, 200–201
    structured ecotourists, 196
Ecotourium concept, 206
Ecumenical Coalition on Third
        World Tourism
        (ECTWT), 39
Education
    visitor *see* Strategies for
        sustainable tourism,
        visitor management
Education tourism *see* Alternative
        tourism, typology
Egypt, 22
    Green Globe 21 membership,
        122
Entertainment *see* Mass tourism
        industry, conventional
Environmental Charter for Ski
        Areas, 103
Environmental movement, 7, 68
Ethics, 60–61
Europe, 3, 62, 101
    ecolabels, popularity of, 116
    golf courses, number, 104
European Commission, 11
European Golf Association, 105
European Travel Agents' and
        Tour Operators'
        Association, 74

Fairmont Hotels, 86
Farm-based tourism *see*
        Alternative tourism,
        typology
Fiji, 4, 22
    Green Globe 21 membership,
        122
Financial sustainability, 25–6
Finland
    golf courses, membership in
        Committed to Green
        Foundation, 124
Florida
    cruise ships, impacts, 84

Food services *see* Mass tourism industry, conventional
Foxwoods Casino Resort, 99
France, 3, 8
  farm-based tourism, 44
  ski resorts, opposition to expansion, 103
French Polynesia
  Green Globe 21 membership, 122
Frontstage *see* Strategies for sustainable tourism, spatial

Galapagos Islands (Ecuador)
  isolation and endemism, 146
  quotas, 175
Gambia, The, sex tourism, 187
Gatlinburg (Tennessee, USA), 134
Germany, 3
  farm-based tourism, 44
  Green Globe 21 membership, 122
  green tourists, 66
Gibbon Rehabilitation project, 45
Giza Plateau (Egypt)
  frontstage and backstage, 155
Goa (India), 48
  development standards, setbacks, 159
Gold Coast (Australia), 139, 140, 150–52
  concentration of tourism activity, 178
Golf Course Superintendents Association of America, 105
Golf courses *see* Mass tourism industry, conventional, attractions
Grand Canyon National Park
  backstage violation by helicopters, 158
  concentration of tourist activity, 178–9
Graubünden ski resort (Switzerland), 103
Great Smoky Mountains National Park (Tennessee/North Carolina, USA), 139
Grecotel, 86, 89–90
Greece
  Green Globe 21 membership, 122

GreenBiz Leaders, 66
Green consumers, 62–8
  incipient markets, 64–5
  magnitude and growth, 62
  segments, 62–4
    cultural creatives, 63, 64
    non-environmentalists, 63–4
    true environmentalists, 64
    veneer environmentalists, 64
Green Globe 21, 118–23, 125, 148
  Affiliated status, 118
  Benchmarked status, 118–19
  Certified status, 120
  critique, 122–3
  membership patterns, 120–21
  Travel Planner, 66
Green Guide Series, codes of conduct, 183
Green Hotels Association ecolabel, 123–4
Green paradigm, 67–8
Green tourists, 65–8
  obscurity, reasons for, 66–7
Grenada
  Green Globe 21 membership, 122
Guernsey
  accommodations, adoption of sustainable practices, 86
Guesthouses *see* Alternative tourism, typology

Habitat for Humanity, 45, 46
Hague Declaration, 12
Hawaii
  cruise ships, impacts, 84
  development standards, setbacks, 159
Heavenly Ski Resort (Lake Tahoe, California), 103–104
Himalayan Tourist Code, 182–3
Holiday Inn Corporation, 98
Hong Kong, 3, 14
  Family Insight Tour, 49
  signage and place identity, 160
Hungary, 29
Hunter Valley (New South Wales, Australia), 133

Iceland
  ecotourism, 198
  Green Globe 21 membership, 122
India, 23, 39
  domestic tourism, 4

green consumers, 64
Green Globe 21 membership, 122
Indicators, sustainable tourism *see* Sustainable tourism
Indonesia, 14, 22
  Green Globe 21 membership, 122
In situ nature of tourism consumption, 61–2
Intercontinental Hotels and Resorts, 85
International Association of Amusement Parks and Attractions, 97–8
International Association of Antarctic Tourism Operators, 202–203
International Civil Aviation Organization, 80
International Council of Cruise Lines, 83–4
International Environmental Film and Video Festival, 147
International Federation of Tour Operators, 77
International Hotels Environment Initiative, 85, 86
International Restaurant and Hotel Association
  Annual Environmental Award, 126
International Year of Ecotourism, 13, 203
Interpretation *see* Strategies for sustainable tourism, education
Ireland
  Green Globe 21 membership, 122
Irridex model, 136
Israel, 22
Italy
  golf courses, membership in Committed to Green Foundation, 124
  Green Globe 21 membership, 122

Jamaica
  Green Globe 21 membership, 122
  Meet-the-People programme, 39

Japan, 3, 14, 101
  golf courses, environmental
      impacts, 104–105
Japan Travel Bureau, 78

Kaikoura (New Zealand), 148,
      193, 207–208
Kakadu National Park (Northern
      Territory, Australia), 143
  user fee increases, hypothetical,
      177
Kenya, 4
  Green Globe 21 membership,
      122
  mass ecotourism, evidence for,
      196
  National Parks, 199
Knowledge-based platform, 4,
      9–10, 51, 68, 137
Kotzebue (Alaska)
  frontstage and backstage, 154
Krakow (Poland)
  districting, medieval town
      centre, 166–7
Kruger National Park (South
      Africa), 143

Lamington National Park
      (Queensland, Australia)
  ecotourism impacts, 202
Lancaster County (Pennsylvania,
      USA), 133
  purchase of development rights
      (PDR) agreements, 169
Languedoc-Roussillon region
      (France)
  dispersal/concentration hybrid
      planning, 179
Laos
  Green Globe 21 membership,
      122
Las Vegas, 98, 139, 140
  signage and place identity, 160
Less developed countries (LDCs),
      3–4
Lowell, Massachusetts, 6

Malaysia, 14
  Green Globe 21 membership,
      122
Maldives, 4, 23, 48, 146
  dispersal of visitors, 178
  Green Globe 21 membership,
      122

Mammoth Lakes ski resort
      (California), 102
Manassas (Virginia, USA)
  Disney plans for historic theme
      park defeated, 108–109
  mitigation strategies,
      battlefield, 170
Manila Declaration, 12
Mar del Plata (Argentina), 139
Marriott, 86
  Green Leaves Award, 126
Mass tourism industry,
      conventional, 40–43,
      51–2, 58–72
  accommodation, 59, 60
  attractions, 59, 60
    casinos, 98–101
    characteristics, 92–4
    golf courses, 104–106
      see also Committed to
      Green Foundation
      ecolabel
    ski resorts, 101–104
    theme parks, 94–8, 108–109,
      161
    typology, 92
  entertainment, 59
  food services, 59
  merchandise, specialized, 59,
      75
    guidebooks, 75
  tour guides, 59
    interpretation, 186
  tour operators, outbound, 59,
      76–8
  transportation, 59, 78–84
    airlines, 80–82
    airports, 80, 81–2
    cruise ships, 82–4
  travel agencies, 59, 60, 74–5
    disintermediation, 75
Mauritius, 39
  Green Globe 21 membership,
      122
  isolation and endemism, 146
Merchandise, specialized see
      Mass tourism industry,
      conventional
Mexico, 3, 6, 14, 29
  dispersal/concentration hybrid
      planning, 179
  Green Globe 21 membership,
      122
Mohonk Agreement, 125–6

Moldova, 14
Montana (USA)
  government incentives for
      sustainability, 170
Montserrat, 22
  ecotourism, 199
More developed countries
      (MDCs), 3–4

Namibia, 44
Napa Valley (California), 133
  purchase of development rights
      (PDR) agreements, 169
National Center for Responsible
      Gaming, 101
National Coalition Against
      Legalized Gambling, 100
National Ski Areas Association
      (US), 103
Navaho Indians, 100
Nefertari's tomb, Luxor (Egypt)
  group size limits, 176
Nepal
  backpacking, 52
  dispersal of visitors, 178
Netherlands, The, 29
  green tourists, 66
Netherlands Antilles
  Green Globe 21 membership,
      122
New York City
  signage and place identity, 160
New Zealand, 3, 14
  Farm-based tourism, 44
  Green Globe 21 membership,
      122
Nice/Cannes (France), 139
North America, 3
  ecolabels, relative obscurity, 116
North Carolina (USA)
  government incentives for
      sustainability, 170
Norway
  Green Globe 21 membership,
      122

Ocean Conservation and Tourism
      Alliance, 84
Old Works golf course (Montana,
      USA), 106
Organization for Economic
      Cooperation and
      Development
      (OECD), 11

Organization of American
    States, 12
Orlando (Florida, USA), 139, 140

Pacific Asia Travel Association
    (PATA), 13
Pakistan, 14
Palau
    Green Globe 21 membership,
        122
Palestinian Territory, 14
Papua New Guinea
    Tufi guesthouses, 53–4
Paradigm shift, 7, 67–8
Pattaya (Thailand), 139
Peru, 14, 22
    ecotourism, 198
    Green Globe 21 membership,
        122
Philippines, 14
    ecotourism, 201
    Luzon, sense of place, 133
    zoning, National Parks, 166
Pleasure periphery, 4, 7, 139
Polynesian Cultural Center, 154
Portugal
    golf courses, membership in
        Committed to Green
        Foundation, 124
    Green Globe 21 membership,
        122
Prairie Dunes Country Club
    (Kansas, USA), 105
Precautionary principle, 20
Psychocentric tourists, 42

Quality control *see* Sustainable
    tourism

Recreation Opportunity Spectrum
    (ROS) *see* Strategies for
        sustainable tourism,
        visitor management,
        redistribution
Redlands Shire Council
    (Queensland, Australia),
    148
Rio Earth Summit, 10, 11, 13, 111
Rothenburg ob der Tauber
    (Germany)
    districting, medieval town
        centre, 166
    infrastructure and service
        limitations, 177

Russia
    Tatarstan, 14
Rwanda, 14

Saba Marine Park (Netherlands
    Antilles), 176
Saint Lucia
    Green Globe 21 membership,
        122
Samoa
    ecotourism, 199
Scandic, 86
Scandinavia, 35–7
    Network Evolution for
        Sustainable Tourism
        (NEST) project, 35–7
Scotland
    golf courses, membership in
        Committed to Green
        Foundation, 124
    Highlands, sense of place,
        133
    ski resorts, environmental
        impacts, 102
Seattle (Washington, USA), 46
SeaWorld, 97
Senegal, 39, 154
Seychelles, 4
    cruise ships, impacts, 82
    Green Globe 21 membership,
        122
    isolation and endemism, 146
Shenandoah National Park
    (Virginia, USA), 139
Sheraton Hotels, 69
Singapore, 3, 14
    Green Globe 21 membership,
        122
Ski resorts
    Banff/Lake Louise, green
        consumers, 66
    see also Mass tourism industry,
        conventional, attractions
Skyrail (Queensland, Australia),
    198
Slovenia, 39
Socially Responsible Investment
    portfolios, 62
South Africa
    Blue Flag ecolabel trials, 123
    casinos, 99
    Soweto, 49
Southeast Asia, 48
South Korea, 3, 14

Spain, 3
    Cataluña, 14
    La Gomera (Canary Islands), 54
Special events, 147
Sri Lanka, 23, 29
    Green Globe 21 membership,
        122
Starwood Hotels, 86
ST-EP (Sustainable Tourism –
        Eliminating Poverty)
        initiative, 13
St. Helena
    Isolation and endemism, 146
St. Jacobs (Ontario, Canada), 142
Strategies for sustainable tourism,
        spatial, 153–73
    development standards, 158–62
        building footprint, size and
            configuration, 159
        building standards, 160
        density controls, 158–9
        height restrictions, 159
        landscaping, 160
        noise regulation, 161
        public access, 161–2
        setbacks, 159–60
        signage and above ground
            utility controls, 160–61
    districting, 166–8
        redevelopment, 167
    frontstage and backstage,
            154–8, 162, 166
        carrying capacity, flexible
            and fixed, 156–7
        formal and informal, 154
        implications for indicators,
            155
        implications for
            sustainability, 155
        violations, 157–8
    government incentives, 170
    purchase of development rights
        (PDR) agreements, 168–9
    trade-offs, 169–70
        mitigation strategies, 170
        transfer of development
            rights (PDR)
            agreements, 169
    zoning, 162–6
        protected areas, 162, 163–6
Strategies for sustainable tourism,
        visitor management,
        174–90
    education, 180–87

interpretation, 185–7
persuasion, 181–5
redistribution of visitors,
    178–80
    concentration, 178–9
    dispersal, 178
    dispersal/concentration
        hybrids, 179
    recreation opportunity
        spectrum (ROS), 179–80,
        181, 204
target marketing, 187
    demarketing, 187
visitation caps, 175–7
    infrastructure and service
        limitations, 177
    quotas, 175–6
    user fees, 176–7
Sundance ski resort (Utah, USA),
    104
Suriname
    Green Globe 21 membership,
    122
Sustainable development, 9–10,
    11, 19, 68
Sustainable tourism
    confined and holistic
        sustainability, 23–4
    definition, 10
    enhancement sustainability,
        20, 144
    flexibility, 19–20
    indicators, 26–31
        aggregate, 27
        benchmarks, 28
        evaluation, 28–9
        internal and external, 27
        measurement and
            monitoring, 27–8
        prioritization, 29
        selection, 26–7
        thresholds, 28–9
    institutionalization, 11–14
    intergenerational and
        intragenerational equity,
        20–21
    minimalist and comprehensive
        composite models, 24–6
    quality control, 110–31
        awards, 126–7, 181
        spectrum, 111
        see also codes of conduct,
            ecolabels
    rationale for Pursuit, 31–3

status quo sustainability, 20, 144
    weak and strong
        interpretations, 19–20,
        28, 140, 143
    see also Strategies for
        sustainable tourism,
        spatial; strategies for
        sustainable tourism,
        visitor management
Sustainable Tourism Cooperative
    Research Centre, 122
Sustainable Tourism Stewardship
    Council, 125–6
Sweden
    golf courses, membership in
        Committed to Green
        Foundation, 124
    green tourists, 66
    public access to private land,
        161–2
Switzerland
    Green Globe 21 membership,
    122

Taiwan, 3, 14
Tamborine Mountain
    (Queensland, Australia),
    142, 150–51
Tangalooma Dolphin Feeding
    Programme
    (Queensland, Australia),
    185–6
Terrorism, 2, 23, 50, 185
Thailand, 4, 14
    backpacking, 52
    demarketing sex tourists, 187
    golf courses, environmental and
        social impacts, 104, 105
Theme parks *see* Mass tourism
    industry, conventional,
    attractions
The Nature Conservancy (TNC),
    12
    private protected areas, 199
Tokyo
    signage and place identity, 160
Tonga
    ecotourism, 199
Toronto
    Green Tourism Association, 50
Tour guides *see* Mass tourism
    industry, conventional
Tourism, 10
    complexity, 21–4

fuzzy boundaries, 21
    indirect and induced
        impacts, 21–2
    influence of external
        systems, 22
    unpredictable cause and
        effect relationships, 23
    geographical expansion, 3–4
    growth forecast, 3
    growth in stayover numbers, 2
    industry, 59–60
    magnitude, 1–3
Tourism Concern, 71–2, 182
Tour Operators Initiative for
    Sustainable Tourism
    Development, 78
Tour operators, outbound *see*
    Mass tourism industry,
    conventional
Transportation *see* Mass tourism
    industry, conventional
Travel agencies *see* Mass tourism
    industry, conventional
TREAD Lightly!, 184
Tree Top Walk (Western
    Australia), 198
Trusthouse Forte, 69
TUI, 77, 78
    ecolabel, internal, 124–5
TUI International Environmental
    Award, 126
Tunica County (Mississippi,
    USA), 99
Turkey
    Green Globe 21 membership,
    122
    Side, 78
Turks & Caicos Islands
    Green Globe 21 membership,
    122
Tuvalu, 146

Uluru National Park (Northern
    Territory, Australia)
    indigenous people, reassertion
        of rights, 145
United Kingdom, 3
    accommodations, adoption of
        sustainable practices,
        86–7
    corporate ethics, 60
    Cotswold Hills, sense of place,
        133
    farm-based tourism, 44

United Kingdom (*contd*)
  golf courses, membership in
      Committed to Green
      Foundation, 124
  green consumers, 62, 63–4
  Green Globe 21 membership, 122
  green tourists, 65, 66
  public access, walking trails, 161
  ski resorts, environmentalist
      tendencies among
      skiers, 104
  tour operators, outbound, 76,
      77–8
United Nations, 10, 11
United Nations Environment
      Programme (UNEP),
      11, 12
United States Golf Association,
      105
United States of America, 3, 22, 29
  casinos, 98, 101
      economic and sociocultural
          costs, 99–100
      economic benefits, 98–9
      problems in Indian casinos,
          100
      resident attitudes toward, 100
      sustainability initiatives,
          100–101
  farm-based tourism, 44
  food services industry, 21
  golf courses, number, 104
  green consumers, 62–4
  Green Globe 21 membership,
      122
  green tourists, 65–6
  indigenous people, reassertion
      of rights, 145

purchase of development rights
      (PDR) agreements, 168–9
  ski resorts, 101–102
      environmentalist tendencies
          among skiers, 104
      support for, 103
United States Tour Operators
      Association
  Sustainable Tourism Awards,
      126
Urban heritage tourism *see*
      Alternative tourism,
      typology
Uruguay, 4
User fees *see* Strategies for
      sustainable tourism,
      visitor management

Vail ski resort (Colorado, USA),
      102
  target marketing of high-end
      tourists, 187
Venice
  visitor management, 189–90
Vietnam
  Green Globe 21 membership,
      122
Vieux Carré (New Orleans, USA)
  districting, 167–8
Visitation caps *see* Strategies for
      sustainable tourism,
      visitor management
Volunteer for Nature, 45

Washington, DC
  Grand Prix, violation of
      backstage, 158
  Shaw Heritage Tours, 56–7

West Coast Trail (British
      Columbia, Canada),
      175, 176
Whale watching, 202, 207–208
Whistler ski resort (British
      Columbia, Canada),
      102, 104
  zoning, 162–3
World Legacy Awards, 126
World Student Games, 147
World Summit on Sustainable
      Development, 13
World Tourism Organization
      (WTO), 10, 12–13, 131
  sustainable tourism indicators,
      29–31
World Travel and Trade Council
      (WTTC), 13, 118, 127
  Blueprint for New Tourism,
      13, 61
World Wide Fund for Nature
      (WWF), 12

Yavapai-Apache Indians, 98–9
Yellowstone National Park
      (Wyoming, USA), 143
Yosemite National Park
      (California)
  quotas, 175
Youth Challenge International, 45

Zoning and districting *see*
      Strategies for sustainable
      tourism, spatial

Lightning Source UK Ltd.
Milton Keynes UK
UKOW011230200412

191158UK00001B/8/P